MUSLIM QUR᾽ĀNIC INTERPRETATION TODAY

Themes in Qur'ānic Studies

Series Editors
Mustafa Shah, School of Oriental and African Studies, University of London, and Abdul Hakim al-Matroudi, School of Oriental and African Studies, University of London

This series aims to introduce critical issues in the academic study of The Qur'ān and offers a variety of topics essential to providing an historical overview of The Qur'ān and the interrelated traditional teachings and beliefs which issue from it.

Published

Philosophical Perspectives on Modern Qur'ānic Exegesis
Key Paradigms and Concepts
Massimo Campanini

The Qur'ān and Kerygma
Biblical Receptions of the Muslim Scripture across a Millennium
Jeffrey Einboden

Forthcoming

Prophets and Prophecy in the Qur'ān
Narratives of Divine Intervention in the Story of Humankind
Anthony H. Johns

Sufism and Scripture
A Historical Survey of Approaches to the Qur'ān in the Sufi Tradition
Harith Bin Ramli

Divine Covenant
Science and Concepts of Natural Law in the Qur'ān and Islamic Disciplines
Ulrika Mårtensson

MUSLIM QUR᾿ĀNIC INTERPRETATION TODAY

MEDIA, GENEALOGIES AND INTERPRETIVE COMMUNITIES

Johanna Pink

equinox

SHEFFIELD UK BRISTOL CT

Published by Equinox Publishing Ltd.

UK: Office 415, The Workstation, 15 Paternoster Row, Sheffield, South Yorkshire S1 2BX
USA: ISD, 70 Enterprise Drive, Bristol, CT 06010

www.equinoxpub.com

First published 2019
First printing in paperback 2020

British Library Cataloguing-in-Publication Data
A catalogue record for this book is available from the British Library.

Library of Congress Cataloging-in-Publication Data
Names: Pink, Johanna, author.
Title: Muslim Qur'ānic interpretation today : media, genealogies and interpretive communities / Johanna Pink.
Description: Bristol, CT : Equinox Publishing Ltd, 2019. | Series: Themes in Qur'ānic studies | Includes bibliographical references and index. | Description based on print version record and CIP data provided by publisher; resource not viewed.
Identifiers: LCCN 2018000424 (print) | LCCN 2018000694 (ebook) | ISBN 9781781797051 (ePDF) | ISBN 9781781791431 (hb)
Subjects: LCSH: Qur'an--Criticism, interpretation, etc.--History. | Qur'an--Commentaries--History and criticism.
Classification: LCC BP130.45 (ebook) | LCC BP130.45 .P555 2018 (print) | DDC 297.1/226--dc23
LC record available at https://lccn.loc.gov/2018000424

ISBN: 978 1 78179 143 1 (hardback)
978 1 80050 027 3 (paperback)
978 1 78179 705 1 (ePDF)

Typeset by Advent Publishing Services, London

CONTENTS

Acknowledgements ix

PROLOGUE: THE CONTESTED QUR'ĀN 1

INTRODUCTION 5
Qur'ānic interpretation today: Tensions and power fields 5
This book's approach 7

1
THE NEW CENTRALITY OF THE QUR'ĀNIC MESSAGE 14
The place of the Qur'ān in premodern Muslim societies 14
The shift to the centre 17
Pedagogy and guidance (*hidāya*): an Indonesian comic book on Q. 49:12 21
Ambiguity, disambiguation and guidance 24
Translation and *da'wa*: a protestantisation of the Qur'ān? 26
Televangelism and *da'wa*: 'Amr Khālid (b. 1967, Egypt) on Q. 23:1–11 29

2
RECONSTITUTING THE EXEGETICAL TRADITION 35
A genealogical tradition 35
The *'ulamā'* as bearers of the tradition 38
An *'ālim* continuing the tradition of *tafsīr*: Muhammad Quraish Shihab (b. 1944, Indonesia) on Q. 95:1–3 40
A Salafi paradigm 48
Reshaping the tradition: Shaykh al-Mubarakpuri's *Tafsir Ibn Kathir (Abridged)* (India/Saudi Arabia) on Q. 38:21–25 52
Present-day Salafi exegesis 61
Takfīr: Seyfuddin El-Muvahhid's *Davetçinin Tefsiri* (Turkey/?) on Q. 4:116 66
Exegetical traditions as a resource 71
Condensing the tradition: 'Ā'iḍ b. 'Abdallāh al-Qarnī (b. 1959, Saudi Arabia) on Q. 9:112 72

3
MEDIA 81
Media transformations: from manuscripts to print and beyond 81
Layers of media: Abdolali Bazargan (b. 1943; Iran/US) on Q. 103:3 85

Visual dimensions ... 94
Tafsīr in pictures: H. Abdul Mustaqim (b. 1972, Indonesia) on Q. 104 ... 95
Preaching and media: audio-visual representations and the internet ... 100
From television to YouTube: Audio-visual interpretations of the Fātiḥa ... 103
YouTube exegetes on Q. 1:6–7 ... 111
Ḥasan b. Farḥān al-Mālikī (b. 1970, Saudi Arabia) on Q. 1:6–7 ... 113

4
MODERNISM AND ITS PARADIGMS 125
Modernism and other labels ... 125
Maqāṣid, or the Qur'ān's higher aims ... 128
Historical contextualisation and its sources ... 131
Tafsīr in the order of revelation ... 134
Reading the Qur'ān in its chronological arrangement:
Muḥammad ʿĀbid al-Jābirī (1935–2010, Morocco) on Q. 109 ... 136
Abrogation (*naskh*) and its opponents ... 141
Chronology, context, semantics:
Talip Özdeş (b. 1954, Turkey) on Q. 16:101 ... 143
Semantics and the 'literal meaning' ... 150
Literary exegesis ... 151
Thematic *tafsīr* (*tafsīr mawḍūʿī*) ... 153
Tafsīr al-Qurʾān bi'l-Qurʾān ... 154
The contested Sunna: from *ḥadīth*-based exegesis to Qurʾānism ... 155
A Qurʾānist approach: Aḥmad Ṣubḥī Manṣūr
(b. 1949, Egypt/USA) on Q. 2:221 ... 158

5
IN DEFENCE OF A PERFECT SCRIPTURE: THE QURʾĀN AS A HOLISTIC SYSTEM 172
Defending polygamy: Karīmān Ḥamza (b. 1942, Egypt) on Q. 4:3 ... 172
Islamist Qurʾānic interpretation ... 181
The 'system' (*naẓm*) and structure of the Qurʾān ... 185
The sacralisation of the Qurʾān's canonical arrangement:
ʿAmr Khālid on the structure of the Qurʾān and the unity of *sūra*s ... 187
ʿAmr Khālid on Sūra al-Nisāʾ (Q. 4) ... 189
Science and the *iʿjāz* paradigm ... 191
The scientific *iʿjāz*: Miracles of Quran on Q. 27:18 ... 197

6
THE GLOBAL QURʾĀN IN A DIVERSE WORLD 202
Negotiating the boundaries of Islamicness through the Qurʾān:
Ali Adil Atalay 'Vaktidolu' (b. 1936, Turkey) on Q. 2:21 ... 202
Centre, periphery and hierarchies of language ... 207

Nation states 210
State building: the Indonesian Ministry of Religion on Q. 12:54–5 214
Sunni and Shiʿi Islam 218
Sufism 223
A female Sufi shaykh: Cemâlnur Sargut (b. 1952, Turkey) on Q. 112 225
New Islamic communities 229
The Ahmadiyya and the death of Jesus: Disputes over Q. 3:55 231

7
CLASHES AND FAULT LINES 244
Gender, queerness and the Qur'ān 244
Debates on same-sex marriage: Mun'im Sirry (b. 1973, Indonesia) on the story of Lot 247
Causes for conflict 257
Doubt versus certainty: Aḥmad Khayrī al-ʿUmarī (b. 1970, Iraq) on Q. 21:51–56 and his critics 259
Postmodern uncertainties and subjective approaches 265
Subjectivity and Qur'ānic interpretation in a Muslim intellectual's blog: Hakan Turan (b. 1979, Germany) on Q. 5:51 269

EPILOGUE: THE QUR'ĀN, TEXTUAL INTERPRETATION AND AUTHORITY, OR: MAY HUSBANDS BEAT THEIR WIVES? 284

Bibliography 296
Index 316
Index of Qur'ānic Citations 323

ACKNOWLEDGEMENTS

I would like to express my gratitude to the Freiburg Institute for Advanced Study for offering me an Internal Senior Fellowship that allowed me to reduce my teaching load and discuss my work with colleagues. During the two periods of my fellowship, I started and finished writing my book.

Many persons have generously provided help with larger and smaller aspects of this book. I am particularly grateful to the following people.

- Karen Bauer for her generous and invaluable help at several stages of this project. Most of all, I thank you for reading much of the manuscript thoroughly and for giving me detailed, constructive and honest feedback. Without that feedback, the book would not be what it is now!
- Walid Saleh and Brett Wilson for visiting me in Freiburg, talking about my project and giving me ideas and, in Walid's case, looking through part of the manuscript. Your input was of enormous value to me!
- Samir Laabous for ceaseless running to the library for me, ordering books from all over the place, scanning chapters and always being helpful and cheerful while doing so.
- Gerard van de Bruinhorst for sharing his thoughts on the power fields in which Qur'ānic exegesis takes place. This concept impacted on me greatly.
- Joas Wagemakers for his unsurpassed expertise on Salafism that he has always been ready to share.
- Fadhli Lukman for our discussions of Qur'ān translations and the Indonesian field.
- Mohammed Abdelfadeel Abdelrahem for giving me the book by Aḥmad Khayrī al-ʿUmarī and his hospitality during many visits to Cairo where I found a host of interesting material.
- Martin Riexinger for helping me out when I needed advice and literature on 'Darwinism'.
- 'Adena Lj' for giving me some inside information on how a Qur'ān *ḥalqa* works.

- Shahrokh Raei and Leila Samadi Rendy for their invaluable help with Persian texts and audio files and their willingness to check my translations.
- Mun'im Sirry and Hakan Turan for looking at my translations and analyses of their work and for giving me feedback and additional information.
- Abdul Mustaqim for answering my questions about his illustrated *tafsīr*.
- Marianna Klar and Younus Mirza for letting me benefit from their insights on Ibn Kathīr.
- Tehseen Thaver for sending me her unpublished work on Cemâl-nur Sargut that had caught my attention when she presented it at conferences.
- Andreas Ismail Mohr for discussing systems of verse numbering with me and pointing me to the reference I needed.
- Ruth Bartholomä, Erika Glassen and Tülin Onas for giving their opinions and answering my questions on my translation of Turkish Alevi and Bektashi rhyming translations.
- Regula Forster for her generous help with aspects of Arabic poetry and metres that I had no experience with whatsoever.
- Hadia Mubarak for inviting me to her workshop on gender and *tafsīr* at the New York University of Abu Dhabi in April 2018, and to all the participants of that workshop for giving me feedback.
- Amir Dastmalchian for his careful, knowledgeable and helpful editing. It really improved the book.
- Rotraud Wielandt for encouraging me to embark on this journey many years ago.
- Stefan Wild for evoking my interest in the Qur᾽ān in the first place, in his memorable class on "The Qur᾽ān as text" with Naṣr Ḥāmid Abū Zayd as a guest speaker, back in 1994.
- Everyone else for bearing with me while I wrote this book. I know how obsessive I can be about such things.

I am profoundly grateful to all of you!

PROLOGUE: THE CONTESTED QUR᾽ĀN

In 2005, Muḥammad Sayf al-Dīn Ṭāhā, an Egyptian accountant working in a Gulf state, submitted a six-volume Qur᾽ānic commentary, or *tafsīr*, to the Islamic Research Council of al-Azhar, the highest Sunni institution of Egypt, in order to obtain approval for publication. He had taken approximately twenty years to write it. The result consisted of 28,000 lines of verse because it was a *tafsīr* in poetry – a format for which, Sayf al-Dīn believed, the time was ripe. The following is one of the only two short samples that became known to the public because an Egyptian magazine reported on the case of this *tafsīr* in 2009.[1] It is the commentary on Q. 9:93:

إِنَّمَا السَّبِيلُ عَلَى الَّذِينَ يَسْتَأْذِنُونَكَ وَهُمْ أَغْنِيَاءُ رَضُوا بِأَن يَكُونُوا مَعَ الْخَوَالِفِ وَطَبَعَ اللَّهُ عَلَىٰ قُلُوبِهِمْ فَهُمْ لَا يَعْلَمُونَ ﴿٩٣﴾

(93) The ones open to blame are those who asked you for exemption despite their wealth, and who preferred to be with those who stay behind. God has sealed their hearts; they do not understand.

On this verse, Sayf al-Dīn Ṭāhā wrote:

ولكن الحساب وكل وقت   على من كانوا قوماً موسرينا
أتوا يستأذنونك فى قعود   فياويل لهم من خائرينا
أرادوا مع النساء يطول مكث   لهم خسئوا وصاروا مدمرينا
على قلب لهم إنا طبعنا   فما كانوا لخير قابلينا
وما كانوا لأضواء ونور   من التنزيل يوماً مبصرينا

God's judgment comes down on those with might
who, despite all their riches, refuse to fight.
Coming to you, for exemption they plead.
Woe unto them, they are weaklings indeed!
A long life they wanted and with the women to stay,
but their lives were destroyed; they were chased away.
Their hearts we have tightly sealed,
the good tidings remain from them concealed.
And revelation with its light
is forever hidden from their sight.[2]

It took the Islamic Research Council four years to come to a decision which, after some initial dissent, was negative and upheld by a court. After that, the author seems to have made no further attempt to publish this work or any other. The reasons the Council members gave for rejecting the book varied, but none of the *'ulamā'*, or religious scholars, involved ever claimed that the content of the *tafsīr* was theologically problematic, let alone heretical. Rather, they criticised the bad style of poetry which uses a traditional Arabic metre.[3] The concluding report used that fact to accuse the author of transforming the Qur'ān's meaning into a superficial and formalistic pattern of metre and rhyme without any artistic value. As such, it deforms and defaces the Qur'ān which amounts to an insult of God. Besides, the reports said, the book does not constitute a work of *tafsīr* and should therefore not be called that because it does not contribute anything to the understanding of the Qur'ān's meaning.[4] This assessment is slightly surprising in view of the fact that even a translation adds to understanding the Qur'ān's meaning and is therefore called *tafsīr* in many non-Arabic contexts, for example in Southeast Asia.

In 2016, the well-established Egyptian journalist Muḥammad al-Bāz took up the case as the twenty-first episode of his Ramadan series *The Qur'ān in Egypt*. The series was published in the print and online newspaper *al-Bawāba*, for which he served as editor-in-chief, and shortly thereafter all thirty episodes were printed as a book under the same title.[5] All in all, the series strove to write a comprehensive story of the modern and contemporary interpretation of the Qur'ān in Egypt. Some of its components are surprising and unusual, such as the chapters on the interpretation of the Qur'ān through music and film. What is striking about this book, though, is not only the unconventional, but extremely plausible attempt to situate the Qur'ān in the specific context of a modern nation state, but also the eminently political character of the narrative. Al-Bāz is clearly not in love with the Muslim Brotherhood, but writing at a time at which the Muslim Brotherhood was completely banned in Egypt, he is much more concerned with al-Azhar. Already in the title of the third episode, he asks: 'Why are the Azhar shaykhs afraid of a contemporary interpretation of the Qur'ān?'

Indeed, Sayf al-Dīn Ṭāhā's case raises many questions that point to the importance of notions of authority and legitimacy in writing about the Qur'ān. Would the work have been deemed acceptable if it had been written in masterful poetry? Would it have been approved if the author had belonged to the *'ulamā'* or would they have excluded him from their ranks? Would he have fared better if he had not called his work *tafsīr*? What, then, are the boundaries of *tafsīr*? What conditions do a work and its author have to fulfil in order to be allowed to carry that title? And, finally, how would any of this have been different if it had happened in another country with different structures of religious authority?

In the case of the failed poet-exegete, al-Bāz surmises that there are several underlying reasons for the opposition of the shaykhs, other than a disapproval of bad poetry: a general fear of innovation; an attempt to prevent anyone from outside the field of the *ʿulamāʾ* to encroach upon their territory, especially in unconventional ways that might raise attention; and also the fear that the Qurʾān and poetry could in any way be associated with each other while the Qurʾān clearly states that it is not the word of a poet (Q. 36:69, 69:41). That fear is indeed a powerful motive. It had similar consequences for an Indonesian Qurʾān translator whose verse-by-verse typesetting choices were deemed too close to poetry by the religious establishment.[6] On the other hand, rhymed Qurʾān translations are published and sold in Turkey.[7] This has much to do with the fact that their authors come from religious groups that are outside the field of Sunni orthodoxy anyway. They also skilfully deploy the powerful Turkish-nationalist discourse as a legitimising factor.

The case of Sayf al-Dīn, the thwarted poet, and al-Bāz's portrayal of the Qurʾān in Egypt clearly show the importance of local power structures to the interpretation of the Qurʾān and to the dissemination of such interpretations. Sometimes, even transnational power structures are invoked when the legitimacy of an interpretive approach is contested. Thus, in 2012, two Saudi-Salafi websites erroneously reported that the rhymed *tafsīr* was finally going to be printed – with money from Saudi Arabia's Shiʿi arch-enemy, Iran.[8]

The *ʿulamāʾ* are still a powerful status group. But they can only exert that power if the state or the society they live in grant them the right to do so; if their pronouncements carry some weight and are considered authoritative expressions of Islam either by the government or by substantial segments of the population. Even when that is the case, though – and it most certainly is in Egypt – it is becoming harder for any type of religious establishment to control the plurality of approaches to the Qurʾān. The field is globalising, and if one country does not offer the liberty to write certain things about the Qurʾān, others will do so. It is increasingly difficult for governments to bar access to such ideas, not least because of the internet. Thus, pluralisation is happening, often because of external pressures. Certain topics, such as global human rights discourses, might be dominant enough to exert pressure to seek justification for Qurʾānic statements that do not seem to conform to them; and specific groups exert pressure in order to achieve such conformity. It is this complex web of power structures and tensions, local as well as global, that this book seeks to elucidate.

NOTES

1. Al-Sibāʿī, 'Qaṣāʾid shiʿr'.
2. Al-Sibāʿī, 'Qaṣāʾid shiʿr'; Bāz, *Al-Qurʾān fī Miṣr*, 190.
3. The excerpt follows the model of a classical Arabic *qaṣīda* where each verse consists of two halves, the second of which carries the rhyme. The metre used is *wāfir.*
4. Al-Bāz, *Al-Qurʾān fī Miṣr*, 191–193.
5. Al-Bāz, *Al-Qurʾān fī Miṣr*.
6. Rahman, 'The Controversy around H. B. Jassin'.
7. See page 202, 'Negotiating the boundaries of Islamicness through the Qurʾān: Ali Adil Atalay 'Vaktidolu' (b. 1936, Turkey) on Q. 2:21'.
8. Al-Barbarī, 'Īrān takhtariq al-Azhar al-sharīf'; al-ʿAnqāʿ, 'Īrān takhtariq al-Azhar al-sharīf'.

INTRODUCTION

QUR'ĀNIC INTERPRETATION TODAY: TENSIONS AND POWER FIELDS[1]

As the case of Egypt's thwarted poet-exegete has shown, Qur'ānic interpretation today is embedded in power structures, and it is also beset by tensions: tensions between localising and globalising forces; tensions between hierarchical and egalitarian social ideals; and tensions between the quest for new approaches and the claim for authority raised by defenders of exegetical traditions.

In Islamic bookstores in Cairo, when asking for recent commentaries on the Qur'ān, the almost uniform answer is 'Why should they be recent?' coupled with a recommendation of the fourteenth-century exegete Ibn Kathīr. Islamic book sellers in Amman, on the other hand, praise the 'simplified commentary on the Qur'ān' (*tafsīr muyassar*) by the Saudi preacher 'Ā'iḍ b. 'Abdallāh al-Qarnī as the most authoritative contemporary work – a work that, in the author's words, aims at avoiding 'speculation' and academic discussion.

At the same time, such 'speculation' and academic discussions take place all over the world. The Iraqi dentist Aḥmad Khayrī al-'Umarī recently proposed a 'Qur'ānic compass' as a medium for developing new perspectives on the world and overthrowing outdated traditions while the American Muslim theologian Aysha A. Hidayatullah, in a thoughtful book, discusses feminist approaches to the Qur'ān, their limits and how those might be transcended.

Such works, of course, have little mass appeal. When searching for more popular presentations of the Qur'ān, a visit to an Indonesian bookstore exposes tables of colourful Qur'ān editions complete with translation – a genre of exegesis that is rarely recognised as such by its readers. Beside them are a plethora of books that promote the Qur'ān as a guide to success, both in the afterlife and in a very material sense, promising a career, wealth and happy marriages based on the Qur'ān's guidance.

Books, though, are generally not the locus of mass appeal. Popular preachers draw huge crowds, and their audiences are multiplied by appearances on television and YouTube. The internet has become hugely influential. Written as well as audio-visual sources available on the internet are so easily accessible that it might have become the most important exegetical resource to many. For example, when a group of young female Muslims in the German city of Freiburg meet for their regular Qur'ān study circle, they cite the above-mentioned Ibn Kathīr as an authority alongside the modernist Muhammad Asad, both of whom wrote Qur'ānic commentaries that have been translated into various languages and are available online. They look up the occurrence of Qur'ānic terms in an internet database with unprecedented ease; and they rely heavily on YouTube videos, ranging from Turkish preachers to the English-speaking Nouman Ali Khan, some of whose talks on the interpretation of the Qur'ān receive several hundred thousand views. Based on all these resources, they discuss their own views on the Qur'ānic text in immediate personal interaction.

The internet does not only provide access to Qur'ān-related information and sermons, it also provides Muslims with a space to discuss questions of interpretation without the need for direct physical contact and without a necessity to reveal their identity. For example, an Ahl al-Ḥadīth message board features a message by an anonymous Muslim who was intrigued by two nearly identical statements in the Qur'ān that only differ by one inconsequential-seeming word, and he decided to ask other board members for their opinion on the issue. This opened a lengthy discussion between many users, none of whom appear to be scholars, about whether this word has a specific purpose, whether or not it makes any difference to the meaning, what the purpose might be and what proofs there are of this.[2]

All these are contemporary expressions of Muslim Qur'ānic interpretation. Describing them as 'modern', though, as is often done, might be misleading; at the very least, the term 'modern' is not a meaningful descriptor. After all, some contemporary Muslims promote approaches to the Qur'ān that they frame as distinctly traditional, even anti-modern; and yet, they often use modern technologies in order to gain followers worldwide. Due to such uses of new media and also due to large-scale migration movements, discourses on the Qur'ān have an increasingly global dimension, yet at the same time, the local embeddedness of many Qur'ānic interpretations is hard to overlook.

How should we make sense, then, of such an ambiguous, broad and conflicting phenomenon? Rather than trying to sidestep, marginalise or smooth over the tensions mentioned above, this book aims to focus on them and identify their causes. At first glance, the main source of conflict lies in divergent views of how the Qur'ān should be interpreted, which techniques and methods are legitimate and how they should be applied. Such views, however, do not emerge in a vacuum. They are embedded in value systems that prioritise certain larger themes over others and frame the Qur'ānic text in a specific way. For example, a committed defender of egalitarianism will find little of value in the Qur'ānic commentaries written by premodern scholars whose thought was shaped by a hierarchical society. Conversely, a believer in the precedence of early opinions over more recent ones will not be interested in 'new', 'fresh' or 'modern' approaches to the Qur'ān, but rather emphasise the authority of Islam's premodern intellectual heritage.

The notion of authority is central to this book. Conflicts over the interpretation of the Qur'ān always touch upon the question who has the authority to talk about the Qur'ān and in what way. Qur'ānic interpretation takes place in power fields. It is not merely about the things that are being said or written; it is just as much, sometimes more so, about the person who says them, the reasons for which they are said, the place in which they are said or published and the opposing parties against whom they are directed. Furthermore, it is about the – imagined or real – recipients of that message. Who are they? Why and how are they supposed to gain access to that message? How is it mediated, and how do media shape the form and contents of the message? Who has control of that media? That last question again leads us to the issue of power.

Not in every case might the existence of power fields and power struggles be as obvious as in the case of the Egyptian poet whose efforts were suppressed by a powerful religious institution. Power relations might not seem particularly important to a Muslim academic who holds a faculty position and may freely publish his works. Even then, however, that work is produced in specific structural conditions that determine the limits of what may be written, its style, its potential for publication and career advancement and its reception. The nation state and its institutions are always part of these structural conditions today, as are national and global media and the audiences they create. If an author attacks the Qur'ān as a violent and patriarchal scripture, the reactions in Muslim-majority societies are just as foreseeable as those in European and North American societies. In both cases, they are made possible, or at the very least multiplied, by mass media. At the beginning of the twenty-first century it is safe to assume that the authors of exegetical works anticipate such effects and take them into account.

THIS BOOK'S APPROACH

This book wants to illuminate the context in which contemporary Qur'ānic interpretation takes place and explain how that context shapes the style and contents of exegesis. It will highlight important themes, arguments and methods in present-day approaches to the Qur'ān. It will examine the exegetical involvement of an increasingly diverse array of Muslims and Muslim communities and the conflicts that it causes. Finally, it will take none of these phenomena as a given, but seek to show where they come from, adding historical depths to the analysis.

In addition to giving an overview of the most important trends, historical antecedents and conditions that shape contemporary Muslim approaches to the Qur'ān, this book substantiates its arguments with an array of case studies of concrete exegetical sources that have been chosen because they illustrate and represent particular phenomena, discourses, communities, exegetical methods, aims or media. They also introduce authentic Muslim exegetical voices into what is otherwise an analytical description.

The sources this book engages with are very recent, dating from the mid-2000s to 2016. The focus, thus, is on the present.[3] At the same time, the perspective I take on present-day sources is a distinctly historical one. I have been inspired by an approach that Michel Foucault called a 'history of the present' and summarised as follows: 'I set out from a problem expressed in the terms current today and I try to work out its genealogy'.[4] In order to make sense of the field of contemporary Qur'ānic interpretation which makes use of historical precedents in many complex ways, the notion of genealogy seems to me to be analytically more useful than, for example, a simplistic paradigm of continuity and change. A genealogical approach is based on a certain scepticism towards writings of history that favour ruptures, innovations and transformations – in short, 'change' – over continuity and that portray change as the irreconcilable antagonist of continuity. In fact, in the history of Qur'ānic exegesis, continuities might be more important than in many other fields. The genre of the Qur'ānic commentary has not been called a 'genealogical tradition'[5] for nothing since it favours interpretations that are traceable to previous authorities over opinions presented as new. The continuing importance of the premodern commentary tradition in present times is a perfect example of the paradoxical nature of the continuity-and-change paradigm: the mere fact that a premodern work of scholarship has been printed and thus converted into a mass commodity signifies not only a remarkable continuity, but also a fundamental change in its function.

In any case, contemporary Muslim Qur'ānic interpretation cannot be reduced to the genre of the Qur'ānic commentary, and the genealogical nature of that genre is not the only, and not even the main, reason for pursuing a genealogical approach. The main advantage of that approach is the fact that it does not focus on 'origins' as much as it tries to take stock of present phenomena and developments and to identify the power struggles, fault lines and concrete decisions they result from. It does not reduce the present to an organic and inevitable outcome of historical processes or to a set of continuities and discontinuities derived from a comparison with an imagined 'original state'. Rather, it…

> traces how contemporary practices and institutions emerged out of specific struggles, conflicts, alliances, and exercises of power…The idea… is to trace the erratic and discontinuous process whereby the past became the present: an often aleatory path of descent and emergence that suggests the contingency of the present and the openness of the future… Genealogy's aim is to trace the struggles, displacements and processes of repurposing out of which contemporary practices emerged…[6]

My analysis of contemporary Muslim interpretations of the Qur'ān, thus, is an attempt, first, to describe the main forms, concerns and structural conditions in which they appear and, second, to understand the genealogy of these trends and conditions, outlining their emergence, their development and their relevance to specific actors.

In other words, I look at contemporary Muslim engagement with the Qur'ān as part of an ongoing discursive tradition.[7] That discursive tradition, much in line with the genealogical approach to history described above, is neither uniform nor unchanging; it undergoes transformations, shifts and possibly even ruptures, but it also retains a core set of symbols and resources. The question that interests me is what meaning and what function such symbols and resources assume for contemporary Muslims who read and interpret their sacred scripture. In that sense, a contemporary translation of the fourteenth-century Qur'ānic commentary by Ibn Kathīr is just as worthy of consideration as a bold and innovative work of feminist exegesis – indeed, I try to avoid this type of dichotomy as much as possible because it is my contention that it obscures more than it does explain anything.

In my analysis and choice of source texts I have tried to select, from among the huge and diverse contemporary Muslim discourse on the Qur'ān, such themes and questions that, to me, seemed to be recurrent and pervasive. For example, why is it that Ibn Kathīr is so important as a premodern source – important enough to have been translated into multiple languages? On the topic of language: what impact do Qur'ān translations have on the ways in which Muslims today understand the Qur'ān? Why is the Qur'ān's view on gender relations such a ubiquitous subject of debate? How do new media shape the way in which the Qur'ān is negotiated? Why and how do so many exegetes use scientific language and paradigms in their Qur'ānic interpretations? What parts of the exegetical tradition have become controversial, marginalised or ignored?

In answering such questions, I have aimed to take stock of the full variety of contributions to contemporary exegetical debates, starting with those erudite exegetical works that are the most common subject of research, but also including the vastly influential Qur'ānic interpretations produced by preachers, teachers, devout lay Muslims and journalists in various types of media, including videos and comic books. These might not always be of the highest intellectual and academic rank, and some of their authors might be little-known or even anonymous, but they are vital means through which many Muslims today negotiate the meaning and importance of their sacred scripture, and thus worthy of scholarly attention.

The field I am looking at is vast, and setting some limitations is unavoidable. One explicit and important condition that I am setting is that I will only look at texts – in the broader sense of the word, including oral utterances and comic strips – that aim at interpreting specific segments of the Qur'ān. These texts need not be complete commentaries on the Qur'ān, but they need to say something about at least one concrete verse or exegetical problem. Thus, I will not discuss general hermeneutical theories although I will, of course, mention them where they are relevant to understanding a particular interpretive approach.[8]

The structure of this book is unique in that each chapter contains a number of case studies that are based on a wide array of recent exegetical sources and which substantiate the main topics and arguments under consideration. Some of the sources are originally in English; most of them I have translated from other languages, specifically, Indonesian, Arabic, Turkish and German. A small amount of material has been translated from Persian and French.[9] Each source text is preceded by a brief introduction into the exegetical work it is taken from and the exegete's background, as well as the Qur'ānic verse it comments on in Arabic and English.[10]

While engaging with these source texts, I repeatedly entered into conversations with their authors. This raised the question, for me, to what extent I want to take sides in the exegetical debates I am writing about, and whether it is even feasible *not* to take sides. After all, Foucault's proposal to write the history of present-day institutions was not a mere exercise in historical analysis. Rather, it had a distinctly critical impetus. He was convinced that the analysis of genealogies has the potential to shake up unquestioned ideas of normalcy, naturalness and normativity and to demonstrate the extent to which present-day institutions are a product of power relations. This critical intention raises problems for me as a non-Muslim scholarly observer. Having been trained as a German Islamicist, I tend to consider it neither my role nor my purpose to be an active participant in Muslim religious debates. However, in today's globalised world, I am not writing in a hermetic field in which would-be objective non-Muslim academic observers interact with each other exclusively, nor would it be desirable to reconstruct such hermetic fields. Through my interactions with contemporary Muslim exegetes, I came to realise that I cannot write on a contemporary discourse without becoming part of it. The least I could do, under the circumstances, was to make a conscious effort not to limit myself to such approaches that I personally empathise or agree with. Rather, I strove to select a diverse array of sources that convey an impression of the manifold contemporary perspectives on the Qur'ān and the conditions that shape them.

It was also important to me to think carefully about the terminology I use to describe various exegetical approaches. Terms such as 'conservative', 'progressive', 'liberal', 'modern', 'traditional' and 'Salafi' abound. Some of them are used as self-descriptors, some as labels that might have positive or negative connotations and some for analytical purposes. Many of them are problematic because of the inherent value they ascribe to particular positions. Furthermore, the fact that a number of exegetical approaches are closely connected not only to an intellectual framework, but also to specific social groups is often neglected when attaching labels to them. Finally, the analytical value especially of dichotomous categories such as 'conservative' versus 'modern' is questionable. For example, an exegete might take up gender concepts from early-twentieth century reformers such as Muḥammad ʿAbduh (1849–1905) whose thought is typically considered 'modern' but was also embedded in an extremely patriarchal society. This might result in an exegetical work that strongly promotes providing girls with an education, but is at the same time adamant that a woman's place is in the home, offering evidence from modern brain research to substantiate the argument. Is this, then, a 'modern' or a 'conservative' position? None of these descriptors would be quite fitting and none of them would be particularly meaningful.

I have decided to largely operate with the following categories. They are characterised not only by a shared general idea of how the Qur'ān should be read, although with a fair amount of variety and overlap, but also by specific genealogies which will be explained at detail throughout the chapters of this book and substantiated by exegetical source texts.

The *ʿulamāʾ* or religious scholars are an important status group and, by and large, embody the continuation of the scholarly tradition of *tafsīr*. It is entirely possible for an *ʿālim* to develop innovative ideas but proposing these ideas in an established form and genre will greatly enhance their chances of being recognised as an important contribution to scholarship.[11]

Modernists propose Qur'ānic interpretations that explicitly aim to make the Qur'ān compatible with the conditions of modern societies and to separate today's understanding of the Qur'ān from that of the premodern exegetical tradition. This is usually achieved by methods that place great emphasis on historical contextualisation and on the Qur'ān's aims, rather than the literal meaning of specific utterances and norms.[12]

Islamists consider Islam a holistic way of life (*manhaj*) or system (*niẓām*), and the Qur'ān the perfect representation of that holistic way of life. Therefore, they emphasise the Qur'ān's relevance for individual believers not only with respect to faith, but also on an emotional and practical level.[13]

Salafis are scripturalists who consider the Qur'ān and the Sunna the only authoritative sources of religion. They advocate a literal reading, resulting in a way of life that follows the beliefs and practices of an imagined original Islamic community in the age of the Prophet and his companions. Salafis, in principle, deny the authority of later scholars although there are, in fact, some scholars whom they tend to grant a high degree of authority for having applied a Salafi methodology.[14]

Postmodern approaches are a rather recent phenomenon and quite rare. Their proponents often share the concerns of modernists, but are highly critical to any claim to having identified the true meaning of the Qur'ān. Rather, they emphasise the subjectivity of any reading of the Qur'ān. They explicitly consider it legitimate to take external factors into account when interpreting the scripture, such as the exegete's conscience or overarching social values.[15]

This book strives to cover this wide variety of approaches, as well as the agents behind them and their genealogy. It treats Qur'ānic exegesis as an intellectual phenomenon that happens in a specific social context in which individual interpretations are pushed to prominence or marginalised. In order to understand this, one has to recognise their embeddedness into a network of local and global power relations and the role of modern media. In sum, this book should be read as a spotlight on a specific period of time, a time of considerable transformations, some of them strikingly obvious and some of them rarely noted.

NOTES

1. I thank Gerard van de Bruinhorst for bringing to my attention the notion that Qur'ānic exegesis is embedded in power fields and for substantiating it so convincingly. For a related case study, see van de Bruinhorst, '"I Didn't Want to Write This"'.
2. Ḥijābī 'Affāfī et al., 'Mā al-farq'.
3. Readers interested in a more long-term account of modern Qur'ānic exegesis have a number of other commendable studies and collections to choose from. See especially Baljon, *Modern Muslim Koran Interpretation*; Campanini, *The Qur'an: Modern Muslim Interpretations*; Ennaifer, *Les commentaires coraniques contemporains*; Jansen, *The Interpretation of the Koran in Modern Egypt*; Taji-Farouki, *Modern Muslim Intellectuals and the Qur'an*; Wielandt, 'Exegesis of the Qur'an: Early Modern and Contemporary'.
4. Garland, 'What is a "history of the Present"?', 367.
5. Saleh, *The Formation of the Classical* Tafsīr *Tradition*, 16.
6. Garland, 'What is a "history of the Present"?', 372–373.
7. For the notion of Islam as a discursive tradition, see Asad, *The Idea of an Anthropology of Islam*.

8. For readers interested in hermeneutical theory, Campanini, *The Qur'an: Modern Muslim Interpretations*, might be a useful introduction.
9. In my translations of the source texts into English, I have avoided shortening the texts wherever possible. In a few cases, inevitably, the texts had to be shortened. In such cases I have indicated the contents of the missing segments. I have slightly adapted the translations to the technical conventions generally used throughout this book, for example by limiting eulogy, by giving sura numbers instead of names, and by using a consistent system of transliteration unless the text was originally in English in which case I have reproduced it as closely as possible. I have also occasionally added life dates and other short explanations in square brackets.
10. The English translations of the Qurʾānic verses discussed in the text samples are the ones contained in the source text if that source text is originally in English. If it is originally in a language that is neither Arabic nor English and contains a Qurʾān translation, I have tried to provide an English translation that captures the choices made by the authors of the source text. If the source text does not provide a Qurʾān translation, as is the case with sources that are originally in Arabic, the translation is my own. In those cases, my aim is to translate in such a way that the exegetical problems discussed in the source text become comprehensible. I have drawn on a number of existing English translations in the process. These are: Abdel Haleem, *The Qur'an: A New Translation*; Ali, *Qur'ān*; Arberry, *The Koran Interpreted*; Asad, *The Message of the Qurʾān*; Droge, *The Qur'ān*; Jones, *The Qur'ān*; Nasr, *The Study Quran*.
11. See page 38, 'The *ʿulamāʾ* as bearers of the tradition'.
12. See page 125, 'Modernism and its paradigms'.
13. See page 181, 'Islamist Qurʾānic interpretation'.
14. See page 48, 'A Salafi paradigm', and page 61, 'Present-day Salafi exegesis'.
15. See page 265, 'Postmodern uncertainties and subjective approaches'.

1

THE NEW CENTRALITY OF THE QUR᾽ĀNIC MESSAGE

Before asking *how* Muslims today are interpreting the Qur᾽ān, we should ask *why* they do it. The answer might seem rather obvious, but in a way, it is not. The Qur᾽ān, of course, has always been the sacred scripture of Islam but it is today central to Muslim discourses on belief, religious identity and moral behaviour to a degree that it had hardly ever been before the late-nineteenth century. The question how it gained this centrality has not been sufficiently explored, and it certainly has no single answer. Nonetheless, what follows is an attempt to describe what happened and offer some explanations for why it might have happened.

The last third of the nineteenth century was a time in which important changes occurred that will be explained below. Therefore, I operate with the notions of 'modern' and 'premodern' periods of Qur᾽ānic exegesis, denoting developments that took place after and before the late-nineteenth century, respectively. This does not imply that either premodern or modern exegetical thought are uniform in any way, nor would it be accurate to assume that there are no continuities or that the same chronology could be applied to every region of the Muslim world. Developments in South Asia, for example, predate those in the Ottoman Empire or Southeast Asia significantly. The rough division between a premodern and modern period is thus no more than an auxiliary construct whose analytical value should not be overestimated.

THE PLACE OF THE QUR᾽ĀN IN PREMODERN MUSLIM SOCIETIES

Premodern Muslim societies were varied and there were vast differences between them with respect to religious practices, the degree of religious observance, educational institutions and the status of religious knowledge in society. However, the core of religious ritual remained the same, and there was also a shared intellectual heritage besides the existence of distinctly local and regional traditions. Despite the immense local variations, it is therefore possible to make some very general remarks.

To practising Muslim believers, some knowledge of the Qur'ān was indispensable for conducting the compulsory ritual prayer.[1] Ideally, they learned the first *sūra* (al-Fātiḥa), some of the short *sūra*s towards the end of the Qur'ān and some segments of other *sūra*s that seemed particularly suitable for prayer. Century after century, however, scholars with a penchant for religious reform bemoaned the low prevalence of such knowledge, particularly in rural areas.[2]

Apart from prayer, the exposure of most Muslims to the Qur'ān was probably through sermons which made use of isolated Qur'ān quotations and possibly through Qur'ānic recitations. Native speakers of Arabic might have had some understanding of the meaning; most speakers of other languages had not. Literacy rates were low. Even for students at Qur'ānic schools and madrasas, who were usually literate, the oral aspect of the study of the Qur'ān was of paramount importance: the goal for the advanced students was to memorise the Qur'ān and to be able to recite it properly, but few managed to master the complete text. Thus, neither the knowledge of the entire Qur'ānic text nor the means to access it were very common, and even where it was taught, this was not necessarily done with a focus on its meaning.[3]

Of course, there were spaces in which the meaning of the Qur'ān, as opposed to the mastery of its recitation, mattered. Students aiming to become religious scholars studied Qur'ānic commentaries in order to understand the Qur'ān; this was normally considered preferable to working with the text itself. The first step was the study of a paraphrastic commentary such as the immensely popular *Tafsīr al-Jalālayn*, a work from the fifteenth century that might be considered an explanatory translation of the Qur'ān into Modern Standard Arabic.[4] Then came medium-length works such as those of al-Zamakhsharī (d. 1144) and al-Bayḍāwī (d. between 1287 and 1316), the most prestigious representatives of this genre, which have been dubbed madrasa-style commentaries for their use in institutions of higher learning where they served to introduce students to the main exegetical debates without going into details of who said what and by what chain it was transmitted. Those details were the domain of the large encyclopaedic commentaries[5] that strove to gather all existing exegetical opinions, or at least those that the exegete deemed important enough not to ignore, and to possibly discuss them, comment on them or add the exegete's own considerations.[6]

All this was an academic activity and, as such, closely interlinked with other academic disciplines such as scholastic theology (*kalām*), law (*fiqh*), philosophy, logic, philology and rhetoric. These disciplines all exerted a strong influence on Qur'ānic exegesis (*tafsīr*); and in all of them there had during the first centuries of Islam emerged a consensus that the Qur'ān was not the only source of religious knowledge. The Sunna – the body of traditions of the Prophet – had equal rank to the Qur'ān in many fields, apart from ritual. Thus, prophetic traditions – *ḥadīths* – and other reports about early authorities were an extremely important resource for *tafsīr* as well as for law and theology.[7]

Tafsīr was certainly a prestigious activity, but it was not the locus of debate about the definition of faith or correct religious practice. Faith (*ʿaqīda*) was mostly the domain of the theologians (*mutakallimūn*) and closely linked to questions of epistemology: which sources and methods should be used in order to determine truth. The relationship between the Qur'ān, the Sunna and reason was fiercely embattled. In contrast to theologians, Qur'ānic exegetes (*mufassirūn*) were rarely concerned with truth. Their aim was to explain the Qur'ān, to decipher its layers of meaning, to discuss specific problems presented by the text, to transmit authoritative past opinions; rarely did they intend to derive from it an unambiguous, coherent message.

If individuals were looking for guidance in matters of religious practice, law or even theoretical questions of belief, they would turn to a qualified jurist (that is, a mufti) and request a fatwa (that is, a qualified legal opinion). Islamic law, as it was practiced by legal scholars was called *fiqh*, and while its function was to provide guidance, it did not necessarily raise a claim to truth. Different muftis could provide different opinions, and they ended their statement by saying 'God knows best' (*wa'llāhu aʿlam*). The existence of schools of law (*madhāhib*) came to be an expression of the legitimacy of divergent opinions. Each scholar was affiliated with one such school and to a certain degree operated within the framework set by it. The mainstream opinion – with certain exceptions – was that the process of establishing legal rulings was not limited to a straightforward application of the Qur'ān and the Sunna, but built upon a complex system of scholarship and the work of past authorities, just as theological dogma was not simply taken from the Qur'ān, but presupposed a complex epistemological system.[8]

Tafsīr, then, was an academic discipline. There were other, smaller academic fields that dealt with the Qur'ān, often focussing on particular sets of problems or narratives discussed in works of *tafsīr*, such as the 'occasions of revelation' (*asbāb al-nuzūl*). Together with *tafsīr*, they formed a broader field of Qur'ānic studies that interacted closely with other fields of learning. While it was not at the centre of debate about correct belief and practice, it often informed them, especially when they used the Qur'ān for polemical and apologetic purposes. Besides, while *tafsīr* and the broader field of Qur'ānic studies did form a distinct discipline, this did not mean that scholars were restricted to working within that discipline. It was perfectly possible and very common for a scholar to be an exegete, a jurist and a theologian and to publish works in each of these fields. However, he[9] would be expected to situate each of his works in the respective discipline by drawing on genre-specific methodologies and sources.[10]

All of this was probably of little relevance for Muslims outside the realm of religious scholarship. They had some exposure to fragments of the Qur'ān and its interpretation through preachers and storytellers who used narrative traditions of various origins in order to expand on Qur'ānic stories and motives. The purpose might have been partly a moral one and partly entertainment. What little we know of these oral activities before the advent of print comes either from collections of sermons by some of the more respectable preachers or from critics. These sources do not give the impression that popular sermons and storytelling were a particularly Qur'ān-centred activity. The same is true for the extremely influential realm of Sufism where ritual practices could be based on Qur'ānic verses, but also on other sources such as the ninety-nine names of God. The Qur'ān played a role in folk beliefs and practices of healing and warding off evil, but again, all that was needed for these were fragments, and an understanding of their meaning was not required.[11] All in all, to most premodern Muslims the Qur'ān seems to have been a device among many: central and irreplaceable in matters of ritual and aesthetics as well as in some areas of folk belief, but not necessarily the main source of guidance – if a need for such guidance was even perceived.[12]

THE SHIFT TO THE CENTRE

The first important reason for an increased emphasis on teaching and understanding the Qur'ān seems to be the activity of some of the revivalist movements that emerged from the eighteenth century onward. Even before then, there had occasionally been scholars who had promoted scripturalist ideas, demanding the direct recourse to the Qur'ān and the Sunna, complemented by reports on the first two generations of Islam. Consequently, these scholars had criticised the reliance on jurists, theologians and their fallible human reason; they had. The most important proponent of this scripturalist trend had been Taqī al-Dīn Ibn Taymiyya (1263–1328) about whom more will be said later. However, before the eighteenth century, these scripturalist tendencies had been a rather elitist endeavour, directed at other scholars and with a strong focus on *ḥadīth* scholarship. They had not been tied to a vision of educating lay Muslims on the Qur'ān.

This changed noticeably with the activities of the scholar Shāh Walī Allāh Dihlāwī (1703–1762) in India who, more than other reformers of his and the subsequent century, attributed an important role to the Qur'ān and Qur'ānic education in his reform project.[13] Deeply troubled by the dramatic decline of the Mughal Empire that he witnessed during his lifetime, he developed a vision of reviving an authentic Islam that was purified from 'aberrations' and divisive aspects. In order to achieve this, a broad consensus beyond the boundaries of schools of law and Sufi orders should be sought, and the Qur'ān – the scripture that all Muslims believed to be a direct revelation from God – was to be at the centre of that consensus. Walī Allāh believed that a reform of education was needed in order to instil in all students an intimate connection to the Qur'ān. His aim was to acquaint students directly with the Qur'ān, as opposed to making them study a paraphrastic commentary which was the common approach in his times. He was also a proponent of translating the Qur'ān into vernacular languages in order to enable a larger number of Muslims to understand its message.[14] He himself penned a Persian translation of the Qur'ān, and his sons produced an Urdu translation towards the end of the eighteenth century.[15]

Other revivalist intellectuals and movements emerged during the eighteenth and early-nineteenth centuries with varying concerns and approaches. Not all of them were as interested in unity and consensus as Walī Allāh was, nor did all of them have an educational ideal that involved for students to achieve an actual understanding of the Qur'ān. Nevertheless, most revivalist movements had features that were conducive to according the Qur'ān a central role: they were critical of the development of Muslim scholarship after the foundational period, sometimes to the extent that they completely rejected the schools of law; as a consequence, they placed great emphasis on the fundamental textual sources and/or the example of the 'early generations' of Islam (*salaf*); and they negatively assessed the state of their respective societies, attributing this perceived crisis to the weakness of religious beliefs and practices which needed to be countered by improved religious education. All this was discernible in various regions of the Muslim world well before European political and military dominance was seen as an issue there.[16]

In the course of the nineteenth century, circumstances changed significantly. The reality of European imperialism led to an increased sense of crisis. At the same time, there was growing interaction with Europeans and European ideas. Christian missionaries were active in many Muslim-majority countries and local rulers strove for reforms based on European models. Finally, around the end of the nineteenth and beginning of the twentieth centuries, nationalist movements started to emerge. All these factors contributed to significant shifts in Muslim religious discourses.

Some responded to the heightened sense of crisis with a renewed revivalist approach that was promoted with increased urgency and, by way of the printing press, with much-improved means. The journal *al-'Urwa al-wuthqā* that two exiles from the Middle East, Jamāl al-Dīn al-Afghānī (1838–1897) and Muḥammad 'Abduh (d. 1905), published in Paris in 1884 for a duration of less than a year proved hugely influential. Besides spreading an anti-Imperialist, pan-Islamist political message, it introduced a novel vision of the role of the Qur'ān. The Qur'ān – from which the journal's title was taken (Q. 2:256, 31:22) – was to be the central source of guidance (*hidāya*) around which all Muslims should unite. Al-Afghānī and ʿAbduh recognised that the Qur'ān, much more than the scholarly traditions of law and theology or the huge and contested corpora of *ḥadīth*s, had a unifying power. The Qur'ān already had high emotional and symbolic appeal through the fact that segments of it were part of ritual prayer and many Muslims were familiar with the aesthetic quality of Qur'ān recitations. Al-Afghānī and ʿAbduh added to these ritual and emotional functions of the Qur'ān the idea that its meaning should be the ultimate guideline for Muslims and their societies, or even more than that: the Qur'ān should be their 'leader'. *Al-ʿUrwa al-wuthqā* particularly focussed on the punishment stories in the Qur'ān where the fate of peoples who failed to listen to a prophet's message is told; it also cited Qur'ānic exhortations that invite its audience to learn from these stories. The lesson Muslims should learn, according to ʿAbduh and al-Afghānī, should be to unite, to stand firm against non-Muslim invaders and to reform their societies both morally and technologically. In order to do so, they should travel and educate themselves so they can develop their societies as well as their countries' military technology. Moreover, they should counsel their rulers not to rely on foreigners. If they did all that, God would fulfil his promises to them.[17]

In his later exegetical works for which he became famous, Muḥammad ʿAbduh abandoned the idea of warfare that had been quite prominent in *al-ʿUrwa al-wuthqā* and focussed on the need for reform and education instead. Much like Walī Allāh had done approximately 150 years earlier, he diagnosed a widespread lack of Qur'ānic education that, in his opinion, prevented both unity and reform. Muslims should gain direct access to the message of the Qur'ān; and their education should focus on precisely that message, not on rote learning or scholarly traditions that seemed sclerotic to him and too far removed from the everyday concerns of Muslim societies. ʿAbduh's idea of taking the Qur'ān as the central source of 'guidance' (*hidāya*) proved extremely influential even if some aspects of his Qur'ān interpretation remained contested or ignored; that was especially true for his rationalism, his use of the Bible as a source to interpret the Qur'ān and his modernist belief in European-style progress, development and the evolution of human societies towards a historical destiny, as well as the realisation of man's God-given potential through the use of reason.[18]

The focus on the themes of guidance and unity meant that interpretive pluralism, which had long been the norm in Qur'ānic exegesis, was suddenly seen as a problem. How could the Qur'ān be a source of guidance if exegetes led endless debates about the myriad linguistic and dogmatic aspects related to any given exegetical problem? Here the ideas of modernists such as Muḥammad ʿAbduh converged with those of conservative scripturalists who, in the wake of the reform movements of the eighteenth and nineteenth centuries and building on the ideas of Ibn Taymiyya, aimed at reconstructing a pure Islamic society from the scriptural sources, based not on the authority of Muslim scholars, but on the imperatives of the Qur'ān and the Sunna.[19] While the two trends differed in many of their opinions, underlying priorities and values, for example with respect to the role of reason, they were united in their fundamental view of the Qur'ān as an undisputable and largely unambiguous normative source.

Thus began a discourse of polemics against all elements of Qur'ānic exegesis that were seen as divisive[20] or pointless both by modernists and radical scripturalists, later often termed *salafī*.[21] The theological heritage of *kalām* rapidly lost its relevance; for what purpose might disputes about the attributes of God serve when the Qur'ān's true aim was to guide believers to progress? The mistrust of philosophy was even larger. Moreover, any kind of esotericism was seen as a distraction from the 'true' meaning of the Qur'ān which was typically understood to refer to behaviour in this world, not in a spiritual sphere. Mysticism continued to be popular, but it came under pressure because modernists regarded it as superstitious and irrational while scripturalist fundamentalists considered it an illicit innovation (*bidʿa*). The existence of schools of law was sometimes accepted and sometimes rejected, but the general focus on unity meant that the differences between them were downplayed, if at all discussed. Narrative traditions surrounding the Qur'ān were often considered superfluous and thus discarded, usually by employing the polemical notion of *isrā'īliyyāt* – *ḥadīth*s purportedly from Jewish sources – about which more will be said below. The general tendency was to refute and abandon anything that was seen as distracting from the 'true message' of the Qur'ān. Until this day, it is very common for Qur'ānic commentaries and other works of exegesis to proclaim their intention to dispense with needless disputes and distractions such as *kalām*, philosophy, technical discussions or *isrā'īliyyāt*. Instead, guidance (*hidāya*) is a pervasive goal of exegesis, and that most commonly means a focus on the legal and ethical contents of the Qur'ān.

Guidance-oriented Qur'ānic interpretation is more common in some contexts than others. It occurs far less frequently in scholarly Qur'ānic commentaries than in exegetical sermons, for example, although it is not uncommon in twentieth and twenty-first-century academic works either.[22] One realm that particularly lends itself to a guidance-oriented approach is that of pedagogy, ranging from formal instruction in schools to educational media meant for home use. The following sample gives an impression of how such an approach is applied to the teaching of ethical injunctions and what distinguishes it from more conventional pedagogical types of exegesis.

Pedagogy and guidance (*hidāya*): an Indonesian comic book on Q. 49:12

Komik-qu, short for *Komik al-Quran* and a play with words (*komik-ku* would be 'my comic strip', the 'q' adds the association of the Qur'ān), is one of those generic works of religious educational literature that are ubiquitous in Indonesian bookstores. It was apparently written and produced by the staff of a provider of modern-style Islamic education for kindergarten and primary school children.

The book has around forty chapters, most of which consist of a topic header, a one-page comic strip leading up to a brief injunction from the Qur'ān and a colouring page or simple game. For example, paint-by-numbers pictures use Arabic numerals in order to help children practice those. The book claims to follow a novel didactic approach towards helping children to master Arabic and memorise the Qur'ān – goals that many Indonesian middle-class parents envisage for their offspring. Catering to those that do not feel comfortable with traditional methods of teaching the Qur'ān, *Komik-qu* wants to present an up-to-date pedagogical concept that emphasises the lessons to be learned from the Qur'ān and sees recitation and memorisation not as an end in itself, but as tools helping to internalise the message (see Excerpt 1.1).

As this sample shows, *Komik-qu* chooses to teach ethical injunctions in the Qur'ān through brief comic strips that typically show an example of 'wrong' behaviour, correct it and explain why it contradicts a specific verse of the Qur'ān. This is done in a very openly didactic manner. Clearly, the focus is not on telling a story, but on teaching a message. The dialogue is written in colloquial Indonesian, not in the formal style that is often used to talk about the Qur'ān. The anonymous authors obviously made an effort to make this book accessible and appealing to children on the linguistic level.

This becomes all the more apparent when contrasted with a recent Egyptian work that is equally targeted at children, 'Qur'ānic commentary for children and the Muslim family'. This five-volume work approaches the Qur'ān by working through the entire text segment by segment. Each group of verses is placed under a heading. The author then explains the meaning of difficult words. After that comes the occasion of revelation if one exists, and then the *tafsīr*, that is, the explanation of the meaning, phrase by phrase. About Q. 49:12, the verse that is the subject of the Indonesian comic strip above, the *tafsīr* says the following:

Excerpt 1.1

Gossip…Gossip…Gossip!!![233]

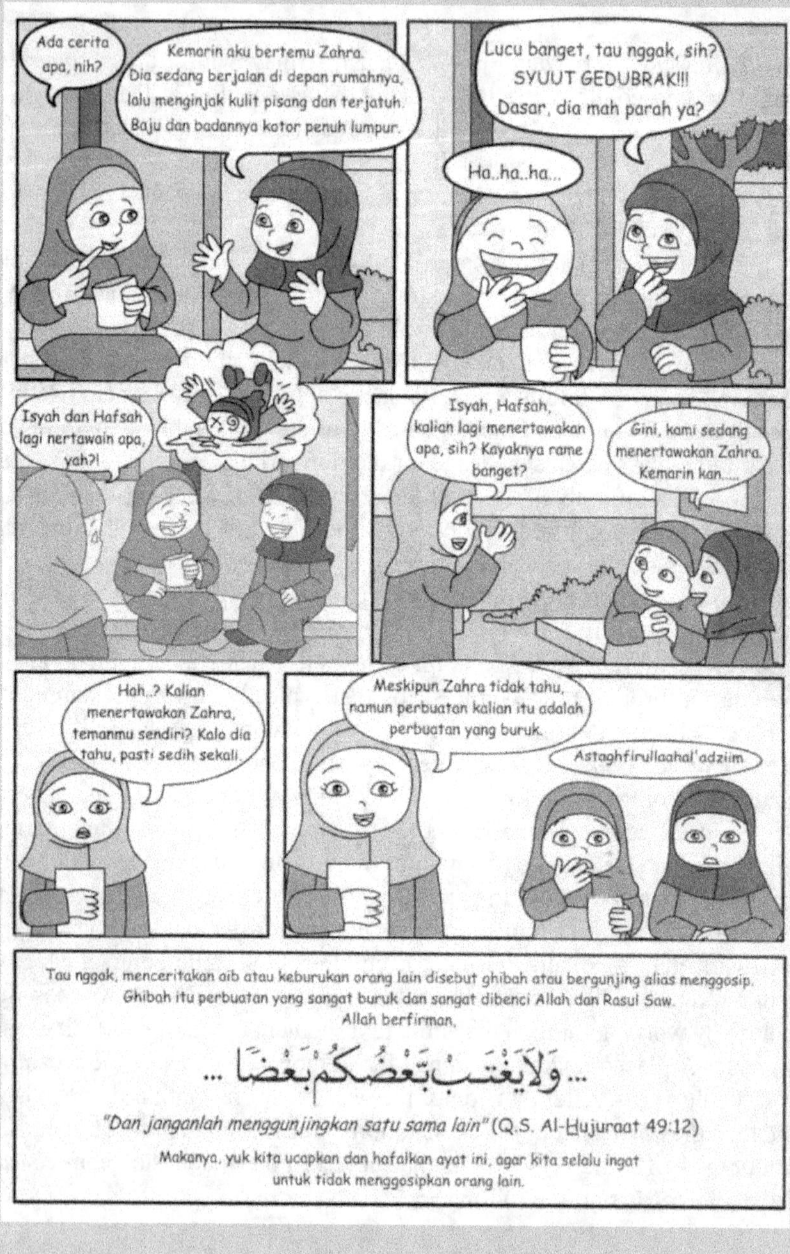

Panel 1:
Girl 1: 'Hey, what's new?'
Girl 2: 'Yesterday I met Zahra. She was walking in front of her house, then she stepped onto a banana peel and fell. Her body and clothes were dirty and full of mud'.

Panel 2:
Girl 2: 'It was so funny, you know? Swooosh – Splaaaash! How clumsy can you be?'
Girl 1: 'Ha ha ha…'

Panel 3:
Girl 3: 'Isyah and Hafsah, what are you laughing about?'

Panel 4:
Girl 3: 'Isyah, Hafsah, what are you two laughing about? Sounds very raucous!'
Girl 2: 'Oh, we were just laughing about Zahra. Yesterday, she…'

Panel 5:
Girl 3: 'What? You are laughing about Zahra, your friend? If she knew, she'd be quite sad!'

Panel 6:
Girl 3: 'Even if she didn't know, what you did there is quite bad'.
Girls 1+2: '*Astaghfiru llāh al-ʿaẓīm* [asking God's forgiveness]'

Text panel below:
You know, recounting a mistake or a bad deed committed by another person is called *ghība* or gossip. Such *ghība* is extremely bad conduct and despised by God and His messenger.

God says:

...وَلَا يَغْتَب بَّعْضُكُم بَعْضًا...

'Do not say bad things about each other' (Q. 49:12)

Therefore, let's recite and memorise this verse in order to always remember not to gossip about others.[244]

> 'And do not say bad things about each other': God prohibited gossip (*al-ghība*). The Prophet explained this term when he was asked 'What is *ghība*?' He said: 'Your saying about your brother that which he does not like'. It was said: 'But what if my brother is like I say?' The Prophet said: 'If he is like you say, then you have gossiped about him, and if he is not like you say, then you have slandered him'. Ibn Kathīr said: 'There is a consensus that *ghība* is prohibited, and the only exception from this is when there is a higher interest (*maṣlaḥa*), for example when discussing the reliability of a person (e.g., as a witness or transmitter; *al-jarḥ wa'l-ta'dīl*) or when giving counsel (*nasīḥa*)'.[25]

This is basically a very much shortened version of the fourteenth-century Qur'ānic commentary by Ibn Kathīr. Quite typical of contemporary Arabic works of *tafsīr* directed at an audience of children and 'families', it does not go to any great effort to accommodate the target audience's horizon of understanding. For example, it contains *ḥadīth* reports in classical Arabic, with no explanation or simplification, and difficult technical terms such as *al-jarḥ wa'l-ta'dīl* which comes from Islamic legal terminology and is not part of a non-specialist's vocabulary. This *tafsīr* makes no attempt to relate the Qur'ān's message to the readers' lives in any way.

Conversely, the Indonesian comic book focusses on themes that the editors consider comprehensible and particularly relevant to their readers, choosing to cover only very short and select fragments of the Qur'ān. They do not present these according to the canonical arrangement. The comic book uses the language of the envisaged audience and tries to situate the message in the context of contemporary Indonesian middle-class children's environment, making it applicable to their lives. The result of this approach is a very clear and unambiguous ethical message that runs no risk of being lost in the distinction between gossip and slander or legal terminology.

AMBIGUITY, DISAMBIGUATION AND GUIDANCE

The unequivocal representation of the Qur'ān's message, as seen in the example above, is central to guidance-oriented approaches. This sharply distinguishes them from the Muslim exegetical tradition whose defining feature is the ability to tolerate ambiguity. In premodern Qur'ānic commentaries, any given exegetical problem can have multiple solutions and an exegete may consider all of them equally acceptable. This was partly the result of a development in which traditions about the opinions of exegetes from the first two centuries of Islam became a central source of Qur'ānic interpretation. This inevitably meant that various, in many cases conflicting, opinions could be brought up with respect to a single exegetical problem.[26]

There were always some limits to ambiguity, however, and areas where it could not quite be accepted. One of them was theology. Theology was ultimately concerned with knowledge about God and His attributes, and it was also the subject of intense polemics. Thus, theological arguments permeate Qur'ānic commentaries. An exegete who was convinced that God's attributes are entirely transcendental would not permit a literal interpretation of Qur'ānic verses mentioning God's hands or face, for example. Similarly, Islamic law, while not being uniform, set some boundaries. For example, while Q 23:5–7 might appear to allow any Muslim to have intercourse with slaves, jurists unanimously agreed that this only pertained to free men and their female slaves, and exegetes just as unanimously followed that assessment.[27] These boundaries to ambiguity still left ample room for presenting multiple opinions on a wide array of questions, some of them seemingly rather technical such as syntactical discussions, debates on the etymology of words, on the information missing from Qur'ānic narratives such as the name of the son whom Abraham was ready to sacrifice and so forth.

It was with the drastic change of the aims and target group of Qur'ānic interpretation that an equally drastic decline in the tolerance of ambiguity ensued. Muḥammad ʿAbduh, for example, while not necessarily rejecting the *tafsīr* of earlier scholars as false, thought that everything had been said on the matters they had discussed and that these matters were of no use to the paramount goal of teaching the Qur'ān's guidance (*hidāya*) to the masses.[28] That guidance was supposed to enable ordinary Muslims to improve and strive for the improvement of their societies.

By the mid-twentieth century, the idea of an unambiguous[29] Qur'ān as a unifying force and source of guidance was rapidly gaining ground. Many factors contributed to this trend: mass literacy, an increasing availability of Qur'ān translations, the ongoing apologetic involvement with Western discourses on Islam and possibly Protestant influences. It was fuelled by the growing Islamist movements that saw Islam as a holistic way of life with clear rules that should govern the laws of the newly emerging nation states. The centrality of the Qur'ān to such a concept was expressed by the slogan of the Muslim Brotherhood, found in Egypt in 1928, that contained the line 'The Qur'ān is our constitution'. The Brotherhood's founder and first leader, Ḥasan al-Bannā (1906–1949), called the Qur'ān 'the comprehensive work which contains the fundamentals of this all-embracing social reformation… God has gathered therein the explanation of all things for this *umma*'.[30]

When Qur'ānic exegesis serves a sole purpose, that of guidance, discussions on semantics, etymology and narrative detail have no place. They are simply a distraction from the true message of the Qur'ān, and that is imagined by modernists, Islamists and Salafis alike to be entirely unambiguous. Religious scholars, or *ʿulamāʾ*, are the ones who most commonly uphold polyvalent readings of the Qur'ān in which multiple interpretations are presented and accepted, but even there, guidance-oriented approaches are not uncommon today. The decision between either explaining the Qur'ān or deriving guidance from it might be the most fundamental hermeneutical decision an exegete has to make.[31]

TRANSLATION AND *DA'WA*: A PROTESTANTISATION OF THE QUR'ĀN?

The shift of the Qur'ān's meaning to the centre of Muslim reform discourses helped in addressing a broader audience beyond scholars and elites which was made possible through increases in literacy and the emergence of mass media. The majority of Muslim audiences did not consist of native speakers of Arabic, however.[32] Acquainting them with the meaning of the Qur'ān required translation.

The mass production of modern Qur'ān translations set in at different times in different parts of the Muslim world, but most commonly during the first half of the twentieth century. The production of Qur'ān translations, as such, long predates that period. However, premodern translations had been different in style and function. They had normally been conceived as devices that helped decipher the Arabic Qur'ān. Often, they were word-by-word translations that gave the meaning of individual terms between the lines of the Arabic text without producing a coherent sentence in the target language. Sometimes, they were simply non-Arabic commentaries on the Qur'ān. Since many languages used by Muslims were written in Arabic script, it was also possible and common to write bilingual paraphrastic commentaries in which a segment of the Qur'ānic text was immediately followed by explanations in a vernacular language and then immediately followed by the next segment of the Qur'ānic text.[33] None of this made sense without having some knowledge of how to read the Arabic Qur'ān.

In the first half of the twentieth century, despite some short-lived resistance especially on the part of Egyptian scholars and intellectuals during the 1920s and 1930s,[34] a different type of Qur'ān translation started to proliferate. These were works that focussed on reproducing the meaning of the Qur'ān in non-Arabic languages in a style that was readable and comprehensible without consulting the Arabic text. Often, they were printed in modernised versions of the respective languages that used Latin script which required new forms of text layout.[35] This development was, in part, a response to Christian missionaries. They not only made ample use of Bible translations to spread their message, but also produced Qur'ān translations specifically for the purpose of refuting Muslim beliefs. This was the case, for example, in East and West Africa.[36] In order to be able to counter that, Muslims needed to be equipped with Qur'ān translations of their own – translations that could be used as a direct reference, not as a reading aid to an Arabic text that was obscure to Christian missionaries and most non-Arab Muslims alike.

Qur'ān translations were not only devices meant to prevent Christian proselyting, they were also useful for the propagation of Islam, and that activity was on the upswing as well. Revivalist movements had been active at least since the eighteenth century in various regions of the Muslim world, calling Muslims to religious observance, sometimes with the explicit aim of improving religious education. By the beginning of the twentieth century, these movements had the printing press at their disposal and they could form professional organisations, such as the Muhammadiyah that was founded in Indonesia in 1911. *Da'wa*, the call to Islam, directed mainly at those Muslims whose religious observance seemed to be deficient to the 'callers', became a central aim among the revivalist movements that were proliferating in the Muslim world.

Perhaps the first such movement that placed the translated Qur'ān at the centre of their *da'wa* was one that most other Muslims considered distinctly heterodox, if at all Muslim: the Ahmadiyya movement that emerged in India in the late-nineteenth century around the teachings of Mīrzā Ghulām Aḥmad (1835–1908) whose messianic claims were rejected by practically all Muslim scholars outside the Ahmadiyya. The movement split in two in 1914.[37] Both branches became very active in the production and distribution of Qur'ān translations not only to Muslims, but also to non-Muslims through their active mission in Western countries. The English translation published by Muḥammad 'Alī (1874–1951) of the Lahore branch in 1917 was widely discussed among Muslim intellectuals and activists; after all, here was finally an English translation written by a Muslim even though he did not belong to the mainstream. In some regions, the Ahmadiyya were the first to publish a vernacular Qur'ān translation by a Muslim author. This induced other Muslim individuals and institutions to follow suit. Today, the King Fahd Complex for the Printing of the Holy Qur'ān in Medina, Saudi Arabia, might be the biggest distributor of Qur'ān translations into dozens of languages; in addition, there are hundreds of other publishers, both local and global.[38]

The use of the translated Qur'ān by these missionary movements shows a strong resemblance to Protestant approaches to the Bible, the difference being that Muslim Qur'ān translations – at least those directed at other Muslims – were typically not called 'Qur'ān' since they were not meant to replace the Arabic Qur'ān, but to provide an overview of its contents. Bilingual editions continue to be more common than monolingual non-Arabic ones which underlines the fact that the Arabic Qur'ān remains indispensable for ritual use; according to predominant Muslim belief, the divine nature of its rhetoric cannot be transferred to other languages.

While the Arabic Qur'ān was thus never actually replaced by translations, their proliferation indicates an increasing focus on the meaning of the Qur'ān and its normative force. This signifies a new understanding of what Islam really is: neither a set of practices and symbols to which different meanings are ascribed nor a multi-vocal, ambiguous tradition[39]; rather, Islam is seen as a coherent doctrine drawn from its fundamental scriptures with a focus on ethical norms of behaviour, which again bears a close resemblance to Protestant ideas of religion. There was also significant interaction between European orientalists and Muslim reformers.[40] Both considered this new understanding of Islam an instrument against the power of Sufi shaykhs and old elites. The focus on the Qur'ān, in particular, seemed to them to be a way to promote rationalism, fight superstition and enable reforms.

These aims were shared by many of the governments of nation states that emerged in the twentieth century. These states promoted mass education in their national languages which led to a further increase in the demand for Qur'ān translations that were accessible to a broad public. Due to mass literacy, reading the Qur'ān and engaging with its message now became hallmarks of piety. Revivalist movements in West Africa started holding public sessions of oral Qur'ānic exegesis in the 1950s;[41] Indonesian women movements formed study circles in order to read the Qur'ān and reinterpret its message on issues such as marital violence;[42] and Turkish Alevis produce Qur'ān translations in order to situate themselves within an Islamic framework.[43] By the second half of the twentieth century, the Qur'ān had taken centre stage in Muslim religious discourses and practices.

This trend has not been entirely uncontested; in fact, it has been criticised as an imported phenomenon influenced by Protestantism, incompatible with an authentic Islamic normativity.[44] It has also not eradicated different attitudes towards the Qur'ān, for example talismanic uses or a veneration of the book in its material sense coupled with a reluctance to actually handle and read it. Nevertheless, at the beginning of the twenty-first century the interpretation of the Qur'ān continues to be the main locus of Muslim debates on belief, religious practice and ethics.

Today's Qur'ān is also a much more uniform and standardised text than the Qur'ān of the nineteenth century, a fact that might have further supported its elevation to such a central role. Under the influence of print, the edition published in Cairo in 1924 became a near-standard. Consequently, many hitherto accepted differences concerning variant readings, verse numbering and names of *sūra*s all but vanished for all practical intents and purposes (if not from the theory of Qur'ānic studies), making it easier for Muslims to perceive of the Qur'ān as an unambiguous, canonical text. *Da'wa* activities rarely have a use for technicalities or ambiguities. They typically want to provide a clear message, as the following example shows.

Televangelism and *da'wa*: 'Amr Khālid (b. 1967, Egypt) on Q. 23:1–11

'Amr Khālid (b. 1967, Egypt), a famous television preacher, is an accountant by training. His degree in accounting, dating from 1988, is in fact mentioned on the back cover of all of his books since it is one of the many aspects that distinguish him from traditional religious scholars. His suit, tie and moustache make him look like a businessman, rather than a shaykh, and he usually talks in Egyptian dialect, rather than in Modern Standard Arabic. He started preaching among members of the Egyptian educated urban middle and upper-class in the 1990s, calling himself a *dā'iya*, someone who offers *da'wa* or the call to Islam, and proved to be especially successful at addressing young people. These became his main target audience when he started hosting television shows on satellite channels. From 2002 onwards, he moved back and forth between Europe and Egypt, acquiring a doctorate in interreligious tolerance in the UK. He used his media presence to promote a message of self-improvement, ethical behaviour, piety, health and success. He encouraged his audience to quit smoking, save the environment, engage in charity and build up a personal relationship with God through the Qur'ān and through the stories of the Prophet and the early Muslims.[45]

His book on the Qur'ān was published in 2004 and written in a very simple, accessible form of Modern Standard Arabic. If it is adamant about one thing, then it is its insistence on not being a work of *tafsīr*. Its title, *Khawāṭir Qur'āniyya* (Reflections on the Qur'ān), bears a striking resemblance to the Qur'ānic commentary by the famous Egyptian television shaykh Muḥammad Mutawallī al-Sha'rāwī (1911–1998) who likewise emphasised the fact that his work was not intended to be an explanation of the Qur'ān, but rather a collection of personal thoughts on the Holy Scripture.[46] This might be a preventive measure against accusations of not following an established methodology of interpretation, but more importantly, it reflects the preachers' aim to use the Qur'ān as a basis for the call to Islam (*da'wa*).[47]

Excerpt 1.2 is a rather typical excerpt from his book, commenting on the first section of the *sūra* 'The Believers' (Q. 23).

Many aspects are striking about this text when compared to conventional Qur'ānic commentaries. Perhaps the most obvious is the thoroughly modernised style; the rhetoric of exams and quiz shows, of check-marking, scoring points, succeeding in tests and winning prizes. The possibility of failure is ostensibly not addressed. Another thing that is conspicuously

Excerpt 1.2

Q. 23:1–11

قَدْ أَفْلَحَ الْمُؤْمِنُونَ {١} الَّذِينَ هُمْ فِي صَلَاتِهِمْ خَاشِعُونَ {٢} وَالَّذِينَ هُمْ عَنِ اللَّغْوِ مُعْرِضُونَ {٣}
وَالَّذِينَ هُمْ لِلزَّكَاةِ فَاعِلُونَ {٤} وَالَّذِينَ هُمْ لِفُرُوجِهِمْ حَافِظُونَ {٥} إِلَّا عَلَىٰ أَزْوَاجِهِمْ أَوْ مَا
مَلَكَتْ أَيْمَانُهُمْ فَإِنَّهُمْ غَيْرُ مَلُومِينَ {٦} فَمَنِ ابْتَغَىٰ وَرَاءَ ذَٰلِكَ فَأُولَٰئِكَ هُمُ الْعَادُونَ {٧} وَالَّذِينَ
هُمْ لِأَمَانَاتِهِمْ وَعَهْدِهِمْ رَاعُونَ {٨} وَالَّذِينَ هُمْ عَلَىٰ صَلَوَاتِهِمْ يُحَافِظُونَ {٩} أُولَٰئِكَ هُمُ
الْوَارِثُونَ {١٠} الَّذِينَ يَرِثُونَ الْفِرْدَوْسَ هُمْ فِيهَا خَالِدُونَ {١١}

(1) Prosperous are the believers (2) who in their prayers are humble (3) and who from idle talk turn away (4) and who at almsgiving are active (5) and who guard their private parts (6) – save from their spouses and what their right hands own; then they are not blameworthy; (7) but those who seek beyond that, those are transgressors – (8) and who preserve their trusts and their covenant (9) and who observe their prayers. (10) Those are the inheritors (11) who shall inherit Paradise in which they will remain forever.

Can you compare to them?

This *sūra* mentions the most important qualities of believers [...], thus asking the reader of the Qur'ān: how do your qualities compare to those of the prosperous believers that have been shown to you? It directs your attention at something important, which is that those qualities combine morals with acts of worship: the first property is one of ritual worship, then comes a moral one and so forth. Examine yourself according to the following properties and give yourself a check mark next to each of them:

The examination of belief

The *sūra* begins with the words 'Prosperous are the believers' (v. 1). So, who are they? And how well do we score when compared with them? Join us in answering the pivotal questions of this exam:

- 'Who in their prayers are humble' (v. 2). How do you perform your prayer? Are you humble when you perform them or not? How many points do you award yourself for that question?
- 'And who from idle talk turn away' (v. 3). Do you slander other Muslims or indulge in gossip? Do you guard your tongue and refrain from useless talk? Do you keep away from gossiping and refrain from listening to it?

- 'And who guard their private parts' (v. 5). Do you lower your gaze [when confronted with members of the other sex]? How about chastity and withholding from everything that could lead to fornication?
- 'And who preserve their trusts and their covenant' (v. 8). How do you protect your trusts? From the most basic trusts (a tape or a book that you have borrowed from your friend) up to the loyalty to your religion, its protection and its spread among the people?
- 'And who observe their prayers' (v. 9). Do you observe your prayer at the beginning of each prayer time? And the communal prayer? How many points do you award yourself for the performance and observance of the ritual prayers?

If you passed the exam: Congratulations!
If you have acquired a large proportion of these properties, rejoice about God's words 'Those are the inheritors who shall inherit Paradise in which they will remain forever'.

Congratulations! You just won a high prize from your Lord; God's testimony in verses 10–12 makes you eligible for inheriting Earth in this world and to be granted the highest [level of] Paradise in the afterlife![48]

missing from the discussion is the clause in verses 6–7 that mentions the option of having multiple wives and concubines, since the term 'what their right hands own', according to the vast majority of exegetes and jurists, refers to slaves.[49] ʿAmr Khālid is not interested in complicating things or evoking negative sentiments; he wants to encourage moral behaviour and piety, rather than doubts.

Islam, to ʿAmr Khālid, is a model for success, and his aim, as a preacher, is to call others to adopting this model. The emotion that his rhetoric wants to inspire is hope, not fear. Discussions of exegetical problems have no place in this discourse, nor do problems or failure. He does briefly refer to the fate of Noah's enemies and other unbelievers who are destroyed by God, as mentioned later in the *sūra*, but only in passing; and he mainly uses that story to place even greater emphasis on the qualities and rewards of true believers. His message is that anyone can and should aspire to being a true believer. This general message is more important than the meaning of an individual verse. The aim is neither to explain the passage comprehensively nor to deliver a consistent exegesis; rather, the aim is the call (*daʿwa*) to Islam and to good religious practice. ʿAmr Khālid's work on the Qurʾān is a sermon in the form of a commentary.

This is not an entirely new phenomenon. It has its origins in the spread of mass media that offered a new kind of pulpit to popular oral exegesis, a genre that has doubtlessly existed since the early days of Islam. In Egypt, it has a long-standing tradition, from the famous Qur'ānic commentary of Sayyid Quṭb (1906–1966) that was originally published in instalments in a newspaper to the popular television show by the above-mentioned Shaykh al-Sha'rāwī (1911–1998).

Like many of his forerunners, 'Amr Khālid is concerned with providing guidance, but his target audience is neither the intellectual elite to which Muḥammad 'Abduh reached out at the beginning of the twentieth century, nor the lower and middle-class Muslims with which al-Sha'rāwī was particularly popular. 'Amr Khālid attained fame for winning the hearts of the Egyptian urban middle and upper-class youths who were starting to discover religion in the 1990s. His rhetoric is adapted to the world of that audience, a world where financial success and self-improvement go hand in hand. That audience wants to be motivated, not threatened; it wants to be applauded for having attained most of the required checkmarks, not blamed for missing out on one or two of them. They appreciate religion most when it makes them feel good, rather than frightened or confused; and it should never be boring. This brand of Qur'ānic interpretation can only fulfil its purpose when it is entertaining. It would be misleading to dismiss it as superficial or empty, though. Its concern with what its author perceives as the 'true message' of the Qur'ān is as sincere as the quest for the Qur'ān's emotional relevance.

Scholarly exegetical traditions seem to be entirely irrelevant for the ubiquitous genre of the unambiguous, guidance-oriented Qur'ānic interpretation. Yet they continue to be of tremendous importance in many ways and on many levels that will be explored in the next chapter.

NOTES

1. For a useful overview of the juridical debates about the degree to which knowledge of the Arabic Qur'ān was considered compulsory, see Zadeh, *The Vernacular Qur'an*, 53–91.
2. This is apparent, for example, from the criticism of such eighteenth and early-nineteenth-century reformers as Muḥāmmad al-Shawkānī (1760–1834), Usman Dan Fodio (1754–1817) and Muḥammad al-Sanūsī (1787–1859). See Dallal, 'The Origins and Objectives of Islamic Revivalist Thought'.
3. This is, of course, a very generalising description of a picture that emerges from a number of studies of pre-modern educational traditions. See, for example, Messick, *The Calligraphic State*; Saad, *Social History of Timbuktu*.
4. For the immense importance of the *Tafsīr al-Jalālayn* to Islamic education in West Africa, for example, see Brigaglia, '*Tafsīr* and the Intellectual History of Islam in West Africa'. Shāh Walī Allāh of Delhi (1703–1762) explicitly criticised and sought to reform this practice of teaching the Qur'ān through a paraphrastic commentary; see Jalbani, *Life of Shah Wali Allah*.

5. Saleh, *The Formation of the Classical* Tafsīr *Tradition*, 16–18.
6. Exegetes themselves commonly referred to the division between short, medium and extensive commentaries in the description of their works; see Bauer, 'Justifying the Genre: A Study of Introductions to Classical Works of *Tafsīr*'.
7. On the rather complex relationship between *tafsīr* and *ḥadīth*, see Tottoli, 'Interrelations and Boundaries between *Tafsīr* and Hadith Literature: The Exegesis of Mālik b. Anas' *Muwaṭṭà* and Classical Qur'anic Commentaries'.
8. See, for example, as a case study on the differences between the laws on rebellion in law and Qur'ānic exegesis Sauer, '*Tafsīr* between Law and Exegesis: The Case of Q. 49:9'.
9. Until the twentieth century, Qur'ānic exegesis, at least in written form, was practically exclusively a male endeavour. This has changed somewhat in recent years and is arguably even less the case in oral, informal and/or educational settings, but there is still a marked overall dominance of male exegetes. Therefore, I use the male form of personal and possessive pronouns when speaking about unspecified exegetes, but I mean for it to potentially include women.
10. On the distinction between Qur'ānic exegesis within and without *tafsīr*, see McAuliffe, 'Genre Boundaries'. An illuminating case study of distinctly exegetical writing outside *tafsīr* is Mirza, 'Ibn Taymiyya as Exegete'.
11. O'Connor, 'Popular and Talismanic Uses of the Qur'ān'.
12. Doorn-Harder, 'Teaching and Preaching the Qur'ān'.
13. It has to be pointed out, however, that he widely published in areas other than Qur'ānic exegesis, such as Sufism and theology, and granted the Qur'ān nowhere near as exclusive a role as some later reformers did.
14. Pink, 'Striving for a New Exegesis of the Qur'ān', 767–768; Baljon, *Religion and Thought*, 74, 77.
15. Robinson, 'Perso-Islamic Culture in India', 119.
16. Dallal, 'The Origins and Objectives of Islamic Revivalist Thought'.
17. Jomier, 'La revue "Al-'Orwa al-Wothqa"'.
18. Pink, ''Abduh, Muḥammad'. For the broader context of Muḥammad 'Abduh's life and works, see Sedgwick, *Muhammad Abduh*.
19. See Lauzière, 'The Construction of Salafiyya'; Lauzière, *The Making of Salafism*.
20. The term generally used here is *fitna* which may mean seduction or temptation, but also sedition, strife or unrest.
21. More on this scripturalist trend that also goes by the label of 'Salafism' – a label which was not used in the early-twentieth century – will be said below: page 48, 'A Salafi paradigm'.
22. Pink, 'Tradition, Authority and Innovation', 72.
23. This is the original Indonesian title, using an English loanword.
24. Tim Rumah Qurani, *Komik-Qu*, 41–42. Text originally in Indonesian.
25. Abū 'Azīz, *Tafsīr al-Qur'ān al-karīm lil-aṭfāl*, vol. 5, 62–63. Text originally in Arabic.
26. Calder, 'Tafsīr from Ṭabarī to Ibn Kathīr'. For the general role of ambiguity in Islamic intellectual history, see Bauer, *Die Kultur der Ambiguität*.
27. Pink, *Sunnitischer Tafsīr in der modernen islamischen Welt*, 147–153.
28. Pink, ''Abduh, Muḥammad'.
29. On the loss of ambiguity in Muslim religious discourses in modern times, see Bauer, *Die Kultur der Ambiguität*.
30. Al-Bannā, *Five Tracts*, 14–15.

31. On the competing aims of explanation and guidance, see Pink, *Sunnitischer Tafsīr in der modernen islamischen Welt*, 301–306; Pink, 'Tradition, Authority and Innovation', 72.
32. Today, around twenty per cent of Muslims worldwide are native speakers of Arabic.
33. For a very good study of early Persian translations and Qur'ānic commentaries, see Zadeh, *The Vernacular Qur'an.*
34. Masterfully described in Wilson, *Translating the Qur'an in an Age of Nationalism.*
35. Pink, 'Form Follows Function'.
36. Lacunza-Balda and Westerlund, 'Translations of the Quran into Swahili, and Contemporary Islamic Revival in East Africa'; Solihu, 'The Earliest Yoruba Translation of the Qur'an'.
37. I will return to the Ahmadiyya movement below. page 229, 'New Islamic communities'.
38. Wild, 'Muslim Translators and Translations of the Qur'an into English'.
39. Bauer, *Die Kultur der Ambiguität.*
40. Jung, *Orientalists, Islamists and the Global Public Sphere*.
41. Brigaglia, '*Tafsīr* and the Intellectual History of Islam in West Africa'. YouTube hosts a large number of videos of such sessions in Senegal that attract large and ecstatic audiences.
42. Doorn-Harder, 'Teaching and Preaching the Qur'ān'.
43. See page 202, 'Negotiating the boundaries of Islamicness through the Qur'ān: Ali Adil Atalay 'Vaktidolu' (b. 1936, Turkey) on Q. 2:21'.
44. Paçacı, 'Sola scriptura?'
45. Rock, 'Amr Khaled'; Wise, 'Amr Khaled'; Pandya, 'Religious Change Among Yemeni Women'.
46. Pink, *Sunnitischer Tafsīr in der modernen islamischen Welt*, 95–98.
47. Khālid, *Khawāṭir Qur'āniyya*, 11–13.
48. Ibid., 251–252. Text originally in Arabic.
49. Pink, *Sunnitischer Tafsīr in der modernen islamischen Welt*, 141–157.

2

RECONSTITUTING THE EXEGETICAL TRADITION

When following contemporary exegetical discourses, it is immediately apparent that the authority of many premodern exegetes continues to rank highly. By referring to them, a contemporary exegete can show his skill at engaging with the tradition and enhance the authority of his own interpretation. The exegetical tradition continues to be a resource of enormous importance for contemporary Muslims dealing with the Qur'ān. It might be used selectively and according to a specific interpreter's needs, just as it had always been, and parts of the tradition might even be rejected, but it is rarely entirely absent from today's exegetical discourses. After all, it is often impossible to make sense of the Qur'ān without some context, whether semantic or historical.

However, 'the' exegetical tradition is not a monolithic entity. Contemporary exegetes who draw on it do not have a dispassionate interest in history; rather, they make use of those works and ideas that they consider important to their own context, which is often very different from the educational and scholarly contexts in which premodern works of exegesis were discussed and transmitted. Perceptions of which works are important and why they are important have changed; as a result, the architecture of the exegetical tradition as a whole has undergone a fundamental transformation and reconstruction. The most salient case in point is the rise of Ibn Taymiyya's hermeneutics to prominence and the promotion of Ibn Taymiyya's disciple Ibn Kathīr to the top of the hierarchy of Qur'ānic commentaries where it currently stands unrivalled as the one work that is most often sold, translated, abridged and cited.

A GENEALOGICAL TRADITION

At the time 'Imād al-Dīn Ibn Kathīr (d. 1373) wrote his Qur'ānic commentary, he built upon an established tradition of *tafsīr*. The characteristics of that tradition as well as its contemporary relevance will be discussed before coming back to Ibn Kathīr, his teacher Ibn Taymiyya and their contemporary reception later in this chapter.

Already by the tenth century, Muslim exegetical scholarship had reached a degree of sophistication that resulted in the production of voluminous encyclopaedic commentaries assembling a vast amount of exegetical opinions and traditions. By the twelfth and thirteenth century, the genre was so well-established that it brought forth authoritative works that were themselves the subject of commentaries and glosses and that were taught in the expanding network of *madrasas*, or institutions of higher learning. New commentaries continued to be written; Ibn Kathīr's was only one among a large number of newcomers to the genre, some more successful and some less so, in an ongoing academic exploration of the meaning of the Qur'ān.

Each work of *tafsīr* had its distinct features, of course; but they were all part of a genre that has aptly been characterised as a 'genealogical tradition',[1] meaning that each new work built upon the entirety of the previous works, or at least those that had collectively been accepted as part of the canon.[2] An exegete might choose to reject some opinions or cite them selectively, but once an interpretation had been admitted into the canon by being made part of *madrasa* teaching and scholarly discourse, it was next to impossible to remove it.

The citation of existing exegetical opinions was an indispensable part of every work of *tafsīr*.[3] This invariably made Qur'ānic interpretation a multi-vocal act in which there were nearly always different solutions to any given exegetical problem. Every exegete who wanted to be recognised as such had to acknowledge the existence of at least some of these opinions. It was acceptable to cite them selectively and to express preferences, but it was by no means required or common to identify a single correct solution to the exclusion of all others. Even a rather categorical exegete such as Muḥammad al-Shawkānī (1760–1834) – who sharply distinguished between 'true' interpretations, based either on scriptural evidence or the 'literal' meaning of the Qur'ān, and 'false' interpretations that had no such basis – acknowledged that the truth might have several equally plausible dimensions, for example when a word has several meanings or might reasonably be understood metaphorically as well as literally.[4]

The recourse to the entirety of earlier exegetes can be read as the manifestation of a high-ranking source of religious legitimacy in Sunni Islam and beyond it: the imagined consensus of the community of scholars (*ijmā'*). An exegete who invokes the *ijmā'* becomes, by this very act, part of the community of scholars and thus contributes to upholding and continuing the genealogical tradition of *tafsīr*.

This tradition was never all-inclusive, though. It had a centre, a periphery and boundaries; it accepted certain opinions and ignored or rejected others:

> ...the early exegetical authorities, in theory, trump later interpreters [...], but in turn, their views can be reinterpreted; there is room for many

> conflicting views, but not every view is tolerated; respected works by respected scholars are read across the boundaries of legal schools; and the correct interpretation is bounded by common practice, common understanding, and ideas of right and wrong.[5]

Opinions that were ascribed to early authorities from the first century or two after the *hijra* had particularly good chances of not being forgotten or ignored although later exegetes might still turn them down if they considered them implausible, dogmatically wrong or unlikely to be authentic.

During the development of Islamic intellectual history there was an increasing distrust of allegorical interpretations, be they of Shiʿi or mystical origin. The motives for that distrust were not purely of an intellectual nature, but also had political causes. Generally speaking, esoteric interpretations never made it into the mainstream of the exegetical tradition which comprised those Qurʾānic commentaries that were taught in *madrasa*s, that other scholars taught, cited and on which they wrote glosses and meta-commentaries (*ḥawāshī*). Esoteric interpretations largely remained confined to specific mystical chains of authority or minority branches of Islam. That is not to say that the exegetical mainstream was an exclusively Sunni affair; it was not. It did, however, exclude such opinions that were too overtly allegorical, for example, by reading statements in the Qurʾān as allusions to mystical stages or the Shiʿi imams. Such opinions were still transmitted, and some continue to be reproduced until this day, but they were usually ignored by mainstream Qurʾānic commentaries.

In sum, the Qurʾānic commentary, or *tafsīr*,[6] constitutes a genre of scholarly literature that has a specific structure and functions according to specific rules. Works of *tafsīr* comment on the Qurʾān in its canonical order and they make reference to existing exegetical opinions.[7] While they usually draw on external frames of reference, such as theology, law or rhetoric, *tafsīr* as a genre is neither arbitrary nor open for all. An individual exegete might, for example, decide to include an argument from the field of philosophy; but the likelihood that this argument is going to be cited by later exegetes is small since it is not rooted in the exegetical tradition. By the tenth century, a body of relevant opinions, *ḥadīth*s and occasions of revelation had been established that later exegetes built upon. From that point onwards, opinions and sources that were not part of this canon occasionally managed to make their way into it, but more often than not were ignored by most exegetes; and even if they were not, it was hardly obligatory to take note of them. The same is essentially true for exegetical methods. Small-scale additions were possible; shifts in the exegetes' interests and preferences occurred; but the genre did not lend itself to fundamental ruptures.

The genre of *tafsīr* is thus extremely persistent. Until this day, Muslim scholars write works of *tafsīr* that comment on the Qurʾān in its canonical order. They generally 'choose to write this type of work to demonstrate their familiarity with the tradition.' Accordingly, 'the genre of *tafsīr* in the modern period is one that is both conservative and circumscribed. Modern works of *tafsīr* do not represent the whole range of modern interpretations of the Qur'ān.'[8]

On the other hand, *tafsīr* has proven able to absorb works that had never been conceived as part of the genre. Some modern Qur'ānic commentaries that were, when first published, seen as attempts to break with the exegetical tradition, have become part of it or even attained the status of modern classics, such as the *Fī ẓilāl al-Qur'ān* (In the Shadow of the Qur'ān) of revered Muslim Brotherhood member, Sayyid Quṭb (1906–1966). Quṭb purposely did not label his work a *tafsīr*, partly because he was not a religious scholar by training and partly because he did not use conventional methods and resources. Nevertheless, his work is today generally treated as a Qur'ānic commentary and cited in later commentaries alongside eminent exegetical authorities who were in no doubt that their books were to be treated as works of *tafsīr*. Obviously, the gravity and attraction of the genre of *tafsīr* are such that they pull in even such works that originally refused to be part of it. This predominantly seems to happen with such works that consecutively comment on the Qur'ān; their structure makes it particularly easy to mine them for opinions.

To a certain extent, the description of *tafsīr* as a genealogical tradition is still valid today, which implies that there is no clear dividing line between 'premodern' and 'modern' exegesis. Even though significant transformations and innovations occurred around the end of the nineteenth century, there was never a complete rupture. Many exegetes writing today find it perfectly legitimate to grant works from the tenth, fourteenth and twentieth centuries equal importance in their interpretations. The tradition is very much alive, and one of the reasons for this is its continuation by a specific status group, the *'ulamā*.

THE *'ULAMĀ'* AS BEARERS OF THE TRADITION

'Ulamā' (sg., *'ālim*), or religious scholars, continue to be among the most important actors with respect to the interpretation of the Qur'ān although they have since the nineteenth century lost their near-monopoly on this activity. This was connected to a dramatic social transformation that fundamentally transformed the exegetical discourse; and yet, the *'ulamā'* as a status group are still there, commenting on the Qur'ān in writing as well as on television and in YouTube videos, and their interpretations are still accorded a high level of authority.

ʿUlamāʾ are characterised by the fact that they have received a higher Islamic education through which they have become thoroughly familiar with the premodern intellectual heritage of Islam, including Islamic law (*fiqh*) and other disciplines such as *tafsīr*. The contents of their curricula and the structure of their education may differ considerably, depending on the country they have received their education in. Some hold formal degrees from state universities while others have studied in a more informal, but often extremely thorough, way in seminaries with high-ranking scholars. In any case, they all hold a scholarly pedigree of some sort.

The social status of *ʿulamāʾ* varies widely. Naturally, they have a comparatively high influence in states that define themselves as Islamic such as Saudi Arabia and Iran. In other states, their political impact may be significantly lower, but even the complete lack of a formal institutionalised position in the system of government does not necessarily correlate with a negligible social impact. The *ʿulamāʾ* are important, if not uncontested, carriers of authority in virtually all Muslim communities across the world.

The *ʿulamāʾ*, thus characterised by a thorough grounding in tradition, draw on this tradition in their work. 'Tradition', in this context, has a rather specific meaning. It refers to the written expressions of the premodern disciplines of Islamic learning. In the case of Qurʾānic exegesis, this includes the study of exegetical opinions and Qurʾānic commentaries from the first centuries of Islam to the nineteenth century and possibly – but never exclusively – the period thereafter. No single *ʿālim* is likely to subscribe to all of these opinions, and of course many *ʿulamāʾ* creatively use and reconstruct the tradition, often alongside other sources, in order to address contemporary concerns; but, being *ʿulamāʾ*, they will not reject the entire exegetical tradition as being irrelevant to understanding the Qurʾān today. The tradition 'remains their fundamental frame of reference, the basis of their authority and identity'.[9] This distinguishes traditional scholars both from modernists searching for new approaches to the Qurʾān and from Salafis who limit their perspective to the Qurʾān and the Sunna.[10]

When traditional *ʿulamāʾ* write Qurʾānic commentaries, they often do so in order to demonstrate their mastery of the tradition, and the main audience of such works are other scholars. As such, these Qurʾānic commentaries – which I have labelled 'scholar's commentaries' elsewhere[11] – are rather likely to conform to premodern criteria for a work of *tafsīr*, even when they incorporate modern sources. However, traditional scholars might also act as teachers, preachers or television show hosts and their exegesis in these contexts might be less restricted than within the confines of the rather formalised genre of *tafsīr*.[12] Traditional *ʿulamāʾ* continue to be the most important group to produce extensive commentaries on the complete Qurʾān.

The fact that *'ulamā'* are grounded in the premodern scholarly tradition might convey the impression that their views are by necessity socially conservative, for example with respect to the status of women. This type of conservatism, however, is neither a prerogative of *'ulamā'* nor is it an unavoidable outcome of their approach to the Qur'ān. It is possible to be a traditional *'ālim*, but to creatively reinterpret classical Islamic law in a way that accommodates reforms of gender norms, for instance; and likewise, it is possible to approach the Qur'ān in an entirely non-traditional way, without drawing on any premodern exegetical authorities, and still arrive at extremely conservative conclusions.[13]

A large number of traditional *'ulamā'* today self-identify as belonging to the *wasaṭiyya* trend. Literally, this term refers to the description of Muslims as the 'community of the middle way' (*ummatan wasaṭan*) in the Qur'ān (Q. 2:143). It could be translated as 'moderate Islam'. The term does not denote a specific theological, legal or hermeneutical stance; rather, it signifies the rejection of revolutionary Islamism and Salafism, on the one hand, and liberal modernism, on the other hand. As such, the contents of the *wasaṭiyya* concept are vague. However, it is often invoked to defend the premodern Islamic intellectual heritage, such as Ash'arī theology or the Sunni schools of law. *Wasaṭiyya* is more of an ideological statement than an analytical tool; one of its many functions is to defend the *'ulamā'* as a status group from attacks against their methodology and fundamental sources. The subsequent text sample will demonstrate both the resilience of the *tafsīr* tradition and the way in which its implicit rules safeguard exegetes against ruptures and extreme positions.

An *'ālim* continuing the tradition of *tafsīr*: Muhammad Quraish Shihab (b. 1944, Indonesia) on Q. 95:1–3

Muhammad Quraish Shihab is among the most prominent contemporary Indonesian Muslim scholars. Born into a family that was proud of its descent from Hadhramaut, in the east of today's Yemen, he received the hybrid education that was typical of his generation, both religious and secular. He studied at the prestigious Azhar university in Cairo and filled high-ranking positions under Suharto's regime in Indonesia, including that of Minister of Religion. After the overthrow of the Suharto presidency, he was often criticised for his affiliation with that regime.

Quraish Shihab's declared aim is to reconcile the global tradition of Islamic scholarship with the specific requirements of today's Indonesian society. Since the 1990s, he has increasingly done so through the interpretation of the Qur'ān in various forms, including a Ramadan television show, a thematic *tafsīr*, a partial Qur'ānic commentary where the *sūra*s are arranged according to the time of their revelation, a Qur'ān translation and his monumental encyclopaedic Qur'ānic commentary *Tafsir al-Mishbah.* As such, he has been part of a growing tendency to move the Qur'ān into the centre of the Muslim religious discourse in Indonesia at the expense of Islamic law or, more precisely, Shāfi'ī *fiqh*.

Tafsir al-Mishbah ('The Commentary of Light') is a fifteen-volume commentary on the entire Qur'ān that was first published between 2000 and 2003. Clearly laid out, professionally produced and written in simple Indonesian, it does not require its readers to have a higher religious education, but the sheer length of the commentary presupposes a deep interest in the Qur'ān. It contains an introduction to each *sūra*. After that, each *sūra* is divided into larger segments which are then discussed at length with a focus on semantic problems and the opinions of previous exegetes. Quraish Shihab distinctly favours twentieth-century Arab sources, but generally gives a diachronic overview of the exegetical debate that also involves premodern commentators such as al-Ṭabarī, al-Zamakhsharī and Burhān al-Dīn al-Biqā'ī (1406–1480).[14]

Muhammad Quraish Shihab firmly situates himself within the 'genealogical tradition' of *tafsīr* with this work. Far from constructing a clear

Excerpt 2.1

Q. 95:1–3

وَالتِّينِ وَالزَّيْتُونِ ﴿١﴾ وَطُورِ سِينِينَ ﴿٢﴾ وَهَـٰذَا الْبَلَدِ الأَمِينِ ﴿٣﴾

(1) By the Tīn and the Zaytūn, (2) and by Mount Sinai, (3) and by this secure city.

[...] The *'ulamā'* disagree about the meaning of the words *al-tīn* [lit. 'figs'] and *al-zaytūn* [lit. 'olives']. Those exegetes who focus their attention on the meaning of verses 2–3 of the *sūra*, which point to the places where the Prophet Moses and the Prophet Muhammad received their revelations, think that *al-tīn* and *al-zaytūn* must likewise be place names: *al-tīn* is a certain place (hill) in Damascus, Syria, while *al-zaytūn* is the place where the Prophet Jesus received his revelation. A different opinion says that *al-zaytūn* is a mountain in Jerusalem where the Prophet Jesus was saved from the attempt to murder him. If this is the case, then the first verse is connected to the Prophet Jesus, the second verse to the Prophet Moses and the third verse to the Prophet Muhammad. There are also some who connect *al-tīn* to the Prophet Abraham. Al-Qāsimī [1866–1914], in his *tafsīr Maḥāsin al-ta'wīl*, goes as far as to suggest that *al-tīn* is the name of the tree where the founder of the Buddhist religion received divine guidance. The Buddhists call this tree Bodhi (*ficus religiosa*) or Holy Fig Tree that can be found in the small town of Gaya in the region of Bihar. Buddha, according to al-Qāsimī, was a prophet – even though he is not part of the group of twenty-five prophets whose names are clearly and precisely mentioned in the Qur'ān which makes it the duty of every Muslim to affirm their prophethood while believing that there are many more prophets who are not mentioned by the Qur'ān.

If we accept this last opinion, it can be said that in verses 1–3, God swears by places of prophets who accepted divine guidance, and these are the prophets who up to now possess the greatest influence and following in human society, namely the followers of the religions of Islam, Christianity, Judaism and Buddhism.

There are also some who understand the words *al-tīn* and *al-zaytūn* as types of fruit. The fruit *tīn* ['fig'] is a very common type of fruit in the Middle East. When it is ripe, its colour is brown, it has seeds like a tomato, tastes sweet and is considered to have high nutritional value as well as being easy to digest. Traditionally, it is even used as medicine to destroy urinary tract stones and as a cure against haemorrhoids. In a tradition that is ascribed to the Prophet, the story goes that he said: 'Eat the *tīn* fruit because it cures haemorrhoids'.

Zaytūn, mentioned four times in the Qur'an, is a shrub plant; the trees are green and grow frequently in the Mediterranean region. The Qur'an calls this plant *shajara mubāraka* (a tree that provides much benefit) (Q. 24:35). Some of its fruit are green, others deep black; they are shaped like grapes, are eaten as pickles and used to produce a very clear oil that can be put to various uses.

The great exegete al-Ṭabarī [d. 923] chooses this opinion on the grounds that the Arabs did not know the word *zaytūn* as a place name, but they knew it in the sense of a type of plant or fruit. This opinion of al-Ṭabarī can be contradicted by saying that, while the Arabs know this word as a name of a plant or fruit, the name of a fruit may very well be converted into the name of a place where that fruit grows in great number. Moreover, Arab society knows a place that is called 'Mount of Olives'. The exegete al-Marāghī [1883–1952] holds yet another opinion. According to this *tafsīr* specialist, *al-tīn* is 'the era of the Prophet Adam' because – he says – when Adam eats from the forbidden tree, he is naked until he finally finds a fig leaf that he fashions into something to cover his sex [*aurat*[15]]. Conversely, *al-zaytūn*, according to him, represents the 'era of the Prophet Noah' because – he writes – several hours before the ark that he was staying in anchored, he saw birds carrying an olive leaf, the sign of safety and security.

This opinion of al-Marāghī is hard to accept since there is not a single verse or *ḥadīth* that supports it. It seems that this scholar, consciously or unconsciously, is influenced by what is written in the Old Testament, Genesis 3:7, that tells the story of how Adam covered his sex with leaves from a fig tree, and Genesis 8:11, that narrates how birds called doves come to greet Noah carrying olive leaves.

Those who think that the first verse means a specific plant or fruit lean towards linking this oath with the fourth verse [of the *sūra*] that says that man has been created by God in the best form. According to them, God swears by the names of plants or fruit that possess great benefit in order to indicate that man who has been created by God in this way also possesses the potential to provide great benefit, just like the above-mentioned plants and fruit. If he uses his potential, he will certainly be as beneficial as the fig and olive trees.

While the connection between the first and the fourth verse, as presented above, seems conceivable, there are many experts who do not find it satisfactory because, they ask, what is the connection between the first, second and third verse? Is there any connection between the fruits of *tīn* and *zaytūn*, on the one hand, and Sinai and Mecca, on the other hand? This connection only becomes clear when the words *tīn* and *zaytūn* are understood as holy places at which God's messengers received His guidance.

There is hardly any controversy among religious scholars about the meaning of al-Ṭūr as the place where the Prophet Moses received his revelation from God. The word al-Ṭūr is understood by some scholars as meaning 'mountain', namely the one where the Prophet Moses received his revelation from God and which is located on Sinai, Egypt. Ṭāhir b. ʿĀshūr [1879–1973] thinks that those commandments of God that were sent down to Moses are known under the name of the place where they were revealed, namely Ṭūr, which was pronounced Tawrāt in Arabic.

Through swearing by these holy places, places that radiate God's brilliant light, it is as though these verses deliver the message that man, whom God has created in the best possible physical and psychological state, will remain in such a state as long as he follows the ordinances that have been sent to the above-mentioned prophets in these holy places.

Ibn Taymiyya [1263–1328] compares the above-mentioned verses with a verse in the Old Testament, Deuteronomy 33:2, that says: 'The Lord came from Sinai, and rose up from Seir unto them; he shined forth from mount Paran'. Sinai is the place where the Prophet Moses received his revelation, Seir is the place of the Prophet Jesus, while mount Paran can be understood to be located in Mecca, or the Cave of Hira, because in the Old Testament, Genesis 21:21, it is said that Hagar (Hajar, the Prophet

Abraham's spouse) and her son, Ismā'īl, resided in Paran. All historians know that Hagar and her child resided in Mecca. Thus, Paran is Mecca.

In this part of the Old Testament, the names listed conform with the [chronology of the] respective eras of the prophets (Moses, Jesus and Muhammad), whereas in the verses of *sūra* 95, while also being listed in a certain order, this is not according to chronology; rather, it is according to the rank of the revelations (sacred scriptures) that they received in the respective places. First come *al-Tīn* and *al-Zaytūn* because it is where the Gospel was revealed which is a sacred scripture that is, in essence, [merely] a supplement to the Tora. Therefore, it is mentioned first. Then comes Ṭūr Sīnīn, the place where the Tora was revealed, which ranks higher than the Gospel. The oath is concluded with *al-balad al-amīn* ['the secure city'] because it is where the revelation of the Qur'ān started. This sacred scripture is the noblest and most perfect for mankind so that man, who likewise was created by God in the most perfect form, could follow its guidance.[16]

and concise meaning, telling a coherent story, entertaining or providing the reader with a set of instructions, he aims at doing what scholars have done for more than a millennium: presenting the whole range of exegetical opinions, or at least much of them, in order to evaluate them without ever explicitly declaring any of them false.[17] There are some implicit restrictions in place, though. Like most mainstream Sunni exegetes, Quraish Shihab is not interested in allegorical or esoteric interpretations. He limits himself to those that can claim to either go back to early authorities or to be based on a, if not literal, then at least immediately plausible reading of the Qur'ān's terminology.

Despite these limitations, the result is an extensive, multi-vocal work that draws upon a wide variety of traditions in an entirely diachronic manner. Whether an exegetical opinion stems from the tenth or twentieth century is not important; it merely matters that it is there and that its author is perceived as an authority by the exegete who quotes him. Gaining a historical perspective on the flow of ideas that come together in Quraish Shihab's commentary requires a direct look at his sources and their interaction throughout history.

Quraish Shihab, in the segment translated above, discusses a rather enigmatic oath. This is a rhetorical device that many *sūra*s, especially the shorter ones towards the end of the Qur'ān, start with. Quraish Shihab's exposition of the existing exegetical opinions on the literal or metaphorical meaning of the fig and the olive is roughly arranged in two parts: first, the group of opinions that consider the fig and the olive metaphors for sacred sites, and second, the group that suggest reading them in a literal sense or as allusions to stories in which figs and olives figure prominently. He then presents arguments for and against these opinions, leading up to what is apparently his preferred solution.

As is typical of many Qurʾānic commentaries, Quraish Shihab provides a lot of generic information: some unnamed exegetes say this, others hold a different opinion. In the first section where Quraish Shihab discusses opinions that consider the fig and the olive substitutes for place names, the only person mentioned by name is al-Qāsimī, an early twentieth-century scholar from Damascus whose Qurʾānic commentary contained some modernist ideas and is quite popular in Indonesia. He is explicitly mentioned because he offers a very distinctive and singular interpretation, specifically, that the fig is a symbol of Buddhism and the Buddha a prophet just like Moses, Jesus and Muḥammad. This unusual claim has the potential to resonate strongly with an Indonesian audience, given the fact that Buddhism is one of the country's major religions. It is, in fact, not al-Qāsimī's own idea, but a direct import from an article that the Egyptian physician and intellectual Muḥammad Tawfīq Ṣidqī [1881–1920] wrote for the journal *al-Manār* in 1913. Al-Qāsimī, in contrast to what Quraish Shihab suggests, does not explicitly endorse Ṣidqī's interpretation, he merely quotes it. It seems as if Quraish Shihab is not quite sure what to make of it either; he leaves it uncommented.

From among those opinions that understand the fig and the olive in their literal sense, Quraish Shihab singles out that of al-Marāghī, again because it is so distinctive and singular. Al-Marāghī was an Egyptian modernist Qurʾānic commentator whose concise and stylistically simple work was translated into Indonesian and is very popular in Indonesia. Al-Marāghī was heavily indebted to the ideas of Egyptian early modernists. In this particular case, al-Marāghī's interpretation is in reality that of Muḥāmmad ʿAbduh, a fact that Quraish Shihab seems to be unaware of. He is simply not concerned with originality or authorship as much as with the contents of an interpretation. In this case, he disapproves of Muḥammad ʿAbduh's and al-Marāghī's interpretation unusually explicitly because he correctly assumes that it goes back to the Bible, rather than the Muslim tradition. Neither the story of the dove and the olive leaf nor that of Adam and Eve covering their nudity with fig leaves is part of the Qurʾān or of the mainstream Muslim narratives about these figures.

On the other hand, Quraish Shihab has no issue with Biblical quotations when they seem to him to confirm the legitimacy of Islam. Such is the case with his extensive quotation of Ibn Taymiyya's understanding of the verses in question. In Excerpt 2.1, Q. 95:1–3 is explained as a parallel to Deuteronomy 33:2 in that it mentions the sites of the revelation of the major scriptures. The Bible lists the sites in chronological order: first Sinai, representing

Moses; then Seir, representing Jesus; then Paran or Mecca, representing Muḥammad. The Qur'ān, on the other hand, according to Ibn Taymiyya lists them in order of hierarchy: first the least important one, the new Testament; then the Hebrew Bible; and finally, the most perfect scripture, the Qur'ān. In this case, Quraish Shihab considers it perfectly legitimate to draw on the Bible, something that Ibn Taymiyya had originally done in the context of an anti-Christian polemic.

Quraish Shihab's main hermeneutical device used to evaluate the various interpretations is a rather recent innovation: he strives for coherence within the *sūra*, and particularly between the segments of the oath contained in verses 1–3. This had not been much of a concern for most premodern exegetes who tended to interpret each verse by itself. There had been exceptions, though. A number of medieval exegetes, especially from Muslim Spain, had clearly read the whole segment as an allusion to the theme of prophethood, with Muḥammad as its culmination. In the times of the crusades and the Reconquista, they had – just like Ibn Taymiyya – clearly written in a context of Christian–Muslim polemics.

In al-Marāghī's and Muḥammad ʿAbduh's case, the recourse to the Bible comes from a different angle. Muḥammad ʿAbduh, who was heavily influenced by European ideas, used the Bible in order to construct from the *sūra* a new vision of human history. In fact, he proposes a more coherent reading of the *sūra* than most exegetes, understanding it as a metaphor for the ascent and demise of peoples according their success or failure in meeting God's demands. The prophets Adam, Noah, Moses and Muḥammad are described as symbols of the evolution of mankind. In al-Marāghī's more concise commentary, that overall message is not as obvious as in ʿAbduh's original one.[18] It is clear that Quraish Shihab has either not understood that message or does not consider it worth being mentioned.

If we take a comprehensive look at the trajectory of ideas that manifest themselves in Quraish Shihab's commentary on this segment (see Fig. 1), it becomes apparent that, despite his attempt to provide an encyclopaedic survey, his sources are predominantly modern. Much of the older material he cites, he has probably quoted from al-Qāsimī. This is certainly the case with Ibn Taymiyya whose interpretation was part of a polemical work, as opposed to a Qur'ānic commentary, and had thus never become part of the *tafsīr* tradition even though Ibn Taymiyya's disciple Ibn Kathīr had cited a few lines from it in his *tafsīr*. None of the exegetes in subsequent centuries quoted this opinion; it was only taken up in the beginning of the twentieth century by al-Qāsimī who was a major proponent of Ibn Taymiyya's revival. Quraish Shihab thus takes part in the reformation of a tradition.[19]

While Quraish Shihab's interest in coherence is a rather modern phenomenon,[20] his interest in philology is not. He is cautious in his translations,

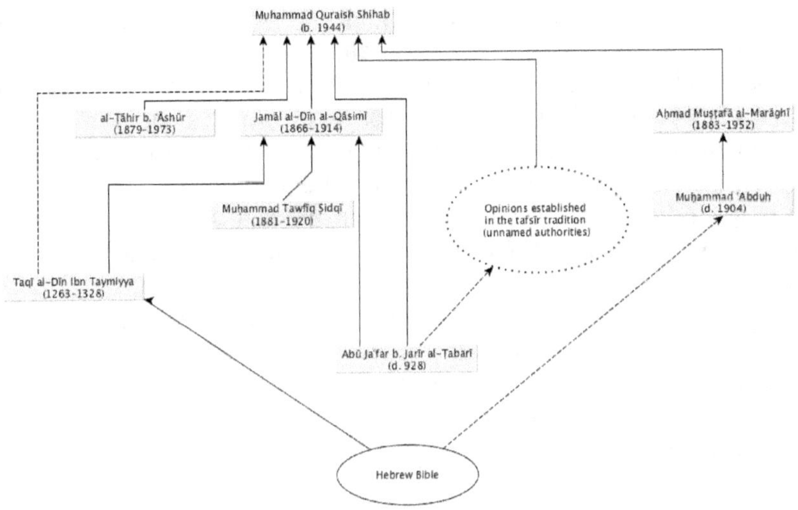

Figure 1. Quraish Shihab's sources in his commentary on Q. 95:1–3.

often opting for retaining the Arabic word and explaining its meaning rather than using an Indonesian substitute. In the case of figs and olives, explanation would, of course, be necessary because Quraish Shihab clearly assumes that his Indonesian readership is not familiar with these types of fruit. It is conceivable that his inclination towards a metaphorical reading of the oath is bolstered by the fact that the benefits of figs and olives are not universal knowledge, which might be more obvious in an Indonesian context than in many others. In any case, Quraish Shihab's interest in semantics and, more broadly, in philological detail is a consistent feature of his work, and one that clearly situates him in a scholarly tradition of exegesis.

The same is true for his approach to the authenticity of his sources. When he assesses them, historical scholarship clearly does not come into the picture, nor do extra-Islamic sources. Quraish Shihab considers a narrative to be plausible when it is corroborated by a *ḥadīth* or has been transmitted by a number of exegetical authorities. To Quraish Shihab, the story of Hagar's exile in Mecca is fact because Muslim scholars largely agree on it, while the story of Adam and the fig leaves is untrustworthy because it does not go back to any Muslim authority.

In sum, Quraish Shihab conceives of his own work as part of an ongoing exegetical tradition. The fact that he makes use of some modern methods, such as the attempt to deliver a coherent interpretation of larger textual units, does not contradict this concept at all because the tradition, as Quraish Shihab perceives of it, is able to integrate these innovations and thrive on them without discarding older elements. He does not aim at overthrowing the tradition, he aims at expanding it. In this framework, twentieth-century exegetes such as al-Marāghī or al-Qāsimī are no different from al-Ṭabarī, even if a millennium of history separates them: both are resources feeding into an ever-growing accumulation of exegetical opinions that any subsequent exegete may draw upon or add to.

Thus, Quraish Shihab's work perfectly embodies, in a contemporary setting, the concept of *ijmāʿ*, the consensus of a diachronic community of scholars that was a hallmark of the tradition of encyclopaedic *tafsīr*.[21] His inclusive approach enables him to integrate a broad range of trends far beyond the conventional Sunni corpus of sources, including the Islamist Sayyid Quṭb (1906–1966), the Shiʿi scholar Muḥammad Ḥusayn Ṭabāṭabāʾī (d. 1981) and various Sufi interpretations. However, Quraish Shihab does not discuss opinions that might be considered overly esoteric, sectarian, revolutionary, violent or otherwise offensive. The emphasis is on unity, a goal that is reached both through including a variety of approaches and through excluding potentially divisive aspects: a contemporary take on the archetypical Sunni doctrine of *ijmāʿ*.

A SALAFI PARADIGM

So far, this chapter might have conveyed the impression that the premodern tradition of *tafsīr*, while continuing into the contemporary period and absorbing some innovations as well as sprouting a few off-shoots along the way, is a more or less monolithic body of sources that has essentially remained unchanged. This is not quite the case, however, because the make-up of the field, with its boundaries, centres of gravity, authorities and outcasts has undergone fundamental changes that influence contemporary discourses on the Qur'ān to a great extent. In order to understand this process, it is necessary to go back into the period in which the Qur'ān started to gain its central role for Muslim religious debates.

Around the late-nineteenth and early-twentieth centuries, a growing number of Muslim scholars and, importantly, publishers were engaged in the rediscovery, rehabilitation and promotion of the works of the Damascene scholar Taqī al-Dīn Ibn Taymiyya (1263–1328) and his disciples. For the field of *tafsīr*, this was most notably the above-mentioned Ibn Kathīr who wrote a major Qur'ānic commentary. In this work, he claimed to apply Ibn Taymiyya's ideas by including the last two chapters of the latter's 'Introduction to the principles of Qur'ānic exegesis' (*Muqaddima fī uṣūl al-tafsīr*) in the introduction to his *tafsīr*, thus presenting Ibn Taymiyya's method of interpreting the Qur'ān as authoritative.

What appealed to readers from the late-nineteenth century onwards about that methodology was Ibn Taymiyya's firmly scripturalist approach. A statement could only be true, he claimed, if it was based on either the Qur'ān itself or the Prophet's opinion. Since the number of exegetical *ḥadīth*s is fairly low and not nearly sufficient to solve all exegetical problems in the Qur'ān, and since a purely intra-textual analysis does not provide solutions to all of the problems either, Ibn Taymiyya broadened the category of exegetical opinions that were admissible sources of interpretation. If no 'proof' (*dalīl*) from the Qur'ān or the Prophetic Sunna was available, it was permitted to look for opinions from the Prophet's companions (*ṣaḥāba*), and if these offered no solution to the problem at hand, the next step would be to look at the generation of their 'successors' (*tābiʿūn*). The idea was that these first generations of Islam, the *salaf*, even if they were not explicitly citing the Prophet's interpretation of the Qur'ān, were close enough to him to transmit it in meaning or spirit. Thus, Ibn Taymiyya managed to shift the idea of the *salaf* – which was not his invention, as such – to the centre of his methodology, to emotionally charge it and to frame it in a way that enabled it to serve as a unifying factor, much as the Prophet's family (*ahl al-bayt*) did in Shiʿi Islam.[22] This was another source of attraction for Ibn Taymiyya's modern proponents who were intensely concerned with uniting Muslims against the threat of Western imperialism.

Ibn Kathīr's Qur'ānic commentary was a work written by a religious scholar engaging with the works of other religious scholars. It was meant to refute some of the paradigms at work in the voluminous Qur'ānic commentary by the Ashʿari[23] theologian Fakhr al-Dīn al-Rāzī (d. 1210), which was arguably the most authoritative encyclopaedic commentary at the time, and to offer a *ḥadīth*-based alternative to that which involved lengthy *isnād*s, or chains of transmitters, and discussions thereof. To achieve this, Ibn Kathīr mined some earlier, tradition-based Qur'ānic commentaries for *ḥadīth* material that he considered authentic while still maintaining many of the standards of the genre such as the acknowledgement of different opinions and the engagement with existing interpretations.[24] For several centuries, his commentary was accepted as part of the *tafsīr* tradition, but not as an outstanding or particularly authoritative one.

The popularity that Ibn Taymiyya's *Muqaddima* and Ibn Kathīr's *tafsīr* attained in the twentieth century was largely owed to efforts by individuals in Cairo, Damascus, Beirut and India to have their works printed and, especially in the case of the *tafsīr*, have them printed in accessible editions in a modern layout in the 1920s and 1930s.[25]

The Taymiyyan idea, in particular, that there is a correct approach to exegesis based exclusively on scriptural 'proof' versus an incorrect approach that makes use of the exegete's 'opinions' has become extremely influential in Muslim and non-Muslim perspectives on the history of Qur'ānic exegesis. Today, this idea is typically expressed in the dichotomy between *tafsīr bi'l-ma'thūr* (exegesis based on transmitted material) and *tafsīr bi'l-ra'y* (exegesis based on personal reasoning) that has become a central part of the modern Muslim narrative of the history of *tafsīr*. This is mainly owed to the standard work that Muḥammad al-Dhahabī (1915–1977) published in the beginning of the 1960s that has been translated into various languages, for example, Turkish.[26] In this work, al-Dhahabī sharply distinguishes between these two types of *tafsīr*, classifying everything that does not fit his concept of *tafsīr bi'l-ma'thūr* into various sectarian subcategories. This perception of exegesis has become extremely influential. It is also highly problematic because there is little consensus about what, exactly, constitutes a *ma'thūr* work and what not. To some, for example, al-Ṭabarī's (d. 923) famous *tafsīr* fits the description while to others, it falls short of the mark. Besides, many contemporary exegetes claim to follow the scripturalist paradigm in their exegesis, but no one ever admits to practising *tafsīr bi'l-ra'y* which is thus not a neutral descriptor, but a label used to denounce others.[27]

This denunciation of various forms of Qur'ān interpretation as not being based on the *ma'thūr* and therefore not conforming to the influential Salafi paradigm typically involves the condemnation of scholastic theology (*kalām*) and philosophy as futile and potentially harmful. Similar diatribes target the use of narrative material labelled as *isrā'īliyyāt*: stories of Jewish, or sometimes Christian, origin that are considered unreliable. These ideas can be found in Ibn Taymiyya's works, which were often polemical in nature, but they only became widely popular in the beginning of the twentieth century as devices to discredit large parts of the exegetical tradition as well as many contemporary forms of exegesis.[28]

It is here that Salafism converges with the modernist trend spearheaded by Muḥammad 'Abduh. The sweeping condemnation of the vast intellectual heritage related to Aristotelian logic, as well as the equally vast heritage related to Jewish and Christian narrative traditions, has its roots as much in Taymiyyan Salafism as in Muḥammad 'Abduh's modernist and rationalist approach.[29] This convergence is personified in Muḥammad Rashīd Riḍā (1860–1935), Muḥammad 'Abduh's disciple and main author of the voluminous *Tafsīr al-Manār*, who was behind the publication of the first modern-style printed edition of Ibn Kathīr's Qur'ānic commentary. This was connected to an increasing affinity to Wahhābism, the ideology of the emergent state of Saudi Arabia that owed much to Ibn Taymiyya, late in Rashīd Riḍā's life.[30]

Despite the similarities between the two trends, the contents of their Qur'ān interpretation are vastly different. Whereas Muḥammad ʿAbduh wanted to limit or even ban polygyny, Salafis want to permit it; whereas Rashīd Riḍā considered an interest-based financial system permissible if the nation's higher interest (*maṣlaḥa*) requires it, Salafis strictly reject it; and so forth. Essentially, the modernist notion of 'reform' had an element of technological, social and institutional progress to it that was absent from the Salafi paradigm.

It will become evident from many of the case studies in this volume that the Salafi paradigm of Qur'ānic exegesis with its emphasis on authentic 'proof' has acquired considerable authority and exerts some pressure on contemporary exegetes to either conform to it or justify their non-conformity. Ibn Taymiyya and Ibn Kathīr have emerged during the twentieth century as major exegetical authorities. This form of reception is a distinctly contemporary phenomenon that is often disjointed from the context and aims of their original works. While they wrote for and – importantly – against other scholars, their modern readers take their scripturalist ideas a step further, with the result that any Muslim who is able to find scriptural 'proof' in the Qur'ān and Sunna is able to construct authority without having to situate his argument in a scholarly discourse, as Ibn Taymiyya and Ibn Kathīr had done.

Ibn Kathīr's Qur'ānic commentary is an example of how certain exegetical texts and ideas have moved from the margins to the centre of Muslim intellectual thought in recent times. Others have taken the reverse direction, attracting criticism for being too steeped in theological debate or including too much *isrāʾīliyyāt* material. Thus, Fakhr al-Dīn al-Rāzī, once possibly the greatest exegetical authority, is often treated with suspicion today due to his penchant for philosophy, just al-Thaʿlabī's (d. 1035) great Qur'ānic commentary, once admired for the wealth of material it contains, is often shunned because much of that material is regarded as overly narrative and potentially unreliable. While these two exegetes, however, are still cited by scholars, the once-ubiquitous genre of the gloss (*ḥāshiya*) – a supra-commentary on a Qur'ānic commentary[31] – has virtually disappeared from use despite the fact that as late as the early-twentieth century, there were some famous *ḥāshiya*s that were taught in all *madrasa*s. The *ḥāshiya* was part of a scholarly tradition that has ceased to be relevant or even intelligible to most Muslims today.

It is not only because of the Taymiyyan concept of exegesis that Ibn Kathīr's Qur'ānic commentary has become a hugely popular resource, dominating contemporary perspectives on the exegetical tradition and the reception of the premodern heritage. It seems to have replaced the exegeses of al-Rāzī and al-Bayḍāwī as the new standard work, and one that is not only used by scholars, but also by students and lay Muslims. The reworking of Ibn Kathīr's commentary into abridged editions and translations was an essential prerequisite to this.[32] The languages into which Ibn Kathīr has been translated include Indonesian, Bengali, English, French, Turkish, German and Urdu. These translations as well as abridged Arabic editions aim to make the *tafsīr* accessible to a broader, non-specialist readership. The following case study will show how they try to achieve that aim.

Reshaping the tradition: Shaykh al-Mubarakpuri's *Tafsir Ibn Kathir (Abridged)* (India/Saudi Arabia) on Q. 38:21–25

Shaykh Safiur-Rahman al-Mubarakpuri's *Tafsir Ibn Kathir (Abridged)* is an English translation of an Arabic digest of the Qur'ānic commentary by Ibn Kathīr. Ibn Kathīr is generally considered by Salafis as a methodologically sound and dogmatically recommendable work of exegesis. Nevertheless, the Riyad-based publishing house Darussalam was uncomfortable with some of the material contained in this *tafsīr* and commissioned a team of scholars with producing a shortened and improved version in Arabic.[33]

Al-Mubarakpuri, who was the main editor of the Darussalam abridged version of Ibn Kathīr's *tafsīr* and also the translator into English, is a Saudi-based scholar of Indian birth.[34] His translation was first published by Darussalam in 2000 and is widely available in various editions as well as on the internet.[35] Mubarakpuri's translation is possibly the most widespread of many translations of Ibn Kathīr's work into various languages and clearly serves the goal of providing Muslims with access to the 'correct meaning' of the Qur'ān, rather than educating readers about the intentions of the historical Ibn Kathīr.[36]

This English translation, as well as the Arabic abridged version it is based on, were undertaken by a publisher in Saudi Arabia, a fact that is closely linked to the ideological context in which the publication, translation and distribution of Ibn Kathīr's *tafsīr* takes place. As the editor of the translation explains in his publisher's note, Ibn Kathīr's work is seen as mostly conforming to a Salafi vision of Islam, as well as a source of guidance to the true meaning of the Qur'ān. The state of Saudi Arabia has since its inception had a strong interest in setting itself up as the guardian of a Taymiyyan or Salafi brand of Islam – which, in its view, is the only correct type of Islam. This ideological trend exerts a tremendous influence on contemporary read-

Excerpt 2.2

Q. 38:21–25

وَهَلْ أَتَاكَ نَبَأُ الْخَصْمِ إِذْ تَسَوَّرُوا الْمِحْرَابَ ﴿٢١﴾ إِذْ دَخَلُوا عَلَىٰ دَاوُودَ فَفَزِعَ مِنْهُمْ قَالُوا
لَا تَخَفْ خَصْمَانِ بَغَىٰ بَعْضُنَا عَلَىٰ بَعْضٍ فَاحْكُم بَيْنَنَا بِالْحَقِّ وَلَا تُشْطِطْ وَاهْدِنَا إِلَىٰ سَوَاءِ
الصِّرَاطِ ﴿٢٢﴾ إِنَّ هَٰذَا أَخِي لَهُ تِسْعٌ وَتِسْعُونَ نَعْجَةً وَلِيَ نَعْجَةٌ وَاحِدَةٌ فَقَالَ أَكْفِلْنِيهَا وَعَزَّنِي
فِي الْخِطَابِ ﴿٢٣﴾ قَالَ لَقَدْ ظَلَمَكَ بِسُؤَالِ نَعْجَتِكَ إِلَىٰ نِعَاجِهِ وَإِنَّ كَثِيرًا مِّنَ الْخُلَطَاءِ لَيَبْغِي
بَعْضُهُمْ عَلَىٰ بَعْضٍ إِلَّا الَّذِينَ آمَنُوا وَعَمِلُوا الصَّالِحَاتِ وَقَلِيلٌ مَّا هُمْ وَظَنَّ دَاوُودُ أَنَّمَا فَتَنَّاهُ
فَاسْتَغْفَرَ رَبَّهُ وَخَرَّ رَاكِعًا وَأَنَابَ ﴿٢٤﴾ فَغَفَرْنَا لَهُ ذَٰلِكَ وَإِنَّ لَهُ عِندَنَا لَزُلْفَىٰ وَحُسْنَ مَآبٍ ﴿٢٥﴾

21. *And has the news of the litigants reached you? When they climbed over the wall into his Mihrāb (private chamber of workship);*
22. *When they entered in upon Dāwud, he was terrified of them. They said: 'Fear not! (We are) two litigants, one of us has wronged the other, therefore judge between us with truth, and treat us not with injustice, and guide us to the right way.*
23. *Verily, this my brother (in religion) has ninety-nine ewes, while I have (only) one ewe, and he says: 'Hand it over to me, and he overpowered me in speech'* [*sic*].
24. *(Dāwud) said: 'He has wronged you in demanding your ewe in addition to his ewes. And, verily, many partners oppress one another, except those who believe and do righteous good deeds, and they are few!' And Dāwud guessed that We have tried him and he sought forgiveness of his Lord, and he fell down prostrate and turned (to Allāh) in repentance.*
25. *So, we forgave him that, and verily, for him is a near access to Us, and a good place of return.*

The Story of the Two Litigants

In discussing this passage, the scholars of *Tafsīr* mention a story which is mostly based upon *Isrā'īliyāt* narrations. Nothing has been reported about this from the Infallible Prophet that we could accept as true. But Ibn Abi Ḥātim narrated a *Ḥadīth* whose chain of narration cannot be regarded as *Ṣaḥīḥ* because it is reported by Yazīd Ar-Raqāshi from Anas, may Allāh be pleased with him. Although Yazīd was one of the righteous, his *Ḥadīth*s are regarded as weak by the Imāms. So, it is better to speak briefly of this story and refer knowledge of it to Allāh, may He be exalted. For the Qur'ān is true and what it contains is also true.

فَفَزِعَ مِنْهُمْ

(*he was terrified of them.*) This was because he was in his *Miḥrāb* (private chamber). That was the noblest part of his house, where he commanded that no one should enter upon him that day. So, he did not realize that these two people had climbed the fence surrounding his *Miḥrāb* (private chamber) to ask him about their case.

عَزَّنِي فِي الْخِطَابِ

(*and he overpowered me in speech.*) means, 'he defeated me'.

وَظَنَّ دَاوُودُ أَنَّمَا فَتَنَّاهُ

(*And Dāwud guessed that We have tried him*)

'Ali bin Abi Ṭalḥah reported that Ibn 'Abbās said that this means, 'We tested him'. (Aṭ-Ṭabari 21:181.)

وَخَرَّ رَاكِعًا وَأَنَابَ

(*and he fell down prostrate and turned (to Allāh) in repentance.*)

فَغَفَرْنَا لَهُ ذَٰلِكَ

(*So, We forgave him that,*)

The *Sajdah* in *Sūrah Ṣād*

The performance of *Sajdah* in *Sūrah Ṣād* is not one of the obligatory locations; it is a prostration of thanks (*Sajdat Shukr*). The evidence for it is the report recorded by Imām Aḥmad from Ibn 'Abbās, may Allāh be pleased with him, who said; 'The prostration in *Sūrah Ṣād* is not one of the obligatory prostrations; I saw the Messenger of Allāh prostrating in this *Sūrah*'. (Aḥmad 1:359.) This was also recorded by Al-Bukhāri, Abu Dāwud, At-Tirmidhi, and An-Nasa'ī in his *Tafsīr*. At-Tirmidhi said, '*Ḥasan Ṣaḥīḥ*'. (*Fatḥ Al-Bāri* 2:643, Abu Dāwud 2:123, *Tuḥfat Al-Aḥwadhi* 3:176, An-Nasā'ī in *Al-Kubrā* 6:342.) In his *Tafsīr* of this *Āyah*, An-Nasā'ī also recorded that Ibn 'Abbās, may Allah be pleased with him, said, 'The Prophet prostrated in *Ṣad*, and he said:

«سَجَدَهَا دَاوُدُ عَلَيْهِ الصَّلَاةُ وَالسَّلَامُ تَوْبَةً، وَنَسْجُدُهَا شُكْرًا»

"*Dāwud prostrated as an act of repentance and we prostrate as an act of thanks*"'.

This was recorded only by An-Nasā'ī. (An-Nasā'ī 2:159.) The men of its chain of narration are all reliable.

In his *Tafsīr* of this *Āyah*, Al-Bukhāri recorded that Al-'Awwām said that he asked Mujāhid about the prostration in *Sūrah Ṣād*. He said, 'I asked Ibn 'Abbās, may Allāh be pleased with him, "Why do you prostrate?" He said, "Have you not read:

وَمِن ذُرِّيَّتِهِ دَاوُودَ وَسُلَيْمَـٰنَ

(*and among his [Nūḥ's] progeny Dāwud, Sulaymān*) (6:84)

أُوْلَـٰئِكَ الَّذِينَ هَدَى اللَّهُ فَبِهُدَاهُمُ اقْتَدِهْ

(*They are those whom Allah had guided. So follow their guidance*) (6:90)".

Dāwud, peace be upon him, was one of those whom your Prophet was commanded to follow. Dāwud prostrated here so the Messenger of Allāh also prostrated here.' (*Fatḥ al-Bāri* 8:405)

Abu Dāwud recorded that Abu Sa'īd Al-Khudri, may Allāh be pleased with him, said, 'The Messenger of Allah recited *Ṣād* while he was on the *Minbar*. When he reached the prostration, he came down from the *Minbar* and prostrated, and the people prostrated with him. On another occasion when he recited it, he reached the prostration and the people prepared to prostrate. He said:

«إِنَّمَا هِيَ تَوْبَةُ نَبِيٍّ، وَلَكِنِّي رَأَيْتُكُمْ تَشَزَّنْتُ»

"*This is repentance for a Prophet, but I see that you are preparing to prostrate*".

Then he came down (from the *Minbar*) and prostrated'.

This was recorded only by Abu Dāwud and its chain of narration meets the conditions of the Two *Ṣaḥīḥ*s. [...][37]

ings of the Qur'ān, and one of the ways in which it does so is through the distribution of Ibn Kathīr's *tafsīr*.

In Excerpt 2.2, it is easy to see why Ibn Kathīr's commentary, or at least most of it, appeals to a contemporary Salafi publisher from Saudi Arabia. In the first paragraph, Ibn Kathīr mentions a story based on *isrā'īliyyāt*, which is the term he uses to denote traditions that he considers to be borrowed from Jewish or Christian sources and weak with respect to their authenticity.[38] He apparently deems the story he alludes to important enough to be mentioned, but declines to provide any details. Any reader unfamiliar with the background of his remarks will be left in the dark, and Ibn Kathīr's editor does nothing to clarify the matter. In fact, what Ibn Kathīr refers to is an exegetical debate about the reasons for which David sought forgiveness from God. Many exegetes assumed that David must have sinned in order to ask for forgiveness, and most of them identified the Biblical story of David and Bathsheba as the cause of the sin. According to this story, David had intercourse with a married woman, impregnated her and arranged to have her husband die in battle so he could marry her, which makes the sin rather remarkable. The Hebrew Bible also tells the story of how God sent Nathan the Prophet to David to tell him a parable that is very similar to the story of the two litigants. The Bible continues to narrate how David – unsuccessfully – prostrated himself for seven days in order to save the child born out of the illegitimate relationship from dying (2 Sam 12:1–18). The Qur'ānic story of the two litigants seems to be an obvious reference to this Biblical narrative – especially if one looks one verse further, to Q. 38:26, where God warns David not to follow his desires.

However, in the course of the centuries an increasing number of Islamic scholars came to believe that prophets were by definition free from sin (*'iṣma*). If one subscribes to this dogma, the story of Bathsheba and especially the murder of her husband is unacceptable. Since the story is of Jewish origin, it seems an obvious solution to declare it an untrustworthy *isrā'īliyyāt* narrative. The *isrā'īliyyāt* motive was a device that Ibn Kathīr frequently used.[39] He obviously felt compelled to at least hint at the story in order to show that he knows of it, which would be expected of him as an exegete of the Qur'ān; but he refuses to give details, he expresses his doubts and he concludes with the pious and undebatable statement that the Qur'ān itself is the truth – which could be understood to mean that extra-Qur'ānic narratives may very well be false.

Ibn Kathīr's actual thought was probably more complex than his modern adherents give him credit for, but his approach here, to them, seems congruent with the contemporary Salafi stance on how exegesis should be performed: with an emphasis on authentic traditions, but also with an eye on dogmatic coherence.

Despite the appeal of Ibn Kathīr to modern audiences, though, it is not Ibn Kathīr's *tafsīr* as such that is presented in this English edition, but an abridged translation. This translation has a number of features that distinguish it from Ibn Kathīr's original commentary beyond the degree to which any translation is bound to differ from the source text. These features turn *Ibn Kathir (abridged)* into an original contemporary *tafsīr*, rather than a mere rendition of a work from the fourteenth century. The differences from the original are not random. They have reasons that are rooted in contemporary concerns. The differences can be subsumed in five main categories.

First, each section of commentary is preceded by a translation of the Qurʾānic segment in question. The authors here have opted for using the Hilâlî-Khân translation that is published by the King Fahd Complex for the Printing of the Holy Qurʾān in Medina. In some cases, the use of this translation adds an interpretive dimension that is not present in Ibn Kathīr's work. In the example above, the translation explains the term 'brother' (*akh*) in Q. 38:23 as 'brother (in religion)' as opposed to an actual blood relation, which is neither evident from the Qurʾān nor something that Ibn Kathīr saw a need to discuss.

Second, and in the same vein, the translation of Ibn Kathīr's commentary itself sometimes reflects the translator's dogmatic perspective more accurately than it does Ibn Kathīr's. An example can be found at the very end of the text. Ibn Kathīr's original commentary about Ibn Dāwud's narration on the Prophet's prostration concludes with the statement: 'Its chain of transmitters (*isnād*) fulfills the criteria of authenticity (*ʿalā sharṭ al-ṣaḥīḥ*)'.[40] The translation, on the other hand, says: 'Its chain of narration meets the conditions of the Two *Ṣaḥīḥ*s', meaning the two *ḥadīth* collections of al-Bukhārī and Muslim that Sunnis generally consider to be the most authentic. It is highly doubtful that Ibn Kathīr, who quotes traditions from a wide variety of collections up until his own time, had such a narrow understanding of authenticity as the translator wants to make his readers believe.

Third, the translation adds headings to the text, thereby presenting the commentary as a set of narratives and instructions on coherent themes, which the original is not.

Fourth, it contains bibliographical references that point to Sunni *ḥadīth* collections containing the traditions cited by Ibn Kathīr, conforming to the Salafi paradigm that only such statements are credible that are based on authoritative sources about the Prophet and his companions. On the other hand, the full chains of transmitters (*isnād*) that Ibn Kathīr provides are missing from the translation, suggesting that the editor expects readers to trust his judgement on the authenticity of traditions, rather than being interested in technical details that would allow for verification. Moreover, it suggests that he considers the inclusion of a *ḥadīth* in a major *ḥadīth* collection more relevant to judging its authenticity than the actual chain of transmitters.

Fifth, and maybe most strikingly, the translation of the commentary explicitly omits material from the original work. It is based on an abridged Arabic version that claims to 'refine' Ibn Kathīr's *tafsīr*[41] and that had been produced by the same editor – together with a team of scholars – and the same Saudi-based publishing house. Some of the omissions are related to linguistic discussions requiring an academic knowledge of Arabic, but most of them concern explicatory and narrative exegetical traditions that the editor apparently does not consider authentic.

In the above commentary on the story of David and the two litigants, the omissions and alterations are significant; it could be argued that they fundamentally change the nature of Ibn Kathīr's Qur'ānic commentary in order to make it conform to a contemporary Salafi paradigm.

First, explanations of the wording of the Qur'ān that Ibn Kathīr gives are omitted from the translation. An example of this is related to David's prostration described in v. 24. Here, Ibn Kathīr tried to clarify an exegetical problem that arises in the Arabic text of the Qur'ān. A more literal translation of the phrase in v. 24 that Hilâlî and Khân render as 'he fell down prostrate' would be 'he fell down, bowing (*kharra rākiʿan*)'. This is slightly confusing: did David fall down or did he bow? The act of prostrating oneself in prayer is normally expressed by the verb *sajada*, which the Qur'ān does not use here, but exegetes usually agree that it is what the text means by the verb *kharra*. However, the participle used here, *rākiʿan*, refers to the act of bowing in the prayer ritual which is distinctly different from the prostration. Ibn Kathīr tries to solve the problem by saying that in all likelihood, David first bowed and then fell down prostrate. He also mentions traditions according to which David spent forty days in prostration. All this is missing from the translation.

Moving on to the problem of the sin for which David sought forgiveness, Ibn Kathīr quotes a saying that suggests that the act David sought forgiveness for was not sinful by normal standards, but only by the high standards of a person close to God. For example, David might have lost his exclusive focus on God for a while which would not be reprehensible in an ordinary believer. This, too, is missing from the translation. Although both segments concern exegetical issues that every scholarly commentary on the Qur'ān would be expected to address, the editor probably feared it might confuse the intended readership and might make the Qur'ānic text appear imperfect and contradictory. He might also have considered the traditions about the forty days David spent in prostration untrustworthy.

Next comes a paragraph that the editor has not deleted in its entirety, but shortened in a way that rather subverts the original intention. Ibn Kathīr starts out, as any self-respecting premodern exegete would have done, by stating that there is a difference of opinion among the earlier authorities. Their controversy concerns the question whether the prostration mentioned in v. 24 refers to the obligatory prostration that is part of ritual prayer. According to Ibn Kathīr, there are two opinions on this matter. Presumably, the first – which he does not explicitly mention – answers the question in the affirmative. Ibn Kathīr only mentions the second, and more recent, opinion. He ascribes it to the Shāfiʿī school of law that he himself adhered to. According to this opinion, the Qur'ān here refers to the prostration of thanks. Ibn Kathīr proceeds to provide evidence for this opinion, thereby suggesting that it is the one he considers more likely to be correct. The abridged translation, however, bypasses all references to the existence of a difference of opinion and merely states that the prostration in this verse is a prostration of thanks.

Taken together, the omission or extreme abbreviation of the first segments of Ibn Kathīr's commentary in the abridged translation convey the rather misleading impression that Ibn Kathīr's commentary is neither interested in the exegetical tradition nor in engaging in exegetical debates, but rather focusses on providing the one correct interpretation of the verse. Moreover, the Salafi paradigm upon which the translation is based, rejects the mere existence of schools of law and would therefore not risk 'discrediting' Ibn Kathīr's opinion as a Shāfiʿī one. Rather, it is presented as the only opinion supported by scriptural proof (*dalīl*) or, more precisely, not even as an opinion, but as the true meaning of the verse. Ibn Kathīr's Qur'ānic commentary was originally situated in a scholarly tradition and participated in ongoing scholarly controversies. The way in which its editor presents it to a contemporary readership, however, transforms it into a guidance-oriented manual of correctly understanding the Qur'ān.

The main part of Ibn Kathīr's commentary consists of *ḥadīth*s and other exegetical traditions related to the verse. From his account of traditions on David's prostration and its significance, two are conspicuously missing in the translation. Both of these involve colourful dreams in which trees or objects prostrate themselves, reciting the verse on David's prostration, whereupon the Prophet advises believers to perform this type of prostration.[42] They thus belong to the genre of *faḍāʾil* traditions, that is, traditions that establish the excellence and benefits of a *sūra* or verse in the Qur'ān. The reason for which these traditions were eliminated from the abridged Ibn Kathīr edition is clearly neither a Judeo-Christian background, which is not discernible, nor a weak chain of transmitters. Both traditions are included in major *ḥadīth* collections that the Saudi editors of the abridged Ibn Kathīr considered acceptable in many other instances. They are also reported by Jalāl al-Dīn al-Suyūṭī (1445–1505) in his *al-Durr al-manthūr*, a Qur'ānic commentary that exclusively collects those exegetical traditions that al-Suyūṭī, after having examined their chain of narrators, considered authentic.[43] Thus, the reason for the omission of these traditions is probably not so much that the editors found fault with the *isnād*; it is rather more likely that they found fault with the contents.

Possibly, the editors simply did not see the point of *faḍāʾil ḥadīth*s, assuming that they do not contribute to better understanding the verse in question. Indeed, on a superficial level, they do not, but Ibn Kathīr might well have included them with an explicit exegetical purpose: as further evidence for his opinion that the prostration mentioned in the verse does not refer to any particular sin committed by David, but rather to a more general act of repentance or gratitude.[44]

Another likely explanation for the omission of these *ḥadīth*s is their endorsement of the belief in spiritual, even divine, dreams. Stories of dreams of divine provenance were commonplace in Ibn Kathīr's time, but to a modern reader, they might appear questionable and superstitious. How could the Prophet recite words that a tree had said to someone in a dream? Why should it be relevant that a companion of the Prophet imagined his inkwell – a rather anachronistic item, by the way – to prostrate itself? The editors of Ibn Kathīr's commentary avoided such questions by omitting the colourful and mystical in favour of the straightforward and respectable. By the same token, they avoided the connotation of Sufism that is associated with divine messages in dreams; after all, official Saudi-Salafi doctrine is rather hostile to Sufism.

Ibn Kathīr's Qur'ānic commentary has certain features that appeal to contemporary audiences, especially his tendency to identify a 'correct' solution to exegetical problems above others and his emphasis on *ḥadīth* material. However, he also situated himself within the scholarly *tafsīr* tradition by analysing problems posed by the Qur'ānic text and by acknowledging dissenting opinions. He excluded certain narrative traditions whose authenticity he doubted, but unlike his editor, he did not have a narrow vision of the Sunna as a corpus of sources mainly embodied in a few authoritative collections, nor was he sceptical of transcendental experiences. None of these typical aspects of a premodern Qur'ānic commentary is discernible in the abridged translation of his *tafsīr*. Through a number of changes and omissions that might seem small at first glance, the Saudi-based editor and translator of Ibn Kathīr has managed to fundamentally alter the nature and exegetical perspective of his work. Far from striving to faithfully transmit Ibn Kathīr's thoughts to today's readers, he has produced a new – and distinctly contemporary – contribution to the canon of *tafsīr*.

As mentioned at the outset, this is not an isolated phenomenon. For example, the Jordanian Salafi Muḥammad b. Mūsā Āl Naṣr published in 1426 AH (2005–6 CE) an abridged Arabic version of Ibn Kathīr's *tafsīr* that pursued the declared aim of purifying it from weak *ḥadīth*s and occasions of revelation as well as *isrā'īliyyāt*. Other goals included the exclusion of *ḥadīth*s that do not contribute to understanding the meaning of the verse, the omission of *isnād*s and the elimination of legal and linguistic details that the editor considers irrelevant.[45]

Paradoxically, Ibn Kathīr's immense importance as a contemporary exegetical authority seems to be both enhanced and called into question by such works. They enhance his status by contributing to the popularisation and accessibility of his Qur'ānic commentary, but at the same time they call into question authoritativeness of his *tafsīr* by explicitly aiming for its purification. It is unlikely, however, that many contemporary readers of abridged translations are aware of the fundamental changes to which the original work is subjected. It is rather more probable that they are under the impression to be dealing with the actual Ibn Kathīr, an icon of Salafi exegesis.

PRESENT-DAY SALAFI EXEGESIS

What does it mean to talk about 'Salafi exegesis' How did a scripturalist paradigm related to the ideas of Ibn Taymiyya come to be known as 'Salafism'? In the course of the twentieth century, the term 'Salafism' (Ar., *salafiyya*) has changed its meaning to a remarkable degree, at least in the Western academic discourse. It has transformed from an elitist intellectual movement associated with modernist ideas to a global fundamentalist religious movement that, on a worldwide scale, probably attracts more attention than any other such movement. Both the nature of that astonishing transformation and the diversity of the contemporary forms of Salafism are the subject of intense academic debate.

Even in fairly recent Western works on Qur'ānic exegesis, 'Salafi' Qur'ānic interpretation is not remotely understood in the sense that contemporary Muslims define Salafism. Rather, for a long time, the label *salafī* has been used by Islamicists to denote the school of Jamāl al-Dīn al-Afghānī, Muḥammad ʿAbduh and their disciples: modernist reformers of the late-nineteenth and early-twentieth centuries invoking the *salaf*, the righteous first generations of Islam, in order to discard the intellectual traditions of previous centuries and focus on the fundamental sources of Islam, especially the Qur'ān. Rather than following the theological reasoning of the Ashʿaris, infused with Aristotelian logic, or the intricate teachings of a specific school of law, Muslims should read the Qur'ān and follow its guidance. The ensuing approach to reading the Qur'ān was rationalist and framed by larger goals of progress and social reform.[46]

As has been mentioned already, this fairly elitist project partly converged with and partly differed from another trend that had its own centres, for example in Damascus, in India and in the newly emergent state of Saudi Arabia. It, too, promoted a return to the sources of Islam to the exclusion of scholastic theology (*kalām*) and the schools of law. However, its understanding of a return to the sources was far more literalist than that of the modernist reformers, and *ḥadīth*s played a much more important role. It was concerned with the purification of Islam from practices that were categorised as *shirk*. The Wahhābī variant of this reform movement, in particular, was extremely polarising in its aggression against anything it classified as *shirk* and its insistence on a narrow concept of correct belief and practice. For this trend, the writings of Ibn Taymiyya were an extremely important source of inspiration and Ibn Taymiyya's invocation of the *salaf* was given much due.

However, the term *salafiyya* as a descriptor of a fundamentalist religious movement seems only to have emerged in the 1920s and was at the time relatively vague. The boundaries between the modernists around Muḥammad 'Abduh and the more literalist trends in Syria, in particular, were not clear-cut. The two groups might not have been equally interested in *ḥadīth*, but they shared some of the same goals as well as a desire to distance themselves from the established *'ulamā'* and their institutions. Moreover, there was a lot of exchange between them. Their positions were strongly influenced by the political situation of their time which is evidenced in the rapprochement of Muḥammad 'Abduh's disciple Muḥammad Rashīd Riḍā to Wahhābism in the 1920s.[47] That movement, which was behind the rise of the Saudi state, had trouble convincing its adherents of the legitimacy of telegraphs at the time and thus seemed to have little in common with the modernist reform project embraced by Muḥammad 'Abduh. However, Wahhābism was made attractive by the person of 'Abd al-'Azīz b. Su'ūd ('Ibn Saud', 1876–1953), the ruler of Saudi Arabia who had managed to establish a state that was not under direct or indirect colonial rule.[48] Rashīd Riḍā was one of the pivotal figures who contributed to the establishment of Salafism as an intellectual trend in the 1920s and 1930s. There were others, among them the founders of the 'Salafiyya' bookstore and publishing house in Cairo.

There is no evidence that Muḥammad 'Abduh himself or his modernist adherents ever adopted the label *salafī*. Whether this means that the Islamicist convention of placing them and al-Afghānī at the centre of an 'enlightened Salafiyya' is entirely inappropriate or not is a matter of scholarly dispute.[49] In any case, it is safe to say that despite some initial vagueness, the term *salafiyya*, in Muslim religious discourse, eventually came to be dissociated from the modernists following Muḥammad 'Abduh and exclusively associated with the adherents of Taymiyyan thought: fundamentalist, *ḥadīth*-oriented, literalist, focussed on purification, religious doctrine and the correct practice of ritual. This includes Wahhābism, but is not limited to it although the centres of learning in the Kingdom of Saudi Arabia were important hubs for the transmission of Salafi thought.[50]

In this book, I exclusively use the term 'Salafi' in the latter sense, as outlined at the beginning of this section, and not for the type of modernist, rationalist thought that Islamicists might conventionally consider to be part of a *salafiyya* movement. The first reason for this is quite simply that with respect to Qurʾānic exegesis, both trends are so clearly different from each other with respect to their methods and aims that there is no analytical value in applying the Salafiyya label to Muḥammad ʿAbduh and Wahhābis alike.[51] The second reason is that in the time span that this book is interested in, namely, the beginning of the twenty-first century, Salafism has emerged as a tangible social and religious movement based on a number of common attributes and beliefs, despite many internal differences. Contemporary Muslims who identify as Salafi and are recognised by other Muslims as such are quite clearly completely opposed to a modernist agenda.

Salafism, in the sense that I use the term, is an exclusively Sunni doctrine, much in contrast to, for example, Islamism or modernism. In the tradition of Ibn Taymiyya, Salafis maintain that religious certainty can be obtained from scriptural proof (*dalīl*), that is, from the text of the Qurʾān and authentic traditions about the Prophet and his companions, and that it can be obtained only from these sources. The focus on certainty means that a defining feature of the tradition of Qurʾānic exegesis, that is, the promotion of polyvalent readings of the Qurʾān, is entirely against Salafi dogma.

Salafis call for a return to the practices and beliefs of the first generations of Muslims, the *salaf*, which includes details of dress, hairstyle and even personal grooming. As such, Salafis are visually distinctive by such aspects as beards and long white gowns for men and face-veils for women, which contributes to their recognisability as a social group. They approve of Ibn Taymiyya's ideas with respect to placing particular emphasis on the notion of *tawḥīd*, the oneness of God, and its opposite, *shirk*. Every act of worshipping someone or something other than God or of accepting another source of authority than the Qur'an and the Sunna is classified as *shirk*. This has to be fought – a conviction that typically results in vehemently anti-Sufi and anti-Shiʿi tendencies. The notion of purifying Islam of all illicit innovations (*bidaʿ*, sg. *bidʿa*) is central. Salafis include action into the definition of belief with the result that Muslims who neglect their religious obligations might be considered non-believers. For Salafis, just as for Islamists, Islam is a complete way of life (*manhaj*), but they understand this in a much narrower sense as an obligation to follow the lifestyle of the *salaf* in every detail.[52] It should be said that they usually approve of the use of modern technology. Many aspects of the Salafi *manhaj*, such as the attitude towards rulers, politics, non-Salafis and the surrounding society in general, are highly contested among Salafis.[53]

Salafi doctrine is polarising. It is based on the conviction that right can strictly be distinguished from wrong and that only those who hold the right beliefs and act accordingly will be saved from hellfire.[54] From this follows a call for rejecting any kind of association with outsiders, classified as unbelievers, and for giving one's exclusive loyalty to those holding Salafi beliefs (*al-walā' wa'l-barā'*).[55] How, exactly, the in-group is defined might be a contentious issue.

What does this mean for the Salafi approach to the Qur'ān? It has already been mentioned that Salafis reject ambiguity and multiple meanings. According to their idea of scriptural proof, the Qur'ān and the Sunna are clear and can be understood by anyone having access to the full corpus of texts.[56] In actual fact, there are some difficulties involved in this method that led to splits within Salafism. Nāṣir al-Dīn al-Albānī (1914–1999) was the protagonist of a brand of Salafism that promoted a critical and detailed study of *ḥadīth* material and embraced the notion of *ijtihād*, that is, independent legal reasoning based on the scriptural sources. The opposing trend, which is common in Saudi Arabia, basically accepts the canonical ninth-century *ḥadīth* collections as authentic and considers *ijtihād* unnecessary, claiming that the Qur'ān and the Sunna can simply be understood literally.[57]

All brands of Salafism oppose metaphorical readings of the Qur'ān as well as modernist attempts to subordinate individual Qur'ānic prescriptions to higher aims or concepts such as public interest (*maṣlaḥa*). They instead aim to identify the most straightforward meaning possible which they consider to constitute unambiguous truth. The question how to put it into practice does not always have an unambiguous answer, though. This leads to doctrinal differences in the application of Qur'ānic prescriptions, especially with respect to the issue of warfare: when is it allowed, or even obligated, and against whom? The Qur'ān talks about warfare in a specific historical constellation, and it is almost impossible to transfer these rulings into the twenty-first century without some analogous reasoning although Salafis, in theory, reject that.

The only extra-Qur'ānic source that Salafis accept is the Prophetic Sunna. In theory, many also accept the interpretations of very early authorities, but only when they had no difference of opinion which makes this a rather problematic source; and not all Salafis agree on this. This is one of the many aspects that distinguish Salafis from Islamists who do not generally reject the interpretations of premodern scholars and who are not categorically opposed to subjective interpretations either.

The Salafi approach to scripture means that it is theoretically possible for anyone to gain religious authority. Despite the lack of a clergy or formal hierarchy, they do have shaykhs whose followers accept their opinions based on the conviction that these rely on scriptural proof. One becomes a Salafi shaykh not by completing a certain program of study or by gaining formal qualification, but by one's command of the Qur'ān and of a large corpus of *ḥadīth*s.[58] It is possible to be both a scholar and a Salafi, but it is not necessary to be a scholar in order to gain authority among Salafis. Whether the two spheres of *'ulamā'* and Salafis converge at all depends on the setting of specific countries. In Saudi Arabia, which officially upholds a specific brand of Salafism as state doctrine, scholars are expected to follow Salafi dogma whereas the Azhar, the most important Sunni religious institution in Egypt, frowns upon it.

Despite the rejection of human authority over scripture, Salafis often do in actual fact have authorities they refer to frequently, most importantly Ibn Taymiyya and his disciples, among them Ibn Kathīr. Many Salafis consider Ibn Kathīr's *tafsīr*, in addition to a few other works such *al-Durr al-manthūr* by Jalāl al-Dīn al-Suyūṭī and *Fatḥ al-Qadīr* by al-Shawkānī, as sufficient for understanding the Qur'ān. They do not believe that the interpretation of the Qur'ān should change in accordance with the transformation of society, but rather maintain that societies should strive to adapt to the timeless prescription of the Qur'ān and the Sunna. Thus, while there have been a few attempts to produce Salafi works of *tafsīr* in the past century,[59] those could never hope to reach the popularity of Ibn Kathīr among Salafis. Nevertheless, the correct understanding of the Qur'ān is constantly negotiated in Salafi circles.

Of course, Salafis, whether ideologically or as a social phenomenon, are not all alike. A basic distinction between Salafi groups that is very commonly applied, with small differences in terminology, goes back to Quintan Wiktorowicz who distinguishes between purists (more commonly called 'quietists' by others), politicos and jihadists. Purists, or quietists, focus on spreading awareness of correct belief and ritual practice, but are opposed to political party activism or armed struggle. Politicos try to reach their goals through participation in elections or political institutions, and jihadists aim to physically fight those that they understand to be unbelievers.[60] This typology has been the subject of substantial criticism. It has been pointed out that it neither explains why some groups shift from one of these categories to another nor does it help to understand the rifts within these categories.[61] Still, the basic distinction between quietists, politicos and jihadists remains useful as long as it is not applied in a way that obfuscates the significant theological, ideological and practical differences within those groups that require further differentiation.[62]

One of the biggest issues within contemporary Salafism, and one of the gravest accusations levelled against Salafis, is that of *takfīr*: the act of declaring as unbelievers persons who identify as Muslim. When to practice *takfīr*, on what grounds, by whom and against whom – these questions are highly contested even emong jihadists. It is therefore unsurprising that *takfīr* is also a recurring theme in contemporary Salafi commentaries on the Qur'ān and exegetical debates.

Takfīr: Seyfuddin El-Muvahhid's *Davetçinin Tefsiri* (Turkey/?) on Q. 4:116

One of the few recent Salafi Qur'ānic commentaries is the Turkish *Davetçinin tefsiri*, or *Tafsīr al-Dā'īya* in Arabic, both of which mean 'The *tafsīr* of the one who calls to Islam'. Its author is entirely anonymous; Seyfuddin El-Muvahhid (Ar., Sayf al-Dīn al-Muwaḥḥid), literally 'The sword of religion, the one who professes and calls for *tawḥīd*', is clearly a *nom de guerre*. Interestingly, Mohammed Bouyeri (b. 1978), the murderer of the Dutch film-maker Theo van Gogh (1957–2004), used to call himself 'Saifu Deen alMuwahhied', but he is doubtlessly not the author of this commentary. On the book cover, the author is called a shaykh as well as a professor and doctor. A discussion on a message board that belongs to the Turkish Salafi site which also publishes Seyfuddin El-Muvahhid's *tafsīr*[63] reveals that no one knows or wants to reveal the author's identity.[64] However, from the style and syntax of Turkish, the sources mentioned in the introduction,[65] and the fact that each volume has a translator, it is clear that the author is not a Turk, but either an Arab or fluent in Arabic. Besides his *tafsīr*, a few other books by him on *ḥadīth*, law, faith and *da'wa* were published in Turkish.

The printed edition of the *tafsīr* was published by the Salafi publisher Hak Yayınları. So far, there are nine volumes that reach up to Q. 8:40 which makes the work quite extensive. It is a cheap, low-quality, pocketbook edition. Only the last volume carries a date: it was published in 2014. The online edition is probably the more important one. It had already been available in 2008 when there were eight volumes reaching up to Q. 7:87. Also in 2014, a German translation of the first volume was published by Hak Yayınları,[66] possibly targeting Germans of Turkish origin.

The commentary goes through the Qur'ān verse by verse. It states that its explicit aim is to deliver an up-to-date interpretation of the Qur'ān that draws attention to the great problems of our time, which are unbelief (*kufr*), association of others with God (*shirk*) and the worship of idols (sg., *ṭāghūt*). Its main sources, which it credits with delivering an interpretation of the Qur'ān that is essentially correct, albeit not sufficiently relevant to the here and now, are the Qur'ānic commentaries by al-Bayḍāwī, Ibn Kathīr and Sayyid Quṭb. The author names fourteen further works of *tafsīr* that he used. Besides a rather conventional set of premodern exegetical authorities, the list contains Muḥammad al-Amīn al-Shinqīṭī's (1907–1973) *Aḍwā' al-Bayān* which was written in Saudi Arabia and is held in high esteem there.[67] It is the only twentieth-century reference mentioned besides Sayyid Quṭb which is in line with the author's ideological orientation.

This Salafi Qur'ānic commentary is conventional, even old-fashioned, in some ways. It comments on the Qur'ān, verse by verse, without any attempt to arrange them in larger units which has become the norm today. When discussing Q. 4:116 (see Excerpt 2.3), it starts out with an occasion of revelation, followed by a *ḥadīth* that emphasises the excellence of this verse. After that comes a paragraph on the punishment of those who commit *shirk*, compared to that of Muslim sinners. All these elements are commonplace

Excerpt 2.3

Q. 4:116

إِنَّ اللَّهَ لَا يَغْفِرُ أَن يُشْرَكَ بِهِ وَيَغْفِرُ مَا دُونَ ذَٰلِكَ لِمَن يَشَاءُ وَمَن يُشْرِكْ بِاللَّهِ فَقَدْ ضَلَّ ضَلَالًا بَعِيدًا ﴿١١٦﴾

(116) God will not forgive anything being associated with Him. He pardons what is less serious than that for those whom He wishes. Those who associate anything with God have deviated to the utmost aberration.

Shirk* and the forgiveness of *shirk
It is narrated that this verse was revealed with respect to Ṭuʿma b. Ubayriq who was a thief. When the Prophet ruled that his hand should be severed, he fled to Mecca and committed apostasy.

Saʿd b. Jubayr [i.e., Saʿīd b. Jubayr, d. 714 (forename misspelt in original)] said: 'Soon after Ṭuʿma had fled to Mecca, he entered a house in order to steal from it. Therefore, the idolaters pursued him and killed him'.

This verse, whether it was revealed about the thief Ṭuʿma or about someone else, is a general ruling [*hükmü amm*].

ʿAlī said: 'The verse [Q. 4:116] is the verse in the Qurʾān that I love most'. (Narrated by al-Tirmidhī considered *ḥasan gharīb*[68] by him)

God will never forgive a person who, despite having received divine guidance, commits greater *shirk*[69] and dies that way, without having repented; He will leave him or her forever in hell. But to a Muslim who has committed sins other than *shirk* without having repented in this world, the option is left to plead with God. Either He forgives or He punishes them in accordance with their sin. But because of their belief, they will not stay in hell forever.

In order to avoid *shirk* which God will never forgive, it is necessary to know *shirk* very well because when a person does not know, they are in danger of inadvertently committing *shirk*. Someone who does not know *shirk* may succumb to it any moment. When people, despite having the opportunity to learn about *shirk*, are too lazy to learn, they are held accountable for the *shirk* they commit and will not be excused.

The first thing that a person who has reached the age of puberty needs to learn, as an individual religious obligation, is how belief can be attained and *shirk* avoided. God has stated the conditions of belief and the types of *shirk* in the Qur'ān and the authentic Sunna in a clear form.

The most important type of *shirk* of our age that most people, without being aware of it, succumb to is to commit *shirk* through legislation. One of the forms of *shirk* most commonly committed by people in our age is to support rulers who throw Islamic law aside and apply laws of different origin, to consider them [those rulers] Muslim, to become members or to elect members of a parliament that is called a legislative council, a council devoted to something that clearly constitutes an act of *shirk*. Just as it is necessary to perform the ritual prayer only for God and only in the way He prescribed it and to take everything connected to prayer from the Qur'ān and the Sunna, it is likewise necessary in an Islamic state to make and apply laws exclusively on the basis of those two sources.

A state that applies other laws instead of God's is not a Muslim state, but a state based on *shirk*. Those in charge of that state, those who lay down laws for that state, those who support that state and are classified as Muslims transgress God's rules and have become *mushrikūn* [idolaters or those who associate something with God].

Everyone who claims to be a Muslim, whichever state they support, must know very well Islam's judgment on those who establish a party in order to enter parliament, participate in the elections of a non-Muslim [*kāfir*] state and become candidates for parliament or elect members of parliament, and they must pass judgement accordingly on whether they themselves and others are Muslim or not. At no time must they forget this word of God: 'Those who associate anything with God have deviated to the utmost aberration'.

Another one of the types of *shirk* that are widespread in our times is to hope for help from the dead, to ask them for help and to appoint them mediators to God.[70]

in Qur'ānic commentaries. After that, however, the author starts describing his own definition of *shirk*, and it is here that the author's views vehemently clash with those of the exegetical mainstream.

The verse itself, Q. 4:116, appears in the *sūra* twice. Q. 4:48 is identical, but occurs in a different context, with reference to the People of the Book, whereas Q. 4:116 is placed before a verse that accuses idolaters of worshipping female idols and Satan. Despite the difference in context, many premodern exegetes conflate the two verses. They mainly comment on Q. 4:48 and, when reaching Q. 4:116, merely remark that they have discussed the verse before. That discussion typically focusses on the theological question of whether Muslim sinners, especially those who have committed major sins, may rely on receiving forgiveness for their sins. Thus, the exegetes are not so much interested in *shirk* as they are in the deeply controversial status of sinners. Seyfuddin El-Muvahhid is no exception to this rule where his commentary on Q. 4:48 is concerned. However, when he comes to Q. 4:116, he uses the recurrence of the verse in order to take a fundamental position on the issue of *shirk*.

His choice of the seemingly conventional material with which he introduces his interpretation underlines that goal. The occasion of revelation that Seyfuddin dutifully mentions concerning the story of Ṭuʿma b. Ubayriq, the thief and apostate, is not the only one narrated about this verse and not even the most widespread one. It does occur in a few Qurʾānic commentaries; al-Baghawī's (d. 1122), in particular, might be Seyfuddin's source. The more common story, however, concerns a bedouin shaykh who is a grave sinner, but the sin of *shirk* is the one sin he has never committed. He consults the Prophet about his status with God whereupon the verse is revealed. Since the fate of the grave sinner is not what Seyfuddin is interested here, he shuns that occasion of revelation in favour of one involving *shirk*. The *ḥadīth* about ʿAlī's preference for this verse, despite not being particularly widespread in Sunni Qurʾānic commentaries, perfectly underlines the importance of the avoidance of *shirk* which is why Seyfuddin quotes it. In this case, the source might be Ibn Kathīr, the main reference for Salafis seeking to interpret the Qurʾān.

However, Seyfuddin El-Muvahhid develops the interpretation of this verse into a direction that is completely absent from Ibn Kathīr's *tafsīr*. He uses the verse in order to expound on a central doctrine of twentieth-century revolutionary Islamism that made its way into jihadi Salafism: the idea that all man-made political systems that are not exclusively based on Islamic law are *shirk* and therefore unbelief (*kufr*).

The idea originated with the Egyptian Muslim Brotherhood in its period of persecution, and specifically with Sayyid Quṭb (1906–1966). Sayyid Quṭb was under the influence of the South Asian Islamist thinker Abū al-Aʿlā Mawdūdī (1903–1979) whose main concern was the establishment of an Islamic state, defined by the exclusive application of divine laws because anything else, to him, constituted a challenge to God's ultimate sovereignty over his creation (*ḥākimiyya*). Sayyid Quṭb connected this with a vehement rejection of all nominally Muslim rulers and governments of his time. From his perspective, they were mirror images of Moses' opponent, the pharaoh, in the Qurʾān: an unjust and oppressive ruler who requires all his subjects to worship and obey him, rather than God. These rulers and their legislature – whether parliamentary or not – are the idols (sg., *ṭāghūt*) of our time. True Muslims are to deny them allegiance. Sayyid Quṭb's ideas were later not so much pursued by the Muslim Brotherhood itself, but by radical Islamist groups who aimed at a total severance of all bonds to their 'un-Islamic' society and a war against the *ṭāghūt* regime.[71]

Later, especially in the context of the war against the Soviet occupation of Afghanistan during the 1980s, these ideas merged with Wahhābi-Salafi thought. Wahhābism had been much concerned with the fight against *shirk* from the outset, but that had mostly pertained to 'incorrect' forms of worship, especially the belief in mediators who could be asked to intercede with God on a person's behalf. Wahhābis therefore completely rejected such acts as praying at tombs. It is this theme that Seyfuddin's last paragraph alludes to.

His main concern, however, is clearly with systems of government. When he mentions 'greater *shirk*' in the beginning, this might be understood to imply that there is also 'lesser *shirk*' which, according to most scholars, does not constitute unbelief. However, he completely drops any such distinction when talking about 'un-Islamic' systems of government and their supporters. He likens a state whose laws are not exclusively based on the Qur'ān and the Sunna to a conscious violation of the prayer rules, which is usually taken to constitute apostasy. Such states are *kāfir* states to him, and those Muslims who support such states become *mushrikūn* and – just like Ṭuʿma b. Ubayriq – apostates. To Seyfuddin, it even constitutes *shirk* to consider the rulers of such a state Muslim.[72]

To be sure, the Qur'ānic commentary of Sayyid Quṭb is not the source of Seyfuddin's *tafsīr* in any direct sense. However, his thought and that of his intellectual descendants are very much at the core of Seyfuddin's ideas. For example, in a commentary on the story of Moses, Seyfuddin discusses the 'pharaohs of our time'. He cites Mawdūdī's concept of *ḥākimiyya*, the absolute sovereignty of God as a law-giver,[73] and he frequently mentions the *ṭāghūt* of our time.[74] At the same time, he employs distinctly Salafi concepts such as that of *al-walā' wa'l-barā'*, of giving one's exclusive loyalty to true believers and severing all ties to anyone else.[75] The idea that Islamic law should be based on the Qur'ān and the Sunna to the exclusion of all other sources is also a Salafi concept that had not yet concerned Sayyid Quṭb much.

Seyfuddin positions himself in a debate about the definition of faith that is central to Salafis. Does a believer become a believer by professing faith only, as the majority of Muslim scholars hold, or is he required to be convinced of the truth of that profession and to act accordingly? Or, in other words: are all those whose actions leave something to be desired unbelievers? That debate is thus ultimately about *takfīr*.[76] The issue of *takfīr*, especially concerning the nominally Muslim rulers of Muslim-majority countries and those who obey them, is one of the most divisive issues for Salafis today.[77]

Seyfuddin clearly thinks that belief encompasses internal conviction as well as action and that actions contradicting his understanding of Islam turn a person into an unbeliever.[78] This matches his classification as *kāfirūn* all those who consider the current rulers Muslim. His Qurʾānic commentary employs the language and concepts connected to a Jihadi-Salafi trend that is not only rejected by most non-Salafi Muslims, but also by a substantial portion of Salafis – or even Jihadi-Salafis – who consider it extreme or *takfīrī*, a term that is always used in a derogatory sense. Seyfuddin thus embraces a contested definition of belief and unbelief, and his *tafsīr* of Q. 4:116 constitutes an attempt to deliver a Qurʾānic justification for it that cannot be drawn from the works of premodern authorities such as Ibn Kathır.

EXEGETICAL TRADITIONS AS A RESOURCE

The Salafi paradigm, while powerful, is not unrivalled in its reading of the tradition. The exegetical tradition is as rich and diverse as the contemporary landscape of Qurʾānic interpretation, allowing for divergent views as well as constant rediscoveries and reassessments. Moreover, many types and genres of exegetical activity allow for a relatively free combination of premodern and modern resources, making it hard or even impossible to categorise the results in any straightforward manner.

There are many exegetes who are revered by some as fervently as they are rejected by others, typically for reasons that have little in common with the reasons for which they were read or not read in the premodern period. For example, the exegete al-Zamakhsharī is denounced by Salafis for his Muʿtazilī[79] approach to theological questions since he advocated the freedom of will and a metaphorical reading of anthropomorphic attributes of God. Others, however, endorse him for much the same reasons, and that is quite a modern development. It is not that this exegete was not famous in premodern times; he was, but that fame was usually based on his linguistic analyses that were the main reason for his popularity especially in the pre-Ottoman period. Only in the twentieth century did rationalists find favour with his theological ideas on a larger scale. When, for example, Indonesia saw the rise of neo-Muʿtazilī ideas in the second half of the twentieth century,[80] there was a renewed interest in what al-Zamakhsharī had to offer and some of his opinions were incorporated into modernist works of exegesis.

The fifteenth-century exegete al-Biqāʿī, on the other hand, only ever gained a large following in the twentieth century. In his times, his plea for drawing on the Bible in order to interpret the Qurʾān was as innovative as his focus on the logic behind the arrangement of the verses.[81] While former exegetes had tended to treat each verse, or even each exegetical problem within a verse, separately, al-Biqāʿī explained the reasons for which, in his opinion, each verse followed the one before it, a technique called *munāsaba*. In a time in which the Qur'ān is increasingly read as a coherent book of guidance, this suddenly seems to be an attractive approach.

The prevailing attitude towards the exegetical tradition in general is slightly ambiguous. While Salafis and many modernists tend to reject much of it for what they consider an incoherent methodology and an exaggerated reliance on the authority of men, rather than scripture, the tradition also enjoys a continuing attraction, possibly because it embodies the consensus (*ijmāʿ*) of a diachronic community of scholars. This becomes all the more important in an age in which many Muslims feel that their religion is under attack and that unity is an important goal. Under such circumstances, it makes sense to uphold the legitimacy of a broad range of relatively uncontroversial sources, but to exclude such elements that might prove divisive. The concrete application of this principle may vary from time to time, from place to place and from person to person; the vast and diverse exegetical tradition is a resource that can be mined according to specific contextual needs. By removing exegetical works from their premodern context and reappropriating them in a contemporary setting, they might change their significance because the concerns of their authors are frequently rather different from the concerns of their modern recipients. In a few cases, the priorities and methods of premodern exegetes clash so dramatically with contemporary perspectives on the Qur'ān that even those exegetes who value their authority feel a need to sidestep them, or at least join them with more recent interpretations. The following case study illustrates this.

Condensing the tradition: ʿĀʾiḍ b. ʿAbdallāh al-Qarnī (b. 1959, Saudi Arabia) on Q. 9:112

ʿĀʾiḍ b. ʿAbdallāh al-Qarnī is a well-known Saudi preacher, religious scholar and author. He was associated with the Ṣaḥwa, an Islamist opposition movement in Saudi Arabia that was particularly influential during the 1980s and 1990s. The Ṣaḥwa blended the country's state doctrine of Wahhābism with the ideas of the Egyptian Muslim Brotherhood. However, al-Qarnī's level of dissidence was fairly low. He mainly clashed with the regime after the stationing of US troops in Saudi Arabia during the second Gulf War in 1991 whereupon he was arrested, but soon released. He is a prolific writer and has authored books on a wide range of religious topics, including a hugely popular Islamic self-help book under the title 'Don't be sad'. Furthermore, he presented series of sermons, including exegetical ones, on major religious television channels, among them Iqraʾ and al-Risāla, and has a strong following on YouTube where many of his sermons are subtitled in English.

Repeated accusations of plagiarism, one of which even resulted in a successful lawsuit against him, had little bearing on his popularity.[82]

Outside the Arab world, he is particularly popular in Indonesia where translations of his works, including his Qur'ānic commentary, are widely available. That commentary, entitled 'A Simplified Commentary on the Qur'ān' (*Al-tafsīr al-muyassar*), was first published in 2006 and reprinted in a second edition in 2013. Several booksellers in 'Ammān, Jordan, praised it as the current standard work of *tafsīr* for lay Muslims in 2014. According to its introduction, it aims at providing easy access to the Qur'ān's meaning without speculation, academic discussions, technicalities and *isrā'īliyyāt* – an extremely common claim in contemporary Muslim exegesis of the Qur'ān. This commentary, in its brevity, appears to be the complete opposite of Quraish Shihab's monumental work.[83] Yet in a way, both are quite similar to each other. Each of them follows a model that is deeply entrenched in the tradition of Qur'ānic exegesis as it was practiced and taught in *madrasa*s until well into the twentieth century. That tradition contained various formats of Qur'ānic commentaries, meant for different target groups. They all built upon the same body of exegetical authorities and drew on the same repository of interpretations, narrations and opinions, but differed in length.[84] The shortest of them were paraphrastic *tafsīr*s; the most famous and important example is the fifteenth-century *Tafsīr al-Jalālayn*. They summarise the meaning of the Qur'ān, reflecting the exegete's preference for what he considers the most plausible and authoritative interpretation. Rarely do they provide more than one opinion. An important resource for students who are only just beginning to understand the Qur'ān, they are extremely reductive, but still based on the entire *tafsīr* tradition from which they derive their meaning.[85] Al-Qarnī's Qur'ānic commentary is a new take on the old genre of the paraphrastic commentary. It is also fairly Salafi in its selection of the sources it uses.

Q. 9:112 seems to be a straightforward verse listing a number of qualities of believers, and al-Qarnī's commentary is for the most part equally straightforward (see Excerpt 2.4). However, the verse contains one problem that has puzzled exegetes from an early time and that induces al-Qarnī, against his custom, to provide more than one possibly interpretation. In a long list of obvious religious virtues, the fourth of the mentioned qualities, 'wandering' (*siyāḥa*), does not quite seem to fit in. It is unclear in what sense it is a religious virtue, if it is a virtue at all. The term *siyāḥa* is mentioned in the Qur'ān in only one other comparable context, in Q. 66:5, and there it refers exclusively to women. This made a literal understanding in the sense of 'travelling' appear all the more unlikely to premodern exegetes. This scepticism is obviously shared by al-Qarnī who offers two possible

Excerpt 2.4

Q. 9:112

التَّائِبُونَ الْعَابِدُونَ الْحَامِدُونَ السَّائِحُونَ الرَّاكِعُونَ السَّاجِدُونَ الْآمِرُونَ بِالْمَعْرُوفِ وَالنَّاهُونَ
عَنِ الْمُنكَرِ وَالْحَافِظُونَ لِحُدُودِ اللَّهِ وَبَشِّرِ الْمُؤْمِنِينَ ﴿١١٢﴾

(112) Those who repent, those who serve, those who praise, those who wander, those who bow, those who prostrate themselves, those who enjoin what is considered right and who forbid what is considered wrong, those who keep God's bounds – give good tidings to the believers.

Those pious warriors [described in the preceding verse, Q. 9:111] to whom their Lord has promised the Garden, those are the ones who repent their sins, the obvious and the hidden ones; who are sincere in their obedience to their Lord; who praise God in good and bad times; who fast or contemplate God's creation; who persevere in their prayers and increase their benefits; who enjoin what God and His messenger like and who forbid what God and His messenger hate, who take care to keep God's bounds, follow His ordinances and refrain from doing what is forbidden – give you, oh Messenger of God, to the believers good tidings of the gardens of bliss that are the reward for their good deeds.[86]

interpretations, both of which are not or not closely related to the literal sense of 'wandering:' fasting and contemplating God's creation.

The first of these, fasting – far-fetched though it may seem if one does not look beyond the Qur'anic text – is in fact an obvious choice if one takes into account the exegetical tradition. Many of the earliest Qur'ānic commentaries know no other interpretation. A small number of exegetes, however, offered alternative readings, possibly out of a certain irritation with the semantic incompatibility between 'wandering' and 'fasting'. They proposed to understand 'wandering' as a reference to, among others, wandering the Earth like a homeless person, jihad, the *hijra*, the quest for knowledge, the exploration of God's signs on Earth or, in the case of mystics, the mystical journey of the self. These interpretations could never rival the dominance of the fasting interpretation, however, since it was corroborated by a great number of *ḥadīth*s and reports on early authorities who apparently agreed that the Prophet Muḥammad himself had settled the question unambiguously. There were a few *ḥadīth*s that ascribed some of the alternative interpretations to the Prophet as well, but those were isolated and could not compete with the mass of traditions stating that the Prophet said something along the lines of 'Wandering means fasting' or 'The journey of my *umma* is fasting'. When al-Qarnī promotes this interpretation, he thus has a sound basis in *ḥadīth*.

Interestingly, however, the fasting interpretation entirely lost its dominance in twentieth-century exegesis. This has two reasons: for one thing, exegetes tended to pay more attention to the literal meaning of the words used in the Qur'ān, as opposed to semantically unrelated interpretations attributed to earlier authorities. For another thing, early twentieth-century exegetes, most notably Jamāl al-Dīn al-Qāsimī (1866–1914) and Muḥammad Rashīd Riḍā (1865–1935), fiercely rejected the fasting interpretation and promoted the value of travelling instead, calling into question the previously dominant position that travelling was dangerous, tiresome, at best a necessary evil and definitely not a virtue. Travels, they maintained, educate people, helping them to acquire knowledge and to learn from the fates of other peoples. Any interpretation that discourages Muslims from travelling is morally reprehensible since it robs them of their ambitions, makes them lazy and denies them the opportunity of progress.[87]

Al-Qarnī, by mentioning the fasting interpretation as the first of two possibilities, expresses both his opposition to these utilitarian readings and a firm belief in the guiding role of *ḥadīth* in Qur'ānic interpretation. In that, he follows Ibn Taymiyya, the main source of inspiration to Salafis; and as a Saudi preacher, al-Qarnī generally follows Salafi paradigms on which the official religious doctrine of his state is based.

His second interpretation explains 'wandering' as a synonym for the contemplation of God's creation, which might or might not involve actual travelling. This possible meaning had been mentioned in passing by a few premodern exegetes, but was more clearly – although not categorically – endorsed by Muḥammad al-Shawkānī (1760–1834) and Sayyid Quṭb (1906–1966). Al-Shawkānī was a Yemeni exegete who placed great emphasis on both the literal meaning of the Qur'ān and the Sunna[88] which makes him a very acceptable source by Saudi standards.[89] However, al-Shawkānī's method, in this case, leads to a conundrum that he cannot solve: the large majority of *ḥadīth*s point to the meaning of fasting, while the literal meaning of the Qur'ānic term *siyāḥa* does not. Al-Shawkānī still somewhat sympathises with understanding the verse in the sense of actual travel because in his opinion, the contemplation of God's creation encourages humans to obey God. Sayyid Quṭb seems to agree. He points to Qur'ānic verses that endorse humans to consider God's signs in His creation, whereby they may learn about God's custom (*sunan*) in dealing with creation. Quṭb adopted the theme of 'God's custom' (*sunan Allāh*) from early twentieth-century reformers, especially Muḥammad 'Abduh and Rashīd Riḍā. Their idea was that God rewards and punishes not only individuals, but whole peoples according to their merits and vices and that contemporary societies should learn from the example of previous peoples.[90] This was an attractive idea to the Islamist propagandist Sayyid Quṭb. After all, he was trying to call Muslims to abandon their affiliation with what he considered an un-Islamic society and to building a true community of believers instead. The promise of guaranteed divine reward in this world, and not only in the hereafter, tied in with that idea very well.

The concise, educational format of al-Qarnī's commentary forces him to limit the range of interpretations he offers. He rarely even hints at the existence of more than one possible reading. In this case, out of a wide range of options, he presents two, and these two are exactly in line with the main sources of his ideological orientation: on the one hand, Salafism which favours the Prophetic Sunna, and on the other hand, the Islamist exegesis of Sayyid Quṭb that calls on Muslims to contemplate God's creation in order to grow steadfast in belief and to reform society.

NOTES

1. Saleh, 'Preliminary Remarks on the Historiography of *tafsīr*', 14–16.
2. Karen Bauer critically remarks that in the age before print, it is problematic to assume that all books were available to all scholars at all times. She also points out that we know too little of the modes of teaching, book production and distribution in the field of *tafsīr* to know which works might have been available to whom; cf. Bauer, *Gender Hierarchy in the Qur'ān*, 13. This is an important consideration. However, the production and distribution of books might have been subject to similar ideas of the relative importance of exegetical authorities as was the citation of exegetical opinions; it was achieved by different mechanisms, though, and not necessarily by the free and unrestrained decision of an individual author.
3. Norman Calder, in his seminal essay, 'Tafsīr from Ṭabarī to Ibn Kathīr', describes the citation of named authorities as one of the defining features of *tafsīr*. This might be due to the fact that he focuses on extensive Qur'ānic commentaries and thus neglects the existence of subgenres with different functions. As mentioned before, Walid Saleh distinguishes between encyclopaedic and *madrasa*-style commentaries (Saleh, *The Formation of the Classical* Tafsīr *Tradition*, 16–17). The former of these often, but not always, mention by name the authorities to whom specific opinions are ascribed since they aim at providing a resource for scholars; the latter offer a digest of those opinions they consider most important, usually without mentioning names.
4. One example of this concerns the terms 'light' and 'darkness' which might, according to al-Shawkānī, be understood literally, but equally legitimately as metaphors for belief and unbelief or truth and falsehood. Pink, 'Muhammad al-Shawkānī', 331–332.
5. Bauer, *Gender Hierarchy in the Qur'ān*, 3.
6. The word *tafsīr* is ambiguous; it may denote the scholarly activity of interpreting the Qur'ān as well as a Qur'ānic commentary.
7. Calder, 'Tafsīr from Ṭabarī to Ibn Kathīr'.
8. Bauer, *Gender Hierarchy in the Qur'ān*, 15.

9. Zaman, *The Ulama in Contemporary Islam*, 10.
10. Bauer, *Gender Hierarchy in the Qur'ān*, 5–6; fundamentally, see Zaman, *The Ulama in Contemporary Islam.*
11. Pink, 'Tradition, Authority and Innovation', 61.
12. Bauer, *Gender Hierarchy in the Qur'ān*, 15–18.
13. Ibid., 7.
14. Ikhwan, An Indonesian Initiative to Make the Qur'an Down-to-Earth; Pink, *Sunnitischer Tafsīr in der modernen islamischen Welt*, 74–78.
15. *Aurat* is derived from the Arabic *ʿawra* and denotes those body parts that should not be exposed other than to close relatives. However, in a more limited sense, it might denote the sexual organs. Since this story is taken from the Hebrew Bible, this is likely to be the intended meaning.
16. Shihab, *Tafsir al-Mishbāh: Pesan, kesan dan keserasian Al-Qur'an*, vol. 15, 372–377. Text originally in Indonesian.
17. Saleh, *The Formation of the Classical* Tafsīr *Tradition*, 14; Calder, 'Tafsīr from Ṭabarī to Ibn Kathīr'.
18. Al-Marāghī, *Tafsīr al-Marāghī*, vol. 30, 193–194.
19. For the history of the interpretation of Q. 95:1–3 and detailed references on the above-mentioned interpretations, see Pink, 'The Fig, the Olive'.
20. For more detail on this aspect, page 185, 'The 'system' (*naẓm*) and structure of the Qurʾān'.
21. Saleh, *The Formation of the Classical* Tafsīr *Tradition*, 14–18.
22. Saleh, 'Ibn Taymiyya'.
23. Ashʿarism is a major school of Islamic theology that largely supported traditionalist views in that it placed God's omnipotence, as opposed to humans' free will, in the centre of its reasoning and affirmed the uncreatedness of the Qurʾān. However, unlike traditionalists, Ashʿarīs based their arguments on the methods of scholastic theology (*kalām*) derived from Aristotelian logic.
24. Mirza, 'Ibn Kathīr, ʿImād al-Dīn'.
25. Cf. Saleh, 'Preliminary Remarks on the Historiography of *tafsīr*', 10–11.
26. Al-Dhahabī, *Al-tafsīr wa'l-mufassirūn.*
27. Saleh, 'Preliminary Remarks on the Historiography of *tafsīr*'.
28. Tottoli, 'Origin and Use of the Term *isrāʾīliyyāt* in Muslim Literature'.
29. Muḥammad ʿAbduh was extremely and explicitly critical of the existing exegesis of the Qurʾān for some of the reasons mentioned here; see Pink, 'ʿAbduh, Muḥammad'.
30. Pink, 'Riḍā, Rashīd'.
31. Saleh, 'The Gloss as Intellectual History'.
32. Mirza, 'Ibn Kathīr, ʿImād al-Dīn'.
33. Mubarakpuri, *Tafsir Ibn Kathir*, vol. 1, 5–6.
34. See Dar-us-Salam Publications, 'Safi-ur-Rahman al-Mubarakpuri.'
35. See, e.g., QTafsir.com, *Quran Tafsir Ibn Kathir.*
36. For a useful discussion of the goals of translations of premodern works of *tafsīr*, see Rippin, 'Contemporary Translation', 480–481.
37. Mubarakpuri, *Tafsir Ibn Kathir*, vol. 8, 321–323. Text originally in English.
38. It is a matter of debate whether he actually considered these stories reprehensible and potentially harmful, as is assumed by his modern readers, or whether he simply deemed them irrelevant for his Qurʾānic commentary. Often, he discusses stories in his work on history that he dismisses as *isrāʾīliyyāt* in his *tafsīr*. This

will be discussed in Klar, 'Ibn Kathīr's (d. 774/1373) Treatment of the David and Uriah Narrative: The Issue of Isrā'īliyyāt and the Syrian School of Exegesis.'

39. For a discussion of this and further examples, see Calder, 'Tafsīr from Ṭabarī to Ibn Kathīr'.
40. Ibn Kathīr, *Tafsīr al-Qur'ān al-'aẓīm*, vol. 7, 62.
41. Ibn Kathīr, *Tahdhīb Ibn Kathīr*.
42. Ibn Kathīr, *Tafsīr al-Qur'ān al-'aẓīm*, vol. 7, 60–61.
43. The first tradition is one that Ibn Kathīr says he learned from his father-in-law, the Damascene Shāfi'ī *ḥadīth* scholar Abū al-Ḥajjāj al-Mizzī (d. 743/1342). He provides the complete, extensive *isnād* that goes back to Ibn 'Abbās, a cousin of the prophet and much-respected transmitter of exegetical *ḥadīth*s, and he also mentions a few early *ḥadīth* collections that contain it. According to Ibn Kathīr, al-Tirmidhī considers it *gharīb* which means that there is only one known narrator or sequence of narrators at one point in the chain; some *ḥadīth* scholars consider this type of tradition weak although the *isnād* itself is sound. The other *ḥadīth* is contained in the collection of Aḥmad Ibn Ḥanbal (d. 855). According to Ibn Kathīr, this is the only source, but al-Suyūṭī names other sources in his *al-Durr al-Manthūr*.
44. For an interesting discussion of possible exegetical functions of *faḍā'il ḥadīth*s, see Burge, 'Jalāl al-Dīn al-Suyūṭī', 291–295.
45. Al-Shihrī, 'Ṣadara ḥadīthan Al-Durr al-nathīr'. I thank Joas Wagemakers for pointing me to this work.
46. For this use of the label 'Salafī', see, for example, Campanini, *The Qur'an: Modern Muslim Interpretations*, 8–20.
47. Boberg, *Ägypten, Nağd und der Ḥiğāz*, 290–314.
48. When the Saudis conquered the Ḥijāz in 1924 and expelled the Hāshemite rulers who had close ties to the British since World War I, this was widely perceived as an act in which 'Abd al-'Azīz courageously faced off against British interests although the British had at that point already tacitly withdrawn their support for the ruler of the Ḥijāz. For the history of Saudi Arabia, see Al-Rasheed, *A History of Saudi Arabia*.
49. Lauzière, 'The Construction of Salafiyya'; Griffel, 'What Do We Mean By "Salafī"?'; Lauzière, 'What We Mean'.
50. For the conceptual history of Salafism, see Lauzière, *The Making of Salafism*.
51. Presumably for the same reason, the term Salafi is used exclusively in the sense of Taymiyyan fundamentalism in some of the secondary literature dealing with the recent history and historiography of Qur'ānic exegesis. See, for example, Saleh, 'Preliminary Remarks on the Historiography of *tafsīr*'.
52. Haykel, 'On the Nature of Salafi Thought and Action'.
53. Wagemakers, 'Revisiting Wiktorowicz', 14–15.
54. Haykel, 'On the Nature of Salafi Thought and Action', 34.
55. Wagemakers, 'Al-walā wa al-barā'.
56. Haykel, 'On the Nature of Salafi Thought and Action', 38–39.
57. In actual fact, this often simply results in the application of Ḥanbali law, cf. ibid., 42–44.
58. Ibid., 36.
59. For example, the 'Simplified *tafsīr*' (*aysar al-tafāsīr*) by the Saudi-based scholar Abū Bakr al-Jazā'irī (1921–2016) that presented itself as a Salafi alternative to

the popular paraphrastic *Tafsīr al-Jalālayn*. See Pink, 'Tradition and Ideology', 18–19.

60. Wiktorowicz, 'Anatomy of the Salafi Movement'.
61. See, for example, Hegghammer, 'Jihadi-Salafis or Revolutionaries?'; Alshech, 'Doctrinal Crisis'; Wagemakers, 'Revisiting Wiktorowicz'.
62. For an up-to-date nuanced categorisation of Salafism based on the doctrinal differences that inform their political attitudes see Wagemakers, 'Revisiting Wiktorowicz'.
63. See the 'reading salon' of the Davetulhaq.com website at <http://www.davetulhaq.com/tr/mkportal/kategoriler/kitaplik/okuma_salonu/okuma_salonu.htm>.
64. The thread was publicly available on <http://www.davetulhaq.com/tr/forum/index.php?topic=8239.0>, on 17 May 2017, but is now password-protected.
65. El-Muvahhid, *Davetçinin tefsiri*, 8–9.
66. Al-Muwahhid, *Tafsir ad-Da'iya*.
67. El-Muvahhid, *Davetçinin tefsiri*, 3–9.
68. *Ḥasan* and *gharīb* are slightly ambiguous categories from *ḥadīth* scholarship that imply, in al-Tirmidhī's case, that there are no strong objections against the *ḥadīth*'s authenticity, but that it has only been narrated through one chain of transmitters, at least in its present form.
69. The distinction between greater and lesser *shirk* refers to the difference between associating other Gods with God (greater *shirk*) and acknowledging God's oneness, but violating that principle in the practice of worship (lesser *shirk*). That distinction was common among legal scholars, but rejected by Muḥammad b. ʿAbd al-Wahhāb (1703–1792).
70. El-Muvahhid, *Davetçinin tefsiri*, vol. 5, 322–323. Text originally in Turkish.
71. For an overview of these ideas and developments, see Kepel, *Muslim Extremism in Egypt*.
72. For a very good analysis of the rejection of democracy by Jihadi-Salafis and its causes, see Wagemakers, 'The *Kāfir* Religion of the West'.
73. El-Muvahhid, *Davetçinin tefsiri*, vol. 9, 103–105.
74. Ibid., vol. 1, 7.
75. Pink, 'Tradition and Ideology', 41; On the concept itself, see Wagemakers, 'The Transformation of a Radical Concept: *Al-Wala' wa'l-Bara'* in the Ideology of Abu Muhammad al-Maqdisi'; and Wagemakers, 'Revisiting Wiktorowicz', 19–23.
76. Wagemakers, 'Revisiting Wiktorowicz', 11–12.
77. Wiktorowicz, 'Anatomy of the Salafi Movement', 28–34.
78. El-Muvahhid, *Davetçinin tefsiri*, vol. 9, 525.
79. A theological trend, particularly successful in the ninth century, that upheld belief in human freedom of will, prioritised God's justice over his omnipotence, professed the createdness of the Qurʾān and relied on rational methods of producing religious knowledge.
80. Saleh, *Modern Trends*, 196–307.
81. Saleh, 'A Fifteenth-Century Muslim Hebraist'.
82. Mühlbeyer, 'Aid al-Qarni'.
83. See page 40, 'An *ʿālim* continuing the tradition of *tafsīr*: Muhammad Quraish Shihab (b. 1944, Indonesia) on Q. 95:1–3'.
84. See page 14, 'The place of the Qurʾān in premodern Muslim societies'.
85. Calder, 'Tafsīr from Ṭabarī to Ibn Kathīr', 104.
86. Al-Qarnī, *Al-Tafsīr al-muyassar*, 244. Text originally in Arabic.

87. Pink, *Sunnitischer Tafsīr in der modernen islamischen Welt*, 230–233.
88. Pink, 'Muhammad al-Shawkānī'.
89. Haykel, *Revival and Reform in Islam*, 190–229.
90. Nispen tot Sevenaer, *Activité humaine et Agir de dieu.*

3

MEDIA

MEDIA TRANSFORMATIONS: FROM MANUSCRIPTS TO PRINT AND BEYOND

No attempt at interpreting the Qur'ān will have an impact unless it is shared with others – orally, visually or in writing. The media used to convey a message to its audience has a profound impact on the style and nature of the message. The same message changes its character, and usually also its wording, when it is transferred from one media to another. The effect of media on the shape, contents and transformations of Muslim Qur'ānic interpretation is hard to overestimate. Media changes effected changes in authorship, audience, topics and style. It is no coincidence that discussions of the inimitability (*iʿjāz*) of the Qur'ān have shifted from rhetoric and rhyme to the identification of scientific information and historical predictions in the Qur'ān:[1] the former can only be understood with background knowledge that few Muslims today possess, whereas the latter opens spaces for discussions that anyone able to read Wikipedia can participate in.

During the past 150 years, massive transformations in media landscapes have shaped the production of new exegetical works. Moreover, the demise of manuscript culture as well as the ascent of print and subsequently of further new media were central agents of change in the reception of premodern exegetical traditions. Works that had previously been accessible only to some scholars, or in a few cases to a larger number of scholars and advanced students, now had the potential to reach a mass market. This was based on several preconditions: access to technical requirements; funding; actors willing to invest time and money in the production of print, audiovisual or digital editions of manuscript material; and a target group willing to buy, watch or otherwise consume the result.[2]

It is tempting to describe the history of how media shaped Qur'ānic exegesis as a neat succession of consecutive media: oral exegesis was replaced by manuscripts and manuscripts by printed books; then came radio, television and finally the internet. Of course, reality was more complex and messier. For example, while one might think of oral exegesis as a mainly premodern phenomenon, in West Africa it was actually part of a revivalist trend that came up in the mid-twentieth century,[3] and study circles devoted to the discussion of the Qur'ān are a contemporary reality in many places on the world. The shift from manuscript to print culture did not occur simultaneously everywhere and there was a long period of overlap between both. Even the rather famous extensive Qur'ānic commentary by the Damascene Salafi Jamāl al-Dīn al-Qāsimī (1866–1914), completed in 1911, at a time when printed Qur'ānic commentaries had been around for several decades, remained in manuscript form until the late 1950s.[4] Nevertheless, al-Qāsimī included a large number of printed sources that would not have been accessible to him a few decades earlier. He extensively quoted the printed Qur'ānic commentary by the Indian Ṣiddīq Ḥasan Khān (1832–1890), a proponent of the fundamentalist *ahl-i ḥadīth* movement, probably unaware that the bulk of this work is a *verbatim* transcript of the early nineteenth-century Qur'ānic commentary by the above-mentioned Yemeni scripturalist scholar Muḥammad al-Shawkānī.[5] He also made use of journal articles, for example, from Rashīd Riḍā's journal *al-Manār*.[6]

Print culture allowed for the global distribution of ideas in a very short period of time. Journals such as *al-ʿUrwa al-wuthqā* and *al-Manār* spread across the Muslim world and had significant impact on exegetical thought. Indian and Malay intellectuals printed and distributed books in Istanbul and Cairo if they had the necessary funds. This new wave of globalisation, enabled by the medium of print, bolstered ideas of Muslim unity that seemed all the more important given the political situation at the time, when much of the Muslim world was under direct or indirect Western rule.

Among the few states that appeared to be exempt from that problem was the Kingdom of Saudi Arabia, which was one of the reasons for Rashīd Riḍā's attraction to that state's official ideology. In the course of the twentieth century, but particularly after the ascension of King Fahd to the throne in 1982, the kingdom emerged as a major actor in the mediatisation and distribution of exegetical ideas, old and new, the works of Ibn Taymiyya and Ibn Kathīr featuring prominently among them. The King Fahd Complex for the Printing of the Holy Qur'ān was established as a centre for the production and publication of Qur'ān translations into dozens of languages read by Muslims. The universities in the kingdom as well as private publishers were a source of even more Qur'ān translations – for example, the widely read *Saheeh International* translation into English – as well as Qur'ānic commentaries. The case of Saudi Arabia demonstrates that only by taking into account specific actors and their source of funding is it possible to explain how specific texts and ideas were spread and gained popularity. The above-mentioned Ṣiddīq Ḥasan Khān was only able to publish works of Ibn Taymiyya and al-Shawkānī on a large scale because he had married a wealthy local ruler, Shāhjahān Begum; al-Shawkānī, in particular, might not have gained the importance that he has today without such exposure.[7]

In a previous age, even more so than now, it was time-consuming and expensive to typeset and print multi-volume *tafsīr* works. Only works that were deemed worthy by a publisher or wealthy donor had that good fortune. The selection of works that appeared in print throughout roughly the first half of the twentieth century distinctly shaped most Muslims' perception of what was important within the exegetical tradition and what was not. The skill, the means and the willingness to use manuscript libraries eroded quickly, after all, and became the domain of a very small number of specialists. Thus, media changes were thresholds in the transmission of earlier material. Some Qur'ānic interpretations made it across the threshold strengthened, others weakened, and some did not make it at all.

Towards the end of the twentieth and the beginning of the twenty-first centuries, a wave of editions broadened access to the premodern exegetical heritage in print, but around the same time, digitalisation took over with some effects that are fairly similar to those of print in its beginnings. Websites provide much broader audiences with access to exegetical works than books do, saving their users the time and money required to buy books or visit libraries. Digitising extensive works of *tafsīr* consumes resources, though, and therefore has to be carried out by individuals or institutions with the necessary means; and it invariably involves a selection that shapes users' impression of which parts of the exegetical tradition are important. Consequently, platforms such as *Altafsir.com*, operated by the Jordanian Royal Aal al-Bayt Institute for Islamic Thought that pursues an ecumenical agenda and promotes 'moderate' (*wasaṭiyya*) Islam,[8] today have a marked influence on the ways in which users, from lay Muslims to scholars, make use of the exegetical tradition.

Media changes of course had far wider effects than merely shaping the reception of the premodern heritage. The printing press made it possible to print religious literature in editions that addressed a market beyond that of the scholars and elites who had been able to afford such things before. The expansion of schooling also led to an increase in literacy and the emergence of a literate class that had received little or no religious education. These new audiences had neither the interest nor the capacity required to read scholarly works of jurisprudence or theology. As a result, new texts were written that were designed to reach new audiences; and often, these texts were written by new types of authors who had not received a traditional Islamic education. The twentieth century thus saw the rise of educational works of *tafsīr* that were simple and accessible to readers without a background in Islamic learning; and it witnessed the emergence of a brand of mass-medial *tafsīr* that was not only meant to offer guidance, but also to entertain. An early example is the *Tafsīr al-Manār* that was first published as part of a journal and incorporated a broad range of material such as magazine articles, letters, excerpts from books, political and social commentary and anecdotes. This was not the last work of *tafsīr* that had its origins in periodical publications. With the advent of mass media, the boundaries between academic and popular *tafsīr* – which had probably never been entirely rigid – blurred even more, as did those between written and oral *tafsīr*.

During the twentieth century, radio and television overtook journals as the most important form of mass media (more on television, in particular, will be said below). At the beginning of the twenty-first century, the spread of the internet constituted another massive transformation. After websites, blogs and YouTube channels, the latest trend in exegetical media is the creation of apps for smartphones and tablets. Some of these do little more than present the content of a book or file in a more structured manner; others distinctly emphasise the devotional aspects that Qur'ānic exegesis may take, dividing Qur'ānic translations and commentaries into daily portions and including audio files in order to enable users to consume them during commutes, for example. There is a world of difference between low-quality, home-made videos of sermons on the Qur'ān, sometimes offering no more than an audio file with pictures, and the well-structured, inviting website of the American preacher Nouman Ali Khan's (b. 1978) *Bayyinah.tv* that offers a large amount of professionally produced content for purchase with the aim of teaching Muslims about the Qur'ān.

Media has the potential to popularise Qur'ānic interpretations and make them accessible. Nevertheless, the extent to which individual Muslims listen to them, read them or watch them is not a direct and inevitable result of their availability. From among two Qur'ānic interpretations that are equally accessible, one might prove to be popular while the other one might not. The decision to choose one over the other is linked to the authority that the audience accords both the exegete and the interpretation he has produced; and this, in turn, will motivate most exegetes to try and enhance the authority of their interpretations, for example, through dropping the names of renowned scholars. Thus, the emergence, persistence and disappearance of exegetical paradigms is not only caused by publication decisions and the formats required by specific media, but also by ideas of authority. One important reason for the continuing relevance of premodern exegetical traditions – however much, since the nineteenth century, they might have been restructured and repositioned – is the authority they offer. This is particularly true in a scholarly context in which Qur'ānic exegesis serves to demonstrate one's familiarity with the tradition,[9] but it is also true for many brands of popularising Qur'ān interpretation where references to earlier authorities bolster the exegete's authority in the eyes of his audience.

Despite all the media changes that have taken place over the course of the nineteenth, twentieth and the beginning of the twenty-first centuries, many

Muslims' only source of information on the Qurʾān is still a local preacher or teacher. However, that preacher or teacher might choose to spread his message in various ways. A sermon might be published on the internet, put into writing and eventually become part of a printed book. Books might be translated. The same core message may be directed at different audiences in a variety of ways. As a result, it may change its form and sometimes its content, making it advisable to think carefully about what we mean when talking about the *tafsīr* of a specific person. The following example illustrates this point.

Layers of media: Abdolali Bazargan[10] (b. 1943; Iran/US) on Q. 103:3

From reading the author's biography in the English translation of his Qurʾānic commentary, one gains the impression that this intellectual's most distinguished feature is the fact that he is Mehdi Bazargan's (1907–1995) son. Mehdi Bazargan, an engineer and part of an early generation of Iranians who had the opportunity to study in Europe, had entered politics after World War II, opposed the regime of the Muḥammad Riḍā Pahlavī and was a proponent of democracy and human rights. Given that he was a well-known public figure, he became prime minister of an interim government after the Islamic Revolution of 1979. He submitted his resignation after a short while due to his lack of power which rested almost completely with Ayatollah Khomeini. However, Khomeini, who had not yet established an Islamic Republic and needed a government that was acceptable to the secularist and democratic segments of society, rejected the resignation. After the takeover of the US embassy in November 1979, Bazargan resigned all the same. He tried to continue playing a political role, but was given little chance to do so. In 1995, he died of a heart attack. He had displayed an interest in social and religious themes and had drawn on his scientific background to elaborate on them, a method that his son Abdolali adopted as well.

Abdolali Bazargan largely took over his father's legacy and – contrary to the impression conveyed by his biography – is quite a well-known public intellectual in his own right. He is an architect by training, but also studied with traditional Shiʿi scholars and some modernist intellectuals in Iran and was deeply influenced by the ideas he learned in that milieu. Among them was a strong concern with political and social questions, especially the theme of social justice. Bazargan, like his father, never identified with the idea of an Islamic state ruled by the clergy, but nor did he pursue an entirely modernist agenda. Many of Bazargan's religious writings, encompassing twenty books and many more articles, focus on the Qurʾān. Others reveal an interest in mysticism and in *Nahj al-Balāgha*, an important Shiʿi collection of traditions, sermons, letters and Qur'ānic interpretations attributed to 'Alī b. Abī Ṭālib which Bazargan frequently quotes in his Qur'ānic commentary.

Bazargan migrated to the United States in 2001 for political reasons and settled in California where he continued to publish, teach and give lectures.[11] In contrast to Abdolkarim Soroush (b. 1945), with whom he frequently interacted and disputed, he firmly upholds the eternal and divine nature of the Qur'ānic text.

Excerpt 3.1

Q. 103:1–3

وَالْعَصْرِ ﴿١﴾ إِنَّ الْإِنسَانَ لَفِي خُسْرٍ ﴿٢﴾ إِلَّا الَّذِينَ آمَنُوا وَعَمِلُوا الصَّالِحَاتِ وَتَوَاصَوْا بِالْحَقِّ
وَتَوَاصَوْا بِالصَّبْرِ ﴿٣﴾

(1) By the declining time [day or epoch], (2) Truly, humanity is (always) in a state of loss, (3) Except those who have faith and do good deeds, urge one another to truth and urge one another to patience.

Urging and counselling one another to be actively patient in standing for the truth (*tawāsaw bi-s-sabr*) [commentary on the last part of v. 3]:

Those who struggle to uphold the truth often face many adversities. In 31:12–49, Luqman advises his son on various life-shaping matters, such as treating one's parents kindly, worshipping the one God and being humble. In verse 17, he instructs his son to '*enjoin the moral and forbid the immoral*', to be patient and to persevere in the face of the ensuing difficulties. That is to say, cast aside your apathy and become proactive and stand for truth and justice. [Author's Note: permission to go to war in Islam is restricted to those who fight against you, in the path of God (i.e., divine imperative) and in self-defense to some extent: 'Fight in the way of God those who fight you but do not commit aggression for God does not love aggressors' (2:190). Those who flee the battlefield are not to be pursued, the wounded cannot be killed, and immunity is granted to non-combatants (e.g., women, children, the aged, disabled, monks and nuns). None of these innocents can be persecuted or harassed. Thus, the collective punishment or genocide found in the Hebrew Bible has no sanction in the Qur'an, for only those who have been assaulted are allowed to fight: 'Permission (to fight) is given to those who have been attacked because they have been wronged' (22:39). The notion that the so-called 'sword verse' (9:5) has abrogated (*naskh*) these verses is flimsy and baseless.] They might throw you in jail, deprive you of some of your rights or fire you from your job, but exercise some fortitude and be resolute and steadfast: '*Oh Prophet, urge the believers to battle* (*in order to defend themselves against pagan transgressors*)*: if there are twenty of you who are steadfast* [*actively patient;* sābir], *they will overcome two hundred*' (8:65).

No matter where or when, history shows that such people expose themselves to persecution. Most of the world's powerful people are not necessarily benevolent individuals who chose public service to improve their fellow citizens' condition or do God's work; rather, it is far more likely that they will exploit their positions for personal gain, oppress and intimidate people and be unjust and tyrannical. Hence, there is always a need for the *mu'mins* to take a stand and willingly accept the consequences. These are the ones who will attain salvation. They should encourage other citizens to do the same.

Ali underlines the mutual and reciprocal nature of the relationship between rulers and citizens: rulers will not reform themselves unless citizens hold them accountable and 'enjoin the moral and forbid the immoral'. Moreover, citizens will not reform themselves unless their rulers behave in a fair and virtuous manner. As such, the public is obliged to be fair and equitable in its dealings with the rulers and, at the same time, be vigilant that they do not exceed the boundaries established by God. Of course, under ordinary circumstances this does not mean that they should resort to violence, lawlessness or vigilantism. Rather, they should take a keen interest in their community's affairs and be proactive to ensure that those in charge cannot abuse their power. [*Nahj-ul-Balāghah*, Sermon 215.]

These two characteristics work symbiotically and draw energy from one another. Rulers will not behave morally unless citizens stand for truth. The reverse is also true. Hence, citizens who are indifferent to everything but their own affairs should not expect to end up with a just and ethical government. It should be clear by now that a responsible citizenry is a prerequisite for a flourishing society, one in which the citizens are fully engaged in their communities' affairs.

According to Ali, if you accumulate all of the good deeds performed in this world, add *jihad* to them and then compare it to the principle of 'enjoining the moral and forbidding the immoral', it would be like comparing a saliva spit to the oceans' water, because all other norms and obligations emanate from this principle's application. It creates safe inter-state highways and puts the economy on the right path. [Ibid., Aphorism 384.]

In the absence of freedom and justice, everything is but a façade. For example, under Muʿāwiyah people dutifully practiced all of Islam's exoteric aspects, attended the mosque, prayed and so on. But nobody dared to voice the slightest criticism of his government. Thus, Ali underscores the vital need to activate this principle. In another place, he states that if the people are negligent and self-absorbed and abandon this principle, then the worst type of people will rule over them. In such a situation the former will plead with God to release them from their predicament, but He will not accept their prayers. [Ibid., Letter 47]

This is a reminder that those of us who want to improve our society cannot be indifferent and passive individuals who rely on prayer alone. How could such a passive society ever improve? This principle can be compared to a healthy blood system's white blood cells, for one of these cells' functions is to destroy the foreign bacteria that infect the body. If they fail, the body suffers and eventually dies. While those who have faith and do good deeds are not in a state of loss, they need to oppose their society's lack of freedom and equity, for such things indicate that the truth is being suppressed. Ali repeatedly emphasizes that truth cannot exist in a selfish, egotistic and apathetic society.

It is important to appreciate the relationship between this chapter and the previous one, Vying for More (at-Takāthur), which points out our tendency to compete with others to acquire more worldly possessions and power. This rivalry only stops when death finally comes for us. The discourse is about indulgence, competition and the struggle for power and money; however, this chapter pointedly asks if it is worth spending our life in the pursuit of these goals. Is doing so not a great loss? It warns us that only those who are aware, have faith, do good deeds, enjoin one another to do the right thing and struggle to uphold the truth are not in loss.

As observed earlier, the Qur'an addresses a subject in one chapter and follows the thread through to the next one, just as pearls are tightly connected with one another by a chain to make a necklace.[12]

Glancing at the luxurious, carefully designed hardcover edition of Abdolali Bazargan's commentary on the last part of the Qur'ān, the *juz' 'amma* (Q. 78–114), it seems to be a typical printed work of *tafsīr*, possibly the most prominent features being the illustrious author and the work's Imami Shi'i leanings. However, this book is not the result of an intellectual's decision to sit down and write it. Rather, it is the last link in a chain of representations of the author's Qur'ānic exegesis in various media.

The fact that works of exegesis often have several layers and a complex history of publication is not at all a modern phenomenon, of course. Manuscripts of premodern Qur'ānic commentaries are rarely autographs; they are commonly transcripts, copies or redactions, sometimes with editorial comments. Often, they are based on oral lessons the exegete gave, and he might have given these lessons multiple times with varying content. Thus, contemporary printed editions of, for example, al-Zamakhsharī are typically based on several editorial processes. In modern times, we have grown accustomed to thinking of books in a different manner: as works that constitute an author's one-time, deliberate, straightforward, unambiguous expression of his authentic thoughts and words. This is not always the case, however, and Bazargan's exegesis is a good example.

His Qur'ānic interpretation started out as a series of lectures he held at Evecina [Ibn Sīnā/Avicenna] Cultural and Educational Foundation in Irvine, California,[13] which is an organisation that primarily addresses Iranian immigrants and their descendants in the region. It has a distinctly Islamic outlook, but does not identify with the government of the Islamic Republic which is apparent from the fact that the speakers include Iranian Muslim scholars and intellectuals who are critical of the Iranian government.[14] Bazargan's lectures are completely in Persian except for references to the Qur'ān or *ḥadīth*s which are in Arabic. However, he takes care to translate and explain them which makes clear that the target audience consists of Iranian-Americans with a good command of Persian, but no substantial religious education.

The next step was the publication of audio files of these lectures that cover the entire Qur'ān. These audio files are available on Bazargan's personal website.[15] For some lectures, especially those that cover the last part of the Qur'ān, the website additionally offers written versions.[16] These written versions are not verbatim transcripts of the lectures. Rather, the author has converted his oral Persian into writing which naturally results in a different mode of expression. Additionally, all audio files come with a PDF excerpt from a three-volume book on the structure of the Qur'ān (*naẓm-e Qur'ān*) written by Bazargan that explains the connection of each *sūra* to the preceding and subsequent one.

The audio files of the lectures furthermore were converted to a professional app for smartphones and tablets called 'Quran Hakim Farsi Translation by Abdolali Bazargan'. The app was first offered in 2013 and has been continuously developed since then, with added material.[17] It contains the Arabic text of the Qur'ān, its translation into Persian both in written and audio format, and the audio files of Bazargan's lectures on each *sūra*, divided into manageable chunks and accessible verse by verse. The navigation is well-arranged and offers multiple ways to organise the material and listen to it, including an English menu for users who understand Persian, but have not learned to read it, and an enlarged and simplified menu for users who want to access the app while driving. A version of the app for blind users is also available. There is no way to tell how popular this material is, but it certainly reveals an intense desire, on the author's part, to spread his ideas.

The talks, online and audio versions of Bazargan's exegesis are part of a specific type of *da'wa* that only makes sense in the context of migration.

It is clearly directed at second and third generation immigrants who have acquired some knowledge of Persian in their homes, but have not gone to an Iranian and/or Islamic school. Obviously, it is based on the fear that these Iranian-Americans might lose their connection not only to their national and linguistic roots, but also to their religion and, as the Evecena Foundation's website repeatedly mentions, morals. The aspect of *da'wa* is apparent in the style of Bazargan's commentary which employs a narrative prose that is easy to understand and, in the oral version, not spoken too fast.

Realistically, however, many of the Iranian immigrants' descendants would grow up knowing little or no Persian, and it is presumably this group that the English translation addresses – at least partly. Some features point to an attempt to reach wider audiences, though. The introduction and the blurbs by eminent professors of Islamic studies, the use of an academic transliteration of Arabic terms, the index, the glossary, the professional layout and the high quality of production all point to a desire to reach beyond the Iranian-American Shi'i audiences that the lectures had addressed. They emphasise the universal nature of Bazargan's exegesis and its relevance to all contemporary Muslims beyond doctrinal divisions.

The website and the app almost certainly have editors beyond Bazargan himself, but these remain anonymous. In the case of the English translation, the editor, the translators and even the copy editor are named; only the donors who funded the publication of the book are not. The editor, Hamid Mavani, is an Associate Professor at Bayan Claremont, a graduate school of Islamic theology. He combined studies at institutions of higher learning in Iran and the Arab world with degrees from Canadian universities. As an editor, he seems not only to have played an influential role in the process of translating Bazargan's *tafsīr*, but he also provided the translation of the Qur'ān into English that is used in the book.[18] That Qur'ān translation is an interesting feature of the work because it is generally adapted to Bazargan's preferred interpretation, but in some cases diverges from it as if Mavani does not agree.[19] In one case, Bazargan felt a need to add a footnote that points out the difference between Mavani's translation and his own understanding of the verse.[20]

What does the sequence of medial representations of Bazargan's *tafsīr* mean for the text sample above (see Excerpt 3.1), namely the commentary on the last segment of Q. 103:3? The difference between the audio version[21] and its transcript[22] is mainly one of style. The audio version is in spoken Persian, contains some repetitions and explanations and generally conforms to the mode of expression one would use when speaking to an audience. The written version has been edited to conform with the conventions of written Persian with respect to coherence and syntactical correctness. Differences in content are marginal at most, for example when the 'collective fate' of people becomes their 'fate' in the written version or 'the persons who hold power in different countries' are reduced to 'the persons who hold power'.

This is different with the English translation. It contains some segments that are not present in any of the Persian versions. For example, it adds a footnote about jihad, apparently authored by Bazargan.[23] Obviously, Bazargan sees a need to make clear to this particular audience, which is potentially wider than that of the Persian original, that the notions of perseverance and proactiveness mentioned in the text do not relate to warfare, or only do in exceptional cases. From the text alone, it is not quite clear why this is mentioned at this particular point, and there is no compelling exegetical tradition that connects the verse to warfare either. Of course, the English text cites Q. 8:65, a verse that explicitly makes reference to battle, right after this footnote which is curious because that verse is not part of any Persian version either. The footnote also includes a slightly polemical jab against the Judeo-Christian tradition by its mention of the Hebrew Bible that is not part of the Persian text and probably reflects the expansion of the target audience to include non-Muslims.

Even where it does not add to the source texts, the English translation only follows them loosely. The translators obviously strove for an idiomatic English text, rather than a precise rendition of the source text. Furthermore, the translation sometimes restructures the argument, possibly in order to make the text more coherent. It also largely dispenses with Arabic quotations from the Qur'ān and Arabic–Islamic vocabulary such as *al-amr bi'l-ma'rūf wa'l-nahy 'an al-munkar* (here translated as 'enjoining the moral and forbidding the immoral') and therefore has no need for the explanations that are part of the source text. It makes up for this by expanding on the original text at other points. These expansions result in a noticeable shift in the text's language to more detailed descriptions of state and society in a modernised terminology. For example, the 'people' (*mardum*) from the Persian text become 'citizens' in the English text. Even 'subjects' (*ra'iyya*) are translated as 'citizens' which, in effect, conveys the curious impression that 'Alī b. Abī Ṭālib himself, to whom this Arabic term goes back, was speaking about a modern state.

The expansion of the translation becomes apparent when comparing a sentence from the English version to the Persian source text (see Table 3.1).

Another instance, this time covering an entire paragraph, shows more clearly where the editor and translators condensed the text and where they expanded upon it (see Table 3.2).

The English translation, thus, is not so much a translation, but a version of the text; a separate work of exegesis going back to the same author, but adapted to a different target group and involving an editor, translators and a copy editor. While having been authorised by the original author, it is nowhere near identical to the source text.

Both versions have in common that they focus on the principle of *al-amr bi'l-ma'rūf wa'l-nahy 'an al-munkar* instead of the term *ṣabr* (steadfastness) in Q. 103:3 that this commentary purports to discuss. *Al-amr bi'l-ma'rūf* – enjoining what is right and forbidding what is reprehensible – is a principle that occurs frequently in the Qur'ān, including the verse from Q. 31 that Bazargan cites.[24] It can be understood in multiple ways: as an individual believer's duty to exhort other believers, as an Islamic government's duty towards its citizens or as the citizens' duty towards their government. Bazargan mostly relates it to the relationship between rulers or governments and societies, which is a rather typical theme for Iranian exegetical discourses due to the existence of the Islamic Republic, its repressive nature and the political and religious philosophy that underlies it.

English translation by Mavani	*Direct translation of the Persian text*	*Persian text published on Bazargan's website*
Most of the world's powerful people are not necessarily benevolent individuals who chose public service to improve their fellow citizens' condition or do God's work;…	The persons who hold power are not acting out of piety.	کسانی که قدرت را در دست دارند قربتاً الی الله کار نمی‌کنند.

Table 3.1.

Further aspects of Bazargan's exegetical framework become apparent in his emphasis on the internal coherence of the Qur'ān[25] and his metaphor of the white blood cells. Excurses into scientific phenomena such as neutron stars, the ionosphere, the Earth's crust and, in this instance, the immune system are extremely commonplace in Bazargan's *tafsīr*.

They are more commonplace, in fact, than references to the exegete's Shi'i background that are mostly limited to the abundant citation of Imami Shi'i sources, ranging from *ḥadīth*s about the imams to opinions of eminent Shi'i – and typically Iranian – scholars. Sometimes, however, the specifically Shi'i perspective on early Islamic history comes to the surface, for example in a long narrative excursus on the martyrdom of 'Alī's son al-Ḥusayn (626–680) who is presented as a model of inner peace in the face

English translation by Mavani	*Direct translation of the Persian text*	*Persian text published on Bazargan's website*
These two characteristics work symbiotically and draw energy from one another. Rulers will not behave morally unless citizens stand for truth. The reverse is also true.	Thus, the people will not reform themselves unless their leaders are righteous and possess good manners. This entails two things: that the leaders do not act righteously unless the people exercise their duty [of enjoining good and forbidding wrong] and are truthful; and that the people will not reform unless the leaders are truthful and adhere to justice. These two are mutually dependent on each other.	مردم هم اصلاح نمی‌شوند مگر اینکه رهبرانشان درست‌کار باشند و رفتار نیکو داشته باشند. این دو را با هم فرمود که رهبران درست رفتار نمی‌کنند، مگر مردم به وظیفه‌ی خود قیام کنند و صاف شوند؛ و مردم هم اصلاح نمی‌شوند، مگر رهبران صاف شوند و از حق پیروی کنند. این دو در یکدیگر تأثیر متقابل دارند.
Hence, citizens who are indifferent to everything but their own affairs should not expect to end up with a just and ethical government.	It is known what kind of person wants to govern indifferent people who are only interested in their own concerns and lives.	مردمِ بی‌اعتنا و سرگرم کار و زندگی خود معلوم است که چه کسانی بر آنها حکومت خواهند کرد.
It should be clear by now that a responsible citizenry is a prerequisite for a flourishing society, one in which the citizens are fully engaged in their communities' affairs.	Therefore, the participation of the people in all fields connected to their fate is necessary.	بنابراین، حضور مردم در تمام عرصه‌هایی که مربوط به سرنوشت آنهاست ضروری است.

Table 3.2.

of hardship[26] and in an explanation of the pre-eminence of the Prophet's family, the *ahl al-bayt*.[27] In the text at hand, the jab against Mu'āwiya b. Abī Sufyān (603–680) who was both 'Alī's opponent and successor is clearly a Shi'i theme. But then, Mu'āwiya – in contrast to the first four caliphs – is not particularly revered among Sunnis either. Bazargan tries to present his excurses into Shi'ism in a way that is designed to make them broadly acceptable to non-Shi'is, and he explicitly warns against the dangers of sectarianism.[28] And why should he not? Sunni commentators frequently depict their exegesis as inclusive and even universalist, despite the adherence to a distinctly Sunni view of history which they quite simply see as the norm, rather than one perspective among many. Bazargan, as a Shi'i exegete, merely does the same.

VISUAL DIMENSIONS

The prototypical Qur'ānic commentary consists of text, written or possibly spoken. When the Egyptian modernist Ṭanṭāwī Jawharī (1870–1940) included illustrations into his work of *tafsīr* with the aim of introducing a Muslim readership to Western sciences,[29] this was decidedly innovative. Qur'ānic exegesis, until then, had never had much of a visual dimension. At most, manuscripts of *tafsīr* works had contained some calligraphy or decorations. Other aesthetic aspects were related to recitation and preaching, to a speaker's voice and performance and thus, the auditive level. The inclusion of pictures, however, is a phenomenon originating in the twentieth century. Pictures can fulfil various functions and add dimensions to an exegetical work that are not present in the text alone.

One such dimension is informative and educational. Pictures help readers to understand complex phenomena, especially related to history and the sciences, disciplines that were introduced into Qur'ānic exegesis in the late-nineteenth and early-twentieth centuries. Ṭanṭāwī Jawharī's use of pictures was meant to achieve that function. He was inspired by the encylopaedias and journals that were popular at the time where plants, animals or astronomical phenomena were represented to elucidate scientific explanations.

Images assumed additional functions in some types of Qur'ānic exegesis later in the twentieth century when colour printing, comic strips, advertising and ultimately television started to exert a deepening impact on the visual culture as well as the perceptions and expectations of Muslim audiences. Images may be used to attract attention. Especially in combination with written words, they may add an emotional dimension that is lacking from many Qur'ānic commentaries. Images may speak to the imagination and make a description more concrete, for example by depicting an environment, houses, faces and styles of dress. This effect may be used either in order to present a vision of the Qur'ān's community of origin in Arabia or, quite conversely, in order to adapt a Qur'ānic interpretation to local customs and circumstances, for example, by showing a picture of a rice harvest, rather than a date harvest. The following example illustrates how images may be used to achieve all of the above-mentioned effects in an educational setting.

Tafsīr in pictures: H. Abdul Mustaqim (b. 1972, Indonesia) on Q. 104

H. Abdul Mustaqim is a lecturer at the renowned State Islamic University in Yogyakarta. Born to a Central Javan peasant family, with his father a Qur'ānic school teacher, he received a traditional Islamic education and later went on to study Islamic theology and *tafsīr*. The methodology of Qur'ānic exegesis and the application of religious sources to contemporary social conditions are among his main areas of interest, as is pedagogy – which motivated him to produce a work of *tafsīr* that is mainly targeted at children.[30]

The book mentions ten main sources. These include the encyclopaedic *tafsīr* works by al-Ṭabarī and Ibn Kathīr; the early twentieth-century commentary on the *juz' 'amma* by Muḥammad 'Abduh; the popular work *Ṣafwat al-tafāsīr* by the Syrian scholar Muḥammad 'Alī al-Ṣābūnī (b. 1930), published in 1976, that purports to collect the most authoritative exegetical opinions from the premodern exegetical tradition; two Qur'ānic commentaries by the contemporary Indonesian exegete Muhammad Quraish Shihab; two works on the occasions of revelation; a dictionary of Qur'ānic terms; and the Qur'ān translation by the Indonesian Ministry of Religion.[31] All Qur'ān translations in the book are based on that translation, which is rather common in Indonesia.

The *tafsīr* comes in small booklets that contain a handful of *sūra*s each. The commentary on these is uncontroversial, written in a style that is intelligible for children, but not necessarily in a way that would particularly capture their attention. That is the task of the pictures by an anonymous illustrator that have been designed on the basis of instructions by the author.[32] The *tafsīr* booklets are professionally designed and produced, with a picture on every single page.

This commentary pursues a fairly conventional didactic approach to interpreting the Qur'ān in many ways, starting with the decision to focus on the *juz' 'amma*. Because the thirtieth and last part of the Qur'ān contains the shortest *sūra*s and because these are easiest to memorise; this part – besides the Fātiḥa – is what the teaching of the Qur'ān usually begins with. The structure indicates that the memorisation and at least rudimentary under-

Excerpt 3.2

Introduction[33]
This *sūra* consists of nine verses. It belongs to the Meccan *sūra*s because it was revealed in Mecca before the Prophet emigrated to Medina. This *sūra* was revealed after Q. 75 and before Q. 77. Besides *al-Humaza*, this *sūra* is also known by the name of *al-Ḥuṭama* which is taken from v. 4 [see the Arabic and English text of the *sūra* below].

The main contents of the *sūra* consist of a warning to the two following groups: (1) People who like to slander and denounce others; and (2) people who are busy piling up riches and do not want to spend them in the way of God. They think that the wealth they have collected will make them live forever. God threatens both groups with a chastisement in the hell of *ḥuṭama*, which has a fire so powerful that it burns right up to the heart.

From looking at its contents, it becomes clear that this *sūra* has a close connection (*munāsaba*) to the preceding verses, that is, Q. 103. Whereas Q. 103 talks about people who will not experience loss [Q. 103:2], this *sūra* describes people who experience loss. This can be gathered from the first word with which the *sūra* begins, which is the word *waylun* (woe!). [...]

Occasion of revelation
Ibn ʿUmar said: 'This *sūra* came down in connection with the comportment of Ubayy b. Khalaf who ceaselessly denounced and insulted the Prophet.'

According to a different tradition, it is said that this *sūra* came down in connection with the comportment of Umayya b. Khalaf who always slandered and denounced the Prophet whenever he saw him. Then the *sūra* was revealed as a warning to those who like to denounce and slander others.

Captions: The man's box is labelled 'wealth', the boy's box 'flood victims'.

The text and translation of the *sūra*:

(1) Woe to all those who slander and denounce,	وَيْلٌ لِّكُلِّ هُمَزَةٍ لُّمَزَةٍ {١}
(2) who collect wealth and never cease to count it.	الَّذِي جَمَعَ مَالًا وَعَدَّدَهُ {٢}
(3) He (man) assumes that this money of his can make him live forever.	يَحْسَبُ أَنَّ مَالَهُ أَخْلَدَهُ {٣}
(4) No, never! He will certainly be thrown into (the hell of) *ḥuṭama*.	كَلَّا لَيُنبَذَنَّ فِي الْحُطَمَةِ {٤}
(5) And do you know what (this hell of) *ḥuṭama* is?	وَمَا أَدْرَاكَ مَا الْحُطَمَةُ {٥}
(6) (It is) a fire of (the punishment of) God that was lit,	نَارُ اللَّهِ الْمُوقَدَةُ {٦}
(7) that (burns) up to the heart.	الَّتِي تَطَّلِعُ عَلَى الْأَفْئِدَةِ {٧}
(8) Verily, this fire will close in on them.	إِنَّهَا عَلَيْهِم مُّؤْصَدَةٌ {٨}
(9) (While they will) be bound to long poles.	فِي عَمَدٍ مُّمَدَّدَةٍ {٩}

[There follows one page with explanations of Arabic words]

General explanation of the *sūra*

[Six pages of text and pictures are devoted to the people described in v. 1. They deal with the theme of slandering, gossip and assigning blame. One picture shows a situation from the life of the Prophet, the Prophet being replaced by an oval shape with the Arabic name 'Muḥammad' in it so as to avoid depicting the Prophet. The other pictures are scenes from Indonesian everyday life involving men, women and children. There is also advice on situations in which it is legitimate to 'tell tales', such as reporting a crime to the authorities.]

Captions: 'Beggar' and 'Bourgeois'

The following verses [verses 2–3] make clear that the threat uttered here is also directed at people who like to amass wealth. They assume that this wealth can make them live forever. The meaning of amassing wealth here is when someone likes to collect riches and ceaselessly counts them, which causes a person to become a niggard, not wanting to spend money in God's way. Such persons will be thrown in the afterlife into the hell of *ḥuṭama* for all eternity. It is a hell that is extremely hot, whose fire burns up to the heart. Not only that, but they will also be tied to the poles of hell so they are unable to do anything.

Conclusion
From the preceding commentary on *Sūrat al-Humaza*, we can extract the following messages:

[1. Addresses the issue of slander]
2. Do not find enjoyment in amassing wealth and ceaselessly counting it because this may render the person who does it curmudgeonly (stingy). Someone who likes to amass riches will typically think that his wealth can make him live forever. However, every man will definitely die whereas the riches they have gathered will have to be abandoned. The only thing they can bring to the grave is a shroud, no more than that. As such, if we possess a surplus of wealth, we had better give it as alms to the poor around us.

And God knows best what is correct. [in transliterated Arabic]

Caption: Committee for the distribution of the alms tax (zakāt)[34]

standing of the Arabic text is among the goals of instruction. That structure is commonplace for modern pedagogical works of *tafsīr*, starting with an introduction to the *sūra* that mentions the number of verses and the time of revelation, narrating the occasion of revelation, explaining difficult or rare Arabic words, providing a commentary on the *sūra* and ending with a few conclusions that summarise what the exegete thinks is the main message of the *sūra* or passage in question.

The commentary in Excerpt 3.2 is rather general. It focusses on the moral aims of the *sūra* as opposed to the descriptions of hell which it only mentions briefly, apparently subscribing to a rather literal understanding of them.[35] The text does not make any explicit references to either contemporary or specifically Indonesian conditions. The pictures, however, add precisely that type of localisation and link the seventh-century text with a twenty-first-century society. Some of them – not displayed here – depict historical scenes, but many make connections to contemporary Indonesian life that are absent from the text.

The most obvious example is on the first page where a corrupt civil servant is portrayed. The *sūra* itself does not say anything about the source of the amassed wealth it talks about, nor does the commentary. The picture, on the other hand, gives a clear idea, taking up an issue that has been an – albeit largely ineffectual – part of the Indonesian official discourse since the New Order regime came to power in 1967, that is, the fight against corruption. Themes of statehood and good citizenship are important to contemporary Indonesian Qur'ānic interpretation,[36] and this work is no exception.

The visualisation, whenever it does not depict the Prophet and his environment, portrays an Indonesian Muslim context, but the style of visualisation is clearly influenced by Western models. This is particularly obvious in the image of the Devil. It does not actually conflict with Muslim traditions that are rather vague about the Devil's, that is, Iblīs' or Satan's external attributes, but it has a striking similarity with Western Christian visual conventions, from the red skin to the shape of the tail.

The pictures emphasise the theme of social justice, which is a central theme of the Qur'ān, and especially of the Meccan *sūras*, but had not received much attention in mainstream exegesis until the twentieth century. Then, it became a distinct concern of reformers, particularly in the Muslim mass movements such as the Muslim Brotherhood.[37] This important dimension of modern Qur'ānic exegesis is evoked by Abdul Mustaqim when he chooses illustrations that juxtaposes wealth with poverty.

By showing concrete situations such as the handing over of alms tax shares or a rich man's refusal to give donations to a flood victim, the pictures make it possible for readers to relate the commentary and its message to their lives. Furthermore, they add an emotional dimension that is absent from the text's rather technical style. The pictures make greed, misery and complacency tangible. They are thus a central part of the work, contributing a significant layer of meaning. Far from merely illustrating what the text says, they induce readers to apply the text of the Qur'ānic commentary to specific situations and contexts in their lives.

PREACHING AND MEDIA: AUDIO-VISUAL REPRESENTATIONS AND THE INTERNET

Pictures may achieve a number of functions that written texts may not. Audio-visual media add immediacy to the list: the suggestion of direct personal contact with the exegete. This is possible because, during the second half of the twentieth century, first radio and then television have become the dominant types of mass media.

In most countries, radio and television were largely state controlled at least until the 1990s; consequently, there was only as much room for Islamic themes as governments were willing to allow for. Many governments reacted to the wave of Islamisation that started in the 1970s by incorporating Islamic themes into their broadcasting, especially during the month of Ramadan. The most famous example is the Egyptian shaykh Muḥammad al-Mutawallī al-Shaʿrāwī (1911–1998) whose weekly Reflections on the Qurʾān (*khawāṭir ḥawl al-Qurʾān*) was broadcast in a public television programme from 1977 until his death. In this show, the shaykh was seated in the mosque of his delta town, in front of a male audience, and commented on verses of the Qurʾān in their canonical order, combining classical exegetical themes with education, anecdotes and admonishments in a style akin to that of a sermon, rather than a work of *tafsīr*. While moderately entertaining, the representation of religious authority employed in such programmes was distinctly traditional and its carriers were invariably religious scholars (*ʿulamāʾ*). This also helped to create a distance to Islamist movements that were competing with governments for political authority and whose leadership was notorious for consisting of middle-class academics with secular professions such as engineers and doctors.

The 1990s saw the emergence of satellite television stations, many of them in private ownership. As a result, the influence of governments decreased considerably. Along came a much fiercer competition for audiences, especially from among the young and affluent. In order to captivate such audiences, new types of religious programmes hit the market. They featured performances by younger preachers who were often young, smart and markedly different from religious scholars with regard to their appearance, demeanour and way of speaking. Often, they interacted with their audience; they tried to emotionally engage their viewers and to connect with them on a personal level. This type of religious programme often focussed on particular topics, drawing on all kinds of sources besides the Qurʾān, but the more established these formats became, the more frequently they featured explicitly exegetical content. There were even a few cinematic attempts to engage with the Qurʾān, or specific Qurʾānic verses, in an artistic form.[38]

While the advent of satellite television curtailed the monopoly of individual governments on information and entertainment, it did not automatically amount to a democratisation of supply and demand in these fields. After all, airing a satellite television channel and producing content for broadcast is extremely expensive. This issue of finance increased the influence of wealthy individuals, institutions and even states such as the emirate of Qatar with its successful satellite channel Al Jazeera. A small number of media tycoons – quite a few of them hailing from Saudi Arabia – own a large share of the television networks across the Muslim world. Their main interest might be in profit, but they are also often aligned with political factions or the institutions of a specific state. Both factors – the marketing aspect as well as a channel's political affiliation – have to be taken into account when evaluating the activities of television preachers and exegetes. The tendency is to avoid contents that are markedly controversial or overtly political, but that still leaves a wide range of options. Thus, when, for example, the Indonesian media tycoon Surya Paloh chose to set up the scholar Muhammad Quraish Shihab as the host of exegetical television shows, he opted for a person who is affiliated with his own Golkar party, which was the ruling party under President Suharto (1921–2008); and he opted for an exegete who aims at adapting the Qur'ān to Indonesian society in a way that is relatively open to ethnic, linguistic and religious pluralism as well as different lifestyles.[39] This is important in view of the fact that the projected urban audience includes Muslims, but also other groups such as ethnic Chinese.

Television as an exegetical medium has a much wider and more varied audience than print, but is much more restrictive with respect to the producers of exegetical content; only a handful of them ever manage to use this medium with some degree of success. The internet, however, was revolutionary in this regard.; while not every Muslim has access to it, its reach is rapidly increasing and it offers unforeseen opportunities for anyone to publish content at little or no cost. From academic *tafsīr* to interactive message boards, from sermons on YouTube to missionary sites about the 'miracle of the Qur'ān', from English to Yoruba content, the internet is a medium that has taken over many of the functions of all previous media and reaches most of their audiences, if not more. It also provides the option to interact with one's audience and to encourage their active participation in exegetical debates, and it opens spaces that are meant for interaction only, without an authoritative exegetical voice.

No endorsement by a media tycoon and no academic qualifications are necessary to engage in Qur'ānic exegesis on the internet; any Muslim may discuss how the references to celestial bodies in the Qur'ān match modern astrophysical knowledge and what that means for the nature of the Qur'ān, with no regard to whether these theories would be approved by religious scholars or physicists.[40] Exegetical performances can easily combine the local with the global. Preachers might give sermons or teach lessons to local audiences and have them broadcast to the whole world. Of course, in reality it is not quite as simple as that. While online publishing of text requires hardly any resources, the potential to reach large audiences with professional videos is significantly increased by having some source of funding and technical expertise at one's disposal. Still, the threshold is comparatively low when compared to television productions.

The following section examines the characteristics of audio-visual exegetical content by introducing a range of commentaries on the Fātiḥa, the first *sūra* of the Qur'ān, that are available on the video platform YouTube. After having given an overview of the exegetes, the genre of exegesis and some basic features, I will outline their position on the last two verses of the *sūra*, in particular. This provides the background to a more detailed analysis of one particularly popular YouTube performance on the Fātiḥa, that of the Saudi intellectual Ḥasan b. Farḥān al-Mālikī who focusses on precisely these last verses.

From television to YouTube: Audio-visual interpretations of the Fātiḥa

The Fātiḥa (Q. 1) on YouTube

Interpreting the *Fātiḥa* has always been an extremely popular activity because the *sūra* is not only the first of the Qur'ān, it is also a part of the obligatory prayer ritual and thus needs to memorised by every Muslim. It thus assumes a central place in Muslim ritual practice and piety. Countless *tafsīr* works are devoted to the interpretation of the Fātiḥa alone. The Fātiḥa is also a frequent topic of sermons which is why, in the second half of the twentieth century, cassette tapes, CDs and video tapes of such sermons started hitting the market.

In 2017, YouTube is the most popular platform for free audio-visual content; of course, this will not necessarily always be the case and might change any time. I searched for the terms '*tafsīr*' and 'Sūrat al-Fātiḥa' in English, French and Arabic on YouTube and selected the most-viewed[41] results that contained actual interpretations of that *sūra*, as opposed to recitations or videos that teach its memorisation. The result includes thirteen videos, twelve of which are presented in Box 3.1 and the thirteenth, that by Ḥasan al-Mālikī, in Excerpt 3.3. Some speakers are represented with more than one video, which is due to, first, the fact that they frequently speak about identical topics in various locations and, second, their general popularity.

When comparing these twelve performances, the first observation is that all exegetes are male. The predominance of male exegetes is even higher among high-profile public speakers than among book authors. Female preachers do exist, but they often focus on female audiences and 'women's topics'. Female scholars and speakers are also represented among proponents of liberationist and egalitarian trends, but these attain nowhere near the mass appeal that, for example, Nouman Ali Khan does. Indeed, none of the speakers considered here, all of whom were selected for the relative popularity of their take on the Sūrat al-Fātiḥa, come from the modernist field – the only exception being Ḥasan al-Mālikī who will be discussed later. Rather, they include traditional scholars such as al-Shaʿrāwī and al-Qazwīnī or, from a younger generation and a minority context, Yasir Qadhi and Ismail Menk. Then there are Salafis such as al-ʿArīfī and Kabir who received substantial religious training in Saudi Arabia. Interestingly,

Box 3.1 *(reference codes in square brackets)*

Yasir Qadhi

A Ramadan series by Yasir Qadhi (b. 1975), an American scholar of Pakistani descent who conducted studies in Saudi Arabia and was strongly influenced by Salafism at that time, but later took a critical stance towards it. The entire series, which consists of nineteen parts with a length of 10 to 20 minutes each, deals with the Fātiḥa. The language is English, the location Memphis, Tennessee, and the year 2014.[42] [YQ]

Nouman Ali Khan

Rediscovering the Fatiha, a lecture with a duration of nearly three hours held by Nouman Ali Khan (b. 1978) who is also an American scholar of Pakistani descent. He is a professional preacher and speaker. Through his Bayyinah Institute for Arabic and Qur'anic Studies, he provides large amounts of high-profile, professionally produced Islamic audio-visual content that is hugely popular. The language is English, the location Singapore, and the year 2013.[43] Translations, by way of subtitles, into several other languages such as Turkish, Urdu and French are available. [NAK1]

Another lecture by the same speaker of slightly shorter duration at 2 hours and 30 minutes. The language is English, the location a mosque in Malaysia, and the year 2014.[44] [NAK2]

A five-part lecture series on the Fātiḥa at a total length of approximately 3.5 hours. It was produced by the Bayyinah Institute. The language is English, the location not identified, but probably in the US, and the year 2018.[45] [NAK3]

GET TO KNOW: Ep. 1 – Surah Al-Fatihah, a 25 minute presentation on the Fātiḥa by Nouman Ali Khan that is part of a Ramadan series encompassing twenty-nine parts, each on a different *sūra*, on the YouTube channel Quran Weekly. The language is English, the location is unclear, but likely to be the Dallas area where Khan is based, and the year is 2016.[46] [NAK4]

Ismail Menk

A lecture at a length of 56 minutes, published on the Qatar-based platform Digital Mimbar. Ismail Menk (b. 1975), also known as Mufti Ismail Menk, is an Islamic scholar from Zimbabwe who studied in Medina. He gives lectures and speeches worldwide; the Fātiḥa is a common subject of those. Ismail Menk is the only one from among the preachers presented here who consistently recites the Qur᾿ān, as opposed to merely quoting it, during his speeches. The language is English, the location is an Islamic cultural centre in Doha, and the year is 2012.[47] [IM1]

Another lecture by the same speaker at a Muslim Student Union. This one is longer at 1 hour and 20 minutes. The language is English, the location is Leicester, Great Britain, and the year is 2011.[48] [IM2]

Sofiane Kabir

A Friday sermon on the interpretation of the *Fātiḥa* at a length of a little more than half an hour, which is common for such sermons. Sofiane Kabir (b. 1987) is a French preacher who studied sharia at the University of Medina. The language of the sermon alternates between Modern Standard Arabic and French, with the preacher himself translating his Arabic statements into French. The location is Villetaneuse in the northern suburbs of Paris and the year is 2012.[49] [SK]

Shaykh al-Shaʿrāwī

Six instalments at 50 minutes each of a popular Friday television show in which the Egyptian shaykh Muḥammad al-Mutawallī al-Shaʿrāwī (1911–1998) interpreted the Qur'ān in weekly sessions for more than twenty years until his death. They were broadcast on state television and also distributed on video tapes and DVDs. There are multiple identical versions of this content on YouTube.[50] The language is Egyptian colloquial Arabic, and the location is the mosque in the shaykh's home town Daqādūs in the Nile Delta where he held all his sessions. The date of the original sessions on the Fātiḥa is unknown. They were probably held in the late 1970s and uploaded in 2011. [ShSh]

Muḥammad al-ʿArīfī

A sermon, possibly a Friday sermon, at a length of 25 minutes. Muḥammad al-ʿArīfī (b. 1970) is a Saudi preacher who is extremely popular and has a wide following on social media. He is also staunchly Salafi. He is frequently accused of jihadi leanings and connections to al-Qāʾida. The language is Modern Standard Arabic, the location is unknown. Since this video has the same background as many others by al-ʿArīfī, it was probably filmed at the mosque in Saudi Arabia where he usually preaches. The year is 2015.[51] [MA]

Muḥammad Rātib al-Nābulusī

An audio file that has been converted into a video by combining it with either a static picture of the speaker or – in a different version – with an Islamic background image: an Arabic calligraphy of the slogan *Muḥāmmad ṣallā Allāhu ʿalayhi wa-sallam*. At a length of 1 hour and 47 minutes, this lecture is part of a series that is devoted to the consecutive interpretation of the entire Qurʾān. Currently, the series includes fifty-seven videos covering the first *sūra* and half of the second. Al-Nābulusī (b. 1938) is a Syrian university professor with degrees in Arabic language and in education from Syrian and European universities. He publishes and lectures widely on Islamic themes. The popularity of his audio files points to the fact that a substantial part of the content on YouTube is primarily used for listening, not for watching. The language is Modern Standard Arabic and the location is unknown, but possibly Damascus. The year is unknown as well; the various identical audio files of his lecture were uploaded between 2013 and 2015.[52] [MRN]

Āyatollāh al-Sayyid Murtaḍā al-Qazwīnī

A three-part lecture at a total duration of 2 hours and 45 minutes, held at the shrine of al-Ḥusayn in Karbala, one of the holiest sites of Shiʿism. It was apparently recorded for several media outlets as is apparent from the range of microphones and the presence of *tafsīr* clips by al-Qazwīnī that were clearly broadcast by a television station. Al-Qazwīnī (b. 1931) was born in Karbala into a family of prominent Imami Shiʿi scholars and descendants of the Prophet. His father was a grand ayatollah. He fled to the US in 1986 and returned to Iraq in 2003. He was then appointed imam at the shrine of Karbala where he holds daily lectures. The language is Iraqi colloquial Arabic and the year is 2014.[53] [MQ]

the popular speaker al-Nābulusī and the highly successful preacher Nouman Ali Khan have much weaker scholarly credentials. They do, however, draw on the discourses and sometimes even the habitus of traditional scholars, combining them with the eclectic approach of a *dāʿī*, someone whose mission it is to 'call to Islam'. This is most obvious in Nouman Ali Khan who is no scholar by training, but relies all the more heavily on his knowledge of classical Arabic and mainstream scholarly Qur'ānic interpretation to corroborate his standing. He combines this with the skills of a public speaker, employing didactic methods, stories, examples from everyday life and humour to engage his audience.

The twelve *tafsīr* sessions examined here represent five different types of audio-visual exegesis that are broadly representative of YouTube as an exegetical medium.

1. Presentations that are exclusively recorded for online distribution on YouTube and other platforms. This is only true for NAK4 which is a professional studio production. In a Muslim majority context, this type of content might have been produced by a television station, but in Nouman Ali Khan's Muslim minority context, digital distribution is a more feasible way to address an international English-speaking Muslim audience.
2. Recordings that are an unprofessional side product of a sermon or lecture, typically fan videos taken with mobile phones. Such is the case with the recordings of Nouman Ali Khan's lecture in Malaysia (NAK2) and with Ismail Menk's lecture in Britain (IM2).
3. Semi-professional recordings of Friday sermons undertaken, for example, by mosque staff. Sofiane Kabir's *tafsīr* (SK) is an example. The sound quality is low, but the image is good despite the speaker's face often being obscured by the microphone.
4. Public lectures or performances that have been set up to be professionally filmed, which is most frequently the case in the sample (YQ, NAK1, NAK3, IM1, MA, ShSh, MQ). There are vast differences in quality, even among the televised material. Only the few (NAK1, NAK3, ShSh) that have been filmed by several cameras allow for changing perspectives and views of the audience. In most other cases, the existence of an audience can be assumed, but it cannot be seen. When there is only one camera, the speakers are invariably static in order to remain in the focus. Occasionally, this might be intentional since the speaker is standing on a pulpit anyway (YQ, MA).
5. Audio sermons that are similar in function to the audio tapes and CDs that have been vastly popular for several decades among

> Muslim audiences interested in religious instruction.[54] Obviously, they still have their uses since there are many situations in which a person might listen to a sermon, but have no time or opportunity to watch a video. In Muḥammad Rātib al-Nābulusī's case, the acoustic quality is fairly low, indicating that this might be a recording of a lecture, rather than a studio production, which is something that is not uncommon.

Furthermore, the videos represent three different types of exegetical performance, with some overlap:

1. the sermon (*khuṭba*);
2. the religious lesson or teaching session (*dars*); and
3. the public lecture that borrows from the techniques of motivational speakers.

The distinctions between these formats is not clear-cut but there are a number of considerations that suggest a performance should be placed into one category rather than another. For starters, a preacher is typically standing whereas in a religious lesson, the instructor sits. A public lecturer or motivational speaker, on the other hand, might move around, stride across the podium and even enter the auditorium. Nouman Ali Khan is the only speaker who pursues this dynamic approach in three of his four videos (NAK1, 2, 3); the fourth one shows him sitting behind a desk, entirely static (NAK4), which emphasises the stark distinction between his public lectures and his role as an instructor. In Muḥammad al-ʿArīfī's case, the genre of the Friday sermon is emphasised by showing at the outset how the preacher rises from his seat; while standing, he is filmed slightly from below, in a 'hero shot' perspective that underlines his authority as a preacher and that is equivalent to how the seated congregants would see him.

Preachers typically stand on a pulpit (YQ, SK) or the existence of a pulpit is at least indicated, for example by an arch-shaped illumination in their backs (MA). Others, especially the older scholars, sit in a preacher's chair that is reserved for giving lessons (ShSh, MQ). A religious lesson may also be given in a nondescript setting, of course (IM1, IM2), possibly enhanced by a bookshelf with Arabic books (IM1). Nouman Ali Khan, in his public lectures, favours a lectern, a podium and large, stylish banners whereas in his Ramadan series (NAK4), he uses a vaguely premodern Arabic–Islamic setup.

The differences between the types of presentation are also reflected in the speakers' clothing, physical attributes and the locations in which they preach. Nouman Ali Khan is the only speaker wearing a suit and tie which distinguishes him from a traditional scholar. All other speakers wear some type of Islamic garb, depending on their background and affiliation. Sofiane Kabir, for example, clearly self-identifies as a Salafi by his white clothes and beard style while Yasir Qadhi's clothes reveal his South Asian background. Al-Nābulusī is the only one who does not have a beard, only a moustache.

Depending on whether a sermon, a lecture or a lesson are intended, the aims, contents and interaction with the audience might differ. A preacher aims to exhort his audience and to transmit a message; he will not typically interact with his listeners. A teacher will make more of an effort to explain a Qur'ānic verse, including linguistic details, and might ask the audience questions that are often rhetorical or affirming what he has already said. A lecture might combine both elements. In the videos, only al-Shaʿrāwī and Nouman Ali Khan (NAK1, 2, 3) clearly interact with their audience; Nouman Ali Khan sometimes even answers individual questions in the break (NAK2). In al-Shaʿrāwī's case, the answers given by members of the audience are audible. So too is al-Qazwīnī's audience, not so much in response to his questions, but through emotional exclamations that occur when he mentions the Shiʿi imams. The only speaker who is shown as having a mixed-gender audience is Nouman Ali Khan. In the other cases, the audience is either exclusively male (ShSh, MQ) or their gender is not clear.

Language is also an important consideration. From the four videos that are in Arabic only, two are in Modern Standard Arabic (MA, MRN) which is the language typically used in Friday sermons, but also generally preferred by Salafis. The other two are in Egyptian (ShSh) and Iraqi (MQ) dialect, respectively, signalling that this is pedagogical content and that the focus is on helping the audience understand the message. In the non-Arabic videos, the amount of Arabic quotations differs vastly. If used in abundance, they might make it harder for a non-specialist audience to follow, but might enhance the speaker's authority (e.g. NAK4). Ismail Menk is the only speaker – including those who preach in Arabic – who does not only quote the Qur'ān in Arabic, but recites it with considerable skill. His mastery of Qur'ānic recitation (*tilāwa*) doubtlessly adds to the attraction of his lectures.

The length of the clips differs vastly, from the roughly half hour that a typical Friday sermon takes (SK, MA) to Nouman Ali Khan's three-hour lectures. Several videos are part of a series of either daily (MQ) or weekly instalments (ShSh). A particularly popular format is the Ramadan series with daily instalments (YQ, NAK4). Such series with religious content are generally pervasive during Ramadan, and since Muslims are recommended to read the complete Qur'ān during that month, exegetical themes are an obvious choice.

YOUTUBE EXEGETES ON Q. 1:6–7

بِسْمِ اللَّهِ الرَّحْمَـٰنِ الرَّحِيمِ ﴿١﴾ الْحَمْدُ لِلَّهِ رَبِّ الْعَالَمِينَ ﴿٢﴾ الرَّحْمَـٰنِ الرَّحِيمِ ﴿٣﴾ مَالِكِ يَوْمِ الدِّينِ ﴿٤﴾ إِيَّاكَ نَعْبُدُ وَإِيَّاكَ نَسْتَعِينُ ﴿٥﴾ اهْدِنَا الصِّرَاطَ الْمُسْتَقِيمَ ﴿٦﴾ صِرَاطَ الَّذِينَ أَنْعَمْتَ عَلَيْهِمْ غَيْرِ الْمَغْضُوبِ عَلَيْهِمْ وَلَا الضَّالِّينَ ﴿٧﴾

(1) In the name of God, the Merciful, the Compassionate! (2) Praise belongs to God, Lord of all beings, (3) the Merciful, the Compassionate, (4) Master of the Day of Judgement. (5) It is You we worship; it is You we ask for help. (6) Guide us on the straight path: (7) the path of those You have blessed, not of those who incur anger and who have gone astray.

The Fātiḥa is possibly the most frequently interpreted *sūra* of the Qur'ān. The commentaries on it are detailed and extensive, often discussing individual words such as "the Merciful" at length since, in the exegetes' opinion, the *sūra* sets the stage for the entire Qur'ānic discourse. Summarising and analysing what the twelve videos introduced above have to say on it would require a book of its own. I will thus focus here on outlining their approach to the last two verses of the *sūra*, Q. 1:6–7, because these are, as we will see in the next subsection, what Ḥasan b. Farḥān al-Mālikī focusses on as well. A very brief overview of the YouTube exegetes' interpretations will permit to situate al-Mālikī's approach and to appreciate the reasons for which it was promoted on YouTube as a 'shocking' *tafsīr*.

All exegetes deliver a specific explanation of these two verses with the exception of Ismail Menk who does not go into details of interpretation. Many of them draw attention to the way in which the *sūra* uses pairs of opposites as a rhetorical device. For example, it contrasts those whom God has blessed with those who incur wrath and those who go astray. Yasir Qadhi calls this technique 'affirmation and rejection'.

As for the identity of those whom God has blessed, the implicit consensus seems to be that they include Muslims only although not necessarily all Muslims fall into that category. Sofian Kabir quotes Q. 4:69 for further explanation: 'Those will be among the ones God has blessed: the prophets, the truthful, the *shuhadā'* and the righteous – what excellent companions these are!' He goes on to explain that the word *shuhadā'* means 'martyrs' and that the 'righteous' are either the Muslims or the believers.

The identity of those who incur wrath and of those who go astray is a thorny issue since there exists an exegetical *ḥadīth* that is cited in most premodern Qur'ānic commentaries that does not cohere with contemporary standards of interreligious diplomacy. According to this *ḥadīth*, Muḥammad said that those who incur wrath are the Jews and those who go astray are the Christians. From among the YouTube exegetes discussed here, al-Qazwīnī most unequivocally embraces that *ḥadīth*. In his opinion, the Jews are the ones who incur God's wrath more than anyone else; other groups such as hypocrites and those who kill believers come second to them. Furthermore, he states that the modern state of Israel demonstrates the wickedness of the Jews and the extent to which they deserve God's wrath. When he talks of the Christians, he is less emphatic. The Saudi Salafi Muḥammad al-ʿArīfī likewise takes the *ḥadīth* literally, but implies that the verse applies to some Muslims as well, such as those who adopt 'illicit innovations' (*bidaʿ*).

Nouman Ali Khan, Yasir Qadhi and Sofiane Kabir have a different take on the *ḥadīth*. They deliver what is probably the most common contemporary explanation of Q. 1:7, sometimes also put forward without any reference to Jews and Christians (NAK4, ShSh, MRN): those who incur wrath are people who have knowledge, but do not act according to that knowledge, and those who go astray might try to follow the truth, but do not have sufficient knowledge. According to Yasir Qadhi, the Jews and Christians are merely examples of those two types of person. The true Muslim avoids both paths: knowledge without action and action without knowledge. The path of those whom God has blessed therefore has two conditions, knowledge (*ʿilm*) and action (*ʿamal*). Nouman Ali Khan goes one step further in discussing this 'most misunderstood *ḥadīth* ever', stating that the verse is not about the Jews and the Christians at all although they might be examples of the issues that the verse addresses. It is about human behaviour, about doing a wrong thing that one knew was forbidden or doing it without such knowledge: 'the *āya* is about us'. He also specifies that no Muslim has an excuse for going astray because all Muslims have an obligation to learn.

Another exegetical problem related to v. 7 is the fact that the Qur'ān does not specify whose wrath it is that is incurred. In contrast to the blessing in v. 6, v.7 does not mention a subject. Many either do not see this as a problem or simply assume that the verse speaks of God's wrath (MQ, SK). According to Nouman Ali Khan, God does not mention himself in this verse because this demonstrates the enormity of his anger (NAK1). Yasir Qadhi, on the other hand, rejects the notion that God would feel anger. Rather, he says, the use of the passive is intentional. The message of the verse, then, is that there is a group of people who thoroughly deserve to incur anger. Those who are angry with them include angels and other humans, but not God who is above such emotions.

There are marked differences between the eight exegetes considered here with respect to their thematic foci, their readiness to rely on the exegetical *ḥadīth* about the Jews and Christians and their tendency to read it literally. However, they also have much in common. Their sermons, lessons or lectures are grounded in the tradition of *tafsīr* and the exegetical resources it offers. They talk exclusively to other Muslims. While not all of them pay the same amount of attention to the issue of Jews and Christians, none of them rejects the exegetical *ḥadīth* referring to them, nor does any of them make an effort to develop an inclusive perspective. This is entirely different to the approach taken by Ḥasan b. Farḥān al-Mālikī.

Ḥasan b. Farḥān al-Mālikī (b. 1970, Saudi Arabia) on Q. 1:6–7

Ḥasan b. Farḥān al-Mālikī is a prominent and controversial Saudi intellectual representing a post-Wahhābi trend in the kingdom, highly critical not only of the contemporary manifestation of the state ideology, but also of its religious underpinnings and even of Sunni Islam itself. Born in the South of Saudi Arabia, he adopted the Wahhābi-Salafi approach to Islam in his youth, subscribing to the ideas of the Saudi mufti ʿAbd al-ʿAzīz b. Bāz (1910–1999) and dreaming of jihad in Afghanistan. During his studies of communication, he started to realise the extremist potential of that ideology, broadened his intellectual outlook and developed an interest in history. While working for the Ministry of Education, he started publishing articles. One of those caused him to be sentenced to two months in jail. He also wrote several books all of which were banned in Saudi Arabia. In 2001, he published a book that vehemently criticised Saudi school curricula whereafter he was dismissed from his job.

He not only attacked the authority of Ibn Taymiyya who is central to Wahhābi-Salafi thought, but also the equally important idea of the quasi-infallibility of the *salaf*. He denounced Wahhābism in general as a rigid doctrine, or even a 'school' (*madhhab*), that calls for aggression against all non-Wahhābis and thereby is directly responsible for extremism and jihadism.[55]

He became increasingly known as a protagonist of a call for reconciliation between Sunna and Shiʿa, connecting this to a pro-ʿAlid view of early Islamic history that questioned the legitimacy of some of the first caliphs and especially the Umayyads. In the course of his career, the Sunna in the sense of prophetic *ḥadīth*s lost much of its importance to him. He came to consider the Qurʾān as the principal source of religion, combined with reason and the collective memory of the prophetic practice with regard to issues such as prayer rules. In 2012, he was arrested and detained for a short period of time after which he was forbidden from appearing on Saudi television; he was detained again in 2014. He continued, however, to spread his ideas on other channels. For example, his Ramadan series *The Life of the Most Noble Prophet* on the Kuwaiti station Al-Kout saw four seasons. Ultimately, his aim is to deconstruct Sunni and Shiʿi Islam as they are currently known. Instead, he promotes a unified version of Islam that follows the tradition of the Prophet and venerates the Prophet's family. His call for reconciliation with marginalised Islamic movements goes as far as to include the Ahmadiyya which most non-Ahmadi Muslims consider heretical. He is also active in interfaith discourses, emphasising the positive contributions of Jews and Christians to Islamic history.[56]

What follows in Excerpt 3.3 is the English translation of his televised interpretation of the Fātiḥa.This is Qur'ānic exegesis in the form of a religious lesson (*dars*), broadcast on television, published on YouTube and thus watched by hundreds of thousands of viewers. The way in which it is performed and the media in which it is broadcast have a profound impact on its style and presentation.

The exegete, Ḥasan b. Farḥān al-Mālikī, speaks extemporaneously to a large extent although he occasionally reads Qur'ānic quotations from a laptop computer on his desk. My translation does not entirely represent the transcript of the original Arabic speech because that includes many more pauses, corrections, changes of words or sentences; translating all these would have made for a rather awkward written text. Despite this, the speaker does not appear to be confused or unsure about what he wants to say. He simply speaks naturally, occasionally gathering his thoughts, as opposed to reading from a script. He conveys the impression of giving a personal talk rather than a public speech. The setting contributes to this impression: he sits at his desk, he occasionally puts on his glasses, reads something off his screen, takes off his glasses and looks at his audience again. It is not an expensive set; there is no studio audience either. Al-Mālikī speaks in Modern Standard Arabic, with a very small amount of colloquialisms where anything else might have appeared too stiff.[57]

The lecture, which has a length of less than 13 minutes, originally constituted the second of two parts – interrupted by a commercial break – of an instalment of al-Mālikī's series *The Life of the Most Noble Prophet* (*Sīrat al-nabī al-akram*) on the Kuwaiti television station Al-Kout TV that was founded in 2010.[58] Nearly every television station in Muslim-majority countries has its Ramadan shows which run in daily instalments. This particular show already saw its second season in Ramadan 1434 when al-Mālikī gave his lecture on the Fātiḥa. The lecture was part of the third instalment of the season. The television station uploaded it to YouTube on 13 July 2013.[59] It did not attract much attention there; by April 2017, it had less than 2,300 views.

On 15 July 2013, however, a Saudi fan of al-Mālikī uploaded the second part of the instalment to YouTube under a new title: 'A shocking interpretation of the Fātiḥa, different from what the exegetes say' (*Tafsīr ṣādim li-sūrat al-Fātiḥa khilāfan li-mā qālahu al-mufassirūn*). By mid-April 2017, it had more than 270,000 views, between 150 and 200 per day. Nearly 3,000 viewers left a feedback; more than 80% of those liked the video.[60]

This clearly shows how the media of television and YouTube interact with each other. The television show probably had more viewers when it

Excerpt 3.3

In the name of God, the Merciful, the Compassionate, the Lord of all beings. Prayer and Peace be upon our prophet Muḥammad and upon his family and descendants who are good and pure. May God be pleased with his companions, those who migrated from Mecca, his helpers in Medina and the generation who followed them, and look kindly upon them until the Day of Judgement. *Ammā baʿd…*[61]

Of course, we have mentioned in the previous sessions of this show some points of reflection, some answers to the question whether we believe God in His book, whether we believe in what the Qurʾān tells us. We should not underestimate this question because there are degrees of faith; it may increase and decrease. There may be a progression with regard to belief in the words of God, mighty and majestic is He. Not everyone follows the same approach.

In the last session, we mentioned the group of those who will be saved (*al-firqa al-nājiya*). Today, I want focus on another point of reflection, which is none other than the Fātiḥa (the first *sūra* of the Qurʾān). This will be easy for everyone to follow because there is no Muslim today who doesn't know the Fātiḥa. However, the information that we already have in our minds diverts us from its actual meanings. Of course, knowing that – I seek refuge with God from the cursed Satan[62] – from the Basmala [Q. 1:1] to His utterance 'Guide us on the straight path [Q. 1:6]; the path…' – why did I skip ahead to the 'straight path' [i.e., why did I not discuss verses 1–5]?[63] Because the explanation of issues such as praise and mercy would be extensive. It might happen in other sessions. But the explanation of the straight path, that's easy. God said 'guide us on the straight path'. What is it? Unfortunately, the average exegete or *madrasa* teacher will all give you the same meaning; a meaning that is not helpful. What is the straight path? They say that it is the clear way, unobscured by anything; the clear way; the obvious way; sometimes it's the way of Islam. God says in the same *sūra* – and why do we not wait for God to explain it, with just a little patience? – 'guide us on the straight path, the path of those you have blessed'. Who are those whom God has blessed?

Don't just say 'the believers'. Extract the meaning from the Qur'ān. 'Those will be among the ones God has blessed: the prophets, the truthful, the *shuhadā'* and the righteous – what excellent companions these are!' [Q. 4:69] These four types of people are the ones God has blessed. It is necessary to clarify, to explain who they are. Because, for example, the word *shuhadā'* does not mean [as is usually claimed] 'those who have been killed in God's way'. Rather, it means 'one who says the truth', one who bears witness for God's sake. 'O you who believe, be witnesses for God'. [Q. 4:135] Calling the martyr in battle *shahīd* was derived from this meaning, not the other way around. Thus, being a *shahīd*, in the Qur'ān, means telling the word of truth, 'not fearing the blame of any blamer', [Q. 5:54] for God's sake. 'O you who believe, be witnesses for God'. [Q. 4:135] And He said: 'And [those] who stand by their testimony' [Q. 70:33].[64] This is just a small aspect of the explanation of those God has blessed. Those whom God has blessed are the four types of people: the prophets, the truthful, those who bear witness and the righteous.

'The path of those You have blessed, not of those who incur anger and who have gone astray', this is also of amazing depth. The commonplace opinion on those who have gone astray is that they are the Christians, sorry, the Jews – no, those who incur anger are the Jews and those who have gone astray are the Christians. However, this meaning that I would like for all, be they specialists in religious law or not, to pursue – of course it would require long explanations or reflections. If you wanted me to expand on it, I could do it in, like, seventy sessions because all of it are signs (*āyāt*). For example, with respect to the straight path, every verse from the Qur'ān that refers to the straight path needs to be mentioned if you want to expand on the topic. If you want to limit yourself to the Fātiḥa, then the straight path is the path of those You have blessed. Who are they? Then you can provide the *tafsīr*, as I just did.

Those who incur anger, who are they? Those who incur anger are not just the Jews. They are all those who have incurred God's anger according to the Qur'ān. After all, there are some Christians and Jews that He was pleased with or at least they did not incur His anger. God has also mentioned exceptions. 'There are some among the People of the Book who are upright' [Q. 3:113]; He does mention exceptions. What I am getting at is this. Now, of course, if we expanded on the reflection of the Fātiḥa, that would be beautiful, but also very extensive, and it would distract us from what I am getting at; here, we want to be brief. So, those who incur anger, who are they? Fractions from among the People of the Book of whom God said they ended up with wrath – that is, He said 'O People of the Book' – let's see – I seek refuge with God from the cursed Satan – let's see – they ended up with wrath upon wrath as it says in the second *sūra*: 'Low indeed is the price for which they have sold their souls by denying the God-sent truth, out of envy that God should send His bounty to any of His servants He pleases. They have ended up with wrath upon wrath' [Q. 2:90]. Those, for example, belong to the ones who incur anger.

The Qur'ān mentions certain types of People of the Book who have incurred God's anger. But doesn't it also mention types of Muslims who incur God's anger? Someone who kills a human being, for example. 'God is angry with him, curses him and has prepared a tremendous torment for him' [Q. 4:93].[65]

Alright, so why did we come to consider 'the path of those You have blessed' – why did we come to consider us Muslims the ones whom God has blessed while the ones who incur wrath are supposed to be the Jews and the ones who have gone astray the Christians? This division, this cultural sabotage, it was produced by – now, of course, we would need to go into more detail about this; I don't want to say anything harsh – but it was produced by a mix of politicians, People of the Book, hypocrites, criminals and simple-minded preachers. This mix of people produced, or brought forth, a culture of simplifying, of rendering the Book of God simplistic, not arriving at its actual meaning.

When we come, for example, to the straight path – alright, I'll make a very quick comment. The straight path belongs to the clearest things in the Book of God. That is, when someone asks you what the straight path is, then we are obliged to look for the straight path in the Qur'ān itself. For instance, among the most outstanding evidence for explaining what is the straight path is God's utterance in the sixth *sūra*: 'Say, Come! I will tell you what your Lord has really forbidden you. Do not ascribe anything as partner to Him; be good to your parents; do not kill your children fearing poverty. We will provide for you, and for them. Stay well away from committing obscenities, whether openly or in secret; do not take life, which God has made sacred, except by right. This is what He commands you to do, so that you may use your reason. Stay well away from the property of orphans, except with the best [intentions], until they come of age; give full measure and weight – *give full measure and weight – I seek refuge with God from the cursed Satan* – according to justice; we do not burden any soul with more than it can bear. When you speak, be just, even if it concerns a relative. Fulfil God's covenant. This is what he commands you to do so you may be reminded. This is my path, leading straight, so follow it, and do not follow other ways lest they take you away from His path. This is what he commands you to do so you may be Godfearing'. [Q. 6:151–153]

From these verses in the sixth *sūra*, the researcher may – now, among you, there may be ordinary people who don't have the means – for example, he may not know what the straight path is, so God provided an explanation in the Fātiḥa itself: the path of those You have blessed. But the researcher may add to this explanation of the straight path in the Qur'ān by searching and by finding the aforementioned attributes. That is, whoever, from among all religious groups, possesses these attributes is on the straight path. So, everyone who doesn't ascribe anything as partner to Him, is good to his parents, doesn't kill, you know, his children, fearing poverty, gives full measure and weight, and is just, and fulfils God's covenant, and so forth – these attributes are part of the straight path.

They show, by the way, that the Qur'ān is a book that speaks to human nature [*kitāb fiṭrī*], that is, a human book, not a book particularly for Muslims. Whoever thinks that it belongs to us, not to, you know, the West or the East – that is, the other peoples, the non-Muslim peoples, maybe they possess these attributes more than we do. Justice in speech, in particular, and not killing, not diminishing the goods of people [Q. 26:183], compassion with orphans: all these things are there, they have them in abundance. And therefore, we have to be careful not to be misled by the issue of Muslims and similar notions, us being Muslims and the others being unbelievers (*kuffār*, sg. *kāfir*) and so on. According to the Book, according to the Qur'ān and the Arabic language, the *kāfir* is only called a *kāfir* when he has knowledge and then renounces it. This is another topic that we need to clarify. We do not call a Muslim a Muslim in the full sense of the word either unless he submits himself to the decree of God. There may be people who are outwardly Muslim and inwardly unbelievers (*kāfir*); God knows their unbelief best. And there may be people who are outwardly unbelievers and inwardly Muslims according to the insights and knowledge they possess. So, let's not look down upon our fellow human beings, whether they be Muslim or non-Muslim.

This Qur'ān is a beacon of divine guidance. It breathes fresh air into you; your conscience is uplifted rather than falling asleep. And you see all these millions of people in hell and wonder about God's justice. And you have come very close to yourself, to your soul. And God gives you, he gives you peace of mind and confidence that God does not burden any soul with more than it can bear and that God is the Lord of all beings and that God does not unjustly deprive people even of 'the weight of a speck of dust' [Q. 99:7–8]. These meanings are among the blessings of God's book.

In my occupation with the Prophet's biography in the upcoming session we will discover that the social groups among whom the Prophet lived did not recognise these meanings, or most of them did not; they squandered knowledge and neglected reflection. This is mentioned in the Book of God in acerbic criticism; criticism of those social groups that existed in the time of the Prophet. Of course, we cannot generalise; there is also praise for those who believe and observe. But the Prophet faced the reality that there was a lack of reflection, of obedience [to God] and of certainty in many things. And this, this – the disease is old; the disease that we suffer from today was there. Its treatment is the Qur'ān, which is what the Prophet tried to explain. But hypocrisy was much more widespread towards the end of the Prophet's time than at its beginning. There was a lot of hypocrisy at the end of the Prophet's time, as evidenced by the fact that the Medinan *sūra*s, such as *sūra* nine and five – the fifth *sūra* being the last one, we will begin our next session with it – mentions severe criticism of the people. And this severe criticism comes at the end of the Prophet's lifetime, in the fifth *sūra* and in the ninth, which they called 'the pecking [or: scrutinising] one;' it hardly spared anyone.

So, in the next sessions, we will start to look at the life of the most noble prophet. Peace be upon you, God's mercy and blessings.[66]

was first aired although there is no reliable way to know this. The long-term impact of YouTube, however, is potentially much higher, and this is predominantly made possible by the existence of a fan base and of social media influencers who like and share content.

What makes this *tafsīr* so 'shocking', though? Why did it attract so many views and a relatively favourable rating?

It is certainly a more thoughtful interpretation than the average *tafsīr* sermon or lesson. But what really makes it different, as the YouTube title claims, can only be understood in relation to those mainstream interpretations that al-Mālikī politely renounces which are precisely the ones that have been described in the previous section. Furthermore, al-Mālikī's Saudi context needs to be taken into account. His talk has a defensive quality in that he continuously expresses his regret over not being able to discuss his subject matter at more detail, referring to the deep and complex nature of the issues he is only able to superficially address.

Both in the mainstream commentaries and in the Saudi context, the exegetical *ḥadīth* that identifies those who incur wrath as the Jews and those who go astray as the Christians is pervasive. In Saudi Arabia, it is accepted as the correct interpretation of Q. 1:7 to the degree that it was made part of several Saudi Qur'ān translations published by the King Fahd Complex for the Printing of the Holy Qur'ān in Medina, such as the English translation by Hilâlî and Khân and the Indonesian translation.[67] The application of this *ḥadīth* to the interpretation of the Fātiḥa fits the Salafi paradigm that is dominant in the country, both in its reliance on *ḥadīth* as a source of exegesis and in its content that clearly distinguishes Muslims from non-Muslims and those who are saved (*al-firqa al-nājiya*) from those who will go to hell. Al-ʿArīfī with his insistence that only true Muslims are blessed by God is typical of this trend. The other YouTube exegetes largely subscribe to the exclusion of non-Muslims from those whom God has blessed as well, albeit in softened terms – with the exception of the Imami Shiʿi al-Qazwīnī who is even harsher than al-ʿArīfī.

Al-Mālikī, however, sharply rejects the interpretation of 'the average exegete or *madrasa* teacher'. He does not even link it to a *ḥadīth*, but merely dismisses it as 'not helpful'. He then proposes his own interpretation that he purports to derive from the Qur'ān. That al-Mālikī is no trained religious scholar is evident from the fact that he needs to read Qur'ānic quotations off his computer screen. Still, the Qur'ān is so central to his argument that one might call his method *tafsīr al-Qur'ān bi'l-Qur'ān*[68] which is exactly what he means when he asks his listeners to 'extract the meaning from the Qur'ān'. His talk is interspersed with Qur'ānic quotations that are not always marked as such. Their function is often to explain segments of the Fātiḥa such as that referring to those whom God has blessed. Here, al-Mālikī refers to Q. 4:69 which describes that group. That reference is not exactly innovative in this context; Sofiane Kabir, for example, has it as well. But while Kabir simply and conventionally explains *al-shuhadā'* as 'martyrs' and *al-ṣāliḥūn* as Muslims or believers, al-Mālikī goes to great lengths to first expose the notion of martyrdom as un-Qur'ānic and, secondly, to deconstruct the sharp division between Muslims and non-Muslims.

The deconstruction of the notion that Muslims are identical to believers and constitute the only group that will be saved is the central message of al-Mālikī's *tafsīr*, and it is indeed an exceptional message in popular interpretations of the Fātiḥa. Al-Mālikī points to those occasions in the Qur'ān on which Jews and Christians have not incurred anger and to other occasions on which Muslims have incurred anger. Mainstream doctrine nevertheless ended up identifying those who are blessed as Muslims and those who incur wrath and go astray as Jews and Christians. Al-Mālikī calls this 'cultural sabotage' and, much in contrast to the Salafi paradigm of the rightly-guided first generations of Islam, attributes it to corruption in the very early period of Islamic history and even in the Prophet's lifetime. He firmly states that justice, compassion and good deeds are not the exclusive possession of Muslims and that non-Muslims may even surpass Muslims in these areas. In order to further weaken the sharp distinction between non-Muslims and Muslims, he deconstructs the terms *muslim* and *kāfir* which is much in line with modernist perspectives on Qur'ānic semantics such as that of Fazlur Rahman.[69] He also seems to have a conception of *shirk* that differs starkly from that of Saudi mainstream doctrine since he does not see in the reference to those who associate partners with God in Q. 6:151 a cause for concern regarding his positive assessment of non-Muslims. Apparently, he does not link the notion of *shirk* with contemporary non-Muslims at all.

It is not only the deconstruction of Muslim eschatological exceptionalism that makes al-Mālikī's interpretation a rather bold one, especially in a Saudi context, but even more so the corruption narrative that he connects with early Islamic history, including the last years of the Prophet's life. By claiming that the correct understanding of the Qur'ān has been subverted even then, he questions fundamental assumptions of Sunni Islam which is the most controversial aspect of his thought in general. This ties in with the marked reverence he shows to the Prophet's family and descendants in his preamble which is indicative of his sympathy for Shi'i views on early Islamic history.

Al-Mālikī employs a number of interpretive methods and strategies that have become popular in modernist approaches to the Qur'ān, but that have also faced a lot of opposition. Broadly speaking, they are characterised by an emphasis on historical contextualisation, a renewed look at Qur'ānic semantics and utterances from the perspective of the Qur'ān's first audience and a sceptical attitude towards both the corpus of *ḥadīth*s and the premodern exegetical tradition. These methodological approaches and their application to concrete exegetical problems will be the subject of the next chapter.

NOTES

1. See page 191, 'Science and the *i'jāz* paradigm'.
2. For the impact of print culture on the reception of the Islamic tradition, with a focus on the field of law and the works of Abū Ḥanīfa, but with a description of

many of the same actors that were instrumental in shaping the modern reception of the *tafsīr* tradition, see Khan, 'Islamic Tradition in an Age of Print'.

3. Brigaglia, '*Tafsīr* and the Intellectual History of Islam in West Africa'.
4. Al-Qāsimī, *Jamāl al-Dīn al-Qāsimī wa-ʿaṣruhū*, 679–685.
5. Pink, 'Muhammad al-Shawkānī', 355.
6. Pink, 'The Fig, the Olive', 311.
7. Preckel, 'Islamische Reform im Indien des 19. Jahrhunderts'.
8. See their website at <http://www.aalalbayt.org>.
9. Bauer, *Gender Hierarchy in the Qur'ān*, 73.
10. In Persian transliteration, ʿAbd al-ʿAlī Bāzargān. In this section, I use the spelling Bazargan himself uses in English.
11. Bazargan, *Zindigīnāmih*; Bazargan, *In the Presence of the Sublime Qur'an*, xii–xv.
12. Ibid., 360–362. Text originally in English.
13. Ibid., xiv.
14. See the website of the Evecina Cultural and Educational Foundation at <http://www.ecef.org/index.php>.
15. Bazargan, *Kilās-i Qurʾān.*
16. Bazargan, 'Maqālāt wa-āthār-e qalamī: Sharḥī bar sūra-hā-yi Qurʾān'.
17. At the time of writing this section in late March 2017, the last update had been on 6 February 2017. Bazargan also has produced several other apps on Islamic themes, such as a class on the correct performance of the hajj and an introduction into the life and thought of the Iranian revolutionary Islamic thinker ʿAlī Sharīʿātī (1933–1977).
18. Bazargan, *In the Presence of the Sublime Qur'an*, x–xi.
19. See ibid., 194, n. 1.
20. Ibid., 159, n. 2.
21. Bazargan, Sūra-yi ʿAṣr.
22. Bazargan, 'Tafsīr-i sūra-yi ʿAṣr'.
23. The notes in the book are usually carefully marked either as 'author's note' or 'editor's note'.
24. See Q. 3:104, 3:110, 7:157, 9:71, 9:112, 22:41, 31:17.
25. For more on the exegetical trend to assume a coherent structure (*naẓm*) underlying the Qurʾān, which Bazargan subscribes to, see page 185, 'The 'system' (naẓm) and structure of the Qurʾān'.
26. Bazargan, *In the Presence of the Sublime Qur'an*, 207–208.
27. Ibid., 404–406.
28. Ibid., 313.
29. Jansen, *The Interpretation of the Koran in Modern Egypt*, 44–45. So far, there is no study specifically of Ṭanṭāwī Jawharī's use of pictures.
30. Mustaqim, *Tafsir Juz 'Amma for Kids*, vol. 2, 80.
31. Ibid., vol. 2, 79.
32. Source: an instant messenger conversation (i.e., online chat) with Abdul Mustaqim on 13 April 2017.
33. This section aims at giving an accurate impression of the complete commentary on Q. 104 in order to enable the reader to understand its didactic approach. However, since the commentary extends over 16 pages with just as many large pictures, a selection had to be made. Therefore, the translation focusses on the second part of the commentary's message, concerning its warning against the amassment of

wealth. It only shows the pictures that have a bearing on this and significantly shortens the content that is unrelated to this topic.

34. Mustaqim, *Tafsir Juz 'Amma for Kids*, vol. 2, 1–16. Text originally in Indonesian.
35. With respect to the description of hell, the translation of v. 9 contains a lot of interpretation. The verse itself merely refers to towering, long or extended columns, which might as well be columns of fire, and does not mention people being tied to columns. A few early exegetical opinions exist that understand the verse as referring to a kind of pillory (cited, e.g., by al-Zamakhsharī and in Abū Ḥayyān's *al-Baḥr al-Muḥīṭ*), but these were not very prominent in works of *tafsīr* and do not seem to have convinced any author of major English translations. In Indonesian Qurʾān translations, however, the explanation presented here as the meaning of the verse is widespread and seems to have prevailed since Mahmud Yunus' (1899–1982) translation which dates from colonial times which might be an interesting indication of the emergence of national exegetical traditions. The illustrated Qurʾānic commentary analysed here uses the Indonesian government translation. It is unlikely that the rendition of v. 9 goes back to a conscious decision by the author.
36. This is discussed at length in Federspiel, *Popular Indonesian Literature of the Qur'an*.
37. See page 181, 'Islamist Qurʾānic interpretation'.
38. Al-Bāz, *Al-Qurʾān fī Miṣr*, 69–76.
39. Ikhwan, An Indonesian Initiative to Make the Qur'an Down-to-Earth.
40. Görke, 'Redefining the Borders of *Tafsīr*'.
41. The actual number of views for each of the exegetical performances represented in the videos is difficult to figure out since there are often numerous versions of the same material available online, sometimes with different intros, subtitles or partitions into shorter videos, but in each case, at least one of those videos was ranked very high among the relevant material in the respective language.
42. Qadhi, 'Tafsir Surat al-Fatihah 18'. See also Qadhi, *Shaykh Dr Yasir Qadhi: Official YouTube Channel.*
43. Khan, 'Rediscovering the Fatihah'. See also Free Quran Education, 'The Life of Nouman Ali Khan'; Bayyinah.com, *History*.
44. Khan, '*FULL* Divine Speech'.
45. Khan, 'Deeper Look at Al Fatihah'.
46. Khan, 'GET TO KNOW'.
47. Menk, 'Tafseer of Surah Al Fatiha'. See also Menk, *Mufti Menk*.
48. Menk, 'Mufti Menk'.
49. Kabir, 'Explication de la sourate Al Fâtiha'. See also Comité Jeunesse de la mosquée Assakina de Farciennes, 'Qui est Sofiane Kabir?'
50. The version I have used here is al-Shaʿrāwī, *Tafsīr sūrat al-Fātiḥa*. On al-Shaʿrāwī see also Pink, *Sunnitischer Tafsīr in der modernen islamischen Welt*, 95–98.
51. Al-ʿArīfī, 'Maʿānī sūrat al-Fātiḥa'. See also Al Arabiya News, 'Britain Bans Controversial Saudi Cleric'.
52. Al-Nābulusī, 'Tafsīr sūrat al-Fātiḥa 001'; al-Nābulusī, 'Tafsīr sūrat al-Fātiḥa 002'; al-Nābulusī, 'Tafsīr sūrat al-Fātiḥa kāmila'. See also Mawsūʿat al-Nābulūsī, 'Al-Sīra al-dhātiyya'.
53. Al-Qazwīnī, 'Tafsīr al-Qurʾān al-karīm'; see also Office of Ayatollah Sayid Mortadha Al-Qazwini, 'Biography'.
54. Hirschkind, *The Ethical Soundscape*.

55. Lacroix, 'Between Islamists and Liberals', 350–352.
56. Husayn, 'Pro-Alid Sunnis'; Al Bawaba News, 'Saudi Officials Arrest Sunni Cleric'; Haidar, 'After the Prophet'; Wikipedia contributors, 'Ḥasan Farḥān al-Mālikī'. See also al-Mālikī's personal website at <http://almaliky.org/index.php>.
57. For instance, he occasionally uses *wa-kadhā* for 'and so forth' and once *shwayy, shwayy* for 'slowly'.
58. See the Al-Kout TV website at <http://alkoutnews.net/من-نحن>.
59. Tilifizyūn al-Kūt, 'Barnāmaj sīrat al-nabī al-akram'.
60. Al-Mālikī, 'Tafsīr ṣādim li-sūrat al-Fātiḥa'.
61. Arabic sermons and some other genres of texts such as letters start with a preamble that may contain prayers, greetings, expressions of gratitude, eulogies of varying length. These may be generic or adapted to the occasion of speech. After the preamble, the phrase *ammā baʿd* signals the beginning of the main text.
62. An invocation that is typically uttered when reciting the Qurʾān, based on Q. 16:98. Al-Mālikī also uses it when he has made a mistake in his recitation.
63. The sentence is incomplete and changes track twice in the original.
64. Q. 70:35 concludes the sentence of which v. 33 is a part: 'These will be honoured in Gardens'.
65. The verse specifically talks about the intentional killing of a believer (*muʾmin*). Most premodern exegetes are not concerned with whether the same applies to the killing of any human, as al-Mālikī implies; they are more interested in the theological controversy over whether it is possible for a Muslim to sin so gravely that he is condemned to eternal hellfire as a result, and if it is possible, whether this is only true for those who do not repent their deed.
66. Al-Mālikī, 'Tafsīr ṣādim li-sūrat al-Fātiḥa'. Text originally in Arabic. The English translation is based on my own transcript of the video, slightly modified to correct for mistakes, repetitions and pauses.
67. Wild, 'Muslim Translators and Translations of the Qurʾan into English', 173–174; Pink, '"Literal Meaning" or "Correct *ʿaqīda*"?', 112–113.
68. See page 154, '*Tafsīr al-Qurʾān bi'l-Qurʾān*'.
69. See page 150, 'Semantics and the 'literal meaning''.

4

MODERNISM AND ITS PARADIGMS

MODERNISM AND OTHER LABELS

The central theme of modernist exegetical trends, when they emerged in the late-nineteenth century, was to read the Qur'ān as a guide to social reform. Depending on the exegete, the concrete aims of that reform might include an improved system of education in which foreign languages, science and technology were taught, an overhaul of existing structures of government in order to lessen corruption and increase accountability, the abolition of slavery and the improvement of the status of women. Freedom from traditional modes of thinking, which were labelled *taqlīd* – the blind following of earlier authorities – and equated with authoritarianism and superstition, is a common demand. Thus, at least a certain degree of liberalism and egalitarianism is always involved in modernism. The rejection of violence is a more complex issue since some modernists tied the notion of jihad to anticolonial resistance and thus considered it legitimate.[1] In more recent decades, modernists have increasingly come to reject all forms of religiously legitimated violence; the propagation of defensive jihad in the sense of warfare, by contrast, was mostly upheld by parts of the Islamist spectrum which will be discussed later.[2]

Modernist readings of the Qur'ān often advocate the use of reason, rather than the authority of existing interpretations, in order to arrive at the correct understanding of the Qur'ān. Modernists typically aim at reading the Qur'ān in its historical context and in light of its higher aims (*maqāṣid*), rather than literally applying every individual prescription. When modernists speak in favour of treating the Qur'ān as 'divine guidance' (*hidāya*), as opposed to an obscure text with metaphysical power, an object of detached academic scholarship or a specific penal code, it is to these higher aims that they usually refer. They tend to focus on ethical norms. While rationalism, egalitarianism and the values of liberal democracy are defining features of modernist exegesis, not every aspect of these is necessarily endorsed to the same degree – an exegete might well advocate women's rights, but be opposed to the acceptance of homosexuality. Sometimes, but not always, there is an apologetic impetus associated with these ideas. Whereas Salafis would rather tend to defend the existence of gender hierarchies as being appropriate to human nature and beneficial to social order, a modernist might maintain that any kind of gender hierarchy is against the true intention of the Qurʾān and that accusations of misogyny against Islam are therefore baseless. Often, this amounts to the claim of having uncovered the 'true meaning' of the Qurʾān after it had lain dormant for centuries due to the exegetes' embeddedness in patriarchal and authoritarian societies.

Modernist exegetes do not necessarily reject every single component of the premodern scholarly tradition, but nor do they regard it as authoritative. Some hardly make use of it while others draw on it selectively when a component of it suits their intention. An increasingly popular reference, for example, is al-Shāṭibī's (d. 1388) theory of *maqāṣid al-sharīʿa*, the higher aims of Islamic law by which the individual prescriptions should be interpreted, an idea that is often transferred to the interpretation of the Qurʾān. Modernism has also brought forth its own exegetical authorities such as Muḥammad ʿAbduh, his disciple Aḥmad Muṣṭafā al-Marāghī (1883–1952) and the Austrian-born convert from Judaism Muhammad Asad (1900–1992). This has the paradoxical effect that some types of modernism – those that mainly reproduce the views of earlier modernist authorities – might actually appear fairly conservative in a twenty-first-century setting, for example when men are encouraged to provide women with an education so that they are better suited to be good wives and mothers.

Modernists emphasise the need to find individual, rational solutions to concrete problems, solutions that are appropriate to their place and time. Therefore, they make ample use of the pragmatic instruments provided by Islamic law. This includes legal devices such as the public interest (*maṣlaḥa*), overriding need (*ḍarūra*) and the assumption that God has made it easy for humans to follow His religion and therefore places no undue burden on any one (*taysīr*). Generally, discussions of ethics and social questions are far more common in modernist Qurʾānic interpretation than those concerning theological issues such as the nature and duration of hell or the attributes of God, which does not mean that the latter do not occur at all.[3]

Modernists are sometimes *ʿulamāʾ* by training. In those cases, it is their sceptical attitude towards traditional Islamic learning that qualifies them as modernists. Muḥammad ʿAbduh, who had studied at al-Azhar in Cairo, but was rather disenchanted with this institution, is a case in point. Others, especially in the late-nineteenth and first half of the twentieth centuries, received a hybrid education in both traditional Islamic schools and secular institutions although these secular institutions might still have drawn on Islam as a source of morality. A third group, especially among the more recent modernists, have received no formal religious education at all.

This development is closely connected to the loss of the scholars' monopoly on education and the rise of print culture in the late-nineteenth century which brought forth a new class of intellectuals operating outside the social domain and traditional discourse of the *ʿulamāʾ*. Today, the extent to which *ʿulamāʾ* operate by modernist paradigms – or to which religious intellectuals adopting modernist paradigms would describe themselves as *ʿulamāʾ* – depends much on the religious and educational institutions of the country they work in. For example, modernism is fairly widespread in Turkish university theology, albeit frequently under attack and often contested. Its proponents are more similar to university professors from other disciplines than to traditional *ʿulamāʾ* with regard to the way they dress, speak and write. In Saudi Arabia, much the opposite is the case. Iran's Shiʿi seminaries host a wide variety of scholars, some of whom clearly identify as clerics but are staunchly modernist at the same time.

There is an activist component to modernism. Some of its proponents come from a context of social reform or the fight against specific kinds of discrimination, for example women's activism[4] or campaigns against racism. Here, a modernist interpretation of the Qurʾān can be an important instrument aimed at convincing Muslim communities that the person's or group's agenda does not clash with Islam but is instead the result of a rational reading of the Qurʾān.[5]

What I call 'modernist' is labelled as 'reformist' or 'revisionist' by other authors. Revisionism and reformism might pertain to a wide variety of aims, though, whereas modernism is connected to the idea of making Islam 'modern', adapting it to the requirements of our time and the standards of our age, which are broadly considered to entail rationalism, egalitarianism and liberalism. These are also the aims of the reform project connected with modernism, and as such, modernism is by definition reformist; but there are other strands of reformism whose idea of reconstituting an idealised past leads them towards a Salafi paradigm and drives them to reject the ideas connected to the modernist project. Therefore, modernism is not only defined by its hermeneutics, but also by the broad content of its aims and by its proponents' self-identification. These last two aspects also distinguish it from exegetical projects that use modernist hermeneutical tools, but pursue socially conservative aims, which happens both in scholarly and in Islamist contexts.[6]

A 'modernist' approach to the Qurʾān is not identical to a 'modern' one. The term 'modern' has many layers of meaning. It is sometimes used in a normative sense, as a synonym for liberal democracy and therefore superior to less 'modern' approaches, erroneously suggesting that 'modernity' is an exclusively positive force. At other instances, it is used in a purely chronological sense, denoting all developments that occurred since the nineteenth century. The term thus has the potential to create confusion.

As for the increasingly popular label of 'progressive Islam', it is a self-descriptor for such ideas that pursue a liberal and egalitarian agenda. In that respect, it is much in line with modernism, but also includes the hermeneutically more open approaches that I call postmodern.[7] As an analytical tool, the label of progressivism is problematic because it implies a historical movement – or progression – into a direction that is considered desirable, which is a normative assessment that would be out of place in an analytical study.

This chapter will give an overview of the most common exegetical strategies and methods proposed and used by modernists. These might as well be called 'hermeneutics', but I use the term sparingly. Among Muslim exegetes, scholars and intellectuals, the concept of 'hermeneutics' is heavily contested because it is often taken to refer to a specific theory of text interpretation that does not presuppose a fixed and clear meaning, but takes into account the understanding of the historical and contemporary readers. This approach to Qur'ānic interpretation is considered indispensable by some Muslims and heretical by others.[8] When I talk of hermeneutics, in this book, I use the term in a more general sense unless otherwise noted; not in the sense of a specific theory of text interpretation, but as an umbrella term for the interpretive frame of reference and the sum of the methods applied by an exegete. Since this book focusses on applied exegesis exclusively, this chapter will limit itself to discussing those strategies that exegetes use to extract meaning from the text of the Qur'ān and on the results that they generate, rather than presenting larger hermeneutical models.[9] In as far as these models have a discernible impact on current exegetical projects, this will of course be mentioned.

MAQĀṢID, OR THE QUR'ĀN'S HIGHER AIMS

Literally, *maqāṣid* – an extremely popular term in contemporary legal methodology as well as exegesis – denotes goals, intentions or objectives. At the core of this methodology is the idea of overarching aims that should govern the interpretation of individual utterances. The *maqāṣid* approach allows an exegete to move away from the straightforward meaning of a specific Qur'ānic utterance and embed it in a larger system of meaning.

The term *maqāṣid al-Qur'ān* is not entirely new, but most premodern exegetes who mentioned it simply understood it in the sense of large, general themes such as theology and not so much in the sense of specific goals. Al-Biqāʿī (1406–1480) wrote an extensive work on the *maqāṣid* of the *sūras*[10] which was innovative in its time, but seems to have only found recognition in the twentieth century when interest in the *maqāṣid* methodology rose.[11]

Rashīd Riḍā was possibly the most important early proponent of the *maqāṣid* idea in the twentieth century. He published a long programmatic excursus as part of his *Tafsīr al-Manār* in 1930 and converted it into a separate book under the title 'The Muhammadan Revelation' (*Al-Waḥy al-Muḥammadī*) that was published in 1933. After an intensely apologetic first part, Rashīd Riḍā expounded his vision of the Qur'ān's ten main aims (*maqāṣid*) that should define how specific statements within the text are understood. The first of these contains the basic tenets of religious belief and practice and the second the existence and purpose of prophethood. The remaining eight *maqāṣid* focus on the theme of reform: the development of man's intellect and the prohibition of *taqlīd* (blind following of a school of law or, more generally, earlier authorities); social and political reform through Muslim unity; the instigation of responsibility through duties and prohibitions; the principles of an Islamic political order; economic reform; the main tenets of just war; the improvement of women's rights; and the emancipation of slaves.[12]

Other important modern exegetes who emphasised the need to conceptualise the *maqāṣid* dimension in any work of *tafsīr* were al-Ṭāhir b. ʿĀshūr (1879–1973), who was strongly influenced by modernist debates on legal methodology, and Muḥammad ʿIzzat Darwaza (1888–1984) who advocated a comprehensive look at the Qur'ānic message and its historical development. Darwaza distinguished between the essential goals of the Qur'ān, or its fundamentals, and the secondary details of implementation (*wasā'il*), warning against focussing on the secondary details at the expense of the essentials.[13]

More recent concepts of the Qur'ān's higher aims have outlined a clearer methodology that allows for applying the idea to a concrete exegetical project. Possibly the most prominent proponent is Fazlur Rahman. His assumption was that the Qur'ānic message is based on general ethical values, but mainly responds to specific problems of Arab society at Muḥammad's time. Therefore, interpreting the Qur'ān today requires a 'double movement'. The present-day reader has to move into the past, to the historical context of the Qur'ān's revelation, and then back to the present. First, the reader needs to study the historical situation or the problem to which a Qur'ānic statement was the answer. Then, the general intent and the *ratio legis* behind those specific answers have to be identified so that general moral and social objectives, rather than responses to a specific problem that might be irrelevant to today's society, can be distilled from the text. Finally, the general objective has to be applied to a specific contemporary social context.[14] All this is based on the assumption that the exegete possesses a full understanding of both the past and the present. While Fazlur Rahman never applied this hermeneutical theory to a concrete exegetical project, it proved hugely influential on later modernist and postmodern exegetes.

The main field to which the *maqāṣid* theory is applied is that of social ethics. For example, with respect to polygamy as it appears to be permitted in Q. 4:3, a stereotypical *maqāṣid*-based argument would be that in pre-Islamic society, men could have an unlimited number of wives with no fixed obligations concerning their treatment. Islam came to improve this situation and to introduce restrictions on men's rights over women, but could only do so to the extent that would have been acceptable in seventh-century Arab society and compatible with its social structure. Therefore, the number of wives was limited to four and the Qur'ān enjoined men to treat them equitably. An exegete might now focus either on those secondary rules, as exegetes have done for centuries, or on the general goal behind them, which is to ensure fairness, happiness in marriage and the best possible situation for wives. If the latter, *maqāṣid*-oriented approach is pursued, the result might be that in today's society, monogamy is a better option for achieving the Qur'ān's larger ethical goals than the detailed prescriptions about polygamy in the Qur'ān.[15] More traditional or Salafi exegetes, on the other hand, would argue that the Qur'ān set these detailed prescriptions for all societies at all times and that they *are* the goals of the Qur'ān. Islamists often consider them part of the Islamic system or way of life. They would argue that it is presumptuous for a human to distinguish between essential and less essential, or eternal and time-bound parts of the Qur'ān when, in reality, all of them are essential, especially since the Qur'ān itself does not explicitly state that the validity of some of its prescriptions is limited.

At the core of the controversy is the exegetes' perspective on history and on the Qur'ān's place in history. A teleological, *maqāṣid*-based approach argues that the Qur'ān was revealed in a particular historical context and that this historical context shaped the ways in which God's higher aims were put into practice – a practice that was not meant to be prescriptive for all eternity, but only for a specific society. This assumption requires some knowledge of that society, for example concerning its marriage practices.

The *maqāṣid* approach is connected to a dynamic view of history according to which societies evolve towards an ideal of egalitarianism and tolerance which is associated with the Qur'ān's higher aims. Opposing views essentially embrace a static view of history according to which differences between societies are negligible and unrelated to evolutionary principles. Proponents of such views might accommodate for a certain degree of variation, for instance by pointing to the fact that Islam allows polygamy, but does not make it obligatory, thus leaving some room for individuals to adapt their lifestyles to a specific society's needs; but there would be no reason to ban the practice altogether. An even more poignant example is slavery. An evolutionary view of the Qur'ān's social ethos would argue that the abolition of slavery is the ultimate goal whereas exegetes with a static view of history argue that it is possible to abolish slavery when there is no need for it in a given historical situation, but it is just as possible to reintroduce it at a later moment in history.[16] History, the view of history and its function for the interpretation of the Qur'ān are thus central points of contention in contemporary exegetical methodology.

HISTORICAL CONTEXTUALISATION AND ITS SOURCES

Visions of history and particularly of early Islamic history assume a number of functions in the exegesis of the Qur'ān. Some of them go back to premodern scholarly traditions while others are fairly recent methodological innovations. All of them are contested.

Before early Islamic history can assume any function in the interpretation of the Qur'ān, the historical events surrounding the origins of the Qur'ān in general and the first proclamation of particular *sūra*s or verses in particular have to be established. After all, the Qur'ān is said to have been revealed throughout a period of roughly 22 years (*c.* 610–622) during which the circumstances of Muḥammad and the early Muslim community were subject to dramatic changes. This leads to the question of what sources on the history of the Qur'ān might be reliable and legitimate.

The most obvious historical source of exegesis would be the so-called 'occasions of revelation' (*asbāb al-nuzūl*). These are stories telling an event from the life of the Prophet, for instance a litigation or an occasion on which he was asked for advice. Subsequently, a specific verse is revealed that offers an answer to the problem at hand, confirms the Prophet's opinion or, in some cases, corrects it.

Problems with this material abound. For a start, occasions of revelation are only available for a minority of verses. When they are, it frequently happens that several contradictory occasions of revelation are reported. In other instances, an identical story is cited as occasion of revelation for different verses. Occasions of revelation are usually related to one verse or a small group of verses only. The result is that consecutive verses might be connected to occasions of revelation that point to widely divergent periods of revelation, regardless of whether the verses form a textual unit or not. This was not usually a problem for premodern exegetes who went through the Qur'ān, verse by verse, gathered the relevant material connected to each verse and rarely aimed at establishing a larger context. They also were not usually interested in historical criticism of the *asbāb al-nuzūl* material for its own sake.[17] Only if there were conflicting traditions on the occasion of revelation of a verse, they sometimes made a selection based on plausibility – historical, contextual or otherwise. At other times, they ignored the contradiction or tried to harmonise the divergent stories.

In the twentieth century, criticism of the transmitted occasions of revelation became more frequent. Critical scholarship has shown that a large proportion of the material comes from the biographical tradition and has only been connected to the Qurʾān at a later stage.[18] Even if an exegete does not take that critical scholarship into account, as is often the case, there are several reasons for which contemporary exegetes tend to assume a more sceptical approach to the material. First, they more commonly look at larger units of text or even entire *sūra*s. This causes them to wonder whether the *sabab al-nuzūl* of a verse fits the larger context, the occasions reported about previous or subsequent, verses and the assumed timing of the entire *sūra*.[19] Second, modernist exegetes in particular have a dynamic view of history according to which societies change and these changes have meaning.[20] Therefore, many of them are acutely aware that an occasion of revelation needs to be plausible on more than a semantic level; it needs to be historically plausible both in relation to the verse and to the timing of the entire *sūra*. Third, many contemporary exegetes are not willing to tolerate the ambiguity involved in reporting several conflicting narratives; they prefer to settle for one unambiguous solution which forces them to critically look at the material. It has to be pointed out, however, that not all contemporary exegetes take a critical perspective on the *asbāb al-nuzūl*. There are still many interpreters of the Qurʾān who are perfectly content to take them at face value.

Another problem with the material is that, while many occasions of revelation provide a narrative context for a specific verse, they are not necessarily helpful for dating it. When unspecified persons come to the Prophet seeking advice, this does not tell us very much. At most, it might be taken to indicate the Medinan period, after the *hijra*, because only then did the Prophet hold a position of authority. Even that deduction is only possible, however, when the basic mainstream narrative of the Prophet's life and of the revelation of the Qurʾān is taken for granted.

The history of Muḥammad's life and the revelation of the Qurʾān are taken from works of prophetic biography (*sīra*), the related genre of the *maghāzī* literature that focusses on the Prophet's expeditions and battles and from *ḥadīth* reports.[21] Virtually all exegetes, no matter what their approach, take these at face value unless a dogmatic problem or an apologetic context force them to reconsider specific details. This occurs, for example, in controversies between Sunnis and Shiʿis or out of a desire to defend Islam against a Western Orientalist and/or Christian audience. The latter reason might lead exegetes to present purified or idealised versions of potentially problematic episodes of the Prophet's biography such as his supposed love for Zaynab bt. Jaḥsh (d. 641) who was repudiated by his foster son Zayd b. Ḥāritha (d. 629) before Muḥammad married her, based on Qurʾānic justification, or the infamous incident of the 'Satanic verses' that seemed to involve an outward acknowledgement of three Meccan goddesses on Muḥammad's part.[22] The details of particular events might thus be questioned by exegetes, but the validity of the overall narrative is rarely doubted, nor is a critical discussion of the sources and their authenticity a typical feature of exegetical works, regardless of whether they are written by traditional scholars or modernists.[23]

With the historical context thus more or less established, the question is what to do with it, which leads to the fundamental and unavoidable hermeneutical controversy around the question whether God's word was adapted to the specific historical circumstances of Muḥammad's society or not. If one accepts the premise that it was, which has been theorised in various ways,[24] this opens a whole new field of exegetical engagement with the Qurʾān. For if God's word was adapted to specific historical circumstances once, it could be adapted to today's circumstances as well. If it was transmitted in a code meant to be understood by seventh-century Arabs, it has to be translated into the code used by humans today. Furthermore, if previous exegetical works did no more than translate the Qurʾān into the code of their authors' times, this means they are not authoritative for a contemporary reader.

This approach can be framed in terms of modern communication theory, as the Egyptian Naṣr Ḥāmid Abū Zayd (1943–2010) did. Abū Zayd was also much indebted to the Japanese Islamicist Toshihiko Izutsu (1914–1993) and his works on the semantics of the Qurʾān.[25] Other exegetes seek to legitimise historical contextualisation within the framework of Muslim scholarship. For example, Muslim exegetes from a fairly early time onwards have distinguished between the general (*ʿāmm*) meaning of a verse and its particular (*khāṣṣ*) circumstances of revelation or the specific context of its first application. Unless there was a strong reason to limit its meaning to the particular circumstances, rather than the general meaning, the broader and more general interpretation was preferred. By reversing this principle, it is possible to understand many prescriptions in the Qurʾān as being suited to the specific circumstances of a by-gone era, not as timeless obligations.[26]

Most premodern approaches to Qurʾānic interpretation, and many contemporary ones that follow in their wake, do not consider context – either the Qurʾān's or the exegete's – an essential prerequisite of interpretation. They assume that the sources are timeless and that therefore the repertoire of exegetical methods and potential outcomes, while allowing for a certain diversity, is 'essentially stagnant and unchanging'.[27] If, on the other hand, the Qur'ān is read as a text that has to be understood in its historical context, for whatever reason, some of its concepts or concrete prescriptions will be seen as expressions of that context, rather than as eternally valid rules, and might consequently be modified or even abandoned today. This is probably one of the reasons for which most modernists and postmodernists, despite their critical approach to the Qur'ānic text, so often retain a fairly uncritical image of early Muslim history: they need that history in order to interpret the Qur'ān as a historical text, to contextualise it and to move away from a literal reading. Historical contextualisation fundamentally shapes the ways in which an exegete will deal with such central notions as that of social hierarchy, which is inherent in the Qur'ān's treatment of gender, religion and slavery. Are these hierarchies an immutable part of the Qur'ān or are they merely the outdated expression of the needs of a hierarchical society, open to an egalitarian reinterpretation?

While the historicisation of the Qur'ān is often undertaken by modernists and postmodernists in particular, hardly any exegetical approach is entirely free from it. Even Salafis employ it occasionally, although rarely explicitly, especially in internal debates about the appropriateness and excessiveness of specific practices described in the Qur'ān. For example, there was a debate, between ISIS and al-Qā'ida, on the applicability of the practice, mentioned in the Qur'ān, of 'smiting' the enemies' necks (Q. 8:12 and 47:4) which ISIS used as justification for the beheading of an American journalist. A representative of al-Qā'ida refuted that justification, arguing that beheading was the most humane method of execution that was at the Prophet's disposal and that it should today be replaced by any of the more humane methods of execution available to modern societies.[28]

The emphasis on historical context in the interpretation of the Qur'ān has become so commonplace that it has brought forth an entirely new genre of Qur'ānic commentary.

TAFSĪR IN THE ORDER OF REVELATION

In the course of the twentieth century, and especially in its second half, there was increasing discontent among intellectuals and scholars with the restrictions that the traditional genre of *tafsīr* entailed. Many of them felt that the method of commenting on the Qur'ān verse by verse in the canonical order created a risk of getting lost in details while missing the larger picture. It made it hard to analyse the Qur'ān's approach to larger themes, the development of semantics throughout the history of the text, to situate verses in a meaningful context and to actually provide the guidance that had become the overarching aim of much exegetical activity. In the second half of the twentieth century, new approaches were developed that were meant to tackle these problems. Some of them retained the label of *tafsīr* because, just like the classical Qur'ānic commentary, their aim was to engage with the entire Qur'ānic text.

One of them, and an increasingly common one, is the '*tafsīr* in the order of revelation' (*tafsīr ḥasab tartīb al-nuzūl*). The first work of this type was written by the Palestinian intellectual Muḥammad ʿIzzat Darwaza who was an Arab nationalist with the aim of reconnecting the Arab youth with their national and religious heritage (*turāth*). In order to achieve his aim he wrote a 'modern *tafsīr*'. He rejected the idea of the Qur'ān being an entirely transcendental, heavenly scripture whose timeless message is disconnected from the environment in which it was revealed. Rather, he thought that the Qur'ān was intimately linked with the biography of Muḥammad as well as the Arab society of the time. Therefore, his 'Modern *Tafsīr*' (*Al-Tafsīr al-ḥadīth*), while fairly conventional in its verse-by-verse approach to the entire Qur'ān, arranged the *sūra*s in the order in which they had supposedly been revealed – or rather, in the order in which he thought they had been revealed since there is no consensus on the precise chronology of the *sūra*s, as the example in the next section will show.

In any case, Darwaza's arrangement was so unusual at the time that he sought out fatwas in order to have its permissibility confirmed. For several decades, his *tafsīr* seems to have had relatively little impact in the Arab world, possibly because its particular notion of 'modernity', which was intimately connected to Arab nationalism and decolonisation, went out of fashion soon after the twelve-volume *tafsīr* had been published in 1961/2. Darwaza's *tafsīr*, however, was translated into Turkish by the 1990s[29] with the result that Darwaza seems to have attained the status of an exegetical authority in Turkey.[30] Between 2007 and 2015, at least seven exegetical works, some of them extensive, as well as several Qur'ān translations or rearrangements of existing works based on the concept of the 'order of revelation' have been published in Turkey.[31] There has also been at least one Indonesian work based on the order of revelation.[32] The phenomenon has hardly been studied as yet.

Despite the innovative arrangement of these commentaries, none of their authors has so far derived from it a radical reinterpretation of fundamental doctrines of faith or Islamic law. The idea of reading the Qur'ānic message in the context of its chronological development does not, to them, entail the far-reaching consequence of identifying certain statements or rulings as specific to their time and society and therefore not applicable to our times. That conclusion could, however, theoretically be drawn from their approach if an exegete wished to do so.

The concept of *tafsīr* in the chronological order of the *sūra*s received renewed attention in the Arab world[33] when the well-known Moroccan philosopher Muḥammad ʿĀbid al-Jābirī (1935–2010) published his three-volume 'clear' *tafsīr* 'in the order of revelation' in 2008,[34] accompanied by a book on Qur'ānic hermeneutics. The *tafsīr* was, maybe unsurprisingly, translated into Turkish. The following section shows what al-Jābirī's approach does and does not achieve.

Reading the Qur'ān in its chronological arrangement: Muḥammad ʿĀbid al-Jābirī (1935–2010, Morocco) on Q. 109

Muḥammad ʿĀbid al-Jābirī was a Moroccan professor of philosophy whose main work, the four-volume 'Critique of the Arab Mind' (1984–2001), attracted much attention in the Arab world and beyond. Late in his life, he embarked on an interpretation of the Qur'ān. His 'Introduction to the Qur'ān' (*Madkhal ilā al-Qur'ān*) was apparently projected to have more than one volume, but only the first of them, entitled 'Getting to know the Qur'ān' (*Fī'l-taʿrīf bi'l-Qur'ān*, 2006), was ever published. It discusses a number of topics from prophethood and the Qur'ān's position towards interreligious relations to the history of the Qur'ān itself. The last part explores stories in the Qur'ān. The work oscillates between hermeneutics and textual exegesis and, as such, distinctly differs from al-Jābirī's three-volume Qur'ānic commentary that was published between 2008 and 2009. Under the title *Fahm al-Qur'ān al-ḥakīm: Al-tafsīr al-wāḍiḥ ḥasab tartīb al-nuzūl* (Understanding the Wise Qur'ān: A clear commentary in the order of revelation), al-Jābirī went through the Qur'ān not in its canonical order, but with the declared intent to 'read the Qur'ān through the Prophet's biography (*sīra*) and the *sīra* through the Qur'ān'[35] – hence the arrangement in the order of revelation. The work received considerable attention and was even translated into Turkish.

Sūra 109, 'The Unbelievers' (al-Kāfirūn), is read by many contemporary commentators as a statement on freedom of religion and interreligious tolerance, or if it is not read that way, these issues are at least discussed.[36] Not so by al-Jābirī (see Excerpt 4.1). Al-Jābirī's exclusive interest is in connecting the *sūra* with the Prophet's biography in a meaningful way. That is why he focusses on assessing the plausibility of the occasion of revelation narratives, and that is also why, in his brief commentary on the *sūra*, he rejects the notion that it takes a disparaging attitude towards the Meccan idols. The reason for which this last notion is important to him lies in his placement of the *sūra* in the internal chronology of the Qur'ān: at the early stage he situates it in, neither the Qur'ān nor Muḥammad had started attacking the Meccan idols yet.

Excerpt 4.1

Q. 109

قُلْ يَا أَيُّهَا الْكَافِرُونَ {١} لَا أَعْبُدُ مَا تَعْبُدُونَ {٢} وَلَا أَنتُمْ عَابِدُونَ مَا أَعْبُدُ {٣} وَلَا أَنَا عَابِدٌ
مَّا عَبَدتُّمْ {٤} وَلَا أَنتُمْ عَابِدُونَ مَا أَعْبُدُ {٥} لَكُمْ دِينُكُمْ وَلِيَ دِينِ {٦}

(1) Say, ‘O unbelievers, (2) I worship not what you worship, (3) and you are not worshipping what I worship, (4) nor am I worshipping what you have worshipped, (5) neither are you worshipping what I worship. (6) You have your religion, and I have mine’.

Introduction

Ibn Isḥāq (d. *c*. 767) mentions in his biography of Muḥammad that some of the Quraysh leaders intercepted the Prophet when he was circumambulating the Ka῾ba and said: ‘Muḥammad, let’s do it like this: we worship what you worship, and you worship what we worship. You and I shall share in the matter. If the one you worship is better than what we worship, then we will be in luck, and if what we worship is better than what you worship, then you will be in luck’. This report, if it is true, and it is likely to be true, is in line with the context of the previous *sūra*s. Besides, it really reflects the mercantile ‘mentality’ of the Quraysh leaders: they were traders and they practiced their religion as part of their trade. What was important to them about their idols was the economic gains they reaped from the pilgrimage of the Arab tribes to Mecca where the tribes offered gifts to the local idols. The Prophet knew this, that is, he knew that what mattered to the Quraysh nobles were their economic interests and they were not going to abandon their idols as long as those interests remained attached to them. Therefore, he attacked those interests through his raids after the emigration to Medina.

There is a different report that the exegetes connect with the occasion of revelation of this *sūra*. In essence, it says that the Quraysh leaders offered to the Prophet money, power, marriage and so forth before they offered to him ‘joint worship’. This report does not conform with the period within which this *sūra* falls since it mentions that they demanded [of the Prophet] in return to ‘stop insulting their gods’! The Prophet hadn’t even started at that point to oppose their gods; this *sūra* is as free from it as the preceding ones. Only in the next period would he start opposing their idols.

The text of the *sūra*

In the name of God, the Merciful, the Compassionate.

(1) Say, O unbelievers,[37] **(2) I worship not what you worship** (now), **(3) and you are not worshipping what I worship** (now), **(4) nor am I worshipping** (in the future) **what you have worshipped, (5) neither are you worshipping** (in the future) **what I worship. (6) You have your religion, and I have mine** (there being no room for compromise).

Commentary

It is clear that this *sūra* does not take a position of either praise or disparagement towards the Quraysh's idols. All that it establishes is that the Prophet shall categorically reject to worship the idols that the Quraysh worship; likewise, it acknowledges the fact that they will not worship what he worships. This is because the compromise that the Quraysh proposed is fundamentally a scam since the Quraysh are the only ones who would have benefitted from it. If Muḥammad had worshipped what the Quraysh worship, it would have meant for him to abandon his religion that does not recognise other gods beside God. If they worshipped Allāh, however, and retained their idols that they consider intercessors to God, they would not lose a thing. Rather, they would keep their religion as it was before because their religion does not need God, but associates partners with him.

The Quraysh wanted to serve this hidden mercantile logic by persuading the Prophet to adopt their opportunistic position when they said to him: 'You and I shall share in the matter. If the one you worship is better than what we worship, then we will be in luck, and if what we worship is better than what you worship, then you will be in luck'. What mattered to the Quraysh was what they would gain in this world by means of religion. Therefore, the [Qur'ān's] refusal [of their proposition] was categorical, refusing that which the Quraysh worship in the present and the future.[...][38]

In the introduction to this volume of his *tafsīr*, al-Jābirī summarises his aim as 'reading the Qur'ān through the Prophet's biography (*sīra*) and the *sīra* through the Qur'ān'.[39] In his book-length introduction to the Qur'ān which is a companion to his *tafsīr*, he expounds on this theme, emphasising the intimate relationship between Muḥammad and the Qur'ān. While the Qur'ān, according to al-Jābirī, is in command and Muḥammad obeys, the Qur'ān reacts to the circumstances of Muḥammad's life and is his companion in every moment. The relationship is not one of mystery, as in other religions, since the Qur'ān never exalts Muḥammad beyond the human pale, but al-Jābirī nonetheless considers the depth of intimacy between Muḥammad and the Qur'ān a mystery that he aims to approach with his *tafsīr*.[40]

This is readily apparent from his treatment of *sūra* 109. Largely following standard Muslim chronologies of the Qur'ānic *sūra*s, he places it at the beginning of the Qur'ān's history, as number fifteen in the total sequence, belonging to the the first of seven periods of prophetic biography and Qur'ānic revelation. Al-Jābirī defines that period as being devoted to the themes of Muḥammad's prophethood as well as God's lordship and divinity.[41] In his introduction to the Qur'ān, he explains that this was a period in which the Qur'ān and its message were not yet publicly promulgated. Thus, the Qur'ān alternatively addressed Muḥammad himself or a small number of individual interlocutors, including some Quraysh elders, but not yet a broader public.[42] Whether this description fits his commentary on Q. 109 is arguable;[43] Muḥammad's message must have had enough of an impact to incite the Quraysh leaders to try and achieve a compromise if one subscribes to the occasion of revelation favoured by al-Jābirī. The main reason for al-Jābirī's placement of this *sūra* at the earliest stage of revelation seems to be the fact that it assumed that place in the Azhari model of the chronology of *sūra*s which al-Jābirī largely follows as will be explained below. This, in turn, informs his discussion of the *sūra*. He clearly rejects one of the transmitted occasions of revelation on grounds of not being in line with this early period of revelation.

Al-Jābirī consciously uses simple language and adopts a narrative style of prose. This, together with his narrow focus on the Prophet's biography, is reminiscent of the storytelling tradition that was an important part of the early development of Qur'ānic exegesis albeit one of which later exegetes often had a disparaging view.[44] The close connection between the *sīra* and *tafsīr* is a part of that tradition. The veneration of the Prophet is a particular type of pious reading of the Qur'ān. Al-Jābirī is not interested in deriving legal, theological or ethical conclusions from the *sūra*. Rather, he uses it in order to educate his readers about the early history of Islam – a history he treats as an edifying story.

Despite the author's fame and the unusual arrangement of his work, it does not attempt to offer groundbreaking new insights into either the Qur'ān or the prophetic biography. Rather, the commentary is relatively cursory. Each *sūra* is introduced by a short description outlining the reasons for its name and the occasion of revelation if one exists. Then, the text of the *sūra* is presented in the form of a paraphrastic commentary with insertions clarifying some words or phrases. A conclusion points to the main message of the *sūra*. Even the first *sūra* of the Qur'ān, the Fātiḥa, receives less than three pages in al-Jābirī's commentary despite the fact that it is at the core of Muslim ritual practice, is often considered to contain the essence of Islamic belief, is interpreted at length in most Qur'ānic commentaries, and is the exclusive subject of many individual works of *tafsīr*. It does not reveal much about the Prophet's biography, however, which is probably why it did not attract al-Jābirī's attention.

The main feature of his work is the chronological treatment of the Qur'ān. In this, al-Jābirī clearly follows the approach introduced by Darwaza whose 'Modern Qur'ānic commentary' was much more extensive and contained many modernist ideas. Al-Jābirī mentions Darwaza only briefly, dismissing his work as 'having brought nothing new' in the sense of not having put the chronological arrangement to any use in terms of elucidating the Qur'ān's history. He does not find in Darwaza's work anything that could not have been achieved by following the canonical order.[45] Al-Jābirī, on the other hand, is not much interested in interpreting the Qur'ān to any other purpose than that of narrating the history of Muḥammad and his community of believers.

The chronology of the Qur'ān's *sūra*s is not a straightforward matter, though. There is no single universally accepted model on which it might be based, and the sources are sketchy. Al-Jābirī is aware of these difficulties. In his introduction, he discusses at length the differences of opinion concerning the distinction between Meccan and Medinan *sūra*s, the first and the last *sūra*s of these periods and other issues of chronology. He briefly describes several models of Qur'ānic chronology by Muslim scholars, among them the one adopted by al-Azhar in its first printed Qur'ān edition of 1924. By virtue of the process of standardisation resulting from print, this is probably by far the most common system among Muslims today. Al-Jābirī claims that the differences between the various systems of chronology proposed by Muslim scholars are negligible and do not affect the overall picture of the Qur'ān's development. He considers it likely that they all go back to Ibn 'Abbās (d. *c.*687), the cousin of the Prophet who is widely credited with having been the first interpreter of the Qur'ān (although the historicity of most of the material ascribed to him is impossible to ascertain).[46] Thus, al-Jābirī's attitude towards Sunni Muslim historical and exegetical narratives is entirely uncritical, sometimes bordering on the apologetic.

Al-Jābirī is all the more critical when discussing the chronological arrangements proposed by Western orientalists, especially Theodor Nöldeke (1836–1930). These, he says, offer 'nothing new', which seems to be a recurring claim on his part. The details of the arrangement, according to al-Jābirī, are arbitrary and much further from the logic of the Prophet's biography than the chronology he ascribes to Ibn 'Abbās. Thus, he is strongly in favour of employing one of the traditional arrangements, such as the Azhari one, but he also wants to subject it to a rational reassessment. This reassessment leads him to independent conclusions concerning the chronology of a small number of *sūra*s. In what reads as an extremely defensive argument, he justifies this by saying that it delivers better results for his goal of connecting the Qur'ān with the Prophet's biography. He also states that, like any chronology, it is based on guesswork, but asserts that it conforms with opinions of earlier authorities and does not contradict the sources and the consensus of scholars. Besides, he emphatically states that he does not intend to replace the existing chronology, but only to slightly modify it based on a number of criteria that he then describes, such as the characteristics of the Meccan versus the Medinan period. The main purpose of his argument seems to be to salvage the authority of Muslim scholarship over Western Orientalism while at the same time justifying his own engagement with the Qur'ān despite his lack of credentials as an *'ālim*.[47]

Al-Jābirī digresses from the Azhari arrangement with respect to the placement of eleven *sūra*s.[48] In five of those cases, he even situates a *sūra* that al-Azhar considers Meccan in the Medinan period or vice versa.[49] A particularly noteworthy disagreement with the Azhari system concerns the *sūra*s that come at the very beginning of the Qur'ānic. Here, al-Jābirī's model is quite different from al-Azhar's, but identical to Theodor Nöldeke's despite his disparaging view of Western orientalists.[50] Generally, though, al-Jābirī, in contrast to Nöldeke, mainly seems to base his arrangement of the *sūra*s on criteria related to content, rather than style.

As has been shown, interpreting the Qur'ān in its order of revelation is not a method in and of itself. Rather, it is a form of arrangement that may or may not yield particular exegetical results. Chronology, however, is important for a number of exegetical methods with far-reaching impact, the most obvious example being that of abrogation.

ABROGATION (*NASKH*) AND ITS OPPONENTS

The principle of abrogation (*naskh*) was developed early in Islamic history due to a perception of contradictions in the Qur'ān, for example between verses calling for peaceful coexistence with non-Muslims and verses calling for war against them. Other cases of conflict more narrowly concerned legal issues such as inheritance law and the ban on alcohol. The solution that was proposed and called *naskh* was to assume that the verse that was revealed later invalidates the one that was revealed earlier. This process through which the Qur'ān was seen as altering the rules it had set up itself was interpreted as a reaction to changing circumstances in the Prophet's lifetime. The rationale ascribed to *naskh* was the deliberately gradual introduction of new regulations. That this principle heavily relies on establishing the order of revelation of the *sūra*s, at least in theory, is obvious.[51]

However, Muslim scholars increasingly saw problems with the excessive application of the principle of abrogation whose validity was eventually narrowed down to legal content. In the course of the centuries there was a tendency to reduce the number of cases to which abrogation was applicable. Outright rejection of the existence of abrogation, however, is a distinctly modern phenomenon[52] that started in the second half of the nineteenth century with the Indian reformer Sayyid Aḥmad Khān (1817–1898) and continues until this day, its proponents including famous modernists such as Muhammad Asad as well as Islamists such as Sayyid Quṭb and many others.[53]

The arguments against abrogation are manifold. At the core of the rejection of abrogation often lies the conviction – particularly among Islamists, but not limited to them – that the Qur'ān is perfect and thus perfectly coherent and devoid of contradictions. In order to further delegitimise the concept of abrogation, the commonly cited Qur'ānic evidence for it is deconstructed and it is argued that the Sunna offers no proof that God or the Prophet ever intended for parts of the Qur'ān to be abrogated. As for the seemingly contradictory verses, opponents of abrogation contend that their meanings are not actually mutually exclusive. Rather, the verses, when properly understood, in reality concern different subject matters, or one of them specifies the other, or both can be applied under certain conditions.

Modernists rejecting abrogation sometimes also problematise the chronology of Qur'ānic *sūra*s and verses, pointing to the fact that there is no single universally accepted system of arranging the *sūra*s in the order of revelation. Furthermore, modernists frequently argue that it would be implausible to praise the Qur'ān's flexibility in adapting its rulings to the changing circumstances of Meccan and Medinan society throughout a time span of twenty-two years whereas those rulings that were last revealed are considered unchanging and eternally valid. This particular type of argument indicates that modernist opposition to abrogation is not motivated by a desire to treat all verses of the Qur'ān as equally sacred, perfect and eternally valid. Rather, modernists tend to take issue with the concept that it is precisely the verses that were revealed last that are considered eternally valid according to the theory of abrogation. If one follows this theory, a clear hierarchy between Meccan and Medinan *sūra*s – based on the chronology developed by premodern scholars – is established, with the Medinan *sūra*s dominating Islamic law. The Medinan *sūra*s reflect the reality of warfare as well as the need to structure a society; they contain references to slavery, gender hierarchy and norms of of retaliation. All these are issues that most modernists do not want to see perpetuated; it is for this reason that many of them are unhappy with abrogation and look for different methods to deal with the Medinan Qur'ān such as the above-mentioned *maqāṣid* approach or the model of treating concrete Qur'ānic prescription as mere options to achieve the Qur'ān's higher aims in specific social circumstances.[54]

A more radical solution to the Meccan–Medinan dilemma was offered by the Sudanese Maḥmūd Muḥammad Ṭāhā (1909–1985) who was eventually declared an apostate and executed by the Islamist Numayrī regime. His disciple Abdullahi Ahmed An-Na'im (b. 1946) continues to spread and develop his ideas. In his book *The Second Message of Islam* (*Al-Risāla al-thāniya min al-Islām*), Ṭāhā argued that God intended for the Medinan message to be valid, as the first message of Islam, only until such time that humans would be able to embrace the Meccan Qur'ān's values of democracy, equality, tolerance, non-violence and spirituality. This, he thought, was the case in the twentieth century when the time had come to apply the 'second message of Islam' contained in the Meccan *sūra*s of the Qur'ān.[55] While the book offers no consistent methodology of distinguishing between Meccan and Medinan content and few Muslims, especially in the Arab world, unequivocally associate with it, Ṭāhā expressed concerns that many modernists share. The chronology of the Qur'ān, the relative importance of the content thought to have been revealed in the different periods of Muḥammad's lifetime, and the distinction between time-bound and eternal prescriptions continue to be among the most pressing and vital questions of contemporary exegetical debates. Entire books are devoted to the rejection of abrogation. The following case study is from one of them. Besides deconstructing a verse that has often been cited as Qur'ānic evidence for abrogation, it also applies a range of modernist interpretive methods, ranging from historical contextualisation to rethinking the Qur'ān's semantics.

Chronology, context, semantics: Talip Özdeş (b. 1954, Turkey) on Q. 16:101

Talip Özdeş is a professor of academic theology (Tr., *ilahiyat*) at Cumhuriyet University in the central Anatolian city of Sivas, Turkey, where he was also born. He graduated from the *tafsīr* department at Ankara University's Faculty of Theology in 1978, then the only Islamic theological faculty at a full university in Turkey. The Ankara faculty was known for its modernist approach and affinity to the humanities, social sciences and systematic disciplines. The option to choose classical Islamic fields of learning such as Qur'ānic exegesis as a specialisation was only introduced a few years before Özdeş obtained his degree. The *tafsīr* program was much influenced by the eminent exegete Süleyman Ateş (b. 1933), a known opponent of abrogation, who had graduated from the same faculty ten years before Özdeş.[56]

After having worked as a teacher for some time, Özdeş benefitted from the changed political climate in the 1980s that gave more importance to Islamic theology, resulting in the foundation of further theological faculties and improved career opportunities for theologians. Özdeş studied Arabic in Saudi Arabia and then acquired a postgraduate degree and a doctorate in *tafsīr* at the Institute for Social Sciences at Erciyes University in the central

Anatolian town of Kayseri during the 1990s. Özdeş has taught at Cumhuriyet University in his home town since 1994.[57]

Most of the published works of Özdeş date from the 2000s. They include books on al-Māturīdī's (853–944) Qur'ānic commentary and on the Qur'ān's attitude to gender relations.[58] His book on abrogation in the Qur'ān, from which the text above is an excerpt, is a pocket book of 160 pages published in 2005. It was printed by *Fecr Yayınevi*, an Ankara-based publisher with a focus on Islamic topics. While not exclusively addressing academics, the book is academic in style with footnotes containing detailed references and a six-page bibliography of Arabic and Turkish works.

In Excerpt 4.2, Özdeş makes use of the fact that the theory of abrogation considers the abrogation of one scripture by a subsequent one – for example, the Jewish Bible and the New Testament by the Qur'ān – one of the established forms of *naskh* and one that he accepts, in contrast to intra-Qur'ānic abrogation. His entire argument against this type of abrogation is embedded in modernist hermeneutical concepts. A look at how a premodern exegetical authority, al-Zamakhsharī, treats the verse in question will throw this fact into sharp relief.

> The exchange of one *āya* against another refers to abrogation (*naskh*). God abrogates religious laws by other religious laws because these laws serve interests, and what was beneficial yesterday might be the opposite, that is, harmful, today. God knows what is beneficial and what is harmful, and He confirms what He wants and abrogates what He wants in His wisdom. This is the meaning of the phrase *and God is well aware of what He sends down – they say, 'You are but a forger'*. They [the Meccan idolaters] found a pretext to challenge [the divine origin of the Qur'ān] and so they did. This is because of their ignorance and lack of knowledge of the concept of abrogation. They said: 'Muḥammad mocks his followers; one day he commands something and the next day he forbids it and brings them something easier'. In actual fact, they were the ones telling lies. In reality, harder rules were abrogated by easier ones, and easier by harder ones, and easier by easier ones as well as harder by harder ones because the purpose [of abrogation] is the implementation of the beneficial intent of the law [*al-maṣlaḥa*], not ease or hardship. [There follows a discussion of the much-debated question, in legal methodology, of whether a Qur'ānic ruling can be abrogated by other sources of Islamic law or only by another Qur'ānic ruling.][59]

For al-Zamakhsharī, there seems to be no question that Q. 16:101 pertains to the concept of *naskh* as it had been well-established in Islamic legal hermeneutics by the time he wrote his Qur'ānic commentary. He quotes the commonplace story about the verse's occasion of revelation, a generic narrative without details of names, place and time, according to which the Meccans

Excerpt 4.2

Q. 16:101

وَإِذَا بَدَّلْنَا آيَةً مَّكَانَ آيَةٍ وَاللَّهُ أَعْلَمُ بِمَا يُنَزِّلُ قَالُوا إِنَّمَا أَنتَ مُفْتَرٍ بَلْ أَكْثَرُهُمْ لَا يَعْلَمُونَ ﴿١٠١﴾

(101) When We exchange one *āya* (sign/verse/revelation) for another – and God is well aware of what He sends down – they say, 'You are but a forger'. But most of them do not know.

The noble verse mentioned in the caption constitutes, together with Q. 2:106, what is considered the classical theory of abrogation's main scriptural underpinning. The *sūra* al-Naḥl of which this verse is a part is Meccan and according to R. Blachère the seventy-third *sūra* in the order of revelation.[60] According to Süleyman Ateş [b. 1933], however, it is the seventieth *sūra* in the order of revelation. Al-Suyūṭī claims that this *sūra* is Meccan, but that its three last verses […] are Medinan. [The same is said about the opinion of al-Rāzī, al-Bayḍāwī and al-Ālūsī (1802–1854).] Also, according to Elmalılı Hamdi Yazır [1878–1942], the *sūra* is Meccan and Ḥasan [al-Ḥasan al-Baṣrī, 642–728], 'Aṭā' [b. Abī Rabāḥ; d. *c.* 732], 'Ikrima [d. *c.* 723] and Jābir [b. 'Abdallāh; d. 697] have related that the entire *sūra* is Meccan. Ibn 'Abbās [d. *c.* 687] said that only three verses are Medinan. Muhammad Asad [1900–1992], pointing out that no evidence or record whatsoever indicates that the last three verses of this *sūra* belong to the Medinan period, states that this claim is merely an exegetical opinion.

As is the case with the other Meccan *sūra*s, the main themes of *sūra* 16 are fundamental matters of belief such as the Divine, revelation, prophethood, life after death, the proofs of God's omnipotence and oneness, the manifestation of His oneness and omnipotence in creation and the veracity of His message. The *sūra* takes its name from a key word from within it, the word *naḥl* (bee). In the *sūra*, God reveals the bee to be among the greatest manifestations of the blessings He has bestowed upon humans, drawing attention to the fact that the bee produces honey for men from what it sucks from flowers, plants and fruit.

Our original topic, the 'exchange verse' (Q. 16:101), is explained by many commentators, despite some difference in opinion, in terms of the theory of abrogation; however, Muhammad Asad's approach to the topic is slightly different. According to Muhammad Asad, when God exchanges one *āya* against another *āya*, this does not mean that He brings one Qur'ānic verse in place of another verse, thereby abrogating the previous Qur'ānic verse, but it means that the Qur'ānic message shall replace the teachings that had specifically been aimed at previous religious communities. Hence, we understand the verse as dealing with the relationship between the Qur'ān and previous divine scriptures. However, illuminating the nature of this relationship doubtlessly requires further explanation.

From the *sūra*'s contents and approach, it has to be understood as directly addressing the idolatrous Arabs in the Prophet's environment. Besides the fact that the *sūra* is Meccan, the verses related to God's oneness, the rejection of idols, the hereafter, revelation and the veracity of His message make it difficult to believe that the *sūra* is centred on the People of the Book.[61] Only in some verses in the last part of the *sūra*, there are references to the Jews, the Prophet Abraham and the Sabbath. [Özdeş now summarises the contents of the *sūra* up to v. 101.]

The fact that the verse in question was revealed in the Meccan period in which none of the specific regulations that were subject to abrogation had emerged yet, as well as the contents and context of the verses before and after this verse make it almost impossible for us to understand it in terms of the classical theory of abrogation. For the point of contention, on the idolaters' part, is not – as an extra-Qur'ānic tradition that is supposedly its occasion of revelation suggests – the question how the Qur'ānic verses are related to each other and whether they exclude each other; it is whether or not Muḥammad's message, which ran counter to the *jāhiliyya*[62] understanding of religion and to part of its traditions, was right and whether or not the Qur'ān which – since it replaced *shirk* with *tawḥīd* – contained rulings that differed from previous religious laws was transmitted from God. [Özdeş now argues that *āya* is *pars pro toto* for an entire scripture.] Therefore, it is immediately decreed in verses 102 and 103: 'Say, The Holy Spirit has brought it down from your Lord in truth to give confirmation to those who believe and as a guidance and good news for Muslims.[63] In truth We know that they say, "It is only a mortal who is teaching him". The speech of the one at whom they hint is foreign, whereas this is clear Arabic speech'.

Actually, verses 102 and 103 clarify to us what the occasion of revelation of v. 101 was [i.e., the Meccans declared the Qur'ān an invention, for which v. 104 threatens divine punishment].

When we approach the *sūra* as a whole, it appears that issues such as God's oneness, omnipotence and blessings, revelation and the veracity of the message – things that humans are invited to observe in the Qur'ān, but which had already been revealed to previous prophets and which are the true religion of the Prophet Abraham – constitute the main theme of the *sūra*. While the *sūra*'s primary speech context is not only to believers, but also to idolatrous Arabs, towards the end it also talks about Jews. Now, it might be thought that those verses related to the Jews were revealed at a date close to the *hijra*. Then again, it might be thought that the Meccan idolaters possessed precise information about the religious beliefs, traditions and customs of the Jews, seeing as they lived close to them and were in communication with them especially due to the trade relationship between them. It is highly likely that the Meccan idolaters, while on the one hand relating themselves to the Prophet Abraham in ancestry and customs through one of his sons [Ismāʿīl] and claiming that the traditions of their forefathers, which they invoke against the proclamations of the Prophet Muḥammad, are true, on the other hand questioned the veracity of Islam and its main source, the Qurʾān since it confirmed part of the Jewish traditions that is usually traced back to Abraham's other son Isaac, Moses and other Jewish prophets, and abolished another part. Islam thus came up with a certain number of rulings that differed from previous legal traditions in form and details, despite coming from the same source. [...] We may also understand the fact that God exchanged one *āya* against another in this context. [...][64]

raised the exact issue to which the verse provides the answer. To him, there seems no doubt that the term *āya* refers to a segment of the Qurʾān – in fact, he uses the indeterminate noun *qurʾān* as a synonym – and that abrogation is a part of the divine intention behind the scripture. The only potential point of contention that al-Zamakhsharī mentions is an issue of legal methodology that takes place within the frame of reference of abrogation theory and takes the concept of abrogation for granted.

Özdeş, however, accepts none of al-Zamakhsharī's premises. His commentary on Q. 16:101 is not so much an exercise in Qurʾānic interpretation as it is meant to refute a core argument in favour of the existence of intra-Qurʾānic abrogation: the claim that this type of abrogation is mandated by the Qurʾān. Özdeş analyses this verse – and others – in order to show that this is not the case; that none of the supposed Qurʾānic evidence for abrogation is convincing. In doing so, he employs a broad array of hermeneutical methods that are representative of contemporary modernist exegetical discourses.

One such concept that is an important part of Özdeş's argument is a critical approach to Qurʾānic semantics. In Q. 16:101, this particularly concerns the meaning of the term *āya*. The ambiguity of this term is directly reflected in recent English Qurʾān translations. Translators who follow a traditional approach render *āya* as 'verse' or even 'ayat'. Other translators, however, opt for its literal meaning, 'sign', or take it to be a *pars pro toto* expression meaning 'revelation' or 'message'.[65]

Refusing to translate āya as 'verse' is a necessary step to make if one wants to read the verse in a way that does not point to the existence of intra-

Qur'ānic abrogation. It is not an arbitrary semantical strategy meant to twist the meaning of words in order to reach the intended result. Rather, it is an attempt to understand the language of the Qur'ān in its textual and historical context. Instead of simply assuming that the word *āya* in the Qur'ān has the same meaning it acquired in later Arabic usage, exegetes employing this strategy explore the context of a term within the Qur'ān and ask from what period this specific bit of revelation dates. From there, they try to reconstruct the circumstances to which this revelation might have responded.

Chronology, thus, is important: the verse is Meccan, as Özdeş takes pains to make clear, invoking the opinions of rather a high number of respectable exegetes as evidence. He needs their collective authority because not only does he disagree with the near-consensus of premodern exegetes on the meaning of the verse, but he also dismisses the story that is commonly quoted – not only by al-Zamakhsharī – as its occasion of revelation. To him, it is no more than 'an extra-Qur'ānic tradition' that some have turned into the verse's supposed occasion of revelation to serve their own purposes. He dismisses it mainly on the basis of chronology: in the Meccan period that the verse originates from, he argues, the question raised by the occasion of revelation was not an important point of contention for the Qur'ān's main interlocutors at the time, the Meccan pagans.

Özdeş corroborates his argument by extensively discussing the intra-Qur'ānic context of the verse. Again, this is a method that did not play a prominent role in the *tafsīr* tradition and was certainly not normally used in order to assess the plausibility of individual occasions of revelation. He pays a great deal of attention to the contents of the previous and subsequent verses and explains how they relate to the issue of God's changing one sacred law against another – in fact, these explanations continue for several pages beyond the excerpt translated here. Interestingly, in these pages it is just as important to Özdeş as it is to al-Zamakhsharī to explain the wisdom behind the concept of abrogation, the difference being that to Özdeş, abrogation only exists between sacred scriptures while to al-Zamakhsharī, it exists within the Qur'ān.

The modernist nature of Özdeş's methodology is completely in line with the sources he quotes. The reference to a number of high-ranking early and medieval exegetical authorities is unsurprising, given the fact that it is central to Özdeş's argument to establish the Meccan origin of the *sūra*. His main source with respect to this particular verse, however, is Muhammad Asad (1900–1992), a distinctly modernist exegete. Asad, in his 'The Message of the Qur'ān', translates Q. 16:101 as 'And now that We replace one message by another' and comments: 'I.e., by substituting the message of the Qur'ān for the earlier dispensations – and not, as some Muslim scholars maintain, "abrogating" one Qur'anic verse and replacing it by another'.[66] To Asad, the concept of intra-Qur'ānic abrogation is untenable.

Özdeş writes in Turkey for a Turkish audience, something which is also apparent from the sources he cites. The Turkish Republic is a striking example of a country that developed its own national tradition of Qur'ānic exegesis. That tradition, while not being disconnected from developments in other parts of the Muslim world, has produced its own authorities and discourses. The toolkit of modernist hermeneutics is deeply entrenched in Turkish academic theology[67] although it is not uncontested by a long shot. Accordingly, Süleyman Ateş, who has published his own – shorter – pamphlet against the doctrine of abrogation[68] besides an extensive commentary on the Qur'ān, is Özdeş's main reference in his book. Another is Elmalılı Hamdi Yazır (1878–1942), the author of the first widely respected annotated translation of the Qur'ān into modern Turkish.

The citation of European sources – such as the French orientalist Régis Blachère (1900–1973) – is not out of character for participants in the Turkish exegetical discourse. In this case, Özdeş quotes Blachère from a Turkish translation of a book on the Qur'ān's internal chronology by Mehdi Bazargan, Iranian intellectual and first prime minister of the country for a short period after the revolution of 1979. While Özdeş has obviously not read Blachère in the original and his list of references includes only Turkish and Arabic sources, his citation of a French orientalist as an authority on the Qur'ān in a prominent place in this chapter does have a symbolic value; it is something that traditional *'ulamā'* or Islamist-leaning exegetes would rather avoid. Furthermore, it is noteworthy that from among four Arabic Qur'ān commentaries that Özdeş quotes as paradigmatic for the conventional interpretation of Q. 16:101, two are Shi'i: one of them premodern, the other from the twentieth century.[69] This indicates a certain openness to, or even interest in, Shi'i Qur'ān interpretation.

Özdeş's interpretation of Q. 16:101 is only one piece of a larger argument on the non-existence of intra-Qur'ānic abrogation; it is interested in hermeneutics more than in applied exegesis. His argument, however, relies heavily, almost exclusively, on deconstructing the scriptural evidence commonly provided for the existence of intra-Qur'ānic abrogation. As such, the text demonstrates that it is impossible to neatly distinguish between scriptural interpretation and scriptural hermeneutics. Any hermeneutical stance towards abrogation relies upon a certain understanding of specific verses in the scripture. The verses need to be interpreted – an endeavour that, as Özdeş's text shows, in turn relies on distinct hermeneutical assumptions. The most striking of those is the approach to semantics where a 'literal' reading of the term *āya* in the sense that a contemporary reader would understand it is rejected and more careful reflection demanded. Discussions of Qur'ānic semantics are a central part of modernist exegetical strategies.

SEMANTICS AND THE 'LITERAL MEANING'

The attempt to read the Qur'ānic message in its historical context often has profound consequences for the interpretation of its language and terminology. If the Qur'ān is understood as a message addressed towards a specific historical group of recipients, then one would need to ask not only whether the recipients and their circumstances have changed, but also whether the code or language in which the message is expressed has changed.[70] In other words, have the Arabic expressions in the Qur'ān always had the meaning that a modern reader with knowledge of Arabic would assign to them?

Possibly the most fundamental case in point is the word *islām*. When the Qur'ān states that 'the religion with God is *islām*' (Q. 3:19) or 'Those who desire a religion other than *islām*, it will not be accepted from them and they will be among the losers in the world to come' (Q. 3:85), a naïve literal reading based on a modern understanding of Islam would assume that this refers to Islam as a religion and to the community of those who believe in Muḥammad's prophethood. Consequently, religions that do not accept Muḥammad's prophethood will not be accepted by God and their adherents will go to hell. If one subjects the verses to a historical reading, on the other hand, one might come to the conclusion that they emerged at a time at which the formation of Islam as a separate religion had not been completed and at which the term *islām* was understood in its original literal sense as 'submission (to God)', thus potentially including Jews, Christians and other monotheists. After all, the Qur'ān calls even Abraham a *muslim* (Q. 3:67).[71] This is a controversy with broad ramifications; it took centre stage, for example, in the dispute between the Turkish modernist exegete Süleyman Ateş and his opponent, the traditional Syrian scholar with Salafi leanings Muḥammad ʿAlī al-Ṣābūnī, on the question whether Muslims have a monopoly on paradise. While al-Ṣābūnī saw Q. 3:19 and 3:85 as evidence for the exclusion of all non-Muslims from paradise, Ateş argued that in Qur'ānic semantics, Islam means no more than the worship of God and the avoidance of polytheism.[72] This was also the reading proposed by the important hermeneutical theorist Fazlur Rahman (1919–1988).[73]

Similar issues are debated with respect to a number of concepts. Does *zakāt* always refer to the alms tax as it was later defined in Islamic law or might it refer, at an earlier stage, to almsgiving in general or even to 'purification'? Is an *āya* always a verse of the Qur'ān or is it more plausible that, at a time at which there was not yet a completed, let alone codified Qur'ān, it carried its original meaning of 'sign'?

Such semantic controversies point to two fundamental insights. First, it is very hard to talk about the 'literal meaning' of the Qur'ān beyond subjective claims to understanding it because there are cases in which each of two entirely different readings will be understood by their proponents as literal. A Salafi would claim that his understanding of Islam as a religion in the modern sense is strictly literal; a modernist would deny that claim and argue that his own understanding of Islam as 'submission' is literal because it is much closer to the original meaning of the word.

Second, whether the first or the second version of 'literally' understanding a Qur'ānic term is taken to be true depends fundamentally on one's conception of the Qur'ānic text, its 'author' and its place in history. For a Salafi, the historical semantics of terms such as *islām* are irrelevant because God revealed the Qur'ān as a scripture for all humans at all times; not specifically for seventh-century Arabs with a potentially narrow understanding of some concepts, but also for later humans who have the benefit of having the full Qur'ānic revelation at their disposal and can therefore understand it accordingly. God might have had the foresight to reveal some verses whose full implications could not be understood by its first listeners; only the appreciation of the entire Qur'ān along with the *ḥadīth* collections gives a full understanding of the meaning of Qur'ānic terms. The opposing view, embraced by modernists and postmodernists, also sees the Qur'ān as a divine message, but one that had to manifest itself in history in order to become relevant to humans. It could only have appealed to its listeners and changed their perceptions and beliefs if it made use of a code they could understand. Each part of the Qur'ān thus manifested itself at a specific moment in time; both its contents and its language evolved as the horizon of its listeners evolved. Therefore, a term might change its meaning in the course of the Qur'ān's revelation. It is thus important to be sensitive to the specific timing of the revelation and to the audience of any given verse.

The idea of understanding the Qur'ān as its first listeners understood it was – and continues to be – upheld by most modernist reformers at varying degrees of sophistication. It has been theorised in different way, both historically, as described above, and in the framework of literary studies.

LITERARY EXEGESIS

The most well-known proponent of a 'literary exegesis' (*tafsīr adabī*) of the Qur'ān was the Egyptian professor of Arabic language and literature Amīn al-Khūlī (1895–1966). He was not the first modern intellectual to show an interest in reading the Qur'ān as a work of literature. Muḥammad 'Abduh had already devoted some attention to the Qur'ān's rhetoric. However, al-Khūlī was more immediately inspired by the famous Egyptian writer and intellectual Ṭāhā Ḥusayn (1889–1973) who had proposed treating the Qur'ān as part of the literary heritage of mankind, independent of its religious status and outside the sphere of the *'ulamā'*. In the same vein, Amīn al-Khūlī maintained that the methods for analysing the Qur'ān, which he considered the greatest work of Arabic literature, are the same that are applied to any other work of literary art. This includes the study of the society in which it originated and of the languages and literatures known to its members, which then enables the researcher to reconstruct the meaning that the text must have had to its first listeners. It also involves the analysis of common figures of speech, text structures and genre characteristics. Al-Khūlī considered a synopsis of Qur'ānic segments speaking about a common theme as preferable to the analysis of isolated verses. His emphasis on treating the Qur'ān as part of the Arabic literary heritage resonated strongly with the nationalist agenda of his time in which cultural identity and the discovery of the Arab heritage were important concerns.

Al-Khūlī emphasised the artistic quality of the Qur'ān which, he argued, primarily lies in its ability to appeal to emotions as is the case with any work of literature. Therefore, according to him, the psychological effect of the Qur'ān on its first listeners has to be taken into account. This reasoning could raise the question – not raised explicitly by al-Khūlī – whether the psychological effect of the narratives or eschatological descriptions in the Qur'ān might not outweigh their factual truth. It is precisely over that sensitive question that al-Khūlī's student Muḥammad Aḥmad Khalaf Allāh (1916–1991) stumbled when submitting, in 1947, a doctoral thesis on the art of narrative in the Qur'ān that was based on al-Khūlī's teachings.

Khalaf Allāh argued that the Qur'ānic narratives, much like other literary narratives, are primarily intended to be psychologically efficient and need not represent historical facts in order to achieve that purpose. Rather, they must be in harmony with the recipients' language, horizon and narrative traditions. They need to resonate with their mindset and must meet the requirements of a well-constructed story. Therefore, Khalaf Allāh concluded, the Qur'ānic stories of prophets are largely not historically true, even though Muḥammad's followers might have believed them to be, but rather were meant to leave a psychological impression on them. To this purpose, God used stories that the Arabs were familiar with and reflected the experience of the nascent Muslim community in these stories. Khalaf Allāh left no doubt about his belief that the Qur'ān was literally revealed by God. Nevertheless, the Azhari scholars considered his ideas sacrilegious, declared him a criminal and achieved the rejection of his thesis. Therefore, subsequent proponents of a literary approach to the Qur'ān tended to be much more cautious; the question of the factual truth behind Qur'ānic narratives or descriptions is usually tackled in an ambiguous manner, if at all.[74]

Chief among these subsequent proponents was al-Khūlī's student and wife 'Ā'isha 'Abd al-Raḥmān 'Bint al-Shāṭī'' (1913–1998) who wrote a literary, or rhetorical, commentary (*tafsīr bayānī*) on some *sūra*s of the Qur'ān in conscious application of al-Khūlī's ideas. She contextualises the *sūra*s both historically and in relation to other treatments of the same topics within the Qur'ān and analyses their stylistic features, explaining their relevance to the topic of the *sūra* and their emotional effect. She also provides in-depth semantic analyses. In contrast to Khalaf Allāh, she carefully avoids controversial topics; therefore, her work was generally accepted as a legitimate approach to the Qur'ān, mainly designed to demonstrate its stylistic perfection. Bint al-Shāṭī''s work was among the first works of *tafsīr* written by women which might have made it even more important to avoid risking its reputation. This might also explain why Bint al-Shāṭi' avoids the discussion of gender issues completely in her *tafsīr*, in contrast to other books she wrote.[75]

Some of the strategies employed by al-Khūlī and his disciples continue to receive much attention especially among modernists; but the factuality of the Qur'ān's statements continues to be a taboo that few Muslim exegetes dare touch upon. The synoptic treatment that al-Khūlī proposed, on the other hand, has become rather popular to the extent that it has informed the establishment of a new exegetical genre, the thematic *tafsīr*.

THEMATIC *TAFSĪR* (*TAFSĪR MAWḌŪ'Ī*)

Tafsīr mawḍū'ī or 'thematic *tafsīr*' is an approach that either covers individual *sūra*s or the entire Qur'ān by general themes, rather than verse by verse, thus fulfilling one of Amīn al-Khūlī's demands. As a specific notion describing a separate type of *tafsīr*, much as the '*tafsīr* in the order of revelation' is presented as a distinct genre, it seems to have emerged around 1970 and been pursued most frequently in Egypt in subsequent decades. There is also an Imami Shi'i tradition of *tafsīr mawḍū'ī* in Arabic and Persian that has received little attention as yet.[76]

There are different ways to structure a *tafsīr mawḍū'ī*. The most conservative approach explores the themes of each individual *sūra* while treating them in their canonical order. This might have been inspired by the prominent Egyptian scholar Maḥmūd Shaltūt (1893–1963) who published a work based on that method, not yet under the title of *tafsīr mawḍū'ī*, in 1959.[77] The most successful adept of his method was probably the Egyptian

Muḥammad al-Ghazālī (1917–1996) whose *tafsīr mawḍūʿī* was translated into several foreign languages.[78] Another one was the Azhari Muḥammad al-Bahī (1905–1982) whose books covered a number of selected *sūra*s.

The more far-reaching method is to mine the entire Qur'ān for statements relevant to a specific theme and to treat them all in context. In 1977, the Egyptian scholar ʿAbd al-Ḥayy al-Farmāwī (b. 1942) published a model for developing such a thematic *tafsīr* that later, starting in the 1990s, proved particularly influential in Indonesia through the activities of local scholars who had studied at al-Azhar University in Cairo. Specifically, the model was applied by the eminent scholar Muhammad Quraish Shihab in a book published in 1996 that discusses thirty-three very diverse themes over nearly 600 pages.[79]

Another important source of inspiration for those pursuing a thematic interpretation was the Pakistani-American theologian Fazlur Rahman's *Major Themes of the Qur'ān* (1980).[80] It was written in English and therefore especially widely used by Muslims working in Western academic contexts, but influential far beyond those. The book is rather slim and does not go into much detail, but points to possible venues for further exploration.[81] Fazlur Rahman is frequently cited by contemporary modernist and post-modern exegetes in the field of gender equality and others.[82]

In recent years, new studies in thematic *tafsīr* have been published in increasing number all over the Arab and the wider Muslim world both by Sunni and Imami Shiʿi authors.[83] More and more often, the label of *tafsīr mawḍūʿī* is used for works that focus on one specific aspect, term or topic in the Qur'ān. They do not differ greatly from books called 'Women in the Qur'ān' or similar, but it is likely that the label of *tafsīr* lends such books some additional weight, especially when they are published with an audience of religious scholars in mind. The focus of these works is often on semantics; typically, exegetes compare all words in the Qur'ān that are derived from a single root. More classical works of *tafsīr mawḍūʿī*, in as far as the genre has established a tradition of its own, usually take a more holistic view at the range of topics within *sūra*s or the entire Qur'ān.[84]

TAFSĪR AL-QUR'ĀN BI'L-QUR'ĀN

Thematic *tafsīr* lends itself to focussing on the Qur'ān as the primary source of exegesis, at the expense of other sources, and this is indeed a prominent phenomenon in contemporary exegesis. Insofar as this phenomenon is based on an explicit method, this method is often called in Arabic *tafsīr al-Qur'ān bi'l-Qur'ān* (explaining the Qur'ān through the Qur'ān). It draws on some of the ideas of literary exegesis and historical semantics, but usually presents itself in a far more traditional manner and is therefore deemed acceptable across the entire exegetical spectrum. The main idea is to solve exegetical problems first and foremost by consulting the Qur'ān itself, either by identifying other uses of the same terms within the Qur'ān or by searching for explanations on a given theme. This approach to the Qur'ān is not new as such, taking up ideas that had already been present in the works of Ibn Taymiyya and other premodern scholars, but the claim to apply it consistently as the dominant exegetical method only gained a significant following in the second half of the twentieth century.

Tafsīr al-Qur'ān bi'l-Qur'ān is capable of producing new insights by interlinking passages from different parts of the Qur'ān and encouraging the reflection about their connection, but it also has its limits. There are topics and specific terms that only appear once in the Qur'ān, for example, or statements that are hard to explain without some historical context. Most works of *tafsīr* that define themselves as being based on this method do, in fact, draw on external sources. Some have been written by eminent traditional *'ulamā'* such as the Mauritanian-born Saudi scholar Muḥammad al-Amīn al-Shinqīṭī (1907–1973) and the Iranian Imami Shi'i exegete Muḥammad Ḥusayn Ṭabāṭabā'ī (1903–1981). In contrast to literary exegesis, this approach does not raise any inherent claims about the historicity of the Qur'ān, the applicability of its prescriptions, nor the authenticity of its narratives.

THE CONTESTED SUNNA: FROM *ḤADĪTH*-BASED EXEGESIS TO QUR'ĀNISM

Despite frequent attempts to use the Qur'ān as the main source of exegesis, the role of the Sunna – the collections of *ḥadīth*s about the Prophet's actions, sayings and general behaviour – is an issue that exegetes can hardly avoid. The question of the relationship between the Qur'ān and the Sunna has from a very early time onwards been central not only to Qur'ānic exegesis, but also to many other disciplines. This is not only true for Sunni Islam, but also for most branches of Shi'ism despite marked differences in their *ḥadīth* collections. The use of *ḥadīth*s does not only provide historical information, such as in occasions of revelation and other material offering historical context, but there is also genuinely exegetical material in which the Prophet is described as having explained particular verses of the Qur'ān.

Since the amount of such exegetical material is too low to provide solutions to all but a small number of exegetical controversies, however, it was soon complemented by reports from other eminent religious figures. In

Sunni Islam, these were the Prophet's companions (*ṣaḥāba*) and the successive generation (*tābiʿūn*); in Shiʿi Islam, these were the imams.

Generally, *ḥadīth* criticism played a less important role in Qur'ānic exegesis than in law, and exegetes were often reproached with uncritically reproducing unauthentic material.[85] Ibn Taymiyya was among those critics. He tried to to come up with a coherent *ḥadīth*-based methodology that, given the lack of authentic exegetical *ḥadīth*s going back to the Prophet, granted special importance to the Prophet's companions, the *ṣaḥāba*, and the first generations of Islam in general, the *salaf*.[86] Today's Salafis invest much in this methodology that ranks exegetical traditions according to their chronological closeness to the Prophet and downplays the differences of opinions between them.

Much could be said about the dynamic premodern debates on the role of *ḥadīth*s for Qur'ānic exegesis. The issue was tied in with larger questions of doctrine and identity and was therefore constantly contested. This is still the case today, but some of the parameters have changed. On the one hand, the Salafi paradigm that strongly relies on *ḥadīth*s and treats them on a par with the Qur'ān, but only after rigorous examination of their authenticity, has become extremely widespread and powerful. On the other hand, starting in the nineteenth century, orientalist scholarship has raised doubts about the authenticity of the corpus of *ḥadīth*s as a whole, pointing to their late emergence as written sources and the obvious reflection, in part, of the material of theological and legal debates that arose long after Muḥammad's death.

Even for the majority of Muslims who entirely reject orientalist scepticism, there is room for debate. In contrast to the Qur'ān whose divine origin is a fundamental tenet of belief, *ḥadīth*s are, by their very nature, open to controversy. The procedures for establishing their authenticity that have been developed by Muslim scholars imply that it is always possible to doubt the status of individual *ḥadīth*s and that their validity can never been definitely proven, only assumed by varying degrees of probability.[87]Another reason for modernist Muslims, in particular, to feel sceptical about *ḥadīth*s has to do with the fact that many of the doctrines and concrete legal prescriptions they reject are derived from *ḥadīth*s, rather than the Qur'ān, ranging from the punishment of stoning to an oft-reported statement saying that the majority of the inhabitants of hell will be women due to their lack of gratitude towards their husbands.[88] The attitude towards *ḥadīth*s is thus an important factor determining possible exegetical outcomes.

One common strategy is to rely on those *ḥadīth*s that are contained in major premodern Qur'ānic commentaries, the selection depending on which works the exegete considers authoritative. There is a distinct tendency to reject overly narrative sources, for example about Biblical figures, as *isrā'īliyyāt*. More ambitious exegetes, especially among Salafis, but not limited to them, might additionally mine *ḥadīth* collections for material. Since the range of material resulting from these strategies is huge and diverse, eclectic approaches abound where some *ḥadīth*s are cited and others ignored depending on whether they match the exegete's goal.

There are also some modernist and postmodern exegetes who tacitly ignore *ḥadīth*s as a source altogether without explicitly stating this. Many contemporary exegetical texts are entirely Qur'ān-centric, but do not take an explicit position towards the Sunna – for good reason, since the topic is decidedly sensitive.

However, there are Muslim exegetes who do not consider these last two approaches intellectually satisfying. Unwilling to either subscribe to the content of the majority of *ḥadīth*s or to reject the entire Sunna as a source, they seek to provide a theoretical foundation for their cautious treatment of *ḥadīth*s. Fazlur Rahman's concept of the 'living Sunna' is one such model, and a popular one at that. He argued that Muslims from the beginning of Islam onwards followed the example of the Prophet in applying the Qur'ān's teachings to their lives; therefore, their customs and norms embodied the Prophetic Sunna. This 'living Sunna' evolved organically as society changed and was distinct and separate from the much later science of *ḥadīth*s which reflected the 'living Sunna' as well as the legal and theological needs of its own times. What mattered to the 'living Sunna' and what should matter today is not the imitation of minute details of the Prophet's actions that are not necessarily identifiable in *ḥadīth*s anyway, but the spirit behind them. That spirit should be applied to the needs of contemporary societies in ways that befits their circumstances and needs. Thus, the prophetic behaviour depicted in a *ḥadīth* can be accepted as an ideal application of the Sunna to one time but need not be followed today as long as the spirit behind it is respected.[89]

Because the status of the Sunna is such a sensitive topic, its outright and complete rejection is a rather marginal phenomenon, but also a fairly visible one due to its presence on the internet.[90] The groups that adopt this position are known as Qur'ānists (Ar., *Qur'āniyyūn*). They had precursors, among them the *ahl-i Qur'ān* group around Abdullah Chakralavi in nineteenth-century India,[91] but rose to greater prominence only during the 1980s. The most well-known Qur'ānist group follows the controversial teachings of Rashad Khalifa (1935–1990) and calls itself 'Submission' in order to signify an attachment to the original, uncorrupted Islam.[92] Some adherents of the Qur'ānist trend faced severe problems in Muslim-majority countries, such as the Kurdish-Turkish intellectual Edip Yüksel (b. 1957)[93] who became affiliated with Rashad Khalifa and eventually emigrated to the US in 1989 due to having received death threats for his beliefs. A similar case is that of the Egyptian Islamic scholar Aḥmad Ṣubḥī Manṣūr (b. 1949) who was expelled from his teaching position at al-Azhar University after he had espoused Rashad Khalifa's ideas in the 1980s; he emigrated to the US in 2000.[94] Despite these difficulties, there are apparently individual Qur'ānists or small groups of them in most countries with a Muslim population.[95]

While Rashad Khalifa is a central figure for Qur'ānists and many of them have links to him, not all Qur'ānists follow his teachings and not all who were affiliated with him share all of his ideas. There are also entirely independent figures who arrive at similar conclusions, such as the Syrian intellectual Georges Ṭarābīshī (1939–2016).

Qur'ānism is a diverse phenomenon which has not yet been sufficiently studied, but it is hard to avoid the impression that the vast majority of Qur'ānists are distinctly modernist. They want to eliminate from Islam legal and ethical concepts that they consider outdated and attribute to the negative influence of *ḥadīth*s. These concepts may include the punishment of apostates, bans on women praying during menstruation, the prohibition of female prayer leaders and male as well as female circumcision. The Qur'ānists' modernist outlook also extends to the interpretation of Qur'ānic statements on issues such as warfare, corporal punishments and the treatment of wives by their husbands. Qur'ānists typically argue that *ḥadīth*s are not only unreliable (that is, largely not authentic and contradictory), but also that there is no indication in the Qur'ān that *ḥadīth*s had ever meant to become a source of religion; on the contrary, they say, the Qur'ān states that it is a clear scripture and the perfect and final message to mankind and that the Prophet Muḥammad never asked anyone to follow anything other than the Qur'ān.

A Qur'ānist approach: Aḥmad Ṣubḥī Manṣūr (b. 1949, Egypt/USA) on Q. 2:221

Aḥmad Ṣubḥī Manṣūr was a graduate of al-Azhar who also taught there. When he criticised the Sufi camp among the Azharis, he received support from the Salafi-leaning scholars. However, when in 1985 he started expressing the view that the *ḥadīth*s are not a divinely-ordained source of Islam and thereby attacking what his colleagues perceived as the foundations of Sunni Islam, Salafis and traditional *'ulamā'* aligned to expel him from al-Azhar in 1987.[96] Aḥmad Ṣubḥī Manṣūr was imprisoned for two months, along with a number of his supporters. He fled to the United States and after his return was detained again briefly. He worked for various secularist causes as well as projects of religious reform and interreligious understanding.[97]

In 1999, he published a proposal for the reform of the Islamic religious education curricula on behalf of the secularist and human-rights-oriented Ibn Khaldun Center for Development Studies. This was part of a project entitled 'Making Egyptian Education Minority Sensitive' which aimed at promoting the value of Coptic history and culture and fostering tolerance. The Islamic religious education curriculum emphasised the values of tolerance and justice. It contained the claim that, according to the Qur'ān, all righteous believers, including non-Muslims, go to paradise. The project created much public hostility, mainly due to the involvement of Aḥmad Ṣubḥī Manṣūr and his Qur'ānist–modernist views on Islam, whereupon the Ministry of Education hastened to distance itself from the project, which was also condemned by the Egyptian parliament.[98]

After the arrest of the head of the Ibn Khaldun Center, Sa'd al-Dīn Ibrāhīm, and an increasing number of his followers and relatives, Aḥmad Ṣubḥī Manṣūr emigrated to the United States in October 2001.[99] The Qur'ānists continue to be subject to harassment and arrests in Egypt.[100]

Aḥmad Ṣubḥī Manṣūr continues to publish on, and work for, his causes which include Qur'ānism, pacifism and interreligious tolerance. His main publication outlet is the website *Ahl al-Qur'ān* from which the article below is taken. The website was established in 2006 by the International Quranic Center, an organisation founded by Aḥmad Ṣubḥī Manṣūr and largely devoted to spreading his ideas,[101] and features large amounts of text and video content, updated daily, in Arabic and English. Aḥmad Ṣubḥī Manṣūr is an important contributor, but by far not the only one. Many of his Arabic contributions are published on the English site in translation. The content on the website is not limited to religious discussions, but also contains news and political commentary with a focus on the Middle East. It strongly opposes – unsurprisingly – the Egyptian regime as well as Saudi Arabia, al-Qā'ida, ISIS and any form of jihadism.[102] The text in Excerpt 4.3 was published on 23 August 2017, in Arabic along with an English translation by Ahmed Fathy. For the sake of brevity I have summarised some of the discussion using my own words; my summaries are included within square brackets.

Excerpt 4.3

Q. 2:221

ووَلَا تَنكِحُوا الْمُشْرِكَاتِ حَتَّىٰ يُؤْمِنَّ وَلَأَمَةٌ مُّؤْمِنَةٌ خَيْرٌ مِّن مُّشْرِكَةٍ وَلَوْ أَعْجَبَتْكُمْ وَلَا تُنكِحُوا الْمُشْرِكِينَ حَتَّىٰ يُؤْمِنُوا وَلَعَبْدٌ مُّؤْمِنٌ خَيْرٌ مِّن مُّشْرِكٍ وَلَوْ أَعْجَبَكُمْ أُولَٰئِكَ يَدْعُونَ إِلَى النَّارِ وَاللَّهُ يَدْعُو إِلَى الْجَنَّةِ وَالْمَغْفِرَةِ بِإِذْنِهِ وَيُبَيِّنُ آيَاتِهِ لِلنَّاسِ لَعَلَّهُمْ يَتَذَكَّرُونَ ﴿٢٢١﴾

(221) Do not marry women who commit *shirk* until they believe; a believing slave woman is better than a woman who commits *shirk*,[103] though you may admire her. And do not marry any of our women to those who

commit *shirk* until they believe; a believing slave is better than a man who commits *shirk*, though you may admire him. Such people call to hellfire, but God calls you to the Garden and to forgiveness, by His permission. He makes His signs clear for people so that they may be reminded.

The *kāfirūn* in Islam legislation on marriage

Introduction:

1. We have received the following question: 'God says "Do not marry women who commit *shirk* until they believe". How can I prove to others I might talk to, drawing on verses of the Qur'ān, that *shirk* in this verse means aggression, rather than taking another deity besides God, whether it be human or made of stone?'
2. The answer to this question needs a lot of detail from the Qur'ān. I hope, God willing, to write a separate study in which I examine all the verses in the Qur'ān that contain the terms *kufr*, *shirk*, crime, injustice, aggression, transgression, sinfulness and disobedience. I will separate them into two categories: do they concern *kufr* in terms of behaviour, where it is up to us to deal with it and treat it according to Qur'ānic legislation, or do they concern *kufr* of the heart and with respect to worship as well as the question how to deal with it according to divine legislation?
3. Because that will require time, I will offer a quick and preliminary answer to the question above, leading up to a more extensive study.

First: the meaning in terms of behaviour when dealing with other people, it is peace. 'Islam' comes from *salām* ('peace').

1. The religion of God with regard to how people treat each other is Islam in the sense of peace. When the Arabs embraced peace, they entered Islam, the religion of God. God said to the Prophet Muḥammad about the victory towards the end of his life: 'When God's help and victory comes, when you see men entering God's religion in throngs' (Q. 110:1–2). The Prophet Muḥammad had no knowledge of what was in people's hearts, including the Islam of the heart, namely the commitment to the pure faith in the one mighty God alone. He could only see outward behaviour, which was Islam in the sense of peaceful demeanour. Thus, 'the religion of God' here means Islam in terms of behaviour, that is, peace.

The hostile unbelievers thus repented of their aggression, conducted the ritual prayer and paid the alms tax, outwardly, so they became brothers in the religion of peace. God says: 'If they repent and perform prayer and give the alms tax, they are your brothers in religion' (Q. 9:11). However, whether these acts come from their heart will be judged by God who recognises treachery and knows what is hidden in people's chests.

2. Therefore, any non-aggressive human is a Muslim in terms of peaceful behaviour, and no one is entitled to judge his belief and religion because the only authority who may judge belief and religion is God on Judgement Day. The hypocrites were unbelievers with respect to faith and religion, but with respect to behaviour, they were Muslims since they lived as citizens in the state of the Prophet Muḥammad whose basic legislative principle was the citizenship for all Muslims. They exerted their right for religious and political opposition peacefully according to Islamic legislation about unrestricted religious freedom.

[3–4.] ['Peace' is the greeting of Islam and of previous monotheistic religions. According to Q. 25:63, 28:55 and 43:88–89, it must be uttered even in response to ignorant and frivolous talk. Q. 4:94 and 4:90 state that enemy soldiers who utter the greeting of peace are to be spared because they became Muslims in terms of behaviour. Hence, Islam in terms of behaviour can be determined based on outwardly peaceful behaviour and it is this outwardly peaceful behaviour that determines marriage rules.]

Second: *kufr* and *shirk* in terms of behaviour signify aggression

1. Conversely, the opposite of peace is aggression, whether it is an individual criminal behaviour violating the rights of others, on which there are norms that tell us how to deal with it, or an all-out attack by a hostile state on a peaceful state. Here, this state is described, based on the direction of its aggression, as the antithesis of Islam, which is *kufr*. *Kufr* in terms of behaviour is the antithesis of Islam in terms of behaviour. Whoever fights a peaceful people by means of physical aggression is a *kāfir* by way of that aggression. We need to judge him according to his clear, uncontested behaviour. This applies to what Saudi Arabia is doing in Yemen, what ISIS is doing in Iraq and Syria and what suicide terrorists are doing all over the world, East and West. It also applies to their supporters and those who help them with words, ammunition, men or intelligence.

2. Hence, it is forbidden to marry them or to give a woman in marriage to them because through their deeds and words, they call to hellfire. The criterion here is the call to hellfire in words and deeds. This is what God refers to in Q. 2:221. [Verse is quoted in full.]

[The third section discusses, based on Qur'ānic references (Q. 2:208, 4:76, 2:190, 2:286, 9:10), God's call to paradise and Satan's call to hell. Satan calls humans to fight for wealth and power whereas God fighting for God's sake is limited to self-defence and the protection of religious freedom. Any act of aggression is forbidden. The Qur'ān describes the *kāfirūn* as aggressors.]

Fourth: there are two kinds of *kuffār*: those who are peaceful in terms of behaviour so that marrying them and giving a woman in marriage to them is allowed; and the hostile *kāfir* who may not be befriended or married and to whom no woman may be given in marriage.

1. The hostile *kuffār* are united by the fact that by their words and deeds they call to hellfire: 'Such people call to hellfire' (Q. 2:221). There are two kinds of them: one kind that directly commits acts of aggression and one that helps and supports them. There are people who don't join aggressors in their acts of aggression physically, by supplying soldiers and weapons, but who call to hellfire just like he they do by speech and incitement to violence, such as the religious scholars of terrorism in our age or those who seduce young people and lie to them in order to incite them to blowing themselves up. Such people have a share in oppression and aggression.
2. Then there are *kuffār* in terms of faith who revere humans or stones as sacred. This is true for most of mankind, such as Christians, Muḥammadans [i.e. Muslims who accept the Sunna as a source of faith], Buddhists, Hindus and so forth. But they are peace-loving, and God said about the rules for dealing with them: 'God does not forbid you to act kindly and with justice towards those who have not fought you over religion and have not driven you from your dwellings. God loves those who act justly'. (Q. 60:8) By their peacefulness, they are Muslims in terms of behaviour and they need to be treated kindly and with justice. Thus, within the scope of peaceful coexistence with them and of kindness and justice, it is allowed to marry them and to give them women in marriage on the basis of equity.

3. And finally, there are *kuffār* who attack Muslims and drive them from their homes, as well as those who help them in word and deed. Those are the hostile *kāfirūn* in terms of behaviour. It is forbidden to support them, to be friends with them or to forge an alliance with them, and thus it is also forbidden to marry them or give them women in marriage. God said: 'God only forbids you to make friends of those who have fought you over religion and have driven you from your dwellings and helped in your expulsion. Those who make friends of them – those are the wrong-doers' (Q. 60:9).

[4–6.] [Discussion of the broader historical context of *sūra* 60 and what it means on a normative level. This leads to the same conclusion that had been mentioned earlier, namely that it is permissible to marry peaceful non-Muslims.]

Fifth: justice and equity in dealing with those of different faith:

1. Equity is the higher objective [*maqṣad*] behind the mission of every messenger in every era. 'We sent down Our messengers with the clear proofs and We sent down with them the Scripture and the Balance that the people might uphold justice; and We sent down iron, in which there is great strength and benefits for the people, so that God might know who helps Him and His messengers in the Invisible. God is Strong and Mighty' (Q. 57:25). So, people should uphold justice between each other, in their dealings within the peaceful Muslim society with everyone who might differ with regard to the religion of their heart, but is peaceful in terms of behaviour.
2. This is even true when dealing with the hostile *kāfir*, meaning that the reaction to aggression should not be disproportionate to the original aggression. God said: 'Those who attack you, attack them in the way they attack you. Fear God and know that God is with the Godfearing' (Q. 2:194).
3. God's command to be just and kind in dealing with others is a general command. He said: 'God enjoins justice, doing good and giving to kinsfolk, while He forbids indecent conduct, disreputable deeds and insolence. He admonishes you so that you may be reminded' (Q. 16:90).
4. That is not all. God also warns us, first of all, against being biased against our opponents and prejudiced in favour of our relatives. Typically, most people are governed by their whims in dealing with those who differ from them and easily indulge in unfair

prejudices. God says, confirming the need for treating opponents justly: 'O you who believe, be steadfast for God, bearing witness with equity. Let not the hatred of any people induce you to act unjustly. Act justly – that is nearer to fear of God – and fear God. God is informed of what you do' (Q. 5:8). And He says about favouritism towards relatives: 'O you who believe, be steadfast in justice, witnesses for God, even if it is against yourselves or your parents or your close relatives. Whether the person be rich or poor, God is closer to both. Do not follow whim lest you turn. If you twist or turn away, you will find that God is informed of what you do' (Q. 4:135). Among the Ten Commandments is this Qur'ānic one: 'If you speak, be just, even though it is a relative' (Q. 6:152).

5. In light of the justice inherent in God's laws, we understand that a man who belongs to the People of the Book may marry a believing Muslim woman as long as a believing Muslim man may marry a woman belonging to the People of the Book while each of them may eat that which is permissible to the other. This follows from God's words: 'Today the good things have been permitted to you. The food of those who have been given the Scripture is lawful for you, and yours for them; and the chaste women of the believers and the chaste women of those who have been given the Scripture before you, if you give them their wages, and if you live with them in wedlock, not in some loose arrangement or taking them as companions. Those who do not believe in the faith, their work is in vain, and they will be among the losers in the next world' (Q. 5:5).
6. Justice is an objective [*maqṣad*] of the law, and all commands and prohibitions have to be measured against it. The execution of any command or prohibition must be subjugated to the standard of justice. Unfortunately, the Muḥammadans discarded justice in their religious laws and codified injustice. God does not love the injust, just as He does not love aggressors.[104]

The Qur'ānist nature of this text is apparent, first of all, from its method. It relies solely on Qur'ānic references to the exclusion of *ḥadīth*s, *tafsīr* works and the tradition of *fiqh*. When it does include some references to Muḥammad's life, this is mostly for background information on the original relevance of Qur'ānic verses. The author labels mainstream Muslims who do not reject the Sunna as a source of belief and religious law as 'Muḥammadans'. He thereby insinuates that, much like Christians and Buddhists, they deify a fallible human, rather than submitting to God alone.

The text further emphasises Muḥammad's human nature by stating that he could assess a person's belief no more than any other human.

The application of the Qurʾānist paradigm is framed by a thoroughly modernist approach to the Qurʾān that is typical for many proponents of Qurʾānism. The emphasis is not on detail, but on the *maqāṣid*, the higher aims of the Qurʾān, the foremost of which the author defines as justice. This is evident, for example, in the fact that the author insists on treating women and men equally where interreligious marriage is concerned, a view that is diametrically opposed to the traditional rules of *fiqh* according to which a Muslim woman may not marry a non-Muslim. While Aḥmad Ṣubḥi Manṣūr maintains the *fiqh* terminology of "giving a woman in marriage to a man" (*tazwīj*), he makes clear that any unequal treatment of men and women would contravene the higher divine principle of justice. Presumably on the same grounds, he makes no distinction between the People of the Book and adherents of other religions despite the fact that the Qurʾān often talks about the People of the Book specifically, and he certainly does not seem to consider 'Muḥammadans' above any of them.

Aḥmad Ṣubḥī Manṣūr completely rejects conventional definitions of *shirk* and *kufr* which, intriguingly, he treats as identical categories without elaborating on this. While he concedes that they have a semantic dimension related to religious belief, he maintains that this dimension is only known to God and is therefore not the subject of verses related to human behaviour and the treatment of others. That treatment should exclusively be based on the empirical categories of peacefulness versus aggression. He cites a number of Qurʾānic verses to support his view. Their place in the Qurʾānic chronology does not concern him. This might be due to the fact that he is an explicit opponent of the doctrine of abrogation[105] and therefore accords no special importance to verses from the late Medinan *sūra*s.

His focus is on peace, which he supports with reference to the semantic field of the root *s-l-m* from which the word *islām* is derived. Much of his discussion on peacefulness and inclusivism is couched in the language of modern statehood, possibly owing something to the Egyptian religious discourse in which the concept of equal citizenship (*muwāṭana*) for adherents of all religions, or at least the officially recognised ones, is hotly debated. The proponents of *muwāṭana*, much like Aḥmad Ṣubḥī Manṣūr, frequently talk about the 'state' of Medina, about its 'government' and the constitutional and political rights it granted, including the right to religious freedom.

The text's emphatic condemnation of Muslim terrorism is typical for the *Ahl al-Qurʾān* website, but it is also a particularly prominent feature of contemporary American discourses on Islam where links between Islam and terrorism are frequently made and vehement attempts to refute them are their natural consequence. Aḥmad Ṣubḥī Manṣūr rarely misses an opportunity to attack Saudi Arabia, ISIS or Muslim suicide bombers, and this text is no exception. It is clearly more than an apologetic text directed at Western non-Muslims, though. Rather, it constitutes a radical attempt to redefine Islam as a faith in relationship to other faiths, on the one hand, and as an attitude towards humanity, on the other hand. That attempt is based on an ingenious hermeneutical move. Rather than trying to make sense of the conflicting Qur'ānic statements on the status of unbelievers and the seemingly contradictory prescriptions for their treatment by applying the principle of abrogation or by reading the Qur'ān in a chronological fashion, as traditional scholars and many modernists do, Aḥmad Ṣubḥī Manṣūr distinguishes two levels of discourse, faith and behaviour. This allows him to harmonise divergent statements without having to prioritise or discard some of them – an essential prerequisite for reading the Qur'ān as a scripture that is comprehensive, clear, sufficient in itself, and dedicated to peace, mercy, justice and freedom.[106]

NOTES

1. Even within the writings of Muḥammad ʿAbduh alone, conflicting answers to that question can be found from the rather militant Qur'ānic interpretation advanced in *al-ʿUrwa al-wuthqā*, written together with Jamāl al-Dīn al-Afghānī, to the more education-oriented later writings. Cf. Pink, 'ʿAbduh, Muḥammad'.
2. See page 181, 'Islamist Qur'ānic interpretation'.
3. See, for example, Pink, 'Ein Monopol aufs Paradies?'; Khorchide, *Islam ist Barmherzigkeit*.
4. Wesselhoeft, 'A Hermeneutics of Intimacy'.
5. See Rahemtulla, *Qur'an of the Oppressed*.
6. The definition of modernism that I propose here is largely my own, but builds upon others, not all of which use the same terminology. For the historical emergence of modernist thought, see Kurzman, *Modernist Islam*; Hourani, *Arabic Thought in the Liberal Age*. For modernist (and other, especially postmodern) exegetical perspectives, see Wielandt, 'Exegesis of the Qur'an: Early Modern and Contemporary'; Taji-Farouki, *Modern Muslim Intellectuals and the Qur'an*; Körner, *Revisionist Koran Hermeneutics in Contemporary Turkish University Theology*. For a discussion of terminology and categories, see also Bauer, *Gender Hierarchy in the Qur'ān*, 6–7.
7. See page 265, 'Postmodern uncertainties and subjective approaches'.
8. On the Indonesian controversy, see, e.g., Ikhwan, An Indonesian Initiative to Make the Qur'an Down-to-Earth, 57–58.
9. For more information on some such models see, in particular, the chapters in Taji-Farouki, *Modern Muslim Intellectuals and the Qur'an*. For a shorter overview, see Campanini, *The Qur'an: Modern Muslim Interpretations*; Wielandt, 'Exegesis of the Qur'an: Early Modern and Contemporary'.
10. Al-Biqāʿī, *Maṣāʿid al-naẓar*.
11. For more information on historical and modern precedents of the methodology, see Tazul Islam, 'Maqāṣid al-Qur'ān'.

12. Pink, 'Riḍā, Rashīd'.
13. Tazul Islam and Khatun, 'Objective-Based Exegesis', 41–42.
14. Rahman, *Islam and Modernity*, 5–7; see also Wielandt, 'Exegesis of the Qur'an: Early Modern and Contemporary', 135.
15. This is a very commonplace position in a broad range of exegetical works. See, for example, al-Marāghī, *Tafsīr al-Marāghī*, vol. 4, 180–183; Mudzakir, 'Indonesian Muslim Women'. For a case study of an exegetical approach to the topic, see page 172, 'Defending polygamy: Karīmān Ḥamza (b. 1942, Egypt) on Q. 4:3'.
16. Pink, *Sunnitischer Tafsīr in der modernen islamischen Welt*, 153–157.
17. Al-Shawkānī is a notable exception. This seems to be a fairly late development, derived from a trend towards more vigorous *ḥadīth* criticism. Cf. Pink, 'Muhammad al-Shawkānī', 18–19.
18. Rippin, 'Occasions of Revelation'.
19. See, e.g., Pink, *Sunnitischer Tafsīr in der modernen islamischen Welt*, 212.
20. Cf. Pink, 'The Fig, the Olive'.
21. For more on the exegetical role of the Sunna, see page 155, 'The contested Sunna: from *ḥadīth*-based exegesis to Qur'ānism'.
22. Muḥammad ʿAbduh wrote individual treatises to specifically reject these stories, both of which are connected to specific passages of the Qur'ān. See ʿAbduh, *Tafsīr al-Fātiḥa*, 72–123.
23. Raven, 'Sīra and the Qur'ān'.
24. A good overview with further references is given in Wielandt, 'Exegesis of the Qur'an: Early Modern and Contemporary', 135–137.
25. Kermani, 'From Revelation to Interpretation: Nasr Hamid Abu Zayd and the Literary Study of the Qur'an'; Izutsu, *God and Man in the Koran: Semantics of the Koranic Weltanschauung*; On Abū Zayd's indebtedness to Izutsu, see Kermani, 'From Revelation to Interpretation', 177.
26. Hidayatullah, *Feminist Edges of the Qur'an*, 65–86.
27. Bauer, *Gender Hierarchy in the Qur'ān*, 19–20.
28. Wagemakers, 'Salafi Source Readings between Al-Qaeda and IS', 59–62.
29. The earliest edition I could find is Derveze, *Et-tefsirü'l hadîs*. It dates from 1997 and is marked as the second edition. The publisher is based in Bursa where Darwaza spent the last period of the Second World War and started writing his *tafsīr.*
30. Pink, *Sunnitischer Tafsīr in der modernen islamischen Welt*, 215, 290, 308, 311.
31. Based on a search in Turkish online bookstores and library catalogues. There might well be more such works. The commentaries I have found have been written by Hakkı Yılmaz (first published in 2007), Zeki Duman (2008), Ali Bulaç (2008), Mehmet Türk (2011), Recep İhsan Eliaçık (2011), Atilla Fikri Ergun (2013) and Mustafa Islamoğlu (2015).
32. Shihab, *Tafsir Al-Qur'an al-Karim*.
33. If we exclude the incomplete *tafsīr* 'in the order of revelation' by the Syrian scholar ʿAbd al-Raḥmān Ḥasan Ḥabannaka al-Maydānī (1927–2004); the author passed away after having completed the commentary on the first Medinan sura, Q. 2. The work does not seem to have been received remotely as widely as al-Jābirī's *tafsīr*. Cf. Ḥabannaka al-Maydānī, *Maʿārij al-tafakkur wa-daqāʾiq al-tadabbur*.
34. Al-Jābirī, *Fahm al-Qurʾān al-ḥakīm*.
35. Ibid., vol. 1, 18.

36. See, for example, the Qur'ānic commentary by the pioneer of chronological *tafsīr*, Muḥammad 'Izzat Darwaza, who devotes more than fifteen pages to the *sūra*, as opposed to al-Jābirī's two, and extensively discusses the status of religious freedom in Islam, drawing connections to a large number of later Qur'ānic utterances and *ḥadīth*s on the topic while showing little interest in the occasion of revelation of the *sūra* or the story behind it. Cf. Darwaza, *Al-Tafsīr al-ḥadīth*, vol. 1, 25–40.
37. Al-Jābirī clarifies in a footnote that the term *kāfir* might have another meaning in Arabic, that of ungratefulness, but that it here means a lack of belief in monotheism and prophethood.
38. Al-Jābirī, *Fahm al-Qur'ān al-ḥakīm*, vol. 1, 72–73. Text originally in Arabic.
39. Al-Jābirī, *Fahm al-Qur'ān al-ḥakīm*, vol. 1, 18.
40. Al-Jābirī, *Madkhal ilā al-Qur'ān*, 429–433.
41. Al-Jābirī, *Fahm al-Qur'ān al-ḥakīm*, vol. 1, 23–24.
42. Al-Jābirī, *Madkhal ilā al-Qur'ān*, 250–251.
43. Theodor Nöldeke (1836–1930), whose chronology al-Jābirī rejects, places this sura at the end of the early Meccan period which would be the third of al-Jābirī's six Meccan periods. See, also for the Egyptian chronology and other systems, Bell and Watt, *Introduction to the Qur'ān*, 206–213.
44. Raven, 'Sīra and the Qur'ān'.
45. Al-Jābirī, *Madkhal ilā l-Qur'ān*, 243.
46. Gilliot, ''Abdallāh b. 'Abbās'.
47. Al-Jābirī, *Madkhal ilā l-Qur'ān*, 233–254, esp. 243–245.
48. Specifically, al-Jābirī digresses from the Azhari arrangement with respect to the placement of Q. 1, 13, 17, 22, 55, 68, 71, 73, 76, 97 and 99.
49. In four of these cases, this conforms with Nöldeke's rough periodisation (Q. 13, 55, 76 and 99); his placement of Q. 99 might be inspired by Nöldeke. His placement of Q. 97 (Sūrat al-Qadr) in the Medinan period, on the other hand, is a minority opinion.
50. According to al-Azhar, the first five *sūra*s to have been revealed to Muḥammad are Q. 96, 68, 73, 74 and 1. Al-Jābirī considers three of them (Q. 68, 73 and 1) to be of later origin; he even situates Q. 73 as late as in the last year before the hijra, i.e. 621 instead of *c.* 610. As to the remaining two suras, Q. 96 and 74, he thinks that only their first parts were revealed at the beginning of Muḥammad's prophetic career while the rest of them came at later stages.
51. Which is not to say that, historically, the order of revelation of *sūra*s was established by Muslim scholars before they started discussing abrogation (see Rippin, 'Abrogation'). However, methodologically, and for a contemporary scholar, it might be desirable to base abrogation on a plausible Qur'ānic chronology.
52. Contemporary Muslim intellectuals frequently cite the Mu'tazilī Abū Muslim al-Iṣfahānī (868–934) as a premodern opponent of abrogation. However, he seems to have had little impact before the twentieth century.
53. Rippin, 'Abrogation'; Baljon, *Modern Muslim Koran Interpretation*, 49–50.
54. Taştan, 'Hüseyin Atay's Approach'.
55. Ṭāhā, *Al-Risāla al-thāniya*; Ṭāhā, *The Second Message of Islam*.
56. Pink, *Sunnitischer Tafsīr in der modernen islamischen Welt*, 61, 71–72.
57. See Biyografya, 'Talip Özdeş'.
58. As posted on his faculty website at <http://www.cumhuriyet.edu.tr/ilahiyat> and available at the website of the Turkish online bookseller Kitapyurdu.com in January 2017.

59. Al-Zamakhshsarī, *Kashshāf*, vol. 2, 428.
60. The author provides detailed references in footnotes for this and the subsequent statements he makes. The footnotes are omitted in the translation.
61. That is, the Jews and Christians.
62. Pre-Islamic Arab society; the period of 'ignorance'.
63. Some English translators render the Qurʾānic *muslimūn* as 'those who surrender' or 'submit to God' here to include monotheist believers before Islam, but Özdeş has *müslümanlar* which normally denotes Muslims.
64. Özdeş, *Kur'an ve nesh problemi*, 130–139. Text originally in Turkish.
65. Cf. the instructive collection of translations on <http://islamawakened.com/quran/16/101>, accessed 24 January 2017. Each of the options mentioned above is chosen by several translators.
66. Asad, *The Message of the Qurʾān*, 458.
67. Körner, *Revisionist Koran Hermeneutics in Contemporary Turkish University Theology*.
68. Ateş, *Kuran'da nesh meselesi*.
69. Özdeş, *Kur'an ve nesh problemi*, 132, n. 332.
70. This was expressed, among others, by Naṣr Ḥāmid Abū Zayd in his hermeneutical model based on theories of communication. See Wielandt, 'Wurzeln der Schwierigkeit', 135–136.
71. On the Qurʾānic semantics of 'Islam', see Smith, *An Historical and Semantic Study*; Izutsu, *God and Man in the Koran: Semantics of the Koranic Weltanschauung*.
72. Pink, 'Ein Monopol aufs Paradies?'
73. Rahman, 'Some Key Ethical Concepts of the Qur'ān'.
74. Wielandt, 'Exegesis of the Qur'an: Early Modern and Contemporary'.
75. Naguib, 'Bint al-Shāṭiʾ's Approach to *Tafsīr*'; Wielandt, 'Exegesis of the Qur'an: Early Modern and Contemporary', 131–134.
76. Already in 1969, a Shiʿi Ayatollah published his own exposition of this approach in Najaf in Iraq: al-Abṭaḥī, *Al-Madkhal ilā al-tafsīr al-mawḍūʿī*.
77. Shaltūt, *Tafsīr al-Qurʾān al-karīm: Al-Ajzāʾ al-ʿashara al-ūlā*.
78. Ghazālī, *Naḥwa tafsīr mawḍūʿī li-suwar al-Qurʾān al-karīm*.
79. Shihab, *Wawasan al-Quran: Tafsir tematik atas pelbagai persoalan umat*.
80. Rahman, *Major Themes of the Qurʾān*.
81. Cf. Pink, 'Striving for a New Exegesis of the Qurʾān', 784–785. Further references are provided there. For Indonesia, see also Ikhwan, An Indonesian Initiative to Make the Qur'an Down-to-Earth, 38–39.
82. See, for example, Hidayatullah, *Feminist Edges of the Qur'an*, 31–33.
83. Some recent examples are Dubayshī, *Al-Taqwā fī'l-Qurʾān al-karīm*; al-ʿAssāfī, *Al-Ibrīz fī'l-tafsīr al-mawḍūʿī li-Kitāb Allāh al-ʿazīz*; Jamāl al-Dīn, *Al-Uṣūl al-manhajiyya*; Qarʿāwī, *Dirāsāt min al-tafsīr al-mawḍūʿi*; Yanbuʿī, *Mafhūm al-āya fī'l-Qurʾān al-karīm*. Some of these are part of series that contain more titles of the kind.
84. For an example, see page 247, 'Debates on same-sex marriage: Mun'im Sirry (b. 1973, Indonesia) on the story of Lot'.
85. Fudge, 'Qurʾānic Exegesis in Medieval Islam and Modern Orientalism', 119–124.
86. Saleh, 'Ibn Taymiyya'.
87. Robson, 'Ḥadīth'.
88. For an entirely uncritical Salafi take on this last *ḥadīth* see Islam Q & A, 'More Women in Hell than Men?'

89. Brown, *Rethinking Tradition*, 104–107.
90. Some Qur'ānist websites are <http://www.ahl-alquran.com/arabic/index.php> (in Arabic), <https://www.alrahman.de/koran-hadith-und-islam> (in German), <http://www.quransmessage.com/articles/hadith%20FM2.htm>, <https://www.free-minds.org>, <http://www.quran-islam.org/articles/a_dozen_reasons_(P1153).html>, <https://muslimsforallah.com>, <http://www.islam-koran.net/page/homepage> (in Dutch) and <http://www.ongegrondehadith.nl> (in Dutch), all accessed 4 March 2017.
91. The Oxford Dictionary of Islam, 'Ahl al-Quran'.
92. The group has a number of websites, among them <www.submission.ws>, <www.submission.org>, <www.submission.info>, <www.masjidtuqson.org>, all accessed 4 March 2017.
93. Admin [username], 'Edip Yuksel'.
94. For more on Aḥmad Ṣubḥī Manṣūr and his publications, see the subsequent section.
95. See, for example, for the case of Nigeria: Nigeria Research Network, *Islamic Actors and Interfaith Relations in Northern Nigeria.*
96. Zeghal, *Gardiens de l'Islam*, 320; Zeghal, 'The "Recentering" of Religious Knowledge', 121.
97. This is based on Aḥmad Ṣubḥī Manṣūr's own description of the situation. See Mansour, 'the quranists'.
98. When I was in Egypt in October 1999 conducting research on a subject related to religious freedom and minorities, I talked to Aḥmad Ṣubḥī Manṣūr at the Ibn Khaldun Center and received a copy of his proposal for the reform of Islamic religious education and a folder of collected press articles on the issue. I conducted my own research of press reports in addition to these. Many of them criticised the German source of funding for the project and specifically attacked the Islamic religious education proposal authored by Aḥmad Ṣūbḥī Manṣūr for its derogatory treatment of the prophet's companions that was at odds with a mainstream Sunni perspective on early Islamic history. Some of the more pertinent examples of dozens of press reports and commentaries are Luṭfī, 'Tamwīl ajnabī', and Sulṭān, 'Manāhij tahmīsh al-dīn'. Muḥammad Rajab al-Bayyūmī published an all-out attack on all the religious ideas expressed by Aḥmad Ṣubḥī Manṣūr on behalf of al-Azhar; see al-Bayyūmī, 'Hādhā al-manhaj li'l-tarbiyya al-dīniyya', 41; see also Sulaymān, 'Mashrūʿukum al-taʿlīmī yushʿil al-nār fī Miṣr'. Aḥmad Ṣubḥi Manṣūr himself was interviewed, besides his opponents, in Shafīq, 'Al-tasūmuḥ'.
99. Mansour, 'the quranists'.
100. For media reports and Qur'ānist accounts, see, for example, Daily News Egypt. 'Quranists Still behind Bars'; Minority Rights Group International. *Quranists of Egypt*; The Telegraph. 'Egyptian Quranist Detained, Released'; Montasser, 'The Mistaken Crusade'; Yuksel, 'Another Quranist is Arrested'.
101. See the Ahl al-Qur'ān website's mission statement at <http://www.ahl-alquran.com/English/aboutus.php>.
102. There is also some commentary on Israel and Palestine; this is an issue on which Aḥmad Ṣubḥī Manṣūr takes a complex and nuanced stance, criticising human rights violations perpetrated by both sides. He opposes the attribution of particular religious prestige to the al-Aqṣā mosque; see Manṣūr, 'Hādhā "al-Aqṣā" fī al-Quds huwa masjid ḍarār' This is connected to an ongoing tendency, on his

part, to attribute particular religious prestige to Egypt: Manṣūr, 'Al-Masjid al-aqṣā al-ḥaqīqī fī arḍ Miṣr.' 18.

103. A term commonly translated as 'associating others with God', 'idolatry' or 'polytheism', but since Aḥmad Ṣubḥī Manṣūr does not believe that this verse refers to those meanings and the true meaning of *shirk* is at the heart of his argument, I have left the term untranslated.

104. Manṣūr, 'Al-Kāfirūn fī tashrīʿ al-zawāj al-islāmī'. Text originally in Arabic. The site also offers a loosely translated English version; see Mansour, 'Polytheists and Disbelievers'.

105. Manṣūr, 'Kitāb: Lā nāsikh wa-lā mansūkh'.

106. As per the Ahl al-Qurʾān website's mission statement.

5

IN DEFENCE OF A PERFECT SCRIPTURE: THE QURʾĀN AS A HOLISTIC SYSTEM

Apologetics play a central role in many contemporary exegetical works. This has a number of reasons. Already in the nineteenth century, Muslim reformers had a desire to protect the Qurʾān against attacks and to defend it against orientalists, Christian missionaries and secularists who doubted its divine origin and perfection. They achieved this, for example, by proposing rationalist interpretations of the Qurʾān that portrayed it as being free of superstitions and contradictions and by defending the rationale behind Qurʾānic legal prescriptions. One area of particular interest was science: many exegetes had an interest in showing that the Qurʾān is in harmony with modern scientific insights. In the twentieth century, Islamist movements who understood Islam as a holistic and perfect system and way of life emerged, and exegetical approaches intending to highlight the Qurʾān's perfection, sometimes in unprecedented ways, gained increasing prominence; one of them, the rejection of abrogation, has already been mentioned. The subsequent text will provide an example for the exegetical strategies that are quite frequently used to defend the Qurʾān's statements against competing value systems.

Defending polygamy: Karīmān Ḥamza (b. 1942, Egypt) on Q. 4:3

During the 1990s, at a time at which an increasing number of Egyptian celebrities discovered their faith, Karīmān Ḥamza gained a certain amount of fame as the only woman who was allowed to wear a headscarf on public television, if only briefly, in Ramadan, during one of the religious programmes she anchored. She had been among the early adopters of an Islamisation that swept the country after 1967 and forced the Egyptian regime to make some concessions such as an increased presence of religious topics in state media.[1] Under the influence of the famous shaykh ʿAbd al-Ḥalīm Maḥmūd (1910–1978) who had developed distinct Islamist leanings towards the end of his career, she started donning a headscarf in her twenties, well before it became fashionable for middle and upper-class Egyptian women to do so.[2] Besides presenting religious shows on television, including a program for children on the Qur'ān, Karīmān Ḥamza wrote a number of books such as a spiritual autobiography, *My Journey to the Veil* (1981).[3]

At the end of 2008, Egyptian media announced in rather sensationalist tones that al-Azhar, the highest Islamic authority of the country, had consented to the publication of the first *tafsīr* of the Qur'ān carried out by a woman. In actual fact, Karīmān Ḥamza who, according to the brief introduction to her work, wrote this work in the short span of three years, was supported by a team of seven persons, five of whom were men. They are said to have helped by making proposals and providing references.[4] In any case, al-Azhar's Council of Islamic Research testified that Karīmān Ḥamza's *tafsīr* was completely in line with the exegetical tradition and did not contradict Islamic law in any way, underlining its conformity with the approach to *tafsīr* practiced by traditional scholars.[5] This conformity was confirmed by the eminently traditional title of the work when it was finally published in 2009: *Al-Lu'lu' wa'l-marjān fī tafsīr al-Qur'ān* (roughly translatable as 'Pearls and Corals of Qur'ānic Exegesis'), a poetic two-part title containing a colourful image and a rhyme in the way that many *'ulamā'* have named their works for centuries[6] and still do today, not least at al-Azhar. The same desire to bolster the respectability of her work is apparent in the list of references that contains the most eminent premodern Qur'ānic commentaries, all major *ḥadīth* collections, a scarce selection of premodern and modern works on theology, law and prophetic biography as well as a few twentieth-century *tafsīr* works. These include exegetical efforts by Sayyid Quṭb, some modernists, several proponents of the 'scientific miracle' of the Qur'ān and a number of *'ulamā'*, including the *shaykh al-Azhar* Maḥmūd Shaltūt (1893–1963).[7]

Both al-Azhar and Karīmān Ḥamza herself were quick to reject the sensationalist headlines, pointing out that this was not the first work of *tafsīr* by a woman. An al-Azhar spokesman mentioned the book by a female leader of the Muslim Brotherhood, Zaynab al-Ghazālī (1917–2005), *Naẓarāt fī'l-Qur'ān al-karīm* (Viewpoints on the Noble Qur'ān), first published in 1994.[8] Both al-Azhar and Karīmān Ḥamza herself also emphasised that her work is not a 'women's interpretation' since it neither focusses on women's issues nor does it aim to provide a 'female perspective'. Al-Azhar even denied that such a thing as a 'women's interpretation' of the Qur'ān exists. Karīmān Ḥamza explained that her work was meant to address ordinary people. According to her, her ability to interpret it in a simple language made up for her lack of qualification as a scholar. She underlined her book's educational value; the al-Azhar representative talked about it as a work for children and youths.[9] This relegation of exegetical works by women to the sphere of the education of minors is extremely common. The introduction to *Al-Lu'lu' wa'l-marjān* focusses strongly on the central aim of facilitating access to the Qur'ān's guidance (*hidāya*).[10] This, Karīmān Ḥāmza frequently achieves, by defending the Qur'ān's ordinance against potential criticism, as the following excerpt shows.

This commentary strives to be as traditional in style and content as possible although it was not written by a trained scholar or, rather, precisely because it was not written by a trained scholar. On top of that, it was written by a woman.[11] While not exactly the first Qur'ānic commentary written by a woman, it was the first in Egypt that carried the label *tafsīr* and that was approved by al-Azhar, the highest Sunni institution in the country. It needed that approval, and in order to obtain it, it was probably helpful that it did not transgress conventional boundaries. Nation-state policies regulating publications on the Qur'ān need to be taken into account when trying to understand why specific forms are so persistent.

Nevertheless, it is unlikely that Karīmān Ḥamza would have wanted to produce a less traditional work under different circumstances. Her discussion of Q. 4:3, a verse that is commonly understood as permitting polygamous – or, more specifically, polygynous – marriages, essentially sets out as a classical paraphrastic commentary where the Qur'ān is explained fragment by fragment in running text (see Excerpt 5.1). The one external source that interrupts the explanation is a widely-quoted *ḥadīth* whose origin with the Prophet's wife 'Ā'isha might be emphasised by Karīmān Ḥamza a bit more than usual. This is the only indication that the commentary was written by a woman. Karīmān Ḥamza includes in this unremarkably conventional commentary the opinions of several respected authorities on some of the precise implications of the verse and also on its rationale, which is clearly an important concern to Ḥamza. Her selection is geared to salvage the reputation of premodern exegetes by focussing on such opinions that emphasise justice and explain the benefits of polygyny.

Excerpt 5.1

Q. 4:3

وَإِنْ خِفْتُمْ أَلَّا تُقْسِطُوا فِي الْيَتَامَىٰ فَانكِحُوا مَا طَابَ لَكُم مِّنَ النِّسَاءِ مَثْنَىٰ وَثُلَاثَ وَرُبَاعَ فَإِنْ
خِفْتُمْ أَلَّا تَعْدِلُوا فَوَاحِدَةً أَوْ مَا مَلَكَتْ أَيْمَانُكُمْ ذَٰلِكَ أَدْنَىٰ أَلَّا تَعُولُوا ﴿٣﴾

(3) If you fear that you will not act justly towards the orphans, marry such of the women as it seems good to you: two, three or four; but if you fear that you will not be equitable, one only or what your right hands possess [i.e., female slaves]. That makes it more likely that you will not be unfair.

(If you fear that you will not act justly) If you fear that you will not be equitable **(towards the orphans)** towards the female orphans. The Mother of Believers, ʿĀʾisha, interpreted this as follows: 'It is about a female orphan who is the ward of a guardian who is attracted to her possessions and beauty. Therefore, the guardian wants to marry her without acting justly (i.e., being equitable) with respect to her *ṣadāq* (i.e., her *mahr* or dower) and without giving her the equivalent of what other men would give her. So they [i.e. the guardians] were forbidden from marrying them unless they acted justly towards them and paid them the highest appropriate dower (i.e., paid them the highest amount from the range that equivalent or similar women were given), and they were ordered to marry whatever other women pleased them'. This was narrated by al-Bukhārī. **(Marry such of the women as it seems good to you: two, three or four)** that is, other than the orphans mentioned before. **(Two, three or four)** ʿUrwa b. al-Zubayr, the transmitter of the *ḥadīth* from ʿĀʾisha, explained: leave them alone, for four others were permitted to you. [1] **(But if you fear that you will not be equitable, one only)** If you are afraid that you will not be able to be equitable and that one of them may suffer from unfairness because of it, content yourselves with one. **(Or what your right hands possess)** which refers to the system of concubinage that was widespread among the Arabs and in the world before the advent of Islam, but went into decline in the Muslim world after Islam had dried up its sources. **(That makes it more likely that you will not be unfair.)** That comes closest to preventing you from treating them unfairly and unjustly. [As an alternative explanation,] al-Shāfiʿī [767–820] said: it comes closest to preventing an enormous increase of your descendants so your expenses do not increase to an extent where you would not be able to cover them any longer. Both meanings need to be accepted.

Al-Ṭabarī [d. 923] lists the opinions of a number of exegetes and then says: 'The preferable opinion is the one that says "When you are afraid, then marry no more than those that you do not fear you will treat unjustly, from one to four." If you fear you will treat even one [woman] unjustly, then do not marry her, but rather [have intercourse with] your female slaves; with them, it is easier to avoid treating them unjustly.' Al-Zamakhsharī [d. 1144] says: 'If you fear not to do justice with regard to the rights of orphans and if you also fear to not to do justice between your wives, then lower the number of your wives. It was also said: they did not refrain from fornication while refusing to do their duty by their orphaned wards, and it was said: if you fear injustice with respect to the rights of orphans, fear fornication; marry those women that are permitted to you.' Al-Marāghī [d. 1952] said: 'If you feel fear that you might enrich yourself unlawfully at the expense of your orphaned wife, you may not marry her. God granted you an alternative choice from those orphans, namely those that he allowed you to marry, one, two, three or four.'

[Note 1] When Islam came, some men had four wives or more than that or less. Islam laid down a limit that Muslims were not allowed to transgress, which is four wives. Then it tied that number to the ability to be equitable, else only one wife would be permitted. The required equity concerns one's conduct towards them, their sustenance and intimate relations. Concerning equity with regard to feelings and affection, a Muslim has to make every effort to control them and distribute them fairly. Thus, Islam did not come in order to grant men license in marriage, but to restrict polygyny by equity which, if it cannot be granted, prevents men from making use of the permission they have been given [to marry up to four wives]. Islam wanted to address the circumstances of different societies in different situations, for example when the number of marriageable women is higher than that of marriageable men, especially as a result of war, or when social and economic circumstances are in decline, so that the burden of founding a family becomes too high for many young men, just as in our present days. Or the wife succumbs to a chronic disease and cannot fulfil her marital duties, or the wife is sterile, but the husband wants to procreate, so religious law allows him to marry another wife while the first one may keep her husband and her life. Religious law also gives the wife the right to stipulate before the wedding that there are to be no further wives as well as the right to reject this later on, and it orders husbands to treat their wives well. The Prophet even said: 'The best among you is the one who treats his family best.' Thereby, Islam works to cut down on all options for fornication and illicit relations. Many do not know that Islam was the first religion to restrict the number of wives. In Judaism, there is no restriction on the number of wives. It says in the Bible, the Old Testament, that the Prophet David had numerous wives and the Prophet Solomon had a thousand wives and a concubine. Before these two, the Prophet Jacob had four wives, two sisters and their two slave girls.

[There follow quotations from the book *Women and Jewish Law* by Rachel Biale (New York: Schocken Books, 1984), including a summary of the author's academic credentials, and from the seventh edition of the *New Standard Jewish Encyclopaedia* edited by Geoffrey Wigoder (New York & Oxford: Facts on File, 1992), to the effect that there were nearly no limits to the number of wives a Jew could have until a ban on polygamy was introduced among Ashkenazi Jews around the year 1000 and that even today, while it is not possible to enter into a polygamous marriage in Israel, such marriages, when they exist, are recognised.]

Likewise, there is no explicit text from the four Gospels that limits the number of wives. There is even a parable that Jesus told about the bridegroom who had ten virgins (Mt 25:1–13). Furthermore, Jesus said in the Gospel: 'I have not come to abolish the law', i.e. the Mosaic law which did not set any limits to the number of wives. As to the prohibition of polygamy in Christianity, it was enforced by the Church Fathers, just like celibacy which is against human nature and was not enjoined by the Gospels. Of course, they were unable to comply with it, and so there emerged illicit practices among them from that time onward until this day. The early clergy left their distinct mark on many matters of Christian life. They despised all worldly pleasures, even the licit ones, whether it was good food, beautiful dresses or lawful gains from trade; and even where marriage was concerned, they considered it better to abstain from it. St Jerome considered sexual intercourse between a man and his wife, for the sake of pleasure, wrong. It is worth mentioning that the early Catholic clergy prohibited every Christian from purchasing the Bible in order to retain their monopoly on religion. They were the key to it and its explanation, and anyone who wanted to know it had to resort to them. This ban was upheld, meaning that everyone who was found with a copy of the Bible was punished, until Martin Luther – who said that there is no text in the Bible that limits the number of wives – came at the beginning of the sixteenth century and recorded his objections against the Church, setting off the Protestant Reformation. Martin Luther affirmed in 'Wittenburg Deliberation' [*sic*] the right of King [*sic*] Philipp of Hesse to take a second wife. Melanchthon, Bucer and four other Protestant Reformers shared in this statement. Luther established, adhering closely to the Bible, that it does not prohibit any man to marry a second wife and that this cannot be considered to be contrary to the sacred texts. It was not possible for anyone in Europe to purchase their holy book without fear of punishment until about the middle of the sixteenth century. If we leaf through the book of Pope Shanūda [III; patriarch of the Coptic Orthodox Church, 1923–2012] *The Law of Monogamy in Christianity*, we find that the first page of the introduction which is entitled 'Sources of Religious Lawgiving and Christianity' starts by saying that the first fundamental source of Christianity is the Bible with its two testaments. Then there are traditions and the general consensus. In the second paragraph, he then says that there are also the laws of the Church, and he explains them in the third paragraph: 'All these laws that were put down by the apostles, the synods and the clergy build upon the ecclesiastical authority that the Lord Messiah granted by his words "Truly, I say to you, whatever you bind on Earth shall be bound in heaven, and whatever you loose on Earth shall be loosed in heaven" [Mt 18:18]'. Through this text in the Gospel, the clergy gained the power of permitting and prohibiting things, of forgiving sins or of expelling from Christianity whomever they wanted, of admitting Christians to Paradise or excluding them from it or from salvation. Even though the Pope's book contains more than a hundred pages, he does not provide a single clear and explicit textual reference from Jesus that prohibits marriage with more than one wife. But he allows you to glean some texts such as: 'Therefore, the scholar Tertullianus [d. after 220] said: everyone knows now that it was permitted to our priests – and even their bishops – not only to marry, but also to marry several wives; moreover, they even retained concubines…In past times, it was necessary to uphold practices that need to be annulled or amended in the future'. The early Christians practiced polygamy, and the Church only enforced monogamy several centuries after Christ. It is a custom enforced by the Church, just as it enforced celibacy and just as the Roman Church prohibited Christians from purchasing the Bible.

[There follows a half-page summary of information from the book *After Polygamy was made a Sin: The social history of Christian polygamy* by John Cairncross (London: Routledge and Kegan Paul, 1974), stating that polygamy was customary in the first centuries of Christianity, that it was only banned in the wake of the laws of Emperor Justinian I in the sixth century under the influence of Roman law, that there was opposition to it among Protestant movements, that a number of European monarchs and intellectuals supported polygamy, and that the Mormons practice it until this day.][12]

However, a traditional approach that limits itself to reproducing premodern interpretations is obviously not quite sufficient in this case, which becomes apparent from the fact that Ḥamza felt a need to include a footnote that is at least four times as long as the actual text. This is because it is simply not possible any longer for a contemporary exegete to treat the issue of polygyny as casually as premodern exegetes did.

It is not that exegetes up until well into the second half of the nineteenth century saw no problem with the verse. They did. They devoted long and complex discussions to questions such as the one that Ḥamza quotes from al-Ṭabarī, specifically, whether a man who fears not being able to treat four wives justly should remain monogamous, as the verse literally states, or whether he could at least marry two or three women. They discussed whether it is possible to marry a slave girl or only a free woman; whether intercourse with a slave girl requires her consent; what it means to do justice to a slave concubine as opposed to a free woman; whether the wives whom men are encouraged to marry include orphans; whether the condition of 'fearing' to do injustice only applies when the man is certain that he will not do justice or already when he merely suspects so; and so forth. They did not, however, see any need to justify the mere existence of the institutions of concubinage, slavery and polygamy.

This changed drastically in the late-nineteenth century when colonisers, Christian missionaries and orientalists branded slavery and polygamy symptoms of cruelty and backwardness. Until today, polygamy is a thorny issue and a common topic in anti-Muslim discourses. Muslim intellectuals and scholars responded sometimes by pleading for the abolition of these institutions and sometimes by justifying their existence through an apologetic discourse that focussed on the Qur'ān. As for slavery, it was largely abolished, at least in the Ottoman Empire of which Egypt was a part, due to the pressure of European powers around the turn of the century. Consequently, the matter-of-fact way in which the Qur'ān talks about it threatened to become a source of embarrassment. However, nowhere does the Qur'ān explicitly command Muslims to own slaves; it depicts the institution of slavery as a given fact of life, but also portrays the manumission of individual slaves as beneficial. Therefore, it became a common apologetic argument to say that Islam meant to 'dry up the sources' of slavery anyway, as Ḥamza puts it. This makes it appear as if the eventual abolition of slavery is like a natural result of the teachings of the Qur'ān which is a rather ahistorical concept given the fact that slavery, in various forms, thrived for more than a millennium after the birth of Islam. This cavalier way of dealing with Islamic history stands in stark contrast to the historical details that Karīmān Ḥamza provides on the history of Christianity. Indeed, this technique is a key ingredient of every apologetic discourse: the juxtaposition, on very uneven terms, of two sides, one that is the apologist's own and one against which the own side is defended. On the one hand, there is an idealised, purified image of the own side, based on an ethical reading of its sources that is free of contradictions; and on the other hand, there are the less-than-appealing historical realities of the other side. In reality, contemporary ethical values dramatically clash with historical – and present – realities on both sides, but admitting to that fact would, of course, not serve any apologetic purpose.

The footnote is where both the apologia and the reference to concrete historical and contemporary events take place because these are not part of traditional interpretations of this verse and are therefore not included in the main text. Some, but by far not all of the arguments Ḥamza adduces in the footnote are her own. The discourse on Islamic polygamy has brought forth an apologetic tradition of its own and Ḥamza makes extensive use of this tradition.

First, there is the assertion that Islam came to improve a situation in which there were no ethical or legal limits to the number of wives a man could have. The text gives the impression that Islamic law was the first to set any such limits, calling it 'the first religion to restrict the number of wives'. This might be an acceptable statement if one shares the author's exclusive focus on the religions mentioned in the Qur'ān and does not consider Greek and Roman antiquity an important point of comparison. Comparisons with other historical cultures that appear convincing at first glance, but upon further scrutiny turn out to be highly selective, are a standard feature of apologetics.

The same can be said for the conflation of ethical and legal norms. When Ḥamza says Islam 'came to restrict polygyny by equity which, if it cannot be granted, prevents men from making use of the permission they have been given', she avoids addressing the question whether this is an actual legal restriction that may be enforced any time, granting each wife rights that she may successfully claim, or whether it is more of an ethical exhortation that only takes effect when the husband is pious enough to strive at obeying it. Besides, the general concept of equity and just treatment is relatively vague and not all of its components, as outlined by Ḥamza, seem easily enforceable.

Ḥamza further underlines the superiority of polygamy by the argument that Islamic norms allow for flexible adaptation to a particular society's or individual's needs. Here, Ḥamza inserts an implicit reference to what is often called the 'marriage crisis' in Egypt: the inability of many young men, for financial reasons, to marry and found a family. This is a serious problem that her readers will be well able to relate to although it is unclear how the verse in question contributes to its solution since the option of having intercourse with female slaves instead of marriage does no longer exist and the option of having multiple wives is hardly helpful for a man who cannot even afford one wife.

The main part of the footnote is devoted to proving that polygamy is part of Judaism and originally also of Christianity. The latter is the focus of Ḥamza's argument since Christians are obviously the main counterpart of the apologia. The argument is bolstered by many detailed references to English-language sources – another common apologetic device. The intention is to impress readers with seemingly impartial knowledge. Western non-Muslim authors frequently have an important function as chief witnesses since they can be assumed to have no pro-Islamic apologetic intention. Besides, the references give the footnote a rather scientific flair although a closer look reveals the sources to be popular scientific at best. This is rather typical since the objective is not to summarise up-to-date scholarship, but to collect evidence that supports the apologetic argument.

The presentation of various aspects of Christian attitudes to polygamy contains an unusual amount of details and is more precise than many Muslim apologetic texts on that subject. For example, Ḥamza is aware that contrary to Qur'ānic terminology, there are four Gospels in the Bible, not one, although she frequently reverts to Muslim conventions when she talks of 'the Gospel'. On the other hand, Ḥamza's argument jumps between centuries and denominations, partly addressing the Coptic Orthodox Church which is relevant to the Egyptian context but to which some of the author's arguments pertaining to the Roman Catholic Church or Protestantism – derived from her English-language literature – do not apply at all. Many of the details are imprecise, such as the spelling of 'Wittenburg' (in Latin letters) instead of 'Wittenberg' and the designation of Philipp of Hesse as a king, instead of a landgrave. In any case, the reference to Luther is standard fare in Muslim apologetic discourses on polygamy, as is the presentation of Mormonism as a Western example of polygamous practices.

The discussion of the Jewish and Christian positions on polygamy serves several purposes. Most obviously, it is meant to demonstrate that the Qurʾānic permission of polygyny is not a deviation from some universal ethical norm, but rather in line with the teachings of all major religions. It also bolsters the belief that the Qurʾān was revealed to confirm the Jewish and Christian scriptures and that differences between the religions are mainly the result of later distortions. Finally, it suggests that Islam is superior to earlier religions, especially to Christianity whose history is cast in a rather negative light. Ḥamza spends much effort on criticising the Christian clergy for having introduced innovations that contradict the Bible, such as celibacy, and for having tried to prevent Christians from reading the Bible. The result is that Christianity is portrayed as a significant aberration from the divine law which is, by contrast, preserved in Islam. The argument rests on the assumption that religion should exclusively be defined by the contents of its foundational scriptural sources. Later developments are not granted any legitimacy.

Karīmān Ḥamza does not pull out all the stops of Muslim apologetic discourses on polygamy, though. Her argument on the social and individual benefits of polygamy is cursory and there is no attempt to back it up by references to the natural sciences, such as male hormones, female dispositions and other biologist claims. Clearly, she primarily wants to treat this as a question of faith. That this is even necessary, however, is a rather modern development. The need to justify and defend the institution of polygamy is so strong that it forces the author to transcend her general focus on the Sunni exegetical tradition.

ISLAMIST QURʾĀNIC INTERPRETATION

Islamism is not the only source of modern apologetic discourses which started far earlier, with reformers such as Sayyid Aḥmad Khān and

Muḥammad ʿAbduh, but it is an important one. Islamist movements started out in opposition to Western imperialism and the hegemony of Western culture. They presented an Islamic system as a superior, even perfect, alternative, and that system was supposed to be based on the Qur'ān.

Islamist Qur'ānic interpretation brought forth two major exegetical works that have inspired many others within the Islamist ideological context and outside it: those of Sayyid Quṭb (1906–1966) and Abū al-Aʿlā Mawdūdī (1903–1979). Islamist *tafsīr* has thus developed a set of exegetical authorities of its own. It is also defined by a number of shared ideological considerations that are contained in Islamist works of exegesis, besides other themes and interests. Finally, it occupies a specific social space. Sayyid Quṭb was a member of the Muslim Brotherhood that was founded in Egypt in 1928 while Mawdūdī founded the Jamāʿat-e Islāmī in colonial India in 1941 and was its head in Pakistan after the division of India. Both exegetes were thus part of activist movements with a political agenda, namely the creation of both an Islamic society and an Islamic state.

While the works by Sayyid Quṭb and Mawdūdī differ greatly from each other in scope, method and some of their conclusions, they also have many things in common. Most importantly, they advocate a return to the original sources, the Qur'ān and – although to a much lesser extent – the Sunna, and want to let them speak directly to today's believers. The immediate relevance of the Qur'ān for contemporary Muslims is to be limited neither by previous interpretations nor by attempts to bring the Qur'ān into line with modern ideas; conversely, the goal is to bring contemporary society into line with Qur'ānic ideals.

Sayyid Quṭb's extensive Arabic Qur'ānic commentary *Fī ẓilāl al-Qur'ān* (In the Shadow of the Qur'ān) is presented as a continuous narrative of personal musings on the message of each *sūra*. It was written between 1951 and 1965. In that period, Sayyid Quṭb was the Muslim Brotherhood's chief ideologue, and he spent much of that time in prison due to the Nasserist regime's persecution of this organisation. His musings reflect the ensuing ideological radicalisation. They exhort believers to renounce their obedience to any ruler who tyrannically sets his own, man-made laws above those of God and requires his subjects to worship him; to worship God alone; and to give their allegiance to neither the tyrannical ruler nor his servants, but only to the small avant-garde of true Muslims who are going to give birth to a renewed Islamic society. Present-day Muslim societies are denounced as *jāhiliyya*, a new age of ignorance of God's laws worse than the one before the revelation of the Qur'ān.

However, Sayyid Quṭb's Qur'ānic commentary cannot be reduced to an attempt to read the Qur'ān along the lines of this ideological paradigm. His radicalism went much beyond a social and political vision, extending to his hermeneutical approach. He reads the Qurʾān as a coherent text that is directly relevant to a contemporary believer. It needs no mediation, no rationalisation, no historical contextualisation; rather, it has a direct emotional impact. This search of 'a new immediacy to the Qurʾān'[13] was novel and set Quṭb apart from the modernists who were typically far more rationalist. It is probably the main reason for the attractiveness of his work even to audiences who do not share his religio-political convictions. Sayyid Quṭb's holistic perspective on *sūra*s and larger textual units within *sūra*s, as well as his quest for a coherent structure in the Qurʾān, also proved extremely influential.[14]

Mawdūdī's Urdu work *Tafhīm al-Qurʾān* (lit., making the Qurʾān comprehensible) was published between 1942 and 1972. In 1947, the state of Pakistan was founded, and from the 1950s onwards, Mawdūdī was politically active, trying to convert the 'state for Muslims' into an 'Islamic state'. This development is somewhat reflected in his work on the Qurʾān which is at the beginning mostly a translation with notes meant to facilitate understanding, but gradually, and with increasing frequency, adds extensive sections of commentary that discuss an Islamic lifestyle, an Islamic system of governance and any number of contemporary issues. Mawdūdī's work has been translated into English at least twice, and from there into other languages. It has been commended for its masterful prose to which, apparently, none of the translations do justice.[15] Its clear structure and style distinguish it from older Urdu works. It incorporates information from the exegetical literature, such as 'occasions of revelation' narratives, more frequently than Sayyid Quṭb's work; Quṭb had no access to these resources while in prison. The focus, however, is on providing a practical interpretation that modern-day believers can apply to their lives and that helps them make sense of their world.[16] For example, when Q. 21:105 says that 'the Earth shall be inherited by my righteous slaves', Mawdūdī makes clear that this does not mean that any ruler who has 'inherited the Earth' by having gained domination of a territory could be called righteous, and he states that this pertains to the Qurʾānic pharaoh as much as it does to 'communist despots'.[17]

Such direct reference to contemporary events was unthinkable for premodern exegetes. The degree to which it occurs in Mawdūdī's and – usually couched in more general terms – Quṭb's Qurʾānic commentaries might in part be owed to the influence of early modernists such as Rashīd Riḍā. It is even more compelling to attribute it to the origin of both works in mass media. They started out as instalments in journals, much like Riḍā's *Tafsīr al-Manār*, and although they are clearer and more accessible in style, they share with the *Tafsīr al-Manār* the desire to make Qurʾānic interpretation directly relevant to their readers and connect it to recent events, in line with the needs of a periodical.

Neither of the two authors called their work a *tafsīr* since they did not intend to situate it in a scholarly tradition, but rather to make their view of the Qur'ān's message comprehensible to a readership that consisted of literate Muslims without an advanced religious education – and indeed, none of the authors was a trained scholar either. This brand of pious activism called for a reading of the Qur'ān that was directly applicable to their attempt to lead an Islamic life and work towards the foundation of an Islamic society or even an Islamic state.

Islamist Qur'ānic commentaries do not usually reject the exegetical tradition outright. They use it wherever they find it helpful or convenient, but it is subordinate to other considerations. The first of those is the concept of an Islamic way of life (*manhaj*) that encompasses every aspect of individual, social and political life, especially the legal system which should not be based on any man-made laws. It follows that the Qur'ān is the main guide towards this way of life, a notion that is clearly inspired by the modernist idea of reading the Qur'ān as a book of guidance (*hidāya*). This results in a marked tendency to understand the Qur'ān not so much as a spiritual text but as a book that both explains events in this world and provides rules for human behaviour. Thus, the story of Moses is not so much about belief in God and prophethood, but about the fight against an unjust ruler who wanted to elevate his own laws above those set by God and turn himself into an idol (*ṭāghūt*).

In contrast to most modernists, Islamists target 'the masses', rather than an intellectual elite. The result is a strong focus on social justice. In fact, social justice is a prominent theme in the Qur'ān, and it does not require much effort to read it that way. However, the conditions of the poor had not been a prime concern of premodern exegetes, nor had previous reformers such as Rashīd Riḍā, who wrote for an elite audience, paid much attention to these conditions. Sayyid Quṭb, on the other hand, devoted an entire book to them.[18] Islamist exegesis thus contributed significantly to establishing the theme of social justice as part of the field of Qur'ānic interpretation. This also explains some of its appeal beyond adherents of revolutionary Islamism.

In general, an Islamist outlook encourages a literalist reading of legal prescriptions in the Qur'ān. The idea is that God's laws should be obeyed, rather than subverted, critically re-assessed or reformed. The ensuing views on the rights of women and non-Muslims or on issues such as slavery are usually restrictive and the discourse on them is apologetic, involving either references to *ḥadīth*s and premodern exegetical authorities or to modern science that justify the Qur'ān's rulings. While socially conservative in this respect, the Islamists' interpretation of the Qur'ān is often not quite identical with the views of traditional *'ulamā'*. For example, with respect to the punishments mentioned in the Qur'ān, such as cutting off the hand of a thief, the Islamist discourse is often more literalist than that of traditional scholars and lacks the intricacies that they have come up with in order to restrict the application of these rules.

At the same time, the Islamists' literal reading is not always as literal as it might seem. The desire to treat the Qur'ānic message as timeless and unchanging results in an uncritical superimposition of quite modern concepts onto the Qur'ān. For example, to Mawdūdī, the idea of an 'Islamic state' was central and he constantly sought to relate it to the Qur'ān. Whether the concepts and vocabulary of the Qur'ān are even compatible with the notion of modern statehood was not a question that occurred to him. Thus, he had no issue with understanding the Qur'ānic notion of *shūrā* (originally referring to the consultation of the community's elders by the leader) as akin to a formal general election.

Of course, there are many aspects in which individual Islamists' views or priorities differ, also depending on their own situation. For example, while Sayyid Quṭb and his follower, Sa'īḍ Ḥawwā (1935–1989), a member of the Syrian Muslim Brotherhood, promoted a revolutionary reading of the Qur'ān, influenced by the persecution that their organisations faced from totalitarian regimes, Mawdūdī was more concerned with ideas of governance.

Today, there are a few clear-cut Islamist Qur'ānic commentaries,[19] but the influence that Islamist exegesis exerts goes far beyond them. There is a continuing intense reception of Quṭb's and Mawdūdī's works. Furthermore, parts of the Islamist exegetical framework have been appropriated by traditional scholars and a wide range of intellectuals and preachers while others, especially the revolutionary ideas developed by Sayyid Quṭb, have merged with parts of the Jihadi-Salafi movement.

THE 'SYSTEM' (*NAẒM*) AND STRUCTURE OF THE QUR'ĀN

One feature that Quṭb, Mawdūdī and Sa'īd Ḥawwā have in common is the holistic approach to the *sūra*s of the Qur'ān, or even to the entire text, and their concern with coherence. Among the main aims of Mawdūdī's introductions to the *sūra*s and of his notes is to explain the logic behind the sequence of topics.[20] Sayyid Quṭb discusses large segments of text at a time and identifies complex structures even within the longer *sūra*s that, in his opinion, revolve around an 'axis' (*miḥwar*) consisting of some central verses. Sa'īd Ḥawwā developed this system even further and sees an intricate structure permeating the whole Qur'ān.

The trend towards identifying structural coherence within the *sūra*s of the Qur'ān and even an overarching structure to the entire text stands in marked contrast to the verse-by-verse treatment common in most premodern works of *tafsīr.* Even those premodern works that had explained the logical connection between verses (*munāsaba*) had usually limited this to immediately consecutive verses or segments of text. By contrast, the quest for a logic to the Qur'ān's structure has become common today and it has several sources, besides the above-mentioned Islamist exegetes. It also may take a variety of forms. The earliest of those consisted of introductions to *sūra*s stating their central themes. This approach was taken by the *Tafsīr al-Manār* and, roughly simultaneously, by the Indian exegetes Ashraf ʿAlī Thanawī (1863–1943) and Ḥamīd al-Dīn al-Farāḥī (1863–1930). Their ideas were taken up and further explored by a host of exegetes from subsequent generations, including Sayyid Quṭb, Bint al-Shāṭiʾ, Muḥammad ʿIzzat Darwaza and Muḥammad Ḥusayn Ṭabāṭabāʾī.[21] There was clearly a modernist influence here, besides the Islamist one that was already mentioned, since the idea of a central theme of *sūra*s or larger textual units is closely connected to the concept of *maqāṣid al-Qur'ān* – reading the Qur'ān in the light of its higher aims.

- Besides introductions to *sūra*s, the engagement with the Qur'ān's structure and the quest for a perfect logic to its arrangement may include some or all of the following elements:
- The treatment of larger segments of text in the commentary, instead of a verse-by-verse analysis.
- The division of *sūra*s into thematic sections that enables readers to recognise a structure, especially in the longer *sūra*s.
- The discussion of the logical connection (*rabṭ* or *munāsaba*) between verses, segments and sections within the *sūra.*
- The identification of one central theme, doctrine, thesis or verse around which, according to the exegete, the whole *sūra* revolves and that a reader needs to be aware of in order to understand it. Sayyid Quṭb called this *miḥwar* ('axis'), Farāḥī *ʿamūd* ('pillar').[22]
- A few exegetes go even further and identify a connection between the *sūra*s or even an overarching structure within the entire Qur'ānic arrangement, attributing it not to human decisions, as the conventional Muslim narrative of the Qur'ān's genesis assumes, but to some form of divine planning. For example, Saʿīd Ḥawwā proposed a system according to which the Qur'ān is divided into larger parts. Each of those has an axis around which the *sūra*s within these parts revolve. Ḥawwā considers this structure a proof

of the Qurʾān's divine origin and inimitability (*iʿjāz*) because of its superhuman complexity.[23]

The quest for coherence thus ranges from a literary analysis of the structure of *sūra*s to the sacralisation of the Qurʾān's entire arrangement.

The treatment of *sūra*s as coherent textual units has been described as a wholly indigenous development, not influenced by Western Qurʾānic Studies.[24] This is true in the sense that the early proponents of this trend have certainly not borrowed their ideas from Western scholars; but they might well have reacted to the orientalists' dismissive treatment of the Qurʾān's arrangement. From the nineteenth-century proponents of Western Qurʾānic Studies until at least the 1980s,

> the hypothesis of an artistically valuable composition – be it of the qur'ānic corpus or of the single *sūra*s – has...been negated, and existing literary forms have been considered to be the result of a haphazard compilation.[25]

The trend towards treating the Qurʾān as a coherent whole obviously runs counter to these assumptions. It is often – but not always – intended to demonstrate that the divine nature of the Qurʾān exceeds individual verses or segments of text and extends to its canonised form.

This idea is not shared by all contemporary exegetes, however; there are conflicting opinions. For example, the trend to interpret the Qurʾān in the order of revelation calls into question the importance of the canonical arrangement of *sūra*s[26] while the opposing trend, pursued by exegetes such as Saʿīd Ḥawwā, sacralises precisely that arrangement as one form of *iʿjāz al-Qurʾān*, the inimitability of the Qurʾān, besides others. The following case study exemplifies that trend.

The sacralisation of the Qurʾān's canonical arrangement: ʿAmr Khālid on the structure of the Qurʾān and the unity of *sūra*s

The introduction to ʿAmr Khālid's *Khawāṭir Qurʾāniyya* (Reflections on the Qurʾān) focusses on his aims, but it also tells us a lot about his method (see Excerpt 5.2). He takes up a number of themes and methodological approaches that are very common in contemporary exegesis despite the fact that they were virtually non-existent in premodern *tafsīr* scholarship.

When ʿAmr Khālid states that his book is no work of *tafsīr*, this is certainly meant to deflect criticism based on his lack of scholarly credentials, but it also implies that he will not deliver the type of verse-by-verse analysis and explanations of difficult terms that even a concise Qurʾānic commentary would entail. His aim, instead, is to enable readers to understand the

Excerpt 5.2

The introduction to ʿAmr Khālid's *Khawāṭir Qur'āniyya*[27]

Praise to God who has sent down on His servant the Book and has not set in it any crookedness. [Q. 18:1]

Praise to God who has guided us to this. We would not have been guided if God had not guided us. [Q. 7:43]

This book is not a book of *tafsīr*; it does not aim at explaining the verses of the Qur'ān in detail. Whoever wants that should refer to the authoritative Qur'ānic commentaries such as al-Ṭabarī, Ibn Kathīr and other works of *tafsīr* of which the Islamic bookstores are full. The idea of this book is different, and its aim is different as well.

The idea of this book has tempted me for ten years; to be precise, each year [it came to me] in Ramadan, since it is during that blessed month that Muslims all over the Islamic world embark upon reading the complete Qur'ān. I was very sad, however, when I found that this sincere desire to read the Qur'ān is not connected to any clear understanding of the aims of a given *sūra*, the reasons for its revelation and the message it expresses. Therefore, I found people reading the Qur'ān while feeling deep down that the meanings of the Qur'ān remain strange to them. Some even conceive of them as incomprehensible charms that we have to recite without realising their significance or aims. Others understand the meanings of the individual words of the verses, but feel that the verses of each *sūra* are disjointed, without any connection that binds them together, and that there is no single aim to the *sūra* according to which all verses are organised. That was the origin of my idea: to undertake a humble endeavour in order to break the barriers between the Muslim youth and the Book of God.

This book demonstrates to the reader of the Qur'ān that there is a strong connection between the verses of each *sūra*, that each *sūra* has a single topic and a specific aim. While the verses of the *sūra* at first glance appear disjointed and unconnected, you may, upon closer consideration and with an understanding of the aim and central topic of the *sūra*, realise that they are interconnected to an astonishing degree. This interconnection, in return, gives you the capacity to recognise the aim of the *sūra*, which increases your love for the Book of God and your belief that it is indeed a revelation from a Wise and Knowing One: 'If it were from any other than God, they would have found in it much contradiction'. [Q. 4:82] So we see that each *sūra* of the Qur'ān constitutes an integral unit and realises a clear goal, and each verse serves this goal in one or several ways. Even the name of the *sūra* is related to that goal (and thus, we can understand the reason for naming the *sūra*s of the Qur'ān 'The Cow', 'The House of 'Imrān', 'Jonah' or 'The Ants'...) Not only that, but every *sūra* has a strong relationship to the one before and the one after it because the order of the Qur'ānic *sūra*s has also been revealed by God. From that we can conclude that all *sūra*s of the Qur'ān constitute one chain of interconnected links so that, if you understand the aim or aims of the Qur'ānic *sūra*s, you will find that you have understood your Lord's purpose with this *sūra* and what God wants from you in this Book, even if you don't understand every verse and every individual word, because if you have understood the overall aims of the *sūra*s, then you have understood the Qur'ān as a whole. Thus, this book is useful for the masses and ordinary people; it provides them with the basic principles for understanding the Qur'ān. At the same time, it is targeted at those who have memorised the Qur'ān and those who are interested in the discipline of Qur'ānic exegesis (*tafsīr*) as a humble attempt, on my part, to show the 'axes' and the central topics of the Qur'ānic *sūra*s. [...][28]

overall message of the Qur'ān, and that idea is based on a specific vision of the nature of that message: the Qur'ān is seen as a structurally and thematically coherent work in which each *sūra* forms a textual unit with a core message. Even the names and the arrangement of *sūra*s follow a divine logic.

According to 'Amr Khālid, each *sūra* revolves around an axis (*miḥwar*), which is a concept that many contemporary exegetes owe to Sayyid Quṭb. Some exegetes define one or a few central verses, either within the *sūra* itself or a different one, as the axis, but 'Amr Khālid is not usually so specific; for him, the axis is a theme that pervades the whole *sūra* and in the light of which all verses and segments of the *sūra* have to be understood. He generally outlines these themes at the beginning of his discussion of each *sūra* and then goes through the *sūra* segment by segment, explaining how they relate to the axis, but not mentioning, let alone explaining, each individual verse. The goal, here is *da'wa*: to bring across a message at the expense of details.

How does this work, though, especially with respect to the longer and more diverse *sūra*s of the Qur'ān? This might become clearer when looking at 'Amr Khālid's introduction to the fourth *sūra* of the Qur'ān.

'Amr Khālid on Sūra al-Nisā' (Q. 4)

In Excerpt 5.3, 'Amr Khālid makes sense of a very long, thematically diverse and often legalistic *sūra* by reading it in the light of one theme: justice and compassion for the weak. This allows him to integrate even the complex inheritance rules discussed in the fourth *sūra*, since he classifies 'heirs' as belonging to the weak, possibly because they have lost relatives. He also includes the equally complex marriage rules into his argument by establishing a natural order for society: by exerting justice and compas-

Excerpt 5.3

The *sūra* 'Women' (*al-Nisā'*, i.e. Q. 4) is Medinan; it was revealed [chronologically] after the sixtieth *sūra*, has 176 verses, and is the fourth *sūra* in the arrangement of the Qur'ānic codex after the Sūra Āl 'Imrān (Q. 3).

The fourth *sūra* is the *sūra* of justice and compassion, especially with those who are weak. After the second *sūra* had specified Muslims' responsibility for the Earth and presented the concept of their appointment as God's representatives, the third *sūra* came to call for steadfast adherence to the straight path and to the responsibility placed on the believers' shoulders. Then came the fourth *sūra* in order to teach us that those to whom Earth has been entrusted have to be endowed with justice and compassion towards the weak of whom they have been put in charge, indicating that the most important attribute of those who are responsible for Earth might be justice. Therefore, the fourth *sūra* speaks about the rights of society's weakest members. It speaks about the orphans, the slaves, the servants and the heirs and it also focusses on women in a very fundamental way. Moreover, it speaks about the non-Muslim minorities that live under the protection of Islam and about their rights. In addition, it addresses the weak ones directly and tells them how to behave under various circumstances. Besides all this, it talks about travellers and parents and how they should be treated. It is the *sūra* of compassion and the *sūra* of justice. It mentions again and again in each of its verses the weak, justice and compassion in a wonderful fashion: the sublime inimitability of the Qur'ān shows itself in the way it repeats itself without ever boring the reader.

The reason for its name: Your home comes first

The reason for giving the *sūra* this name ['Women'] is that if a man treats his wife justly and with compassion in his home, he will know how to treat other weak members of society justly as well.

This is the *sūra* of the weak; God chose one type of weak creatures, women, to name this *sūra* after. It's His way of telling you: 'Before I put you in charge of Earth, show me your justice in your home. If you exert justice and compassion in your home, then you will be entrusted with upholding justice in society'. Justice towards women at home is a criterion by which the justice of Muslims in their viceregentship of Earth is measured and tested. After this, will we still find someone who claims that Islam is oppresses women and does not treat them fairly?

Such claims will not deceive the reader of the Qurʾān any longer, especially not if he has read the Sūra al-Nisāʾ (the Women). There is a whole *sūra* devoted to treating them justly and with compassion, and it comes right after the third *sūra* that depicts Mary and the wife of ʿImrān as models of steadfastness (by which the third *sūra* paves the way for honouring women).[29]

sion towards their naturally subordinate wives, men will prove themselves worthy of ruling Earth.

Here we have a very common, seemingly paradoxical phenomenon in contemporary Qurʾānic interpretation: the application of modernist methods while following a non-modernist and partly even anti-modernist agenda. The Qurʾān is read in the light of 'higher aims' which is typically a modernist approach. However, the 'higher aims' have little to do with the modernist ideals of egalitarianism and liberalism. ʿAmr Khālid takes it for granted that the *sūra* speaks *to* men and *about* women; that women are just as weak as orphans and slaves; that men, but not women, are entrusted with responsibility and the power to exert justice. He has no issue with controversial topics such as a husband's right to beat his wife or the promise of paradise for those who wage war for the cause of God.[30] That might make his work unsatisfactory to those who expect a contemporary author to expound modernist ideas, but it does not make ʿAmr Khālid's Qurʾān interpretation 'traditional'. There is nothing traditional about the way in which ʿAmr Khālid emphasises the unity of the entire Qurʾānic text, the pivotal message of each individual *sūra* and the divine origin of the *sūra* names. Not even the vision of benign patriarchy that is expressed here is traditional: it expresses rather modern notions of an Islamic family centred around husband and wife, both of whom are attributed natural roles based on assumptions about their biological nature.

While ʿAmr Khālid emphasises the theme of justice, he remains relatively vague about issues of class and poverty, quite in contrast to Sayyid Quṭb's emphatic Qurʾān-based demand for social justice. Given his affluent target group, this is hardly surprising.

SCIENCE AND THE *IʿJĀZ* PARADIGM

The idea of the Qurʾān's divine perfection is pervasive in contemporary exegesis and the search for an overarching structure is only one of the forms of expression that it takes. It is not a new idea as such, but the ways in which exegetes frame the Qur'ān's divine nature have changed drastically. One of the reasons for this is the emergence of a new source of authority – the scientific paradigm.

During the nineteenth and early-twentieth centuries, an increasing number of Muslim intellectuals came to see science as the ultimate arbiter of truth. This was a result of close contact with European models of education and scholarship, and for that precise reason, it was heavily contested. Several modes emerged in which science came to have a bearing on the exegesis of the Qur'ān. While some of them had historical precedents, both the function and the importance that scientific narratives attained for Qur'ānic exegesis in the late-nineteenth and early-twentieth centuries are unprecedented. To be sure, until this day, many exegetes reject the notion that the interpretation of the Qur'ān should involve scientific paradigms. But it rarely happens that commentaries on verses dealing with cosmology, nature or even gender relations ignore the issue altogether.

The idea of science as the arbiter of truth emerged in the same period in which Qur'ānic interpretation was increasingly understood as an activity aiming to reveal an unequivocal truth. This was one of the reasons for which scholars started to search for ways to reconcile both types of truth, the one of science and the one of the Qur'ān. The other reason had to do with apologetics, as was mentioned at the outset of this chapter. Islam was frequently attacked as backwards, irrational and superstitious by colonial administrators, orientalists and Christian missionaries, and the attempt to demonstrate the Qur'ān's compatibility with science – and even its superiority over the Bible in that respect – became an important tool of defence for many Muslims. This was not limited to the natural sciences; historical and archaeological scholarship were also widely studied and used, for example, to explain Biblical history.[31]

Thus, from the late-nineteenth century onwards, Muslim scholars and intellectuals explored various aspects of how the Qur'ān could be understood in the light of science as well as the question whether science affirmed the statements and rulings in the Qur'ān.[32] A particularly prominent, albeit rather atypical, proponent of this trend was Ṭanṭāwī Jawharī who in 1923 published a complete commentary on the Qur'ān with numerous excurses into scientific topics. Strongly influenced by Muḥammad 'Abduh, he was convinced that Muslims need to overcome their backwardness, unite, study science and recultivate an inquisitive mindset. Thus, his Qur'ānic commentary was at least in part – besides various religious, ethical and political considerations – an attempt to use the prestige of the Qur'ān in order to promote science.[33]

Today, the prevailing types of engagement with the relationship between the Qur'ān and science more frequently convey the impression that it is the other way around; that the prestige of natural sciences is projected onto the Qur'ān.[34] The evocation of scientific – or pseudo-scientific – knowledge in the interpretation of the Qur'ān can be roughly divided into three categories.

First, there is the attempt to explain statements in the Qur'ān that appear to contradict the laws of nature in a way that is compatible with science. Especially in its beginnings, this strategy was born out of apologetics, as a defence against accusations of superstition. For example, some exegetes explain the story of how the Red Sea parted to let Moses and the Israelites pass by way of natural occurrences such as a tsunami or a major tidal irregularity, bolstering their argument with quotations from scientific literature. The focus in this approach is on the correctness of scientific paradigms. The Qur'ān is interpreted in a way that is compatible with scientific knowledge. Science takes on the function of a corrective of superstitious and irrational beliefs.[35] This brand of exegesis, if carried out consistently, is sometimes labelled *tafsīr ʿilmī* ('scientific exegesis') and is closely connected to the modernist camp.[36]

The second approach, by contrast, usually takes the Qur'ān's statements and rules at face value and then seeks out scientific evidence to support them. Here, science is not a corrective; its exclusive function is to affirm the plausibility of the Qur'ān. The impetus is apologetic. For example, the prohibition of pork and alcohol, the ritual washing and the movements in the prayer ritual are justified with detailed explanations of their health benefits; or biological arguments are adduced in favour of a hierarchical concept of gender relations in marriage.[37] In fact, biological arguments are particularly common with respect to topics that invite criticism in our times, such as polygyny or slavery. Another common cause for this type of scientific-apologetic argument is a highly literal reading of the Qur'ān that produces interpretations which then have to be justified. Thus, a verse such as Q. 54:1 – 'The Hour has drawn near and the moon has been split'– instead of being read as an apocalyptic metaphor, is taken to refer to a real event for which professional and lay exegetes then try to adduce evidence from sources such as NASA in a rather haphazard and de-contextualised manner.[38] Since the Qur'ān is by definition considered to be correct in its straightforward literal sense, scientific evidence is quoted selectively and without much regard for whether it is reliable and authoritative. Rather, the main criteria for the selection of scientific information is its ability to support a statement in the Qur'ān. An exegete writing on the benefits of polygyny would not want to evaluate the available scientific evidence for and against the practice, but rather focus on searching for evidence supporting it – even if it means tearing a quotation out of its context or resorting to academically questionable sources. The result might be called pseudo-science.

The third approach is called *iʿjāz ʿilmī*, sometimes translated as 'scientific miracle of the Qurʾān'. It involves the claim that the Qurʾān describes scientific facts that nobody at the time of the Prophet, let alone an illiterate man from the Arabian Peninsula, could have known. This is then taken as proof of the Qurʾān's divine origin. Only the combination of these two assumptions qualifies an approach as *iʿjāz ʿilmī*.[39] The *iʿjāz ʿilmī* thus goes way beyond the first two approaches. Those merely try to demonstrate that the Qurʾān makes sense in the light of modern sciences, but do not necessarily combine this with a claim to 'inimitability' which is the most common translation of the Arabic *iʿjāz* – a term that literally signifies the Qurʾān's capacity to render anyone incapable of producing a comparable text.

The idea of the Qurʾān's inimitability goes back at least to the tenth century. In premodern times, it focussed mostly on the perfection of the Qurʾān's language and rhetoric that made mortals incapable of producing something equivalent, although other *iʿjāz* concepts were occasionally put forward.[40] Today, the linguistic and rhetorical type of *iʿjāz* is still sometimes put forward and never outright rejected, but to Muslims without training in classical Arabic rhetoric and literature, this argument is hard to understand, not as compelling as the *iʿjāz ʿilmī*, and it is next to impossible to expand or develop it. By contrast, the internet and *daʿwa* literature are full of variants of the *iʿjāz ʿilmī*. Its function for both apologetics and proselytising is obvious.

The three approaches are not mutually exclusive, but neither are they necessarily present simultaneously. It is possible to follow the first paradigm, but strictly reject the second and third, for example, or vice versa. The second one is probably the most common even in traditional works of exegesis. Just as the modern *iʿjāz* paradigm, it is also very popular with lay Muslims because it constitutes an easy way of lending authority to religious claims that are apparently not trusted to be sufficiently convincing without such support.

Modern-style *iʿjāz* discourses are varied and may cover one or several of a number of arguments.

- The Qurʾān describes contemporary scientific theories such as the theory of an expanding universe.
- The Qurʾān describes natural phenomena more accurately than would have been possible at the time of revelation, for example, the development of the foetus. Embryology, in particular, is a well-established part of the genre at least since the publication of the book hugely popular among *iʿjāz* advocates, *The Bible, the Quran and Science*[41] by French physician Maurice Bucaille (1920–1998) that continues to be cited as a prime witness to confirm the Qurʾān's

potential to convince even non-Muslims of its truthfulness and accuracy.[42]

- The Qur'ān contains information about historical events or other facts that could not have been known to seventh-century Arabs, for example, concerning ancient Egyptian history – again, this was a field that Bucaille had covered and popularised.
- The Qur'ān foretells historical events, discoveries or technologies that only occurred long after its revelation such as space travel, the foundation of the United Nations or the decline and disappearance of the Byzantine Empire.
- In an argument closely related to the second approach, it is assumed that the Qur'ān contains prescriptions that have benefits which can only be explained by modern medicine and which could not have been known to Muḥammad. For example, prayer is explained to have the same benefits as regular exercise and eating pork to be damaging to health.
- Finally, a much-contested, but also quite frequent variant of the modern *iʿjāz* paradigm is related to numerical patterns in the Qur'ān which are sometimes thought to correspond with natural laws or dates of technological discoveries – for example the year of the moon landing.[43] Sometimes, the focus is merely on the numerical patterns themselves, for example in recurrences of specific letters or words. These patterns are said to be so complex that they could only be detected by the use of computers and could therefore not have been constructed by a seventh-century human. This last variant is fairly frequent, but also heavily contested because of its connection with Rashad Khalifa, the main proponent of Qur'ānism. He developed a theory according to which the entire structure of the Qur'ān is based on the number nineteen. Later in life, Khalifa expressed certain messianic ideas. Finally, he fell victim to an assassination. All in all, Khalifa's highly controversial status might have tainted the 'numerical miracle' with a notion of heresy from which the other types of 'scientific miracle' are free.[44] But even then, theories about numerical patterns in the Qur'ān, which Arabic – like any Semitic language – lends itself to, abound.

The *iʿjāz ʿilmī* paradigm, while being extremely popular, has been the object of criticism from various angles. This includes modernist and Islamist exegetes, for example, Amīn al-Khūlī and Sayyid Quṭb. An important argument against it is lexicographic: the *iʿjāz ʿilmī* attributes modern meanings, such as 'atom', to Qur'ānic terms and then deduces that the Qur'ān talks about these things although the modern scientific meaning was unknown at the time of revelation. Critics also argue that it decontextualizes Qur'ānic phrases with the result that, for example, apocalyptic metaphors are read as astronomical descriptions. It does, by definition, not take the horizon of the Qur'ān's first listeners into account for whom the text must have been comprehensible despite their lack of scientific knowledge. More fundamentally, the *i'jāz 'ilmī*, according to its critics, treats the Qur'ān as a scientific textbook, instead of a sacred scripture that offers spiritual insights and religious guidance. It also makes the validity of the Qur'ān's message dependent on the validity of scientific theories and knowledge.[45]

Other critics complain about the distorted understanding of science behind the *i'jāz 'ilmī*. It sacralises science and construes it as neutral, static and universal. The Muslim intellectual Ziauddin Sardar quipped that it is addressed at 'Muslims with a larger-than-life inferiority complex'.[46] It is also accused of being methodologically inconsistent because those Qur'ānic verses that seem to match current scientific knowledge are taken at face value while others for which this is not the case are read metaphorically or thought to describe a supernatural reality.[47]

Even the opponents of a 'scientific miracle', however, rarely ignore science altogether. To a certain extent, scientific interpretations have become part of the exegetical canon and thus have to be at least acknowledged, if not accepted – be it in the relatively 'soft' form of a statement on the 'natural roles' of men and women or in the 'hard' form of debates on embryology or nuclear fission in the Qur'ān.

The core problems and questions inherent in scientific approaches to the Qur'ān become apparent when the attitude towards the theory of human evolution, colloquially called 'Darwinism', is at stake. The fundamental question here is whether the Qur'ān should be interpreted in light of current scientific evidence or whether that evidence has to be reinterpreted in light of the creation story in the Qur'ān. While in the early-twentieth century, many Muslim intellectuals had no issue with Darwinism,[48] the opinions of recent exegetes seem to lean heavily towards creationism[49] which is even true for exegetes who make a point of relying on scientific knowledge in other instances. This was considerably facilitated by creationist discourses in the US which led many Muslim thinkers to believe that the theory of evolution was scientifically controversial or had even been disproved.[50] There are regional and national differences, though. The religious discourse in Turkey, in particular, has given rise to a vehement Islamic creationist movement.[51] That said, some exegetes do make attempts to accommodate current scientific models of the evolution of species, but exempt humans from them.[52] Another 'intermediate' position would accept human evolution, but not the mechanism of natural selection because that, according to them, would interfere with the role of God as creator.[53] Finally, there are

Muslim positions that fully harmonise the theory of evolution with the idea of a divine creator. They claim that the Qur'ān actively confirms Darwinism by asking its audience to observe the process of creation which is thus cast as an observable phenomenon.[54] On the question whether religious scholars and intellectuals are even qualified to make statements about a scientific phenomenon such as evolution, there are widely divergent attitudes.

Interestingly, such divergent attitudes towards science can be identified throughout the exegetical spectrum. Traditional scholars might either read the Qur'ān in terms of modern embryology or vehemently reject such a reading, and the same is true for modernists. Postmodernists are the most likely to take a nuanced view not only of the meaning of the Qur'ān, but also of science, and are most likely to separate the two. In contexts of *da'wa* and preaching, on the other hand, the *i'jāz 'ilmī* narrative is widely popular, promoted by protagonists such as Harun Yahya (a.k.a. Adnan Oktar, b. 1956) in countless brochures and on websites.[55] The following example is one of thousands of the kind.

The scientific *i'jāz*: Miracles of Quran on Q. 27:18

Miracles of Quran is a professional-looking English website with no author details but which, according to ICANN, is registered to Raef Fanous of Beirut, Lebanon. The subtitle of the website is 'From Arithmetics to Astrophysics'. In early 2017, it was ranked such that it consistently came out first in Google searches for the words 'miracle' and 'Quran'. The first snapshot of the page on Archive.org dates back to March 2007. At the time, the page had a very simple generic layout. The current design is the result of a major relaunch that took place in late 2014 or early 2015. The content is continuously expanded; the page on the gender of ants, for example, seems to be an addition made in 2016 (See Excerpt 5.4).

Should a text like this, from a site like this, be taken seriously? Errors in the use of English left aside, the text clearly contains a major misconception. The author's argument about the sex of ants – which is reproduced in a similar fashion elsewhere on the site with respect to bees – betrays both a lack of knowledge of Arabic grammar and a selective reading of the verse. The speaking ant, in the verse, is indeed grammatically feminine, but that is because 'ants' (*naml*) is a collective noun in Arabic and the singular for a collective noun is always grammatically feminine, whether it be trees, tears, bees or ants.[56] Besides, the other ants are addressed as masculine which either means that at least some of them must be male – or, far more likely, the verse might simply use the grammatical gender without implying any information on the biological sex of the ants in question.

Excerpt 5.4

Q. 27:18

حَتَّىٰ إِذَا أَتَوْا عَلَىٰ وَادِ النَّمْلِ قَالَتْ نَمْلَةٌ يَا أَيُّهَا النَّمْلُ ادْخُلُوا مَسَاكِنَكُمْ لَا يَحْطِمَنَّكُمْ سُلَيْمَانُ وَجُنُودُهُ وَهُمْ لَا يَشْعُرُونَ ﴿١٨﴾

Ants
Wingless ants are all females.

All male ants have wings. All worker ants are females. All ants that don't have wings are definitely females. This was only known recently. But 1400 years ago the Quran addressed ants who cannot fly in the female mode:

[Quran 27.18] Until, when they came upon the valley of the ants, an ant said (for females), 'O ants, enter your homes so that you do not be crushed by Solomon and his soldiers while they do not feel it'.

For the word 'said': Kala (قال) is for males. Kalat (قالت) is for females. The Quran used Kalat (female).

If this ant had wings it would have flown off however it didn't have this option, instead it's only option was to hide underground. Since it didn't have wings then this was definitely a female ant. Here the Quran correctly addresses this ant in the female mode.

How could an illiterate man who lived 1400 years ago have known that wingless ants are females?

(The Christian Bible erroneously claims that there are four legged insects[;] Leviticus 11:20. It also claims that there is an animal that has 'flames stream from its mouth; sparks of fire shoot out. Smoke pours from its nostrils as from a boiling pot over burning reeds. Its breath sets coals ablaze, and flames dart from its mouth'. Job 41:19–21)[57]

Nevertheless, such texts should be taken seriously because they are ubiquitous and obviously successful.[58] This specific text's purpose is somewhere between apologetics and proselytisation. It is clearly directed either at Christian readers or at Muslim readers who interact with Christians. The Biblical quotations both refer to the Hebrew Bible, yet are attributed to the 'Christian Bible' which shows that the owner of the site is not much interested in Jews or any other religion besides Christianity and Islam. The aim is not only to demonstrate the Qurʾān's compatibility with science or its truthfulness, but to prove, beyond any doubt, both its divine origin and its superiority to the Bible. Readers who are unfamiliar with Arabic grammar will not recognise the problems with the argument about female ants; rather, they are likely to be impressed.

The site *Miracles of Quran* is entirely devoted to the scientific *iʿjāz* paradigm. It covers a variety of topics from the natural sciences and history that are grouped into several categories and levels of complexity, ranging from standard *topoi* of the genre such as embryology and the make-up of the pyramids to the theory that angels use wormholes for travel. The composition of the site points at an author with a particular interest and background knowledge in astrophysics although probably not a professional, judging from some of his speculations.[59] This matches the observation that very often, the 'scientific miracle' of the Qurʾān is pursued by authors with a background in science or engineering and without theological training.[60]

Apart from the description of 'miracles', the only meta-information on the site consists of the English translations of two Qurʾānic verses that are present on all pages. The first, Q. 42:14–15, refers to Christians and their disunity, which the website attributes to errors in the Bible. It calls Muslims to spread the truth among Christians without quarrelling. The allusion to the erroneous nature of the Bible is mainly a product of the problematic English translation of the Qurʾānic verse; the original is not as clear. The second verse, Q. 6:108, asks Muslims not to curse non-Muslims so that they do not curse God. Obviously, the main goal of the site is thus to provide arguments for interreligious debate and/or proselytising among Christians as is also apparent in the ubiquitous references to 'scientifically false' statements in the Bible at the end of each topic, such as in the above example.

In contrast to many other contemporary Muslim publications on the relationship between Islam and science, this website demonstrates a relatively high level of acceptance of the state of scientific knowledge. For example, it considers humans the product of evolution, it believes in the Big Bang and an expanding universe and it would not dream of promoting, for example, a geocentric model of the universe as some Saudi ʿulamāʾ have done. Rather, it aims at bringing scientific findings in line with statements in the Qurʾān and to prove, in a second step, that the Qurʾān is more accurate about them than the Bible, at least if one subscribes to a literalist reading of the Bible.

NOTES

1. McLarney, *Soft Force*, 154–162. Unfortunately, precise biographical dates are all but absent from the sources on Karīmān Ḥamza.
2. Malti-Douglas, *Medicines of the Soul*, 15–47.
3. Ḥamza, *Riḥlatī*.
4. Ḥamza, *Al-Luʾluʾ wa'l-marjān*, vol. 1, 8.

5. Al-Buḥayrī, 'Majma' al-Buḥūth al-islāmiyya'.
6. Ambros, 'Beobachtungen'.
7. Ḥamza, *Al-Lu'lu' wa'l-marjān*, vol. 1, 9–10.
8. Jādd, 'Tafsīr Karīmān Ḥamza'.
9. See Ibid.; Asharq al-Awsat, 'Al-Azhar Hails First Female Interpretation'; al-Sharq al-Awsaṭ, 'Karīmān Ḥamza: Tafsīrī laysa nisā'iyyan'. Cf. Muslimah Media Watch, 'Kariman Hamzah'.
10. Ḥamza, *Al-Lu'lu' wa'l-marjān*, vol. 1, 7–8.
11. On the widespread conservatism among female Muslim scholars, see Bauer, *Gender Hierarchy in the Qur'ān*, 241.
12. Ibid., vol. 1, 177–180. Text originally in Arabic.
13. Wielandt, 'Exegesis of the Qur'an: Early Modern and Contemporary', 137–138.
14. On *Fī ẓilāl al-Qur'ān*, see Carré, *Mysticism and Politics*.
15. Mir, 'Some Features of Mawdudi's Tafhim al-Qur'an', 234, n. 4.
16. Adams, 'Abū l-A'lā Mawdūdī's Tafhīm al-Qur'ān'; Mir, 'Some Features of Mawdudi's Tafhim al-Qur'an'.
17. These quotations are based on the English ebook version by Hafiz Khan; see Maududi, *Tafheemul Quran*.
18. Quṭb, *Al-'Adāla al-ijtimā'iyya fī l-Islām*; translated into English as Quṭb, *Sayyid Qutb and Islamic Activism*.
19. See, for example, Taji-Farouki, 'An Islamist Tafsir in English'.
20. Mir, 'Some Features of Mawdudi's Tafhim al-Qur'an', 241.
21. Mir, 'The *sūra* as a Unity: A Twentieth-Century Development in Qur'ān Exegesis'.
22. Ibid., 213, 215.
23. Pink, *Sunnitischer Tafsīr in der modernen islamischen Welt*, 103–107. For more on the *i'jāz*, see the subsequent section.
24. Mir, 'The *Sūra* as a Unity: A Twentieth-Century Development in Qur'ān Exegesis', 218.
25. Neuwirth, 'Form and Structure of the Qur'ān', 250–251.
26. It may still be based on the assumption that the suras in themselves form coherent units of text as, for example, Muḥammad 'Izzat Darwaza believes. See Mir, 'The *Sūra* as a Unity: A Twentieth-Century Development in Qur'ān Exegesis', 214.
27. On 'Amr Khālid, see page 29, 'Televangelism and da'wa: 'Amr Khālid (b. 1967, Egypt) on Q. 23:1–11'.
28. Khālid, *Khawāṭir Qur'āniyya*, 11–13. Text originally in Arabic.
29. Ibid., 72–73. Text originally in Arabic.
30. Ibid., 140, 145.
31. I thank Samuel Ross of Yale University, who is working on this issue, for drawing my attention to it in his presentation, The Archaeology of Knowledge and the Knowledge of Archaeology: the Grappling of Modern Qur'anic Exegetes with the New Historiography of the Ancient Middle East, in the AAR meeting in San Antonio in November 2016.
32. Cf. Wielandt, 'Exegesis of the Qur'an: Early Modern and Contemporary', 129–131; Baljon, *Modern Muslim Koran Interpretation*, 88–98; Jansen, *The Interpretation of the Koran in Modern Egypt*, 35–54.
33. Daneshgar, 'An Approach to Science in the Qur'ān'.
34. Bigliardi, 'The "Scientific Miracle of the Qur'ān"', 351.
35. Wielandt, 'Exegesis of the Qur'an: Early Modern and Contemporary' especially with reference to Muḥammad 'Abduh and Sir Sayyid Aḥmad Khān.

36. Bauer, *Gender Hierarchy in the Qur'ān*, 139–142.
37. Klausing, 'Redefining the Borders of *Tafsīr*', 434–435; Bauer, *Gender Hierarchy in the Qur'ān*, 74–81.
38. Görke, 'Die Spaltung des Mondes in der modernen Koranexegese und im Internet'.
39. Bigliardi, 'The "Scientific Miracle of the Qur'ān"', 344.
40. Martin, 'Inimitability'. Shāh Walī Allāh Dihlawī, for example, claimed in the eighteenth century that as part of its *i'jāz*, the Qur'ān accurately describes historical events, later affirmed by historians, and makes predictions for the future. However, he placed the linguistic *i'jāz* first. See Baljon, *Religion and Thought*, 71.
41. First published in French in 1976 and translated into many languages. The English translation was first published in 1978.
42. Bigliardi, 'The "Scientific Miracle of the Qur'ān"', 345.
43. Ibid., 341–342.
44. Khan, 'Nineteen'; for criticism of Khalifa's model, see also Pink, *Neue Religionsgemeinschaften in Ägypten*, 355–358.
45. Wielandt, 'Exegesis of the Qur'an: Early Modern and Contemporary', 130–131.
46. Sardar, *Explorations in Islamic Science*, 31.
47. Bigliardi, 'The "Scientific Miracle of the Qur'ān"', 347–348.
48. Elshakry, *Reading Darwin in Arabic, 1860–1950*.
49. Bigliardi, 'The "Scientific Miracle of the Qur'ān"', 350; Bauer, *Gender Hierarchy in the Qur'ān*, 139–156.
50. Shavit, 'The Evolution of Darwin to a "Unique Christian Species" in Modernist-Apologetic Arab-Islamic Thought'.
51. Riexinger, 'Islamic Opposition'.
52. See, for example, Miracles of Quran, 'Evolution'.
53. Riexinger, 'Responses of South Asian Muslims to the Theory of Evolution'.
54. See, for example, Answering Islamic Skeptics, 'Evolution in Islam'.
55. For Islamic creationist websites in general, Harun Yahya in particular and his popularity far beyond Turkey, see Riexinger, 'Propagating Islamic Creationism on the Internet'. See also the English website <http://www.miraclesofthequran.com>.
56. Fischer, *Grammatik des klassischen Arabisch*, 49.
57. Miracles of Quran, 'Ants'. Text originally in English.
58. In personal talks with several Indonesian graduate students, I found that they had all heard of the argument that ants without wings are female in the context of *i'jāz* discourses. This is, of course, anecdotal evidence, but it shows that the website is far from presenting marginal opinions.
59. See Theoretical [username], 'Is This for Real?'
60. Bigliardi, 'The "Scientific Miracle of the Qur'ān"', 345.

6

THE GLOBAL QUR᾽ĀN IN A DIVERSE WORLD

Qur᾽ānic exegesis is not simply an individual endeavour. It takes place in a specific local setting. It may at the same time be embedded in the discourse of a translocal community. Such translocal, even global, discourses have been much facilitated by the existence of new media, but these have not made local exegetical practices irrelevant. In fact, they might serve to strengthen them, in some way, for example by enabling migrant workers to stay in touch with their home community or exiled scholars to continue offering advice to their adherents.

When analysing Qur᾽ānic interpretations, it is thus often possible to identify specific interpretive communities in which they take place. These might be shaped by a particular approach to the Qur᾽ān; by a locality, a language, a denominational background; by a common set of concerns; by an institutional or organisational setting; by ideology or status. An interpretive community emerges when individuals sharing some of these characteristics take part in a joint discourse, react to each other, make use of the same resources and – maybe most notably – refer to the same authorities.

This chapter starts with a case study that highlights several important factors: language, the nation state, denominational identity and related discourses of orthodoxy and heterodoxy. These structural dimensions of exegesis will then be explored further.

Negotiating the boundaries of Islamicness through the Qur᾽ān: Ali Adil Atalay 'Vaktidolu' (b. 1936, Turkey) on Q. 2:21

'Vaktidolu' is a Turkish Alevi public intellectual by the name of Ali Adil Atalay who originates from a village in Eastern Anatolia and, among other occupations, founded a transport company and a publishing house, the latter of which is specialised on Alevi literature. That publishing house also printed Atalay's *Kuran'ı Kerim: Manzum Meali ve Tefsir Özeti* under his pen name 'Vaktidolu' in 2007,[1] a work that is a rhyming translation of the Qur᾽ān into Turkish. It was inspired by an earlier similar work by the Bektashi Sufi shaykh Bedri Noyan (1912–1997)[2] whom Vaktidolu mentions as an important reference. Vaktidolu also explicitly situates his work in a

Shi'i framework.[3] The relationship of his Alevi identity to Bektashi Sufism and Shi'i Islam requires some explanation.

Alevism and the Bektashi Sufi order are separate phenomena, but there are historical links between them and they are often conflated in contemporary Turkish descriptions and self-ascriptions. The Bektashis are a Sufi order that played an important role in the politics of the Ottoman Empire until it was outlawed in 1826 for political reasons. As with most Sufi orders, it is possible for any Muslim to be initiated into it. In order to be an Alevi, on the other hand, one has to be born into an Alevi family. Alevism unites elements of Sunni and Shi'i Islam and of Sufism with folk customs. Alevi rituals and religious duties differ significantly from those practiced by Sunnis and mainstream Shi'is. While the Bektashis were strong in the cities, the Alevis have always had their base in the countryside. Both groups have some overlap with respect to their ritual practices. They have always used Turkish and sometimes other local languages in their rituals, and the veneration of the trinity of God, 'Alī and Muḥammad plays a major role to both. The veneration of 'Alī is today considered a distinctly Shi'i phenomenon, but it has historically been a feature of popular Islam across denominational boundaries.

Today, the 'Islamicness' of Alevism is heavily contested. Their opponents accuse Alevis of heretical beliefs and immoral practices. Some Alevis counter these accusations by positioning themselves as a branch of the Shi'a and thereby, while not Sunni, perfectly Islamic. Others claim to belong to an independent religious tradition that predates Islam and is, in actual fact, a more authentic manifestation of Turkic identity than the 'Arab' religion of Islam. The debate is thus tied in with discourses on national identity that have dominated the country since the early twentieth century, especially after the foundation of the Turkish Republic in 1923. The fact that Turkish is the Alevis' language of ritual can be used as an argument for either depicting Alevism as a genuinely Turkish religion or as a specifically Turkish brand of Islam, depending on a person's general position on Alevi identity. Since early Turkish nationalists had demanded holding the ritual prayer in Turkish and Atatürk had introduced a Turkish call to prayer for a limited period of time, Alevis can and often do portray their practices as an implementation of that nationalist project.[4]

For Alevis, the mere fact of producing a Qur'ān translation, however unconventional, is a demonstration of Islamicness. It emphasises one of the foundational sources of mainstream Muslim belief and practice, and one that Alevis have rarely engaged with in their history. The work of Vaktidolu thus reflects a quite recent development.

It is a monolingual work that does not include the Arabic Qur'ān. This is not entirely uncommon in Turkey. In Vaktidolu's case, it is unclear whether he referred to the Arabic Qur'ān at all or whether he exclusively worked with Turkish translations. The sources he mentions are all in Turkish. Vaktidolu arranges his material 'in the order of revelation', a method that has been gaining popularity in Turkey in recent years. In his brief introduction, he indicates that this is the original order of the Qur'ān which was distorted later, presumably by Sunni rulers. Vaktidolu also claims that the complete Qur'ān has 6,666 verses,[5] an oft-mentioned, but rarely substantiated number that is considerably higher than the actual count based on any accepted system. In the context of Vaktidolu's partisanship for Shi'ism, this might be understood to imply that the several hundred verses missing from standard Qur'ān editions might have been removed for being references to 'Alī and the *ahl al-bayt*.

Excerpt 6.1 shows an example of his method of translating the Qur'ān in rhyme, including the Turkish text.

The choice of producing a rhyming translation is nearly as unusual as the choice of writing a rhyming *tafsīr* that was the subject of the prologue. Most Turkish Qur'ān translations – and most Qur'ān translations into other languages as well, especially those written by Muslims – are rather prosaic, trying either to follow the Arabic text as closely as possible, with a minimum of concessions to the target language's standards of artful rhetoric, or to present a concise exegesis alongside the translation in a very technical style.

Excerpt 6.1 shows the problem inherent in producing a complete rhyming translation of the Qur'ān. The vast majority of Muslims are committed to refuting any claim that the Qur'ān might be poetry, pointing to the Qur'ān's statements that Muḥammad is not a poet (Q. 21:5; 52:30; 69:41). While parts of the Qur'ān are written in a type of rhythmical rhymed prose (*saj'*), it does not follow one of the metres of classical Arabic poetry.[6] Moreover, the length of verses varies widely. Some parts – especially the short *sūra*s at the end – have a rhythmic structure that lends itself to poetic renditions such as that proposed by the German romantic Friedrich Rückert (1788–1866), which only covered parts of the Qur'ān; other *sūra*s, such as the second, from which the sample above was taken, are rather prosaic in style. In order to translate *sūra*s into poems, the original text, at the very least, needs to be rearranged. Vaktidolu chose, in fact, to significantly expand on it, including many statements that are not part of the source text but make it possible to maintain both metre and rhyme. Thus, his work constitutes not so much a translation as a poetic interpretation of the Qur'ān.

Vaktidolu's Shi'i leanings are not apparent in the text, but are made explicit in the author's footnote. There, he cites a *ḥadīth* ascribed to one of the imams of the Shi'a that underlines Shi'i beliefs in the pre-eminence of 'Alī as well as the Prophet's family and descendants (*ahl al-bayt*).

Excerpt 6.1

Q. 2:21

يَا أَيُّهَا النَّاسُ اعْبُدُوا رَبَّكُمُ الَّذِي خَلَقَكُمْ وَالَّذِينَ مِن قَبْلِكُمْ لَعَلَّكُمْ تَتَّقُونَ ﴿٢١﴾

Yā ayyuhā n-nāsu 'budū rabbakumu lladhī khalaqakum wa'lladhīna min qablikum la'allakum tattaqūn

O people, serve your Lord who created you and those that were before you, so that you may guard yourselves (or: be Godfearing[7]).

Vaktidolu, Kur'an'i Kerim: Manzum Meali ve Tefsir Özeti
Ey Hak yolu unutup gafil olan sınıflar
Gelin kulluk ediniz Tanrı sizi yargılar
Dua edin günahtan sakınanlardan olun
Ondan başka Tanrı yok tanıyanlardan olun
Yoktan var edendir O hem önden sonadır O
O'na kulluk edene rahmeti bol veren O.[8]

O ranks of those who carelessly neglect God's way
Come and serve God who is your judge on Judgement Day
Pray and be among those who guard themselves against sin
Be among those who know that there is no God but Him
The one who creates from nothing is He, from the beginning until the end is He
The one who gives plentiful mercy to those that serve Him, is He.

(Footnote: Imam 'Alī Zayn al-'Ābidīn ordains: 'The most beautiful acts of worship of men are to acknowledge that there is no God but God, to consider Muḥammad His prophet and to trust and come to believe that Imam 'Alī is His legatee [*walī*] and that the *ahl al-bayt* [the Prophet's family] are the most virtuous of imams'.)

Vaktidolu's Shi'i affiliation is also obvious from the title page of *Kuran'ı Kerim: Manzum Meali ve Tefsir Özeti* which is decorated with calligraphic inscriptions of the names of the *ahl al-bayt*, the five members of the Prophet's family around which Shi'i beliefs are centred. The calligraphy uses Latin script but has an Arabic style. Muḥammad's name in the middle is surrounded by the names of Fāṭima, 'Alī, Ḥasan and Ḥusayn. In the translation itself, Vaktidolu frequently performs a type of allegorical exegesis that finds hidden references to ʿAlī, the *ahl al-bayt* and the imams across the Qur'ān. This type of exegesis has been in use in various branches of Shiʿi Islam. Vaktidolu calls it *ta'wīl*, a word that originally denoted exegesis and was often used as a synonym for *tafsīr*, but later came to be negatively connoted in mainstream Sunni Islam as a type of allegorical interpretation that reads meanings into the Qur'ān which are not there.[9] For the Imami Shiʿa, it became less common after the formative period that covered roughly the first three centuries of its development. Ali Adil Atalay, however, unabashedly makes use of this method.

A case in point is his treatment of the disjointed letters at the beginnings of many *sūra*s. There has been much debate about the meaning of these seemingly random combinations of Arabic letters such as *alif – lām – mīm*. Since their significance is less than clear, they have naturally lent themselves to allegorical esoteric interpretations. Contemporary mainstream exegetes tend to keep their distance from such interpretations. Many see these letters as a reference to the fact that some divine secrets are beyond human understanding. Not so Vaktidolu. He 'translates' the verse *alif – lām – mīm*, which contains no more than three letters, into no less than ten lines of poetry where he explains, while upholding rhyme and metre, that *alif* refers to *allāh*, *lām* to ʿAlī and *mīm* to Muḥammad. He also emphasises the deep and enigmatic nature of this symbolism and the fact that to make sense of it, one needs to have knowledge of *ta'wīl*. Without knowledge of *ta'wīl*, Vaktidolu claims, the symbolism (*rumuz*) of the Qur'ān cannot be deciphered.[10] Reading *alif – lām – mīm* as a reference to the triad of God, ʿAlī and Muḥammad is clearly an esoteric Shiʿi interpretation that is not entirely alien to Alevi–Bektashi circles,[11] but it is uncommon in contemporary Twelver Shiʿi works of *tafsīr*. A more common reading in both Sunni and Shiʿi exegesis is to see the letters as references to Allāh, Gabriel and Muḥammad.

Vaktidolu's rhyming translation is thus a clear attempt to situate Alevism within the frame of Islam, albeit not within Sunni Islam, which is the dominant denomination in Turkey. At the same time, it connects with the Turkish-nationalist discourse that has defined the Turkish Republic since its foundation. Even before its foundation, radical early nationalists had demanded a 'Turkish Qur'ān', a Qur'ān that was to replace the Arabic text even in matters of ritual,[12] and this is what a Turkish rhyming translation, in contrast to the rather prosaic and technical translations that are the norm, might conceivably achieve. Of course, the production of a text that lends itself to recitation, potentially replacing the Arabic text, is also something that mainstream Sunnis invariably consider highly sacrilegious.

When Bedri Noyan's rhyming translation was published in 1997, this tied in with a renewed debate about the need to use Turkish in mosques for ritual purposes which occurred against the backdrop of tensions around the possible Islamisation of the public sphere and nationalist demands for a genuinely Turkish brand of Islam. Vaktidolu's rhyming translation follows in the same vein. Just like Bedri Noyan, Vaktidolu emphasises his adherence to Turkish nationalism by choosing to employ, throughout the entire text, the *hece* metre, a metre that had been in use in Turkic literatures at least since the eleventh century. It had not been popular in Ottoman court literature which favoured Arabic and Persianate modes of poetry, but was revived in the nineteenth century as part of a quest for authentic Turkish culture and has ultimately become dominant in modern Turkish poetry. In Alevi–Bektashi poetry, it had been in continuous use. Therefore, the author's choice of the *hece* metre underlines his claim to producing an authentic Turkish Qur'ān. The same is true of his choice of the Turkish word *tanrı* for 'God', instead of the Arabic loanword *allâh*. This is not a unique choice, but one that has clear Turkish-nationalist connotations. Moreover, Vaktidolu makes explicit reference to Atatürk's project of producing a 'Turkish Qur'ān' that had been aborted in the 1930s, positioning his work as an attempt to complete that project and fulfil Atatürk's wish.[13]

Vaktidolu's rhyming translation cannot be understood without taking into account his use of the Turkish language, its position in the Turkish nation state, his denominational background and the ongoing struggle to situate Alevism in relation to both Islam and Turkish nationalism. These dimensions of language, statehood and denomination will now be discussed at more detail.

CENTRE, PERIPHERY AND HIERARCHIES OF LANGUAGE

Talk of 'centres' and 'peripheries' can be controversial. When using these terms, I do not intend to make grand claims about civilisations, cultures, world systems and so forth. Rather, I limit myself to Qur'ānic interpretations and how their origins and the languages in which they are performed influence their movement across the globe.

The first and seemingly self-evident observation, in this context, is that not all languages are equal. Indonesia, for example, might be the country with the largest Muslim population worldwide, but exegetical works written in Bahasa Indonesia are not likely to be read outside the Malay-speaking region. On the other hand, there is a great number of Islamic scholars and graduates of Islamic schools in Indonesia who are able to read Arabic well. Thus, while Indonesian books have virtually no chance of being read by Arabic scholars, a great many Arabic books are read in Indonesia. Moreover, a Turkish, Tanzanian or Pakistani scholar would be extremely unlikely to read an Indonesian work either, but is certain to be quite familiar with many Arabic works.

The degree to which individuals know foreign languages is not determined randomly; rather, it is closely linked to the prestige attached to languages.[14] A language divide can be bridged by translations, but whereas Arabic exegetical works are translated into many other Islamicate languages, the reverse is not the case, one of the reasons being that there is far more prestige involved for an Indonesian scholar citing Arabic sources than for an Arab scholar citing Indonesian sources. There is simply no market for Arabic translations of Indonesian sources.

The prestige attached to Arabic in Islamic religious discourses might be self-evident because it is the language of the Qur'ān and because the bulk of Islamic scholarship throughout history has been conducted in Arabic. However, there was also an important and predominantly Sunni[15] persophone tradition of scholarship, and that has lost much of its importance. The predominance of Persian as a language of literature, learning and the courts from the Ottoman Empire to South and Central Asia was lost to a large extent through the transformation of education, cultural reference systems and the activities of nation states – with the exception of Iran, of course. The result is that most contemporary Islamic scholars, sometimes without being aware of it, are cut off from important parts of the exegetical heritage. Besides Persian sources, this includes Ottoman Turkish and other vernacular languages that have changed drastically, often due to changes in script: the change from Arabic alphabet to Latin or Cyrillic alphabets turned the ability of reading sources predating that change into a skill that needs to be acquired – and that few scholars do acquire.

The situation is complicated by the fact that imperialism and colonisation brought a different set of languages into the picture: English, French and Russian. The new prestige of those languages was the result of asymmetrical power relations and therefore not uncontested. In religious discourses, in particular, there was a considerable level of distrust of the languages of the colonisers who were, after all, non-Muslims.

Today, matters are not nearly as clear-cut. This is most evident when looking at the status of English also much of the same things, albeit to a lesser extent, can be said about French and Russian. Large groups of Muslims live in English-speaking countries, many Muslim scholars teach at English-speaking universities and there is a huge and ever-growing body of original English-language scholarship in Qur'ānic studies. Many works by famous Muslim exegetes writing in English have been translated into numerous languages including Arabic; some examples are Fazlur Rahman, Amina Wadud (b. 1952), Farid Esack (b. 1959), Abdullah Saeed (*Interpreting the Qur'an: Towards a contemporary approach*, 2005) and Abdullahi

Ahmed An-Na'im. There are also *da'wa* activities in English that have a wide impact, as evidenced in the popularity of the English videos by preachers such as Zakir Naik (b. 1959) and Nouman Ali Khan. Some of these publications and videos might not be qualitatively different from texts in Urdu or German, but because they are in English, they have a global impact far beyond English-speaking countries. English has become a 'language of Islam'.[16] Because there are so many English-speaking Muslim audiences, a large amount of exegetical material is not only produced in English, but also translated into English, aimed at readers who are unable to study Ibn Kathīr or Sayyid Quṭb in the original Arabic.[17] The Qur'ānic commentary by the South Asian Islamist Abū al-A'lā Mawdūdī, for example, is probably read more often in the English translation than in the Urdu original.

English, as a global language of Islam, has not replaced Arabic with regard to prestige. It is no coincidence that most of the widely noticed exegetical works written in English come from the modernist and postmodern camp. Traditional scholars, as well as Salafis, continue to accord much prestige to Arabic; many of their English-language activities are *da'wa*-oriented, rather than scholarly. And it is still not common for traditional *'ulamā'* in the Arab world to quote sources in Western languages as exegetical authorities although they do, for example, quote Maurice Bucaille in order to provide evidence for the 'scientific miracle' of the Qur'ān. Here, because a scientific argument is intended, the reference's credibility is enhanced by the fact that it is not written by a traditional scholar writing in Arabic.

Despite the end of colonialism, an element of power relations is still inherent to the prestige of English. Muslim exegetes are part of English-speaking societies for many reasons, the legacy of British imperialism and economic disparities being two of them. Sometimes, scholars migrate due to a lack of freedom to express their ideas in an authoritarian setting. From Fazlur Rahman to Naṣr Ḥāmid Abū Zayd, examples abound. The social and political conditions behind such conflicts will be discussed later.[18]

Migration, of course, is not a new phenomenon. For Muslim scholars to migrate to faraway lands was a frequent occurrence at all stages of the history of the Islamicate world. However, the relatively large numbers in which they occupy academic positions in countries that are not predominantly Muslim is a fairly new phenomenon. Another new phenomenon is the fact that, through the use of digital media, scholars who have migrated may continue exerting a direct influence on their community of origin. Migrants also remain connected to religious discourses in their country of origin quite easily. Often, this results in quite complex networks of relations.

Not only the status of English, but also the contemporary status of Arabic is linked to power relations. It is not merely a matter of tradition and the language of the Qur'ān. When states support institutions of traditional Islamic learning or when they award scholarships for studying at al-Azhar in Cairo, as is very common in Southeast Asia, they make sure that Arabic retains some of its status and prestige. And when the state of Saudi Arabia established numerous schools and universities across the globe and attracted Arabic-speaking scholars from various parts of the Islamicate world to assume positions as teachers, preachers and religious scholars in the kingdom, it contributed to the proliferation of an Arabic exegetical discourse.

The central or peripheral status of a language is an important factor shaping interpretive communities. The reliance on English sources facilitates the establishment of global communities. Not all Qur'ānists are English speakers, nor are all Qur'ānist publications and websites in English, but the central status of Rashad Khalifa's ideas and the publications of his followers even among Egyptian or Turkish Qur'ānists are hard to overlook and certainly also a result of the fact that they are written in a global language. Conversely, the use of a language such as Swahili, Malay, Bengali or Tajik that is spoken only in a limited geographical area might make a Qur'ānic interpretation more appealing to native speakers of that language, but also restrict its impact to those speakers – which might exactly match the exegete's intention.[19]

Languages and their prestige have always been tied to power structures. The extent to which languages have been subjected to control and regulation, however, has changed fundamentally with the advent of modern statehood, and especially of nation states.

NATION STATES

Nation states are an indispensable component of the structures and forces that shape Muslim Qur'ānic exegesis today. The role that they play for exegetical efforts is immense and the ways in which they exert an influence are numerous. One of them is language.[20] For example, when the knowledge of Ottoman Turkish and thus the ability to use the Ottoman exegetical tradition were lost, this was not a natural and organic development, but the result of the deliberate decisions of Turkish language policy makers. When Bahasa Indonesia was introduced as a national language, fast dominating over the many other languages of the Indonesian archipelago, at least in the realm of the written word, this was again the result of a conscious political decision born out of the agenda of the independence movement, but with precedents in colonial times.

Wherever the Arabic script was replaced by the Latin or Cyrillic alphabet, this was usually the result of state policy. Not all countries made attempts to dictate the script, vocabulary or even grammar of their language, but many determined one or several 'national languages' to the exclusion of others; thus, for example, Kurdish and Berber languages were marginalised. All this had a profound impact on the exegesis of the Qur'ān. It determined which exegetical traditions were used and which discarded out of an inability to read them; in which language translations and Qur'ānic commentaries were written; and what kind of vocabulary was used to talk about the Qur'ān.

The imposition and restructuring of national languages were intimately tied to the states' efforts to build systems of public education and regulate – to widely varying degrees – the field of private education which was often synonymous to religious education. The languages that were taught in state schools deeply determined the language in which the majority of the population was literate. Another fundamental policy decision concerned the foreign languages that were to be taught, if any. In many countries, the teaching of Arabic lost much of its importance in relation to English, French and Russian, but this was not true everywhere. For example, after the Iranian revolution in 1979, Arabic was again made obligatory in the country's educational system which exemplifies the highly symbolic nature of such decisions.

Efforts to institute public and more or less secular schooling varied widely. In some states, such as in Pakistan,[21] often due to lack of funding for the public schooling system, private religious schools in which the teaching of Arabic and the study of the Qur'ān play a central role retained much of their importance. In Indonesia, Islamic boarding schools remain popular, not least because many of them have successfully integrated secular subjects into their curricula.[22] In non-religious schools, the extent to which Islam is taught in schools and the contents of that religious education are quite obviously another area in which nation state policies exert an influence. This is not only an issue concerning Muslim-majority societies, but also a field that is increasingly contested in many European states. Religious education is embedded in politics.

The influence of nation states extends to the field of tertiary education, and this is particularly important because it is where religious scholars – *'ulamā'* – are produced and where many of them eventually work. One aspect that should not be overlooked is the varying degree of prestige that religious training possesses in different states; only where studies of religion or theology are considered to be desirable careers do the respective institutions attract good students. The situation varies from country to country and those cannot be described in any detail here. However, the nature of a state's institutions of tertiary religious learning invariably needs to be taken into consideration when studying exegetical works that have been written or performed by scholars trained at state institutions or working in them.

Extensive Qur'ānic commentaries, in particular, are very commonly the work of such scholars because an employment at a higher institution of Islamic learning is one of the few occupations that provides sufficient time and resources for such projects.

Examples of the ways in which university curricula influence exegetical output abound. One of the main reasons for which Turkey has produced so many modernist Qur'ānic interpretations in recent decades is the abolition of all traditional institutions of higher Islamic education by the Turkish Republic and the subsequent foundation of a 'Faculty of Theology' at Ankara University. This faculty had a modernising curriculum that incorporated content from Western humanities and social sciences, rather than focussing on traditional disciplines such as *tafsīr*, *ḥadīth* and *fiqh*. Some of the State Islamic Universities in Indonesia pursued similar projects. On the other hand, the large reform the prestigious Egyptian Azhar underwent in 1961, turning it from a *madrasa* into a university, entailed no fundamental revision of the curricula of the religious disciplines; if anything, it reduced choice and diversity and thus emphasised particular traditional approaches more strongly. Saudi Arabia, at the opposing end of the religious and ideological spectrum from where the Theological Faculty in Ankara was at its inception, uses its educational system to promote its state ideology of Salafism and the multi-national body of scholars teaching at Saudi universities can be expected to represent various shades of that ideology. All these nation state policies translate directly into the content of exegesis performed by affiliates of these institutions.[23]

For Muslims in the diaspora and in countries that have no Islamic educational institutions, such as the former Soviet republics of Central Asia where the Soviet Union had dissolved religious institutions, the question where to obtain trained *'ulamā'* is of some relevance, engendering a certain competition between international actors such as Saudi Arabia and Turkey for gaining influence on the religious fields in these states, for example, by providing scholarships or by sending state-funded imams abroad. Saudi Arabia's wealth obviously makes it a particularly important player in this field. Thus, Islamic religious discourses, including exegetical ones, are not only a subject of interior politics of Muslim-majority states, but also a subject of foreign policy.

State-trained *'ulamā'* are the most likely candidates for state-sponsored exegetical ventures such as the official Qur'ān translation and commentary published by the Indonesian Ministry of Religion[24] or the semi-official translation and commentary produced in Turkey.[25] They are written by committees largely consisting of *'ulamā'*, as opposed to individual scholars, and there is usually an editorial team involved as well.[26] Thus, some states do not content themselves with controlling exegetical discourses indirectly, but intervene directly as exegetical actors.

Another field in which states, usually by means of *ʿulamāʾ*, exert a direct influence on exegetical activities is that of censorship. Many Muslim-majority countries have institutions that control publications about the Qurʾān and that issue certificates of approval or deny them, such as al-Azhar in Egypt or the Indonesian Ministry of Religion. This is a very powerful tool that may be used to suppress militant Qurʾān interpretations as well as works that are deemed overly 'liberal'.

The existence of censorship extends to media which also influences exegetical output. The stronger a state's control on the media, the more likely it is that the type of exegesis published and performed there conforms to the interests of the state. On the other hand, exegetes that oppose the state have always searched for media venues allowing them to express that opposition. The origin of Sayyid Quṭb's Qurʾānic commentary in mass media is a prime example. The internet offers nearly limitless opportunities for such activity.

The question whether the Qurʾān should mean something different to Indonesians from what it means to Turks or Americans and whether it should be applied in different ways is highly contested. Salafis, many (but not all) Islamists, traditional *ʿulamāʾ* and even many modernists claim that there is only one Islam. In general, those who categorically reject the adaptation of Qurʾānic interpretation to historical circumstances equally strongly oppose its adaptation to differences in space, society and political structure. The proponents of such a localisation of the Qurʾān, on the other hand, point to the fact that each society has its own customs pertaining to issues such as dress codes, entertainment, modes of punishment and social hierarchies.[27] They rarely point to the existence of different political structures and systems of governance, but these are, in fact, central to the localisation of exegetical discourses.

National exegetical discourses are already in existence. The deep impact of nation states on the authors, form, media and contents of Qurʾānic exegesis made this unavoidable.[28] These national discourses are not disjointed from the global Islamic tradition; one may find exegetes across the world quoting authorities such as al-Bayḍāwī or Ibn Kathīr. But at the same time, individual nation states have brought forth their own authorities. For example, only Turkish exegetes will quote Elmalılı Hamdi Yazır (1878–1942); he might be far from being a global Islamic authority, but his popularity and importance in Turkey are immense. There are also specific themes connected to exegetical debates in individual states. For example, the discussion about the relationship between Islam and Pancasila – the national doctrine of 'the five principles'[29] – permeates Indonesian Qurʾānic interpretations, but would make little sense to Muslims elsewhere. The following text is an example of how the government of a nation state has produced an exegetical work in order to deliver a specific message on statehood and citizenship.

State building: the Indonesian Ministry of Religion on Q. 12:54–5

In the 1960s, the leadership of the newly founded post-colonial nation state of Indonesia undertook an ambitious project: the Old Order regime led by Indonesia's first president Sukarno (1901–1970) commissioned an annotated Qurʾān translation and a voluminous commentary on the Qurʾān. Priority was given to the production of the translation. The eleven-volume extensive commentary entitled 'The Qurʾān and its interpretation' (*Al-Qurʾan dan tafsirnya*) was started in 1972 and published in 1975. At that time, Suharto's New Order regime had already come to power. Suharto tried to suppress expressions of political Islam while simultaneously co-opting many religious scholars into the regime. The latter objective was achieved by founding a number of state-sponsored Islamic institutions and committees. One of them was in charge of *Al-Qurʾan dan tafsirnya*. The committee consisted of seventeen members, all of whom were employed by the State Islamic Institutes, Indonesia's new institutions of higher religious learning. One of the goals of the commentary was thus to demonstrate the academic potential of these institutions.[30] Both the translation and the commentary saw several revised editions with far-reaching changes to the text that reflected regime changes and changes of general political orientation. The edition used in this book dates from 2004, several years after the fall of Suharto's New Order regime.

This was probably the first Qurʾānic commentary that was written and continues to be revised by a government committee, rather than an individual scholar. The editorial process ensured that the contributions of individual scholars are not discernible. From the outset, this commentary's claim to representing the official Qurʾānic interpretation of the Indonesian Ministry of Religion, rather than a scholar's personal opinion, was novel. Up until today, few states have dared to raise an equally bold claim. The Turkish Directorate of Religious Affairs, for example, published a Qurʾānic commentary in 2003–4, but that was attributed to its four individual authors, all of them religious scholars, and explicitly declared to reflect their subjective opinions as opposed to an official authoritative interpretation.[31] The Indonesian project thus indicates a nation state with an unusual degree of self-confidence and a desire to set the terms of the religious discourse. The government does not have a monopoly on that discourse, though. Under the current democratic system, the Ministry's commentary can be openly criticised, an opportunity that is taken up especially within the Islamist spectrum.[32] Neither has the Ministry's commentary been unrivalled; there is a number of competing Qurʾānic commentaries by individual, reputable scholars. Yet, the case of *Al-Qur'an dan tafsirnya* demonstrates clearly that the various interests the Qurʾān may serve in present times include those of modern nation states.

The commentary in Excerpt 6.2 on the story of Joseph might seem unspectacular at first glance; large parts of it are devoted to the narrative expansion of the Qurʾānic story and to filling the gaps in the Qurʾānic dialogue. That the aim is primarily a pedagogical one becomes apparent from the simple (almost simplistic) style and the clear structure.

Excerpt 6.2

Joseph becomes the state treasurer [Q. 12:54–55]

وَقَالَ الْمَلِكُ ائْتُونِي بِهِ أَسْتَخْلِصْهُ لِنَفْسِي فَلَمَّا كَلَّمَهُ قَالَ إِنَّكَ الْيَوْمَ لَدَيْنَا مَكِينٌ أَمِينٌ ﴿٥٤﴾ قَالَ
اجْعَلْنِي عَلَىٰ خَزَائِنِ الْأَرْضِ إِنِّي حَفِيظٌ عَلِيمٌ ﴿٥٥﴾

Translation
(54) And the king said, 'Bring him (Joseph) to me, so that I can choose him (as a person close) to me'. When he (the king) had spoken with him, he (the king) said, 'Verily, today you (start to) become a person who holds a high position in our domain and who is trustworthy'. (55) He (Joseph) said, 'Make me the treasurer of the land (Egypt); for verily, I am a man who is good at keeping watch and who has knowledge'.

Glossary: *khazāʾini* خَزَائِنِ (Yūsuf 12:55)
Plural of *khizāna*, which means a place to store or collect something. The root of the word is (*kh–z–n*) which means to guard something. *Khāzin* means a guard, its plural is *khazāna*. *Khazāʾin al-arḍ* are the places for storing the riches of the country, that is Egypt. The person who is officially in charge of them is called the state treasurer. The meaning of this verse is thus a request by the Prophet Joseph to be put in charge of the revenues and expenses as well as the places where the riches of the land are stored. At the time of the Prophet Joseph, as well as at any other time, the minister who guards the state treasury holds an office of strategic importance because he controls the lifeline of the national economy.

Munāsaba[33]
The preceding verses had described the Prophet Joseph as saying that man's soul is inclined towards evil unless it obtains mercy from God. This is because the Prophet Joseph was an honest and loyal person since he has

received mercy that has prevented him from wrongdoing. The subsequent verses describe how the king appoints the Prophet Joseph as State Treasurer exactly because of his honesty and loyalty towards the king.

Commentary

(54) In this very moving scene, the king gives orders for Joseph to be fetched from jail and brought to the palace. In the palace, Joseph tells the king all about his experiences from the time he came to live in al-ʿAzīz's[34] palace up until his imprisonment and finally the opportunity to meet the king face to face. When hearing these explanations, the king feels more and more convinced that Joseph is truly an honest and loyal person, with a strong sense of responsibility, a noble character, knowledgeable, perseverant and of firm belief. Due to this conviction, the king proclaims in the presence of all the dignitaries and leaders of the land that he has just appointed Joseph his confidant. All financial affairs of the country are to be transferred to his leadership and responsibility; he is to be the one who completely deserves to control the administration and the only person who may communicate directly with the king. According to a tradition narrated by Ibn ʿAbbās, 'when the king's messenger arrived in prison, he said to Joseph: "Strip off the prison garment that you are wearing, pull on these new garments and come with me to see the king". All the prison inmates prayed for him, and Joseph prayed for them in return. When they arrived at the palace, the king was quite surprised to see that Joseph was still so young (at the time, he was about 30 years old). "That such a young man should be able to interpret my dream with such certainty while all the sorcerers and religious leaders of my country were unable to interpret it!" Then the king ordered him to sit opposite him and spoke forth: "Do not be afraid!" Then he draped a golden necklace around his neck and gave him a silken robe of honour. Furthermore, a saddled horse was prepared for him that was richly adorned and large drums were beaten in all corners of Egypt as a sign and pronouncement that Joseph had been appointed *khalīfa* (the right hand) of the king'. This is what Ibn ʿAbbās narrates. Then the king declared: 'From this day you will hold the highest position at our side and we entrust upon you all affairs of the state'.

(55) Then the king tells Joseph about his dream and asks for his opinion on the measures that should be taken for coping with the seven dry years. Joseph asks the king to put him in charge of all affairs related to the national economy so that he can organise them to the best of his ability in order to prevent famine despite an extremely long dry season. Subsequently, Joseph presents a plan for the full length of that period. He says that in the current long fertile season, farming activity should be increased and all subjects should be ordered to cultivate every plot of fertile land, so

that when the long dry season comes, stores of foodstuffs that have been prepared during the fertile season can be distributed little by little while the grain stalks can be used as fodder for the cattle. The king is very glad to hear Joseph's opinion and places even more trust in Joseph's intelligence and wisdom. He readily accepts all of Joseph's proposals. Not only issues related to agriculture, but all state policies are completely transferred to Joseph. Thus, Joseph has become an authority who is respected, honoured and loved in Egypt.

Conclusion

The king frees Joseph from prison, and because the king is extremely impressed with his honesty, perseverance, trustworthiness, intelligence and knowledge, he is appointed the right hand of the king and put in charge of all affairs of the state.

After the king has heard the opinion and proposals of Joseph, he decides to appoint him state treasurer who holds the reins of Egypt's economy.[35]

In this eleven-volume Qur'ānic commentary, the Qur'ān is consistently explained in segments. After translation into Bahasa Indonesia, one paragraph is devoted to explanations of words and one to the *munāsaba*: the logical connection to the preceding and the subsequent segment of the Qur'ān. There is thus an underlying idea of the Qur'ān as a coherent whole. After the commentary proper, a conclusion sums up the main points so as not to leave any uncertainties.

The sources on which the narrative expansion draws are conventional. There is no direct reference to the Biblical story of Joseph. Rather, the reference is to a tradition on 'Abdallāh b. 'Abbās (d. *c.* 687), the Prophet's cousin and companion who is often considered the forefather of Muslim exegesis, but about whom so many – often contradictory – exegetical traditions are narrated that it is difficult to know which ones actually go back to him.[36] This particular tradition stems originally from the very early book on the conquest of Egypt, *Futūh Miṣr*, by Abū al-Qāsim 'Abd al-Raḥmān b. 'Abdallāh b. 'Abd al-Ḥakam (d. 871) that recounts the history of Egypt from the mythological past to the Arab-Muslim conquest. Its introduction into Qur'ānic exegesis, however, seems to have occurred around six centuries later through Jalāl al-Dīn al-Suyūṭī's *Al-Durr al-Manthūr*. It takes up some Biblical motives, such as the golden necklace, and modifies others in order to bring them in line with the Arab-Islamic cultural environment: the chariot from the Biblical tale becomes a horse, the linen robe becomes a silken robe, and the term *khalīfa* is introduced to describe Joseph's position in relation to the pharao. The Ministry's commentary translates Ibn 'Abbās's account almost faithfully, with one exception: Ibn 'Abbās has the prison inmates pray for Joseph, but it is only the Ministry committee that has Joseph pray for the inmates in return, possibly because the committee thought that this would be the only plausible action that a prophet would have taken under the circumstances and that this would help their general goal of setting him up as a role model.

When the Indonesian government commentary presents the Qur'ānic story of Joseph, it does so in the language of the modern state, and it uses the story in order to send a message to its readers about their role in such a state. It is Joseph's loyalty to the ruler, his intelligence and trustworthiness, as well as his skilful economic planning, that convince the king to hand him control of the state economy. Joseph is not rewarded by God for his faith, nor is he favoured by the pharaoh because of his correct interpretation of the latter's dreams; rather, he is chosen to occupy a prestigious and responsible position because he has both the necessary skill – 'intelligence and knowledge' – and the moral characteristics of a good citizen: 'honesty, perseverance, trustworthiness'. As a reward, he is 'respected, honoured and loved' in his country. In contrast to some premodern treatments of the story that credit Joseph with using his high position in order to spread the faith in the one God, the Indonesian Ministry of Religion describes him, in a very pedagogical manner, as a role model for civil servants. This is consistent with the Ministry's general vision of citizenhood in which religion delivers the moral foundation for qualities such as incorruptibility and hard work.[37] This commentary's primary aim, thus, is neither to contribute to a scholarly debate nor to enhance the faith of believers, but to educate better citizens of a nation state.

SUNNI AND SHI'I ISLAM

The case of the Alevi rhyming translation that, for lack of an Alevi tradition of Qur'ānic exegesis, opted for adopting a Shi'i allegorical approach points to the fact that there is diversity within Islam and that the existence of denominational differences may have a bearing on Qur'ānic interpretation.

Denominational categories have been described as genre-defining in many histories of *tafsīr*: there is Imāmi Shi'i *tafsīr*, Zaydi *tafsīr*, Ibāḍi *tafsīr* and so forth. Frequently, Sunni *tafsīr* is seen as the norm against which all other trends are contrasted which is problematic because it implies that the majority perspective is at the same time either superior or, alternatively, the most neutral one. Sufi *tafsīr*, despite typically being authored by Sunni Muslims, is described as a category of its own, and so are theological tendencies that are perceived as somehow heterodox, particularly those of the Mu'tazila.[38]

In recent years, nuanced studies of a broader array of sources than, for example, Ignác Goldziher (1850–1921) had at his disposal have shown this type of categorisation to be problematic although not entirely obsolete. First of all, from an analytical perspective, there is no reason to assume that a certain type of Sunni *tafsīr* with a specific theological orientation represents some kind of orthodoxy. The concept of orthodoxy itself poses the risk of superimposing dogmatic assumptions on scholarship in intellectual history; if at all, it can only be meaningfully employed to describe power relations at specific places and times where a certain creed was established as normative and others were marginalised or even persecuted. Thus, orthodoxy in today's Iran is not identical to orthodoxy in Saudi Arabia and the latter, in turn, is not representative of Sunni orthodoxy in other places, although it might raise that claim.

Even if Sunnism and its various theological branches were not defined as the norm, but as sects, denominations or schools of thought alongside others, the problem remains that it is often misleading to define an exegete by that type of identity.[39] In fact, most of the phenomena described in this book, whether they be ideological trends such as modernism, structural conditions such as media and nation states or exegetical methods, are relevant across the denominational spectrum.

On the other hand, specific communities such as Sunnis, Imami Shi'is, Zaydis or Aḥmadis do have their own exegetical authorities, genealogies and sources, besides the ones they share with others. They might also use *tafsīr* as a site for inter-denominational polemics or in order to defend their own teachings to a greater or lesser extent. Therefore, it would be equally misleading to completely ignore an exegete's affiliation.

The emergence of Sunni and Shi'i Islam as well as the smaller – and widely vilified – movement of Khārijism was the result of a long process that took several centuries. It involved much polemical and apologetic activity between the groups as well as power struggles and quests for political hegemony. A conflict over authority was at the root of the division. Broadly speaking, those whose claim to the caliphate, during the foundational period of Islam, was successful and those who gave them allegiance came to be known as *ahl al-sunna wa'l-jamā'a*, or Sunnis. This was based on a specific narrative of early Islamic history, where those who attained the caliphate – and in some cases, defeated other contenders – had the legitimacy to do so. The theoretical justification for that legitimacy was largely based on the concept of *ijmā'*, or the consensus of the community. There were also theological questions tied to the issue of legitimate rule. The emerging Sunni community, much like its competitors, was thus the site of significant theological debate which was also carried out within *tafsīr*.[40]

This is not the place to explore the history of Sunni Islam in any depth. I will limit myself to outlining two main features here that are important for understanding contemporary exegetical discourses.

First, there is no central religious authority. It is sometimes claimed that Sunni Islam has no clergy which is true in the sense that there is no priesthood. There are, however, Sunni religious scholars (*ʿulamāʾ*). Many states have had institutionalised positions and hierarchies for these *ʿulamāʾ*, and at least some *ʿulamāʾ* have nearly always been in a position of authority. Throughout the colonial and nation state period, there was an increased tendency to establish formalised structures of religious authority, with the result that today there are many scholars holding more or less official positions, some of them limited to their own state, others with a wider reach. These power structures have to be taken into account when studying specific scholars because it means that in some cases, their opinions hold more weight than that of a random individual Muslim. Yet the fact that there is, formally, no clergy independent of political power structures is often emphasised by individual Muslims defending their right to promote their opinions against the mainstream of Sunni *ʿulamāʾ*.

A particularly relevant phenomenon, in the context of nation states and their respective Sunni religious establishments, is the competition between Egypt and Saudi Arabia that goes back to the first half of the twentieth century.[41] It frequently touches upon fundamental exegetical debates, and that is because of its intimate connection to the second feature of contemporary Sunni religious discourses that I would like to mention here, which is the question what attitude one takes towards the Salafi paradigm.

The tension in Sunni religious discourses – also present in Imami Shiʿism and other non-Sunni communities – between a strictly *ḥadīth*-based approach and other methods, including rationalist ones, is old. The tension was already a defining feature of the formative period. The Sunni tradition of scholarship which emerged from that period accepted the Sunna as a fundamental source of Islam, on a par, or nearly on a par, with the Qurʾān; but it also largely accepted the methods of scholastic theology (*kalām*) based on Aristotelian logic. As has already been discussed, Salafis reject the tradition of *kalām* just as much as they reject the schools of law and Sufism.

The modern state of Egypt hosts the internationally famed al-Azhar, the country's highest institution of Sunni Islam. A reform in 1961 turned al-Azhar into a state institution. Consecutive Egyptian regimes have tried to cast al-Azhar and its *ʿulamāʾ* as heirs to the tradition of Islamic scholarship and as representatives of what is labelled today 'moderate Islam' or *wasaṭiyya*: embracing the tradition of Ashʿari theology, acknowledging the Sunni schools of law, especially the Ḥanafi one that Egypt inherited from the Ottoman Empire, accepting Sufism and building on the premodern genealogy of *tafsīr*. Al-Azhar has also strongly condemned jihadi ideas. In contrast, Saudi Arabia promotes a 'purified' version of Islam that, according to its self-representation, is based on the authority of the fundamental scriptural sources and thereby raises a higher claim to legitimacy. This Salafi paradigm is rejected by many traditional scholars because it ignores or even opposes the imagined consensus of a diachronic community of *ʿulamāʾ*, one of the foundational ideas of Sunni Islam.[42]

This competition between two strong claims for legitimacy demonstrates the impossibility of defining a contemporary Sunni 'orthodoxy' from an analytical perspective. It is entirely possible to speak of either a Saudi, a Salafi or an Azhari orthodoxy, as long as one does not imply that every single Saudi or Azhari scholar follows the same paradigm; but in a global Sunni framework, it is impossible to speak of a Sunni orthodoxy.

Shiʿis describe their movement as having been in opposition to illegitimate Sunni rulers from the outset. They claim for that movement to go back to groups who rallied behind ʿAlī b. Abī Ṭālib (d. 661), the cousin of Muḥammad and father of the Prophet's only surviving male descendants through his marriage with Muḥammad's daughter Fāṭima. ʿAlī became the fourth caliph in 656, but had to fight against opposition from various parties during his entire reign. After his assassination, the Umayyads who, just like ʿAlī's three predecessors, were not close relatives of the Prophet, ascended to power. Umayyad troops were responsible for killing ʿAlī's younger son al-Ḥusayn at Karbala in 680 in order to keep him from raising a claim to the caliphate, a martyrdom that is a central and defining moment in Shiʿi collective memory.

The various branches of Shiʿism that evolved over time are vastly different with respect to their doctrines and views on religious and political legitimacy, but they are united by the belief that the imamate – the leadership of the community – is the prerogative of the Prophet's family, specifically ʿAlī and his descendants. They are divided over the question who, from among those descendants, is the rightful imam, and whether there is a living imam or whether the line of imams ended at some point, at least in this world.

The largest and most influential branch of Shiʿism today – which was not always the case, historically – is Imami or Twelver Shiʿism, which is predominant in Iran, constitutes the denomination of the majority in Iraq and has a strong presence in Lebanon, in Bahrain and the Eastern Province of Saudi Arabia as well as in South Asia. It is also the most productive branch of Shiʿism as far as contemporary exegetical activity is concerned. Imami Shiʿis believe that after the death of the eleventh imam, Ḥasan al-ʿAskarī (d. 874), he left a son who was hidden from people due to the oppression of Sunni rulers and who was later removed into occultation (*ghayba*). According to Imami Shiʿis, the twelfth imam, the son of Ḥasan al-ʿAskarī, will only return from occultation at the end of time in order to establish justice on Earth. In the course of the centuries, the Shi'i *'ulamā'* took over more and more of the tasks that had been thought to be the imam's prerogative such as taxation and jurisdiction, with the result that Imami Shi'ism has a well-established clergy with a clear hierarchy, but also a high degree of independence and diversity.[43]

The first Imami Shi'i works of *tafsīr* were overwhelmingly concerned with defending Shi'i beliefs. They read large segments of the Qur'ān as evidence for the designation of 'Alī as Muḥammad's immediate successor, the precedence of 'Alī and his family, the imamate and related beliefs.[44] To that purpose, they interpreted every reference to right and wrong, righteous people and sinners, God's approval and anger, as references to the Shi'is and their opponents. They also employed allegorical methods, for example by explaining the 'good tree' and the 'rotten tree' in Q. 14:24–6[45] as references to the Prophet's family and the Umayyads, respectively.[46] In the Middle Period starting roughly in the eleventh century, this began to change. Shi'i commentators such as al-Ṭūsī (d. 1067) and al-Ṭabrisī (d. 1154) saw *tafsīr* as a holistic endeavour, concerned with rhetoric, theology and law. They pursued much of the same methods, themes and even sources as their Sunni contemporaries and displayed none of the exclusive focus on Shi'i dogma that had characterised their predecessors. Shi'i identity was still apparent in their works at certain occasions, just as it was common for Sunni exegetes to defend their theological allegiance or the position of their school of law where warranted, but it was no longer the defining feature of their way of interpreting the Qur'ān.[47]

Today, large parts of Imami Shi'i exegesis are virtually indistinguishable from their Sunni counterparts. This is especially true for issues that have contemporary relevance, but do not touch upon topics that usually give rise to Sunni–Shi'i polemics. For example, where women's testimony or the relationship between husband and wife are concerned, the differences between Sunnis and Shi'is are negligible, if they exist at all, while within both denominations, the differences between modernists and conservative *'ulamā'* are profound.[48] Yet where differences with respect to dogma or normative sources are concerned, denominational identities might well come to the surface.[49] For example, the institution of temporary marriage (*zawāj al-mut'a*), which is permitted in Imami Shi'i Islam and forbidden in Sunni Islam, is a subject of great polemic.[50]

Just like in Sunni Islam, nation state politics have a great impact on the exegetical field in Imami Shi'ism. More specifically, Imami Shi'ism is the official denomination of the Islamic Republic of Iran which sponsors religious scholarship, missionary activity and Qur'ān translation. The Iranian-Shi'i field, in particular, still occasionally brings forth distinctly pro-Shi'i apologetic and polemical exegetical projects.[51] Furthermore, views that contradict the Islamic Republic's political or legal system, especially modernist ones that exceed certain limits, are suppressed or punished with the result that a number of Iranian scholars and religious intellectuals are now in exile.

It needs to be emphasised that not every exegete who is Shiʿi by faith or by descent is concerned with Shiʿi doctrines when interpreting the Qur'ān.[52] This is true for many of the Iranian modernist and postmodern scholars and intellectuals who often have a wide following outside Imami Shiʿi Islam, and it is also true for other branches of Shiʿism. For example, the Indian Asghar Ali Engineer (1939–2013) was born a Dawoodi Bohra, which is one of the two existing branches of the Ismaʿili Shiʿa. He was expelled due to his criticism of the community's religious leadership and subsequently headed the Progressive Dawoodi Bohra movement. His Qur'ān-centred writings, however, are ostensibly non-sectarian. They focus on issues such as inter-religious coexistence, secularism and gender justice and have a worldwide readership far beyond disenchanted Bohra.[53]

SUFISM

Forms of Islamic mysticism, commonly called Sufism, have been widely practiced in Sunni Islam and sometimes in Shiʿism. In the Middle and modern period, this typically took place in the framework of mystical orders structured around persons of authority which also means that, besides the focus on the inner dimension of Islam, ritual is important to Sufism. Sufism brought forth its own teaching tradition from which many Sufi commentaries on the Qur'ān emerged. These emphasised, to varying degrees, the 'inner meaning' (*bāṭin*) of the Qur'ān by way of metaphorical and allusive (*ishārī*) interpretations, sometimes to the exclusion of the more conventional elements of *tafsīr* such as linguistic analysis and *ḥadīth*s, and sometimes in addition to it.

In its formative period, up until the thirteenth century, Sufi Qur'ānic exegesis varied widely and, while containing an element of genealogy through the citation of previous authorities, exegetes expressed their own, original interpretations to a larger extent than contemporaneous mainstream exegetes.[54] After that, exegetical authorities and schools of Sufi exegesis started to gain a more important role, with Ibn ʿArabī (d. 1240) emerging as a central figure. His ideas on the 'oneness of being' (*waḥdat al-wujūd*) and a spiritual hierarchy culminating in the 'perfect human' (*al-insān al-kāmil*) were not uncontested, but nevertheless extremely influential.[55]

In the modern period, Sufi *tafsīr* still exists, but it has undergone a few significant developments. For one thing, there is a tendency, at least among some Sufi commentators, to incorporate scientific and philosophical themes into works of exegesis and to address contemporary ethical and social problems. For another thing, since Sufism became a popular phenomenon in Western countries, encouraging some to convert to Islam, but also attracting the attention of non-Muslims interested in spiritual practices, there are a number of Sufi Qur'ānic commentaries which address precisely these audiences.[56]

Premodern Sufi conceptions of esoteric knowledge usually distinguish between those dimensions accessible to the 'masses' (*al-ʿāmma*) and those whose understanding is restricted to an elect (*al-khāṣṣa*), and they adopt their language and the selection of meanings they presented to their readers accordingly. Contemporary Sufi Qur'ānic commentaries usually employ the mode of communication that is directed at a broader public, not presupposing familiarity with Sufi terminology or an advanced stage of progress on the mystical path. Instead, they seek to present the Qur'ān to contemporary, sometimes specifically to secularist or non-Muslim audiences, as an attractive spiritual alternative to a materialist culture, translating the mystical experience into a language that is comprehensible to these audiences which, today, might include reference to scientific concepts.[57]

Modes of religious authority within contemporary Sufism have also changed. Some Sufi writers and exegetes have acquired their authority in a more or less traditional way, having grown up in a predominantly Muslim society and having been initiated into Sufi orders early in their lives. They might come from prominent Sufi families or they might have received the authority to practice and teach a particular brand of Sufism from a renowned Sufi shaykh. Others come from different circumstances, for example, in countries where Sufism had been explicitly banned in the twentieth century, such as in the Soviet republics of Central Asia; or they were born into an educated elite for which Sufism had fallen out of favour due to its perceived backwardness and irrationality; or they were Western converts in search of spirituality who discovered Sufism after forays into Buddhism and other traditions.[58]

In contrast to mainstream Qur'ānic commentaries, with which there might nonetheless be an overlap, contemporary Sufi commentaries emphasise the beauty of the Qur'ān's expression, its aesthetic and emotional appeal and its hidden meanings that sometimes include cabbalistic elements such as frequencies of letters and their significance. The genre of Sufi *tafsīr* thus allows for fairly individual expressions because any Sufi who has sufficiently advanced on the mystical path might have his or her own insights into the Qur'ān's hidden, inner meanings, possibly in addition to those of earlier Sufi authorities or schools. The focus on the inner meaning does not necessarily mean that Sufi exegetes consider the 'outward' (*ẓāhir*) application of legal norms and ritual duties unimportant. Rather, these aspects are only one part of the Qur'ānic message and usually not the one that Sufi exegetes focus on.

Due to the high appeal of Sufism, especially, but not only, in Western societies, and the simultaneous popularity of anti-Sufi Salafi paradigms, Sufi *tafsīr* has the potential to polarise. It is certainly set apart from the mainstream of the exegetical discourse even if it might employ some of its methods and contents as the following case study will show.

A female Sufi shaykh: Cemâlnur Sargut (b. 1952, Turkey) on Q. 112

Cemâlnur Sargut, today a celebrity in the Turkish Islamic field, was born into a family affiliated with the Rifāʿiyya Sufi order; she said of herself that she was 'born as a Rifa'i'.[59] Her mother, Meşküre Sargut, was a Sufi teacher who had studied with Ken'an Rifâî (1867–1950). This was a branch of the Rifāʿiyya Sufi order that, much in contrast to the order's general image of being popular among lower-class peasants, had succeeded in attracting members of the educated, intellectual, urban elites – among them many women.[60]

Despite her family background, Sargut, while never outright rejecting Rifāʿī teachings, at first had little interest in them. She studied chemical engineering and read many works of philosophy, but found her desire for a path that combined happiness with high ideals unfulfilled. Her mother then acquainted her with Jalāl al-Dīn al-Rūmī's (1207–1273) *Mathnawī* which Cemâlnur started reading at the age of 21. Two years later, her teacher, the female Sufi shaykh Sâmiha Ayverdi (1905–1993), asked her to teach the *Mathnawī*. Through teaching, she acquired knowledge of the works of other important Sufis, particularly Ibn ʿArabī (1165–1240). She exclusively relied on Turkish translations since she reads neither Arabic nor Persian.

Over the years, Cemâlnur Sargut gathered male and female students from the urban upper classes[61] around herself. Besides her sessions, appearances on television and other public events, she eventually started writing books. Thus, her work is both directed at a small circle of spiritual disciples and at a larger public. She has been characterised as 'a leading television personality, social welfare and development activist and a much sought out public speaker at various national and international venues.'[62]

Her books – like her speeches – prominently include a number of works of Qur'ānic exegesis. Many of them are commentaries on individual *sūra*s or verses. They are based on the results of weekly Qur'ānic study circles that Cemâlnur Sargut has held with a group of around thirty disciples since the early 1990s, with a few more following on Skype. By the 2010s, these circles had turned into large gatherings in packed conference halls. The books are published by *Nefes*, the publishing house of TÜRKKAD, the Turkish Women's Cultural Association. This Sufi NGO was founded by Sâmiha Ayverdi. Associations of this type were established in order to create a legal framework for continuing the activities of the officially abolished Sufi orders. TÜRKKAD's Istanbul chapter is headed by Sargut.[63]

Another of Sargut's books on the Qur'ān is called 'Existing with the Qur'ān' (*Kur'an ile var olmak*). It is the second part of a series called 'Sufi talks'.[64] The first edition, with a print run of 20,000 copies, was printed in 2014. In this small book, she discusses with her interviewer, Ferda Yıldırım, various aspects of the Qur'ān and some other topics. One might consider this a modern version of the premodern scholar's oral lessons that were written down by his students, only that in this case 'he' is a 'her'.

This is one of the few cases in which *tafsīr* performed by a woman is neither directed at an exclusively female audience nor concerned with 'women's issues'. Sufism is a field in which women may acquire sufficient spiritual and religious authority to participate in a discourse on the Qur'ān that is not gendered, or at least not outwardly so,[65] although even in Sufism the degree of spiritual authority that Sargut holds for her mixed-gender followers is rarely attained by women.[66]

While the names of most *sūra*s are based on a word from the text of the *sūra*, this is not the case with *al-Ikhlāṣ*, one of the last and shortest *sūra*s of the Qur'ān. The term *al-ikhlāṣ* denotes sincere dedication to one's religion. According to a *ḥadīth*, the Prophet said that this *sūra* is equal to one third of the Qur'ān.[67] Mainstream Qur'ānic commentaries usually explain the *sūra* as an affirmation of the oneness of God (*tawḥīd*) as well as a refutation of Christian belief in the Trinity, the Meccan pagans' belief that God has daughters and similar manifestations of polytheism.

Cemâlnur Sargut, however, situates herself in a different tradition, the tradition of Sufi Qur'ānic exegesis. Having acquired her authority through a Sufi lineage and decades of experience on the mystical path, Sargut presents a thoroughly esoteric reading of the Qur'ān. The focus in this interview-turned-book is exclusively on the spiritual dimension of the Qur'ān. There is no discussion of legal verses apart from a few remarks about ritual prayer and what it signifies, but there is ample talk about *sūra*s such as the Fātiḥa (Q. 1), al-Ikhlāṣ (Q. 112) and particularly Yā Sīn (Q. 36) that are commonly used for prayer, contemplation and Sufi rituals. Sargut calls these *sūra*s the heart, the truth and the essence of the Qur'ān.[68] She is not interested in any kind of literal understanding of the text. Rather, she focusses on those parts of the Qur'ān that open venues for spiritual progress, such as the stories about prophets. She also searches for hidden layers of meaning.

For example, the sequence *alif, lām, mīm* (e.g., Q. 2:1), to her, signifies God, Gabriel and Muḥammad.[69]

Her approach to the Qur'ān is thus allegorical, something that is also evident from her treatment of Q. 112 (See Excerpt 6.3). Entirely disinterested in how the *sūra* refutes Christian and other non-Muslim beliefs, she

Excerpt 6.3

Q. 112

قُلْ هُوَ اللَّهُ أَحَدٌ ﴿١﴾ اللَّهُ الصَّمَدُ ﴿٢﴾ لَمْ يَلِدْ وَلَمْ يُولَدْ ﴿٣﴾ وَلَمْ يَكُن لَّهُ كُفُوًا أَحَدٌ ﴿٤﴾

(1) Say, 'He is God the One, (2) God the eternal. (3) He begot no one nor was He begotten. (4) No one is comparable to him.'

[Ferda Yıldırım, interviewer:] May we talk about *Sūrat al-Ikhlāṣ* [Q. 112]? Could you explain to us a little what it's about?

[Cemâlnur Sargut:] While explaining the *sūra*, one actually talks about the [first] four caliphs [Abū Bakr, 'Umar, 'Uthmān, 'Alī]. That is, when we say *qul huwa llāhu aḥad* (v. 1), we say: I have seen that God is One, but it is also the station of Abū Bakr whom I know to be the first. Abū Bakr, through the Prophet's teaching, recognised in the Prophet God's uniqueness and unity. He was the first man [*adam*]; he saw.

After that, when we say *Allāhu al-ṣamad* (v. 2), the name *ṣamad* teaches us that no one but God shall be needed, only God shall be needed. At that point, the ties to man are severed. That term [*ṣamad*] also signifies equity. Equity is to know that we will be accountable to God, not man, and to behave accordingly. *Ṣamad* is an attribute of 'Umar.

The third, *lam yalid wa-lam yūlad* (v. 3). He was not born, he did not procreate; this is the station of 'Uthmān. Yes, there are such persons who do have mothers and fathers. They also have children to whom they attend. But to them, everything is God. Apart from Him, there is nothing.

[Ferda Yıldırım:] However much they might lose, they do not despair, materially and spiritually…

[Cemâlnur Sargut:] Not at all. They understand that high standard. God says: if you want to reach that high standard, you will have to comprehend this name of mine. The fourth, *wa-lam yakun lahū kufuwan aḥad*. It means to know His oneness, to acknowledge it, to be within the oneness. That is the station of 'Alī, may God not separate us from him, *inşallah*.[70]

instead explains it as an allegorical reference to the first four caliphs who were the 'rightly-guided' ones according to Sunni historiography. Furthermore, she presents these caliphs as models of spiritual perfection that believers should follow. This seems to be an interpretation she came up with herself; at least, it is not part of the most well-known Sufi Qur'ānic commentaries.

While the four rightly-guided caliphs are a distinctly Sunni theme, Sargut likewise evokes the Shi'i veneration of the *ahl al-bayt*, the Prophet's family and descendants. She mentions the martyrs of Karbala as examples of submission to God and worship and describes the *ahl al-bayt* as the 'living Qur'ān', the embodiment of the Qur'ān's meaning after the Prophet's death.[71] The veneration of 'Alī and his descendants is a common theme in Sufism. Sargut writes neither as a Sunni nor as a Shi'i, but as a mystic. As such, she draws on the concept of the 'perfect man' (Tr., *insân-ı kâmil*)[72] which is frequently employed by esoteric branches of Sunni and Shi'i Islam. It was made particularly prominent by Ibn 'Arabī who developed an elaborate theory around it, seeing the realisation of oneness with God as the ultimate aim of humans' spiritual progress.[73]

The distinctly and exclusively Sufi nature of Sargut's exegesis becomes apparent not only from the content of her interpretations, but also from the authorities she cites. Leaving aside the Prophet and his companions, all of these authorities, without exception, are Sufis. References to Jalāl al-Dīn al-Rūmī (or *Mevlânâ*, 1207–1273) who is buried in Konya in Turkey and to his monumental collection of poetry, the *Mathnawī*, abound. Other Sufis repeatedly mentioned by Sargut in this book are Ibn 'Arabī[74] and Aḥmad al-Rifā'ī (d. 1182).[75] Both al-Rūmī and al-Rifā'ī are founding figures of important mystical orders and play central roles in Sargut's lineage and spiritual development.[76] Sargut also cites her own predecessors in the Rifā'iyya lineage: her teacher, the female mystic Sâmiha Ayverdi (1905–1993),[77] and Ayverdi's teacher Ken'an Rifâî (1867–1950)[78] – evidence of a tradition of Ottoman Sufism that continued into the twentieth century and is an important aspect of Sargut's spiritual authority.[79] Interspersed throughout the book are names of other famous mystics: Bayram-ı Velî (1352–1430), 'Abd al-Qādir al-Jīlānī (1078–1166), Abū al-Ḥasan al-Kharaqānī (963–1033), 'Abd al-Karīm al-Jīlī (1366–1424), Rabi'a al-'Adawiyya (d. 801) and Aḥmad Sam'ānī (d. 1140).[80] Conversely, there is no mention at all of mainstream Sunni or Imami Shi'i exegetes.

The reliance on a distinct set of authorities is an important criterion that places a work of Qur'ānic exegesis outside the mainstream and in a tradition of its own. Cemâlnur Sargut certainly meets that definition. That is not merely owed to the fact that this book is based on an interview and thus does not formally belong to the genre of *tafsīr*. In a much more detailed and extensive commentary devoted to an interpretation of the 'Throne verse' (Q. 2:255) that extends over approximately 160 pages, the list of references used by Sargut likewise includes no mainstream work of *tafsīr* except the short Qur'ānic commentary by Elmalılı Muhammed Hamdi Yazır (1878–1942), a standard work in Turkey that Sargut uses mostly for purposes of translation.[81] Her Qur'ānic interpretation, thus, is not meant to be a conventional commentary on the Qur'ān that explains its meaning, but a means to progress on the mystical path.

She describes her exegetical efforts as mere rearrangements of the commentaries of 'completed human beings' by which she refers to the Sufi idea of an *insân-ı kâmil* who has completed his journey on the spiritual path. Thus, she essentially perceives of her Qur'ānic interpretation as a compilation of earlier Sufi approaches. In doing so, she expresses the hope to unite all Sufi paths towards the 'Muḥammadan path'.[82] This genealogical view of her own activity is not unlike that of mainstream exegesis although her sources come from a genealogy of its own. She distinctly emphasises the importance of a teacher–student relationship both for learning and for progress along the spiritual path. The aim is to defeat the ego-self (*nafs*) in order to purify oneself and reach oneness with God.[83]

Part of the attraction of Cemâlnur's approach lies in her emphasis on love which, in her view, is preferable to compulsion even where ritual obligations such as prayer are concerned. She considers those an indispensable foundation of the Sufi path, but does not ask her disciples to pray; rather, she hopes for them to start on their own, out of love for their teacher.[84] An important motivation for her middle and upper-class Turkish followers to choose her Sufi guidance over other types of religious activism is the fact that it allows them to seek spirituality while maintaining a 'modern' urban lifestyle. The main symbol of this is clothing, and especially the absence of a headscarf which Sargut does not wear and which, in her opinion, is not obligatory[85] – a symbolic question that has been central to Turkish society since the 1920s and that has bearings both on ideological orientation and on class. Sargut's aim is to distil moral lessons from the Qur'ān in order to create a living Qur'ān community.[86]

NEW ISLAMIC COMMUNITIES

The variety of Islamic faith communities today encompasses not only pre-modern denominations and movements, but also a number of groups that emerged only during the nineteenth or twentieth centuries. Even now, spiritual communities continue to be formed. Today, the use of modern media, from print to the internet, enable some of those new communities, despite being relegated to the margins of, or outside the, fold of Islam by other Muslims, to exert a remarkable influence and lend their ideas a high degree of visibility. This is true, for example, for the Qur'ānists and especially for the 'Submitters' following the messianic ideas of the late Rashad Khalifa. While the group is presumably rather small, its internet presence is very strong.[87]

One community for which this observation is even more pertinent, especially in the field of Qur'ānic exegesis, is the Ahmadiyya movement that had already been mentioned in the context of Qur'ān translations. It emerged in British India in the late-nineteenth century around the reformist ideas of Mirza Ghulām Aḥmad (1835–1908). After the death of his first successor in 1914, the movement split up into two branches. The Lahore Ahmadiyya Movement for the Propagation of Islam rallied around Muḥammad 'Alī (1874–1951); they emphasised the intellectual and modernist nature of Ahmadiyya teachings, saw Mirza Ghulām Aḥmad as a reformer of Islam and rejected the introduction of a caliphate, considering it too autocratic. This part of the Ahmadiyya movement is today very small, but has continuously been active in the field of Qur'ānic exegesis and Qur'ān translation since Muḥammad 'Alī presented his translation of the Qur'ān into English in 1917. His work has repeatedly been updated, translated into other languages and publicised in print and online editions.

By far the larger branch of the Ahmadiyya, the Ahmadiyya Muslim Community which is sometimes named after the town of Qādyān, Mirza Ghulām Aḥmad's birthplace and centre of the movement until the partition of India, believe that Mirza Ghulām Aḥmad was the promised messiah, rather than a mere intellectual reformer. Their organisation is headed by a caliph to whom all members owe allegiance; from the second caliph onwards, they were all descendants of Mirza Ghulām Aḥmad. The Ahmadiyya Muslim Community is often treated as heretical by mainstream Muslims due to their messianic beliefs. Its adherents are subject to persecution in Pakistan and some other Muslim-majority countries. Further areas of disagreement with the Sunni mainstream include: an inclusive concept of religious pluralism, acknowledging the divine origin of religions outside the 'Abrahamic faiths'; the rejection of armed jihad other than in situations of extreme persecution where it is the only option for self-defence; and the rejection of the capital punishment for apostasy. These pacifist ideas were, in Mirza Ghulām Aḥmad's time, embedded in Muslim debates about opposition to British colonial rule which, until today, exposes the Ahmadiyya to the accusation of surrendering Muslims to imperialist rule. The Ahmadiyya is markedly modernist in the field of religious freedom and interreligious coexistence while holding more traditional views on gender relations and sexual identity.[88]

The Ahmadiyya, from the outset, were very active in calling to their particular brand of Islam and, making conscious use of print,[89] Qur'ān translations were central to their efforts. The first Muslim translation of the Qur'ān into Swahili, for example, was an Ahmadi one.[90] Some of the Ahmadiyya caliphs produced extensive exegetical writings, typically written in Urdu and then translated into English, including complete Qur'ānic commentaries, translations and lengthy exegetical speeches and pamphlets, all of which point to the centrality of the Qur'ān to Ahmadiyya teachings. With regard to their hermeneutical approach, the Ahmadiyya reject abrogation, believing all verses of the Qur'ān to be equally valid, but that their application depends on the situative context. They also have a penchant towards modern *i'jāz* theories, interpreting specific verses in the Qur'ān as predictions of historical events or scientific discoveries.[91]

Ahmadiyya Qur'ān translations and interpretations often provoke negative responses. Their high publicity and the Ahmadiyya's sustained effort at distributing them widely challenge individual Muslims, Muslim institutions and governments to react, either by criticising the Ahmadiyya's understanding of the Qur'ān, by calling on Muslims to boycott it, by publishing counter-publications, or by banning Ahmadiyya publications.[92]

The Ahmadiyya and the death of Jesus: Disputes over Q. 3:55

This section portrays the dispute between Ahmadis and other Muslims over the question of Jesus' death. Its focus is not so much on individual texts and their authors as it is on polemics between Ahmadis and their opponents. The following four texts were all taken from English-language websites. It is not always clear when they were written. The Ahmadi positions ultimately go back to Mirza Ghulām Aḥmad's (1835–1908) writings, especially his book *Jesus in India* that was published shortly after his death in 1908. Nevertheless, as the texts show, the controversy is still alive today, partly because it allows for a sharp distinction between Ahmadi and non-Ahmadi Muslims.

The Ahmadiyya Muslim Community, on their official website, explain their position as follows, clearly considering it a doctrine important enough to warrant its own page with numerous supporting documents:

> Strangely enough the three great nations of the world: Jews, Christians and Muslims are at variance with regard […] to […] the death of Jesus Christ who was born among the Jews. […]
>
> - The Jews believe that Jesus died on the cross because he was a false prophet.
> - The Christians believe that Jesus died on the cross in atonement of the sins of humanity, was resurrected soon thereafter, and then ascended to Heaven.

- The orthodox Muslims believe that God saved Jesus from '*death by crucifixion*' and ascended bodily to heaven, and will come down to earth again to smash the cross and what it stands for and to purify the faith of the believers.
- Ahmadiyya Muslim Community declares that Jesus Christ only fell into a swoon on the Cross, but when he was taken down from it, he recovered and migrated to Kashmir, India where he died a natural death at the good old age of 120.[93]

The Ahmadiyya position thus is that, unlike what Jews and Christians believe, Jesus did not die on the cross, but unlike what most other Muslims believe, he did die eventually, after having reached the end of his natural lifespan. The debate on this claim touches upon several verses of the Qur'ān, but the focus here will be on Q. 3:55, a verse that is particularly contested between the Ahmadiyya and other Muslims.

Q. 3:55

إِذْ قَالَ اللَّهُ يَا عِيسَىٰ إِنِّي مُتَوَفِّيكَ وَرَافِعُكَ إِلَيَّ وَمُطَهِّرُكَ مِنَ الَّذِينَ كَفَرُوا وَجَاعِلُ الَّذِينَ اتَّبَعُوكَ
فَوْقَ الَّذِينَ كَفَرُوا إِلَىٰ يَوْمِ الْقِيَامَةِ ثُمَّ إِلَيَّ مَرْجِعُكُمْ فَأَحْكُمُ بَيْنَكُمْ فِيمَا كُنتُمْ فِيهِ تَخْتَلِفُونَ ﴿٥٥﴾

(55) God said, 'Jesus, I will take you / cause you to die [*innī mutawaffīka*] and raise you up to Me: I will purify you of the disbelievers. To the Day of Resurrection I will make those who followed you superior to those who disbelieved. Then you will all return to Me and I will judge between you regarding your differences.[...]'

Excerpt 6.4: Tahir Ijaz of the Ahmadiyya Muslim Community

An important verse is the following:

'When Allah said, O Jesus, I will cause you to die and will raise you to myself, and will clear thee of those who disbelieve and will place those who follow thee above those who disbelieve, until the Day of Resurrection, then to Me shall be your return and I will judge between you concerning that wherein you differ.' (3:56)[94]

The verse clearly indicates that Hazrat Jesus(as) was to die a natural death and then only would he be raised to Allah. The verse does not say that Hazrat Jesus (as) will be raised first then will die.

An important word used in the Quran is *mutawaffi*, derived from *tawaffa*. When God is the subject and a human is the object, *tawaffa* means to take away the soul, i.e, death.

Zamakhshari (467–538 A.H), an Arab linguist of great repute says, 'Mutawaffika means, I will protect you from being killed by the people and will grant you full lease of life ordained for you, and will cause you to die a natural death not being killed *(Kashshaf)*'. Scholars and commentators like Hazrat Ibn Abbas, Imam Malik, Imam Bukhari, Imam ibn Hazm, Imam ibn Qayyin [*sic*], Qatadah, Wahhab and others are of the same view.

Note that the same word *Tawaffa*, has been used in other places in the Quran to indicate death. For example, 2:235: 'and those of you who die (*yatawaffouna*) and leave wives behind, these wives shall wait concerning themselves for four months and ten days'.

Another important word is *rafaa*, which means raising, elevating, lifting, exaltation, honor. When the *rafaa* of a man is spoken of as being towards Allah, the meaning is invariably spiritual elevation and exaltation. For example the Quran says about Prophet Enoch: 'We exalted him to a lofty station (19:58)'.

A commentary of the Quran by Ibn Khatib ('modern' Egyptian Commentary) summarizes: 'And those who assert that Jesus is dead, point to the word of the exalted God: every soul shall taste death, and Jesus, peace be upon him belonged to the human species for which death is ordained. Some people presume that he is dead, and lies buried in a locality which they mention by name, and may be it is India, and God – may He be exalted – knows best what He has said and done'.[95]

The cycle of claim and counter-claim represented in the four texts presented in Excerpt 6.4–6.7 could go on. A French Ahmadiyya website, for example, takes up all the Qur'ānic arguments mentioned on the Jihadi-Salafi website, especially on the semantics of the terms *tawaffā* and *rafa'a*, and dissects them at length, adducing all occasions on which the Qur'ān as much as mentions a term based on the same roots.[96] The debate rages on websites of Ahmadis and their opponents from all walks of life, whether they be medical doctors such as Tahir Ijaz, engineers such as Adel Elsaie (the host of *Usislam.org* where Abdul Wahid Osman Belal's acerbic attack was published) or otherwise; and all of them take a position on what the Qur'ān really means when God says to Jesus *mutawaffīka* in Q. 3:55 because the validity of their respective claims rests on the understanding of that word.

The issue is clearly a subject of intense polemics. Belief in the physical death of Jesus is one of the Ahmadi doctrines that are at odds with mainstream Muslim beliefs and fiercely opposed by many. At the same time, the Ahmadi position is steeped in Muslim–Christian polemics and was indeed born out of interreligious disputes.

The centrality of doctrines about Jesus to Ahmadi thought results from the emergence of the movement in colonial India and the Christian polemics against Islam that took place at the time. These polemics pointed to Jesus' resurrection and divine nature that made him superior to Muḥammad, a human who died of natural causes. In order to counter these claims, Mirza

Ghulām Aḥmad devoted tremendous effort to developing a complex argument, based on the Qur'ān, the Sunna, the Gospels, archaeological findings, Buddhist writings and any other evidence he could muster, claiming that Jesus merely lost consciousness on the cross, rather than dying. After his recovery, he travelled and preached to some of the lost tribes of Israel after which he died and was buried in Kashmir.[97]

Excerpt 6.5: Abdul Wahid Osman Belal disputing the Ahmadiyya interpretation

The Ahamdiyya [*sic*] sect has chosen some of the Holy Qurans verses and explained them, setting the ancient and unanimously agreed upon explanation at naught. Their basic aim is to prove that Jesus (Peace be upon him) is dead and dead people can not come back again to the earth; and all the Quranic verses about Jesus (Peace be upon him) and the *ḥadīth*s about Mahdi – when talking about the second advent – are nothing but a reference to another person other than Jesus (Peace be upon him) and Mahdi. This person is Ghulam Ahamed Kadyani, who founded this movement. This sect is neither Muslim nor Christian. In this short article we will refute their claims; we will mention every fallacy they put forth, and we will give each one a rebuttal. [...]

Fallacy (5) [opinion of the Ahmadiyya]:
The word 'raised' is not peculiar to Jesus (Peace be upon him). It is also used when talking about the other prophets when they died. God says about Idris: 'And We raised him to high station'. (Mariam: 57)

The same words were said when talking about Jesus (Peace be upon him):

'(And remember) when Allah said: O Jesus Lo! I am gathering thee and causing thee to ascend unto Me' (Ale-Imran: 55)

So as Idris was raised (dead), the word 'raised' doesn't imply raising alive.

Rebuttal (5):
The exegetes have different opinions which rebut this paralogism.

First: the first group says that God raised him to the heavens where he died and this rebuts their calumniation.

Second: the other group says that God raised him to the paradise where he lives in flesh and soul.

The two verses concerning Jesus (Peace be upon him) and Idris are different. If the verse concerning Idris implies the high rank and position, the verse of Jesus (Peace be upon him) doesn't imply this because it means openly raising by soul and flesh.

The portion of the verse 'causing thee to ascend unto Me' means raising to where God is while that of Idris implies just rank and position.

The *Ḥadīth*s concerning Jesus (Peace be upon him) are so many, and all of them mean openly that Jesus (Peace be upon him) was raised in flesh and soul.

Narated [*sic*] By Abu Huraira: Allah's Apostle said, 'The Hour will not be established until the son of Mary (i.e. Jesus (Peace be upon him)) descends amongst you as a just ruler, he will break the cross, kill the pigs, and abolish the Jizya tax. Money will be in abundance so that nobody will accept it (as charitable gift).'

The following verse is decisive and silencing:

'And because of their saying: We slew the Messiah Jesus (Peace be upon him) son of Mary, Allah's messenger, they slew him not nor crucified, but it appeared so unto them; and lo! Those who disagree concerning it are in doubt thereof; they have no knowledge thereof save pursuit of a conjecture; they slew him not for certain'. [Q. 4:157]

If he died on the cross, God would have said 'They slew him not nor crucified, but he died'. This verse is in conformity with what the Muslims believe regarding Jesus (Peace be upon him). [...][98]

Excerpt 6.6: Maulana Hafiz Sher Mohammad of the Lahore Ahmadiyya Movement

[...] Seventh Evidence: Holy Quran specifically mentions Jesus' death
Having explained so many general principles on the subject of life and death, it was not necessary that the Holy Quran should speak specifically of the death of Jesus. Nevertheless, Almighty God has particularly mentioned Jesus' death in the Quran. When the Jews succeeded in their plans to have Jesus sentenced to crucifixion, he prayed to God to be delivered from this fate, and was answered by Him thus:

'O Jesus, I will cause you to die, and exalt you to My presence and clear you of those who disbelieve and make those who follow you above those who disbelieve till the day of Judgment'. (3:54)[99]

Here God made with Jesus four promises:

'Cause you to die' (*tawaffa*), i.e., Jesus would not be killed by the Jews, but would die a natural death.

'Exalt you in My presence' (*raf'a*), i.e., he would not be crucified, which the Jews sought to do to prove him accursed, but rather he would receive Divine nearness. In fact, *raf'a* is the opposite of *wad'a*, the latter meaning disgrace and the former meaning honouring.

'Clear you of those who disbelieve' (*tathir*), i.e., he would be cleared of the Jews' allegations against him, as he was by the Holy Prophet Muhammad.

'Make those who follow you above those who disbelieve till the day of Judgement', i.e. his followers would forever have the upper hand over his rejectors.

The above verse proves that Jesus has died, for *raf'a* (exaltation to God's presence) is attained only after death when all the material veils have been removed. Every righteous person is granted *raf'a* to God after his death. The Holy Prophet has said:

When a believer nears death, angels come to him. So if he is righteous, they say: 'O pure soul! leave, you were in a pure body'…So that pure soul comes out, then they take it to the heavens and its gates are opened for it'. (*Mishkat*).

Hence, whenever a righteous individual dies, the angels take his *soul* up to heaven. The very same happened in Jesus' case, so that after his death it was his *soul* that was raised to heaven, and he joined the ranks of the righteous among the dead.

Thus God fulfilled all the above promises in order: he rescued Jesus from the hands of the Jews, and eventually granted him a natural death; after his death, God honoured his soul with Divine nearness; He cleared him of the Jews' allegations against him through the Holy Prophet Muhammad (may peace and the blessings of Allah be upon him) and He gave Jesus' followers the upper hand over his rejectors.[100]

Crucial in refuting the polemics of Christian missionaries, Mirza Ghulām Aḥmad's views on the death of Jesus soon also became a central point of contention between Ahmadis and mainstream Muslims. Both branches of the Ahmadiyya had an interest in defending the ideas of their founder and dispelling criticism. Their members wrote numerous treatises on the issue. There are a host of sermons, books, pamphlets and websites devoted to Ahmadi views on Jesus' death. Frequently, the focus has moved from disputes with Christians to disputes with Muslims, especially such Muslims who consider the Ahmadiyya a non-Muslim sect and its members apostates. The main objection of these Muslims is the messianic status granted to Mirza Ghulām Aḥmad at least by the larger of the branches of the Ahmadiyya. One strategy to dismantle these messianic claims is to demonstrate that Mirza Ghulām Aḥmad's ideas contradict the Qur'ān and Sunna and can therefore not be of divine origin.

Thus, the Salafi website Call to Monotheism classifies Ahmadis as unbelievers, arguing:

> The ahaadeeth regarding the **literal** return of Jesus (peace be upon him) are mutawaatir [...]. To outright reject a mutawaatir belief (which is an established Islamic belief beyond reasonable doubt) for no valid reason is considered major kufr, which takes the person outside the fold of Islam. There is no doubt that rejecting the firmly established statement of the Prophet (peace be upon him) is an act of major kufr.[101]

A former Ahmadi's blog condemns the Ahmadi claims that the Qur'ān proves the death of Jesus, calling them lies, 'distorted interpretations' and attempts 'to twist the verses of the Quran to fit their heretical beliefs'.[102] And the site of *Idara Dawat-o Irshad*, a US-based organisation that has made it their mission to counter Ahmadi *da'wa* with missionary work of their own, accuses the Ahmadiyya of purposefully spreading false translations of the Qur'ān, quoting Q. 3:55 as their prime example. Pointing to the translations by Yusuf Ali and Pickthall, the authors argue that the correct translation of *mutawaffīka* is 'I will take thee' or 'I am gathering thee'.[103]

Excerpt 6.7: A Jihadi-Salafi blog disputing the Ahmadiyya interpretation

Qadianis, also called Ahmadis, the followers of the religion founded by Mirza Ghulam Ahmed of Qadian, say that, Prophet Jesus (PBUH [Peace Be Upon Him]) died a natural death. And moreover these heathens try to prove their point from the Holy Quran, but all in vague. [*sic*] They can only deceive those people who don't know the Quran in detail and the Arabic language. But Alhamdulillah Muslim scholars have done great work and have refuted their false propaganda in an irrefutable manner. All praise is to Allah.

MEANING OF 'MUTAWAFFEKA' & 'TAWAFFAITANI' IN QURAN 3:55 & 5:117.

Qadianis say that the word mutawaffeeka in Quran 3:55 [...] speak[s] of the death of Prophet Jesus (PBUH) and they erroneously translate the verse[s] as;

Lo! God said: 'O Jesus! Verily I shall cause thee to die, and shall exalt thee unto me...' (3:55) [...]

But this is wrong. I present the Islamic view point in detail in the following lines;

Correct Translation:

Quran 3:55 informs believers that Allah will 'take back' Jesus (PBUH), protect him from the unbelievers and raise him to His presence. Many great Islamic scholars and commentators have interpreted this verse to mean that Jesus (PBUH) did not die. As the verse states:

[Q. 3:55 in Arabic]

'When Allah said: "O Isa , I am to take you in full (mutawaffeeka) and to raise you towards Myself, and to cleanse you of those who disbelieve, and to place those who follow you above those who disbelieve up to the Day of Doom. Then to Me is your return, whereupon I shall judge between you in that over which you have differed"'. (3:55)

The part requiring special consideration is the sentence; 'I will take you back (mutawaffeeka) and raise you up to Me'. […]

A close examination reveals a most important truth: the verb carries a sense that differs from what is normally meant by 'to die'. The word translated into English as 'to die' comes from the Arabic root waffaa derived from the verb tawaffaa, which does not imply death, but rather taking the soul, or surrender.

[There follows a list of arguments. Numbers 1–3 contain references in Arabic and English to Ibn Taymiyya and a premodern Arabic dictionary concerning the meaning of *tawaffā*. Furthermore, the usage of the term in the Qur'ān and the Sunna is discussed. Ibn Kathīr's opinion is explained.]

5. Antonym of Hayat (Life) in the Quran?

Further we know that in the Holy Quran only the word mawt (death) is used in contrast to hayat (life) e.g. See Quran 67:2, 25:3, 2:260, 30:19, 2:164, 16:45, 45:5, 3:49, 42:9. But not even once has the Quran used tawaffa against hayat. This is strong evidence that to the Author of the Quran tawaffa is not the opposite of hayat.

6. Views of leading learned scholars:

Islamic scholars agree that mutawaffeeka means that Jesus (PBUH) did not die, but that he was raised to Allah's presence and will return to Earth. For example;

Ibn Jarir Al-Tabari, the famous commentator and scholar, stated that mutawaffeeka is used in the sense of 'removing from Earth' and interpreted the verse in the following terms: 'To me the soundest opinion is to take this word in the sense of "to take into one's possession", "draw (away) from Earth". In that case, the meaning of the verse is: "I shall take you from Earth and into the heavens". [This is] because of the multiple ways it has been narrated from the Messenger of Allah (PBUH) that Jesus son of Mary will descend, [and] kill [the] Anti-Christ (Dajjal)…' (Al-Tabari 3/51)

The great Islamic scholar Ibn Taymiyya stated that Quran 3:55 indicates that Jesus (PBUH) did not die, but most likely experienced a kind of 'sleep death'. […]

So in the light of the Quran, *Ḥadīth* and the views of learned scholars the meaning of mutawaffeeka is 'to take in full' i.e. with both body and soul.

[There follows a discussion of a potentially divergent view of Ibn 'Abbās that understands *tawaffā* as being related to Jesus' death at the end of times. According to the author, this would mean that Q. 3:55 reverts the chronological order since Jesus was first raised into heaven and will only die at the end of times. The author points to another verse in the Qur'ān that reverts the logical order of things which, in his opinion, establishes this as a convention of Qur'ānic discourse.] [...]

All the explanation above refutes the Qadiani position in favor of the Islamic creed.[104]

One might wonder why this aspect of Ahmadi doctrine is debated so much when, in reality, more fundamental issues are at stake. One answer might be that this is a symbolic point of contention. While the death of Jesus is not the cause of the rifts between Ahmadis and other Muslims, it is a tangible difference of opinion that serves to call into question the entire belief system of the Ahmadiyya, its sources and the legitimacy of its leadership, provoking impassioned defences on the part of the Ahmadiyya. Second, it is not only a tangible point of contention, but also one that is highly specific to the Ahmadiyya. While many modernists more or less share their attitude towards jihad and the death penalty for apostates, for example, the idea that Jesus died in Kashmir is distinctly and exclusively Ahmadi and therefore its refutation serves to delegitimise them. Third, the interreligious context of the debates on the death of Jesus is still highly relevant, given the presence of Ahmadis in the West and their high commitment to *da'wa* among non-Muslims. Thus, the question of what the Qur'ān really means when it talks about Jesus' crucifixion and ascension remains strongly disputed.

NOTES

1. Wilson, 'Ritual and Rhyme', 87–93.
2. Noyan Dedebaba, *Kur'ân-ı Kerim.*
3. Vaktidolu, *Kuran'ı Kerim: Manzum Meali ve Tefsir Özeti*, 11–12.
4. Soileau, 'Conforming Haji Bektash'; Wilson, 'Ritual and Rhyme'; Dressler, *Writing Religion.*
5. Vaktidolu, *Kuran'ı Kerim: Manzum Meali ve Tefsir Özeti*, 11–12.
6. Stewart, 'Rhymed Prose'.
7. This is in the same semantic field as the Islamic concept of *taqwā*, often translated as 'piety' or 'fear of God'.
8. Vaktidolu, *Kuran'ı Kerim: Manzum Meali ve Tefsir Özeti*, 556.
9. Poonawala, 'Tȧwīl'; see also Poonawala, 'Translatability of the Qur'an: Theological and Literary Considerations'.
10. Vaktidolu, *Kuran'ı Kerim*, 552.
11. It is mentioned on a Turkish Alevi website; see Seyyid Hakkı, 'Elif-Lam-Mim sıfatları'. A Turkish blog calls it a Bektashi interpretation; see Ersan, 'Elif -Lam

-Mim'. A user on a Dawoodi Bohra, i.e. Isma'ili, forum mentions it as having been recounted to him by a Bohra elder; see porus [username], 'Syedna Is a Star Created by Imam Hussain'.

12. See Wilson, *Translating the Qur'an in an Age of Nationalism*, 157–183.
13. Wilson, 'Ritual and Rhyme', 90–91.
14. This is a vast field of sociolinguistic research that can only be indicated briefly here. See Sairio and Palander-Collin, 'The Reconstruction of Prestige Patterns in Language History'.
15. Persian is today mainly associated with Shi'i Islam that is the predominant religion in Iran. This was not the case before the early-modern period, however, and even after that Persian continued to be in use in many Sunni contexts, for example in South Asia.
16. Wild, 'Muslim Translators and Translations of the Qur'an into English'.
17. Rippin, 'Contemporary Translation'.
18. See page 257, 'Causes for conflict'.
19. For an excellent case study exemplifying the role of local power structures and the intricate relationship between local exegetical discourses, migration and global means of communication, see van de Bruinhorst, '"I Didn't Want to Write This"'.
20. Wright, 'Language Policy, the Nation and Nationalism'.
21. Bano, *Contesting Ideologies and Struggle for Authority*.
22. Azra, Afrianty and Hefner, 'Pesantren and Madrasa'.
23. Pink, *Sunnitischer Tafsīr in der modernen islamischen Welt*, 306–311.
24. For recent editions, see Departemen Agama RI, *Al-Qur'an dan tafsirnya*; Kementerian Agama Republika Indonesia, *Al Qur'an Dan Terjemahnya*.
25. Karaman et al., *Kur'an yolu*.
26. Pink, 'Tradition, Authority and Innovation', 6; Pink, *Sunnitischer Tafsīr in der modernen islamischen Welt*, 78–89.
27. One pertinent example is the current heated Indonesian debate on whether a localised 'archipelago Islam' (*Islam nusantara*) is legitimate and possibly even preferable to an 'Arab Islam' (*Islam Arab*). See, for example, Fachrudin, 'The Face of Islam Nusantara'; NU Online, 'Apa yang dimaksud dengan Islam Nusantara?'; Musa, *Membumikan Islam Nusantara*.
28. Pink, 'The Global Islamic Tradition and the Nation State in the Contemporary Muslim Exegesis of the Qur'an'; see also the edited volume by Taji-Farouki, *The Qur'an and its Readers Worldwide*.
29. Belief in one God, just and civilised humanity, the unity of Indonesia, democracy and social justice. Cf. Ikhwan, An Indonesian Initiative to Make the Qur'an Down-to-Earth, 113–125.
30. Federspiel, *Popular Indonesian Literature of the Qur'an*, 64–69.
31. Karaman et al., *Kur'an yolu*; see Pink, *Sunnitischer Tafsīr in der modernen islamischen Welt*, 81–88.
32. Ikhwan, 'Fī taḥaddī al-dawla'.
33. The *munāsaba* is the relation of a verse to its context within the Qur'ān, i.e., the preceding and subsequent verses.
34. According to the Qur'ān, the mighty man in Egypt in whose house Joseph lived as a slave.
35. Departemen Agama RI, *Al-Qur'an dan tafsirnya*, vol 5, 5–7. Text originally in Indonesian.
36. Gilliot, ''Abdallāh b. 'Abbās'.

37. Federspiel, *Popular Indonesian Literature of the Qur'an*, 64–69.
38. For examples of this type of historiography of *tafsīr*, see al-Dhahabī, *Al-Tafsīr wa'l-mufassirūn*; Goldziher, *Die Richtungen der islamischen Koranauslegung*; Gätje, *Koran und Koranexegese*.
39. A stark example would be al-Dhahabī's classification of al-Shawkānī as Zaydi because he was born into a family of Zaydi scholars in a Zaydi milieu. However, al-Shawkānī had, by the time he wrote his *tafsīr*, long renounced Zaydism and followed a distinctly Sunni paradigm as evidenced in the *ḥadīth*s he relied upon. See al-Dhahabī, *Al-Tafsīr wa'l-mufassirūn*, vol. 3, 285–299; Pink, 'Muhammad al-Shawkānī'.
40. For an introduction to the emergence of Sunni Islam and its competitors, see Berkey, *The Formation of Islam*.
41. This is not to say that there are no further relevant state actors. For example, the Kingdom of Jordan has been quite active in promoting a 'moderate', non-violent Islam in recent years.
42. For the controversy between Egypt and Saudi Arabia and what it means for the approach to Qur'ānic exegesis, see Saleh, 'Preliminary Remarks on the Historiography of *Tafsīr*'.
43. For an introduction to Shi'ism, see Halm, *Shi'ism*.
44. Bar-Asher, *Scripture and Exegesis in Early Imāmī Shiism*.
45. '24 Have you not seen how God has coined a comparison: a good word is like a good tree, its roots firm, its branches reaching into the sky; 25 it gives its fruit every season by permission of its Lord....26 The comparison of a bad saying is that it is like a bad tree which has been uprooted from the earth and has no stability.'
46. Gätje, *Koran und Koranexegese*, 317–318.
47. Fudge, *Qur'ānic Hermeneutics*, esp. ix, 147.
48. Bauer, *Gender Hierarchy in the Qur'ān*, 157; Klausing, 'Redefining the Borders of *tafsīr*'.
49. Bauer, *Gender Hierarchy in the Qur'ān*, 137–157.
50. Ende, 'Ehe auf Zeit'.
51. See, for example, Hubeali.com (ed.), *Tafseer Abu Hamza Sumali*.
52. See, for example, page 85, 'Layers of media: Abdolali Bazargan10 (b. 1943; Iran/US) on Q. 103:3'.
53. On Engineer, see Sagir, *Diversität und Anerkennung*.
54. Coppens, Seeing God in this World and the Otherworld, 283–284. See also Coppens, *Seeing God in Sufi Qur'an Commentaries*.
55. Keeler and Rizvi, 'Introduction', 12–17.
56. Ibid., 16–17; Sands, 'Making it Plain: Sufi Commentaries in English in the Twentieth Century'.
57. Sands, 'Making it Plain: Sufi Commentaries in English in the Twentieth Century', 155–157.
58. See, for example, the two Sufi commentators presented in ibid., 157.
59. Buehler, *Recognizing Sufism*, 190.
60. Neubauer, Celle qui n'existe pas, 11–12.
61. Ibid., 12–14.
62. Thaver, 'The Ambivalences of Modernity'.
63. Neubauer, Celle qui n'existe pas, 89–92; Thaver, The Ambivalences of Modernity; Buehler, *Recognizing Sufism*, 190.

64. The term she uses here is *Sohbetler* which refers to the sessions that Sargut, as a Sufi shaykh, holds with her disciples in order to give spiritual talks. Cf. Neubauer, Celle qui n'existe pas, 86–89.
65. For a discussion of the role of gender in Sargut's discourse, see ibid., 95–120.
66. Ibid., 239.
67. Abdel Haleem, *The Qur'an: A New Translation*, 444.
68. Sargut, *Kur'an ile var olmak*, 18.
69. Ibid., 53–54.
70. Sargut, *Kur'an ile var olmak*, 59–60. Text originally in Turkish.
71. Ibid., 61, 98.
72. Ibid., 93–95, 99.
73. Arnaldez, 'Al-Insān al-Kāmil'.
74. Sargut, *Kur'an ile var olmak*, 31, 53, 81, 90.
75. Ibid., 37, 39.
76. Buehler, *Recognizing Sufism*, 190, 192.
77. Sargut, *Kur'an ile var olmak*, 22, 65.
78. Ibid., 19, 27, 83.
79. Buehler, *Recognizing Sufism*, 190.
80. See Sargut, *Kur'an ile var olmak*, 26, 73, 75, 87, 89, 93, respectively.
81. Sargut, *Âyetü'l-kürsî*, 173–175.
82. Buehler, *Recognizing Sufism*, 190–193.
83. Thaver, 'The Ambivalences of Modernity'.
84. Buehler, *Recognizing Sufism*, 196–197; Neubauer, Celle qui n'existe pas, 75, 97.
85. Neubauer, Celle qui n'existe pas, 140–143.
86. Thaver, 'The Ambivalences of Modernity'.
87. See page 155, 'The contested Sunna: from *ḥadīth*-based exegesis to Qur'ānism' and page 158, 'A Qur'ānist approach: Aḥmad Ṣubḥī Manṣūr (b. 1949, Egypt/USA) on Q. 2:221'.
88. Valentine, *Islam and the Ahmadiyya Jama'at*; Friedmann, *Prophecy Continuous*; Friedmann, 'Aḥmadiyya'.
89. Sevea, 'The Ahmadiyya Print Jihad in South and Southeast Asia'.
90. Topan, 'Polemics and Language'.
91. Comprehensive studies on the Ahmadiyya's approach to the Qur'ān, their translation activity and their Qur'ānic commentaries are still lacking.
92. See, for example, Nur Ichwan, 'Differing Responses to an Ahmadi Translation and Exegesis: *The Holy Qur'ân* in Egypt and Indonesia'. Persecution of Ahmadis is particularly intense in Pakistan.
93. Al Islam, 'Jesus'.
94. The system of numbering verses in the Qur'ān editions of the Ahmadiyya Muslim Community differs from standard editions, largely because they consistently count the Basmala ('In the name of God, the Merciful, the Compassionate') as a verse while the Cairene edition, which is the most wide-spread one today, only does this with the first sura.
95. Ijaz, 'Death of Hazrat Jesus'. Text originally in English.
96. Communauté Islamique Ahmadiyya, 'La mort de Jésus-Christ'.
97. Friedmann, *Prophecy Continuous*, 113–115; Valentine, *Islam and the Ahmadiyya Jama'at*, 18–30.
98. Belal, 'Ahmadiyya Refuted'. Text originally in English.

99. This is yet another system of numbering verses that is based on the Qur'ān translation by Muḥammad 'Alī, first published in 1917, to which the Lahore Ahmadiyya Movement usually refers; see Ali, *The Holy Qur-án*, 159–160. The differences in verse numbering reflect a time that went well into the first half of the twentieth century in which Qur'ān editions were far less uniform than they are today. Mirza Ghulām Aḥmad as well as protagonists of the two Ahmadiyya movements worked with various Qur'ān editions that were in general use in their time. They have since then fallen out of use with the majority of Muslims, but are still authoritative among the Ahmadiyya because their founding figures relied on them.
100. Mohammed, 'The Death of Jesus'. Text originally in English.
101. Zawadi, 'The Ahmadis are not Muslims.'
102. Abu Waleed, 'Refuting the Ahmadiyya Claim'.
103. Idara Dawat-o Irshad, 'Qadiani Changes to the Translation of the Holy Quran'.
104. Mac23190 [username], 'Refutation of the Ahmadiyya/Qadiyaniyya Claims'. Text originally in English. The anonymous website, which was closed down soon after it first appeared, was clearly in support of ISIS. It is unclear where it was based.

7

CLASHES AND FAULT LINES

Qur'ānic interpretation evidently is a discourse fraught with conflict. There are many potential reasons for such conflict: ideological orientation, theology, hermeneutics, denominational differences, political affiliation and competing claims to authority. In the contemporary context, some topics particularly lend themselves to becoming the site of struggles over ideas of society, human nature and Islamicness. First among those topics is gender.

GENDER, QUEERNESS AND THE QUR'ĀN

The fact that gender is seen as a category that is relevant to Qur'ānic exegesis is a distinctly modern phenomenon. *Tafsīr* was an overwhelmingly, maybe exclusively male domain until the twentieth century[1] and continues to be dominated by men until this day. That is true regardless of whether we look at gender as a socially assigned identity or at the increasingly contested notion of 'biological sex'. Moreover, with few exceptions, among them 'Ā'isha 'Abd al-Raḥmān Bint al-Shāṭi' and the Persian scholar Sayyida Nuṣrat Baygum Amīn (1895–1983) whose *Makhzan al-'Irfān*[2] was possibly the first complete written work of *tafsīr* by a woman, twentieth and twenty-first-century female exegetes have disproportionally often either published in the field of gender relations or written works geared towards children, youths, families and/or women.

The question of gender as a subject of Qur'ānic exegesis has become an extremely sensitive topic, for several reasons: apologetic reactions to allegations that Islam oppresses women; the wish for social reform for which an improved education of girls is seen as a prerequisite; women's activism against issues such as domestic violence or discriminatory divorce laws that are typically justified with the Qur'ān; but also the Islamist and Salafi call for a return to a pure Islamic society which is largely seen as being embodied by women, their dress, comportment and social role. The debate on gender roles is pervasive and contested, and no exegete can today refrain from participating in it in some way. The option to simply take for granted institutions such as concubinage and to treat them in such a matter-of-fact, unconcerned way as nineteenth-century exegetes did is no longer available.[3]

At this point, it is important to note that an exegete's gender and the way he or she treats gender issues in the Qur'ān are not necessarily correlated. In fact, there is a large number of female scholars who subscribe to a strictly hierarchical concept of male–female relations in the Qur'ān,[4] and there are many male exegetes who promote egalitarian interpretations of the text. Nevertheless, there is a specific brand of Qur'ānic exegesis that is born out of women's rights activism and is most commonly practiced by women. It is often labelled as 'feminist exegesis' although that term is rather contested and rejected by some of those to whom it is attributed.[5] The label 'feminist' contributes to portraying this type of activist exegesis as a Western phenomenon with US-based writers such as Amina Wadud, Asma Barlas (b. 1950) and Kecia Ali (b. 1972) receiving the largest share of attention while academics as well as grassroots movements based, for example, in the Arab world, South and Southeast Asia often go unnoticed. They do exist, though, including, for example, the Egyptian university professor Umayma Abū Bakr (b. 1957),[6] the Moroccon physician Asma Lamrabet (b. 1961),[7] and the Indonesian Islamic women's organisation Aisyiyah.[8]

The concerns of the types of Qur'ānic exegesis performed by women's rights activists vary widely. Not all of them embrace a fully egalitarian view of gender relations, whether within the family or in public space. Moreover, local conditions have a great impact on the extent to which specific topics such as birth control are seen as important. Some women's rights activists strictly reject polygamy, unequal shares in inheritance and the restrictions on options for women to obtain a divorce, all of which are based on arguments taken from the Qur'ān, while other women's rights activists accommodate some or all of these norms and focus on striving for improvement within that framework. Some issues recur, however; among the most relevant ones is that of domestic violence committed by husbands against their wives[9] which is frequently justified by reference to Q. 4:34.[10]

Nearly the entire debate on gender focusses on the status of women. Concepts of masculinity in the Qur'ān, on the other hand, receive very little attention. Q. 4:34, for example, might well be discussed from that angle, raising the question what it means for the image of man and manhood when a husband is allowed – or possibly even commanded – to discipline his wife. This debate, however, is hardly taking place so far although this might slowly be starting to change.[11]

Beyond the debate on individual verses, exegetes today have to deal with the question whether the gendered language in which the Qur'ān talks about marriage, where women are married by men to other men, reflects the gender conceptions of seventh-century Arab society or whether it presents them as a normative model that all Muslims must follow. In the answers to this question, fundamental, probably irreconcilable, disagreements emerge, most notably concerning the concept of equality. Traditional, Islamist, Salafi and even some modernist readings of the Qur'ān accept the existence of hierarchies between different categories of persons and do not strive to grant them equal status and equal rights; rather, the emphasis is on equity, where each group receives those rights and privileges that are appropriate to its needs and its God-given role. The opposing trend aims for full equality between all humans, arguing that all of them are God's creation and that the Qur'ān emphasises repeatedly that none of them is above the other, for example, by saying:

> O people, we have created you male and female (or: from a male and a female!)[12] and made you races and tribes that you may know one another. The noblest of you in the sight of God is the most Godfearing. (Q. 49:13)

The proponents of an egalitarian reading of the Qur'ān, moreover, point to the central Islamic paradigm of *tawḥīd* (the oneness of God) which, in their opinion, categorically precludes the possibility of raising one type of human over others; that would imply the attribution of divine attributes to God's creation and would constitute a violation of the humans' divinely-ordained status as God's servants.[13]

The same fundamental fault line runs between those who believe in the liberating potential of the Qur'ān and those who read it as a text that is meant to impose norms on humans. Of course, the concept of liberation is fraught with ambiguity; Sayyid Quṭb, for example, firmly believed in the liberating force of an Islamic state that applies Islamic law since it frees society from the tyranny of man and man-made laws. What I mean in this context, however, is the notion of liberation from all forms of this-worldly oppression and discrimination, whether it be racism, the marginalisation of religious minorities, the subordination of women to the authority of men or the suppression of queer identities.[14] The opponents of such an approach point to the need for equity, imposed by the Qur'ān, which would render an equal treatment of unequal groups a profoundly unjust concept. They also believe in the need to apply the distinctions, categorisations and social norms mentioned in the Qur'ān. Leaving the field of sexual relations to the discretion of individuals, they maintain, would result in licentiousness and anarchy. Whether the term 'liberal' is seen as a positive attribute or as a slur depends largely on one's affiliation with either camp.

While new approaches to gender in the Qur'ān have been proposed since the late-nineteenth century, the perspective of queer Muslims is a relatively new addition to the exegetical discourse. On the one hand, the two issues have a lot in common since both of them feature prominently – though not exclusively – the voice of activists fighting against the discrimination faced by their own social group, and both of them concern categories of social identity that are part of the fundamental structures of all present-day societies. On the other hand, the claim that women have dignity and certain God-given rights – although not necessarily the same rights as men – is widely accepted in Muslim communities whereas homosexuality is not. Furthermore, the relationship between men and women, whether it be in creation narratives or in legal prescriptions on marriage and divorce, permeates the entire Qurʾān and therefore needs to be addressed by exegetes whereas there are few or possibly no references at all concerning gay, lesbian and transgender identities. Whether this means that there is no space for them in Islam is a different matter altogether. Historically, homoerotic literature and art tended to coexist with the more restrictive views of Islamic jurists. The concept of 'homosexuality' as a lifestyle or sexual orientation, as opposed to specific sexual acts that individuals might want or not want to commit, was unknown to both the poets and the jurists; it is a creation of the nineteenth century.[15] Contemporary exegetes tend to combine statements of premodern Muslim scholars that condemn illicit acts with elements of modern Christian anti-gay discourses such as the idea that 'homosexuality' is a choice, or even a disease that may be cured.[16] However, in the past few years, different voices, including those of queer actors, have emerged.[17] This is predominantly the case in Western contexts,[18] but not limited to them as the following case study shows.

Debates on same-sex marriage: Mun'im Sirry (b. 1973, Indonesia) on the story of Lot

While print media are of little importance in Indonesia, online media play an increasing role due to the sharp rise in smartphone use in recent years. This has opened a large space for debate that is increasingly used by young, educated Indonesian Muslims to express religious ideas. Among them was Mun'im Sirry who caused a major controversy in Indonesia by calling into question prevailing attitudes about same-sex relationships and their impermissibility in Islam. His exegetical article on the story of Lot was published on 20 February 2016, on inspirasi.co, an Indonesian microblogging site. It was not uploaded by Mun'im Sirry himself, but by Denny JA, short for Denny Januar Ali (b. 1963), an author, intellectual and one of the most successful social media influencers in Indonesia with nearly two million followers on Twitter who has a strong interest in anti-discrimination issues.[19] Thus, the article was guaranteed a high amount of publicity. Indeed, Mun'im Sirry's article received 42,500 views by March 2017. Later, a shortened version was published on the important news site Tempo.[20]

Mun'im Sirry is Assistant Professor of World Religions and World Church at the Catholic University of Notre Dame in the United States. He was born in Sumenep, a town on the island of Madura that belongs to East Java, and received a traditional Islamic boarding school (*pesantren*) education.[21] He then studied at and received degrees from the International Islamic University in Islamabad, Pakistan. Afterwards, he was involved in research and publications on the improvement of interreligious relations at the Paramadina Foundation in Jakarta which had been founded by the prominent Muslim scholar Nurcholish Madjid (1939–2005), one of the most famous proponents of religious pluralism in Indonesia. Mun'im Sirry was the editor of a book with essays on interreligious relations, especially interreligious marriage, in Islamic law[22] that evoked a major controversy in Indonesia, with the Council of Indonesian *'ulamā'* recommending a ban. He then moved to the United States to obtain an MA degree at UCLA. In 2012, he earned his Ph.D. in Islamic Studies from the University of Chicago Divinity School with a thesis that examined passages in the Qur'ān which have often been the subject of religious polemics.[23] Mun'im Sirry's focus is on reading the Qur'ān in a way that is conducive to peaceful coexistence between religious communities.[24]

Even while residing in the US, Mun'im Sirry remains an Indonesian public intellectual who regularly publishes articles in Indonesian online journals and on opinion sites, some of which are highly controversial. Besides his statements on homosexuality, this controversy also pertains to his position on the religious status of Christians in Islam, an issue which became the subject of a heated political debate in Indonesia in 2016. Mun'im Sirry also has a weekly column on the news and opinion site Geotimes.

Mun'im Sirry's article on same-sex marriages appeared at the height of a heated controversy, termed a 'moral panic' by some observers, around LGBT presence in Indonesia. Same-sex and transgender practices are neither outlawed in Indonesia nor are there anti-discrimination laws protecting LGBT persons. While same-sex relationships are socially stigmatised, the new freedoms brought about by the fall of the New Order regime in 1998 gave LGBT groups and human rights groups lobbying against discriminatory practices more opportunities to express and organise themselves. At the same time, there was more space for the articulation of Islamist demands such as the application of sharia law and the implementation of conservative concepts of Islamic morality.

In early 2016, these developments culminated in widespread outrage over the alleged negative influence of LGBT movements, sparked by a statement of the country's Higher Education Minister concerning the need to keep LGBT organisations out of university campuses because of being at conflict with moral standards. Other government officials, medical associations and religious scholars followed suit, including the Council of Indonesian *ʿulamāʾ* (*Majelis Ulama Indonesia, MUI*) with a fatwa that condemned 'homosexuality'. The Ministry of Information demanded of social media companies to remove gay-themed emojis. Islamist organisations executed raids against boarding houses 'in attempt' to create zones free of LGBT people. Fears of a potentially subversive and disruptive LGBT movement (*gerakan*) were supported by moral and religious arguments describing gay and lesbian sexual orientations as unnatural, a curable disease and as condemned by God.[25]

The debate soon died down, to be replaced by other issues, but leaving in its wake a climate in which homosexuals were more and more often subject to arrest and punishment.[26] However, as the debate was still raging, Mun'im Sirry published an article (see Excerpt 7.1), which drew on a number of Qur'ānic texts that all narrate the story of Lot and are all relevant to his argument.

Mun'im Sirry's discussion is an example of a thematic approach to the Qur'ān. He does not focus on a single verse or segment of the text, but on a synopsis of the stories on the Prophet Lot that are scattered throughout the Qur'ān. He touches upon the question of the historicity of prophetic narratives in the Qur'ān that the proponents of literary exegesis in Egypt had already tackled in the middle of the twentieth century and sometimes faced a severe backlash over. It might be with this in mind that Mun'im Sirry does not go as far as to actively question the factual truth of these stories. He merely declares it irrelevant, shifting the focus to the message they want to transport, but implicitly suggesting that the stereotypical content of these stories makes it rather unlikely that they aim to describe the real events surrounding equally real persons. The author is clearly familiar with the well-established American discourse on the compatibility of Islam and 'homosexuality'[27] – a term whose problematic connotations Mun'im Sirry discussed in a later article.[28]

By injecting his contribution into an already heated debate, followed up by a much-noted talk he gave later that year,[29] and by taking a stand that is seen as excessively liberal and contradictory to Indonesian values even by most of those Indonesians who do not actively oppose LGBT practices, Mun'im Sirry doubtlessly was aware that he was going to spark controversy. That controversy was not so much concerned with the historicity of the Qur'ānic prophets although most of his opponents seemed to take that for granted; it was much more concerned with the question whether his argument against the standard reading of the Qur'ān as clearly condemning male–male sexual relations might have some merit or not.

A scholar who publishes on the internet exposes himself to more immediate and direct criticism than an author publishing a book. In this case, the

Excerpt 7.1

سورة الشعراء (٢٦)

كَذَّبَتْ قَوْمُ لُوطٍ الْمُرْسَلِينَ ﴿١٦٠﴾ إِذْ قَالَ لَهُمْ أَخُوهُمْ لُوطٌ أَلَا تَتَّقُونَ ﴿١٦١﴾ إِنِّي لَكُمْ رَسُولٌ أَمِينٌ
﴿١٦٢﴾ فَاتَّقُوا اللَّهَ وَأَطِيعُونِ ﴿١٦٣﴾ وَمَا أَسْأَلُكُمْ عَلَيْهِ مِنْ أَجْرٍ إِنْ أَجْرِيَ إِلَّا عَلَى رَبِّ الْعَالَمِينَ
﴿١٦٤﴾ أَتَأْتُونَ الذُّكْرَانَ مِنَ الْعَالَمِينَ ﴿١٦٥﴾ وَتَذَرُونَ مَا خَلَقَ لَكُمْ رَبُّكُم مِّنْ أَزْوَاجِكُم بَلْ أَنتُمْ قَوْمٌ
عَادُونَ ﴿١٦٦﴾ قَالُوا لَئِن لَّمْ تَنتَهِ يَا لُوطُ لَتَكُونَنَّ مِنَ الْمُخْرَجِينَ ﴿١٦٧﴾ قَالَ إِنِّي لِعَمَلِكُم مِّنَ الْقَالِينَ
﴿١٦٨﴾ رَبِّ نَجِّنِي وَأَهْلِي مِمَّا يَعْمَلُونَ ﴿١٦٩﴾ فَنَجَّيْنَاهُ وَأَهْلَهُ أَجْمَعِينَ ﴿١٧٠﴾ إِلَّا عَجُوزًا فِي
الْغَابِرِينَ ﴿١٧١﴾ ثُمَّ دَمَّرْنَا الْآخَرِينَ ﴿١٧٢﴾ وَأَمْطَرْنَا عَلَيْهِم مَّطَرًا فَسَاءَ مَطَرُ الْمُنذَرِينَ ﴿١٧٣﴾

(26:160) The people of Lot denied the truth of those who were sent. (161) When their brother Lot said to them: 'Will you not protect yourselves? (162) I am a faithful messenger for you. (163) Fear God and obey me. (164) I am not asking you for any wage for this. My reward is only with the Lord of all beings. (165) Do you come to the males from among the created beings, (166) and leave alone the spouses that your Lord has created for you? No! You are a people who transgress'. (167) They said, 'If you do not desist, O Lot, you will be one of those cast out'. (168) He said, 'I am one of those who hate what you do. (169) My Lord, save me and my family from what they do'. (170) So We saved him and his family, all of them, (171) Except an old woman among those who tarried. (172) Then we destroyed the others. (173) We caused a rain to fall on them; and evil is the rain of those who have been warned.

سورة النمل (٢٧)

وَلُوطًا إِذْ قَالَ لِقَوْمِهِ أَتَأْتُونَ الْفَاحِشَةَ وَأَنتُمْ تُبْصِرُونَ ﴿٥٤﴾ أَئِنَّكُمْ لَتَأْتُونَ الرِّجَالَ شَهْوَةً مِّن
دُونِ النِّسَاءِ بَلْ أَنتُمْ قَوْمٌ تَجْهَلُونَ ﴿٥٥﴾ فَمَا كَانَ جَوَابَ قَوْمِهِ إِلَّا أَن قَالُوا أَخْرِجُوا آلَ لُوطٍ
مِّن قَرْيَتِكُمْ إِنَّهُمْ أُنَاسٌ يَتَطَهَّرُونَ ﴿٥٦﴾ فَأَنجَيْنَاهُ وَأَهْلَهُ إِلَّا امْرَأَتَهُ قَدَّرْنَاهَا مِنَ الْغَابِرِينَ ﴿٥٧﴾
وَأَمْطَرْنَا عَلَيْهِم مَّطَرًا فَسَاءَ مَطَرُ الْمُنذَرِينَ ﴿٥٨﴾

(27:54) And Lot, when he said to his people: 'Will you commit abomination when you can see? (55) Do you come to men in lust rather than women? No, you are people who are ignorant'. (56) The only answer of his people was to say, 'Expel the family of Lot from your settlement. They are people who seek to be pure'. (57) We saved him and his family, except for his wife. We decreed that she should be among those who tarried. (58) We caused rain to fall on them, and evil is the rain of those who have been warned.

سورة العنكبوت (٢٩)

وَلُوطًا إِذْ قَالَ لِقَوْمِهِ إِنَّكُمْ لَتَأْتُونَ الْفَاحِشَةَ مَا سَبَقَكُم بِهَا مِنْ أَحَدٍ مِّنَ الْعَالَمِينَ ﴿٢٨﴾ أَئِنَّكُمْ
لَتَأْتُونَ الرِّجَالَ وَتَقْطَعُونَ السَّبِيلَ وَتَأْتُونَ فِي نَادِيكُمُ الْمُنكَرَ فَمَا كَانَ جَوَابَ قَوْمِهِ إِلَّا أَن قَالُوا
ائْتِنَا بِعَذَابِ اللَّهِ إِن كُنتَ مِنَ الصَّادِقِينَ ﴿٢٩﴾ قَالَ رَبِّ انصُرْنِي عَلَى الْقَوْمِ الْمُفْسِدِينَ ﴿٣٠﴾

(29:28) And Lot, when he said to his people: 'You commit indecency such as no creature has ever done before. (29) Do you really come to men and commit robbery and do reprehensible things in your assembly?' The only answer of his folk was to say, 'Bring God's torment to us if you are telling the truth'. (30) He said: 'My Lord, help me against the people who wreak mischief'.

سورة القمر (٥٤)

كَذَّبَتْ قَوْمُ لُوطٍ بِالنُّذُرِ ﴿٣٣﴾ إِنَّا أَرْسَلْنَا عَلَيْهِمْ حَاصِبًا إِلَّا آلَ لُوطٍ نَّجَّيْنَاهُم بِسَحَرٍ ﴿٣٤﴾ نِّعْمَةً
مِّنْ عِندِنَا كَذَٰلِكَ نَجْزِي مَن شَكَرَ ﴿٣٥﴾ وَلَقَدْ أَنذَرَهُم بَطْشَتَنَا فَتَمَارَوْا بِالنُّذُرِ ﴿٣٦﴾ وَلَقَدْ رَاوَدُوهُ
عَن ضَيْفِهِ فَطَمَسْنَا أَعْيُنَهُمْ فَذُوقُوا عَذَابِي وَنُذُرِ ﴿٣٧﴾

(54:33) The people of Lot denied the truth. (34) We sent a storm of stones on them, apart from the family of Lot, whom we saved at dawn (35) as a blessing from Us. Thus we reward those who are thankful. (36) He had warned them of Our assault, but they doubted the warnings. (37) They tried to tempt him concerning his guests, so we obliterated their eyes. Taste My punishment and My warnings.

Islam, LGBT and same-sex marriage

by Mun'im Sirry

The controversy over LGBT (lesbian, gay, bisexual and transgender) may die down over time. But it will leave long-lasting traces in the minds of those who take part in it and, at some point, these will re-emerge on a more far-reaching level. While right now the issue is focussed on the extent to which the legitimate rights of LGBT groups may be recognised and protected or, conversely, rejected and suppressed in the future, the scope of the debate might transcend this to include the question of the validity of same-sex marriage. Once again, religion (in this case, Islam) will become the arena of a fight over textual interpretation.

One important lesson from the above-mentioned controversy is this: the existence of LGBT groups is a social fact that requires a serious discourse imbued with new ethics and new paradigms. Their presence is more and more visible and undeniable. Those who reject LGBT will argue that the phenomenon's visibility in public space does not mean that it may be religiously legitimised just like that. This is true. The question is, do the fundamentals of religion fail to legitimise it?

In this article, I will deconstruct textual arguments that are frequently adduced by the opponents of LGBT rights. I will then take the discussion further towards developing principles that may legitimise same-sex marriages.

Textual arguments and alternative interpretations

In a textbook on Islam, the Saudi Ministry of Education describes 'homosexuality' as follows: 'One of the most repulsive sins and an enormous transgression. God has never tormented a people with a punishment worse than what He has inflicted on Lot's people. He sentenced them to a punishment such as no other people has ever experienced. Homosexuality constitutes a depraved act that is contrary to natural behaviour'. When the Egyptian judge Ḥasan al-Sāyis tapped his gavel sentencing a man who was accused of being gay, he also referred to the story of the people of Lot as the basis for his decision.

Let us discuss the story of Lot in the Qur'ān and see to what extent the verses that have been brought up in this context can be read as an argument to delegitimise LGBT people, including their right to conclude same-sex marriages.

The Qur'ān renarrates the story of Lot from Genesis 19 in the Hebrew Bible (which Christians call 'the Old Testament'). Lot is mentioned in fourteen *sūra*s of the Qur'ān, namely 6:85–87; 7:78–82; 11:73, 79–84; 15:58–77; 21:70–71, 74–75; 22:43–44; 26:160–176; 27:55–59; 29:25, 27–34; 37:133–138; 38:11–14; 50:12–13; 54:33–40; and 66:10. The last of those only mentions Lot's wife, not Lot himself, but it is also relevant.

The story of Lot and his people represents the Qur'ānic paradigm of prophetic mission. I call it a 'paradigm' because all the prophets in the Qur'ān are described in the same pattern: they are sent to a people to deliver a warning and are rejected by part of that people whereupon God sends down a punishment. Even more interestingly, in Q. 26, different prophets utter identical phrases. How can that be? I think the prophetic paradigm that the Qur'ān presents reflects what might be called 'monoprophetic'. That is to say that, although many names of prophets occur in the Qur'ān, they are actually one and the same person, namely the one who is sent to a people and rejected by part of that people, whereupon the threat of divine punishment comes down.

The story of Lot and his people conforms to the same Qur'ānic paradigm. Are the stories of Lot and the other prophets based on historical facts or not? This question is made less relevant by the fact that, according to the 'mono-prophetic' paradigm, the Qur'ān rather emphasises their moral message. Indeed, whether Lot and the others are really historical figures or not is simply not relevant because the Qur'ānic 'prophetology' [English in the original] can be defined as mono-prophetic.

Based on this conceptual introduction, we can analyse the 'moral story' [English in the original] of Lot and his people. When Lot gave his warning: 'Why do you come to the males from among the created beings and leave alone the wives that your Lord has created for you?' (Q. 26:165–166), what does 'come to the males' mean? This is clarified in Q. 27:55: to satisfy their lust. Here, we see that the people of Lot have legitimate wives, but they absolutely want to have improper sexual relations with male visitors who came to stay in their city. This means that their sexual relations happened outside marriage. This needs to be emphasised because, as will be explained below, some of the Islamic schools of law treat sodomy as analogous to illicit sexual relations (*zinā*).

What may we conclude then, if we think about the way Lot's people treated travellers from outside their city? Will these visitors consent to that treatment? Only those who do not have a conscience will answer this question in the affirmative. If that is the case, the depravity of the actions of Lot's people lies in the aspect of satisfying one's lust arbitrarily and at will, and can be categorised as 'rape'.

The Qur'ān does not explicitly state why the people of Lot did this, just as there are not detailed explanations of many other things. Q. 54:37 provides interesting evidence, however. Angels who have reincarnated as men have been targeted for rape, whereupon God blinds them [i.e. the perpetrators]. How, then, does the Saudi Ministry of Education arrive at the conclusion that the people of Lot were punished with an unprecedented sentence because of homosexuality? The Saudi *'ulamā'* are usually literalist in their understanding of the Qur'ān, but why not in this case? If we refer to Q. 29:29, the transgressions of the people of Lot are manifold; besides satisfying their lust with men (certainly outside marriage!), they also committed robbery, did reprehensible things and challenged God.

If those who reject LGBT rights are consistent in their literalist exegesis, they should not be so rash in connecting God's painful punishment with homosexual acts. See how the literalist scholar Ibn Ḥazm (d. 1064) understood the punishment that befell the people of Lot. In his great work, *Kitāb al-muḥallā*, this scholar from al-Andalus rejected the view that connected the punishment of the people of Lot to sexual acts with men per se, but [rather connected it to] their rejection of Lot's call and his prophetic mission. Ibn Ḥazm's explanation is similar to the 'mono-prophetic' idea that I have proposed above (although, of course, I am not a literalist!): Lot was sent to deliver a divine message and was rejected by a part of his people. God punished those who rejected it and blessed those who accepted it.

In a nutshell, the verses of the Qur'ān that concern the story of Lot and his people cannot be taken as a normative basis for discriminating against LGBT people, including a ban on same-sex marriages.

[There follows a discussion of same-sex marriage based on *ḥadīth*s and the rulings of the Sunni and Imami Shi'i schools of law. Mun'im Sirry argues that the textual sources neither explicitly forbid nor allow same-sex relationships; rather, they reject non-consensual and extra-marital sexual acts. Since there is no clear ruling on the issue, it has to be decided according to the principle of *maṣlaḥa*, or public interest, which aims to realise the goals of equality, justice and human dignity under specific social circumstances. This principle might well result in the permission of same-sex marriages in some contemporary societies.][30]

original site of publication allowed for comments of which there are a little more than twenty-five, including three responses by Mun'im Sirry himself. The large majority, save for one commenter who praises the overdue distinction between 'sodomy' and 'homosexual' relationships, is negative, varying in tone from polite disagreement to outrage and insults that lead even other critics to ask for a more respectful attitude. Polemics and expressions of disgust aside, the main argument against Mun'im Sirry's opinion in these comments seems to be that God created humans in pairs. Same-sex relations are declared unnatural because they cannot produce offspring. Mun'im Sirry's position is seen as the result of an overly liberal attitude that knows no bounds. He is reproached with setting himself above previous exegetes who, while fallible humans, cannot collectively have been wrong about everything. He is also accused of claiming to know the interests (*maṣlaḥa*) of the Muslim *umma* better than God. His interpretation is framed as Americanised, giving a Westernised audience what they want to hear.

One of the more erudite commentaries engaging with the substance of Mun'im Sirry's argument points to a Qur'ānic passage on the Lot narrative that Mun'im Sirry did not explicitly mention:

> His people came to him, rushing towards him – and before that they had been doing evil deeds. He said: 'Here are my daughters. They are purer for you. Fear God, and do not shame me concerning my guests. Is there not one right-minded man among you?' They said: 'You know that we have no right to your daughters, and you know what we want.' (Q. 11:78–79)

This, in the commentator's opinion, does not conform with Mun'im Sirry's argument that the Qur'ān is exclusively concerned with banning extra-marital relations or possibly non-consensual sexual intercourse since the point of Lot's proposal is, in their opinion, obviously to deflect the men's attention from his male guests to equally extra-marital and presumably non-consensual acts with his daughters, the reason being that those are at least female, rather than male.[31]

The internet also enables an exegete to directly respond to criticism. As a result, both the arguments of the critics and the response of the exegete are available in one place not only in the moment of debate, but also for an unlimited time afterwards. In this case, Mun'im Sirry responded to some of the criticism directed at him, confessing himself dissatisfied with the frequent argument that his opinion clashes with the interpretations of earlier exegetes such as Ibn Kathīr. Of course, he writes, it is anyone's rights to follow these exegetes' authority, but all the same their works are only interpretations of the Qur'ān, not the Qur'ān itself, and therefore not an arbiter of truth. Mun'im Sirry admits to his limitations as a fallible human making an honest effort to understand the Qur'ān, but the same limitations are in place for all previous works of *tafsīr*, he argues:

> If you want to understand how the Qur'ān was understood by earlier Muslims, read *tafsīr*. It is their understanding of the Qur'an in their times. But if you want to understand the Qur'ān, read the Qur'ān and [about] the climate of the point in time at which this sacred scripture emerged, including the social conditions, culture and literature in those times; do not (merely) read *tafsīr*. This is the basis of the epistemology that I adhere to. You are welcome to disagree.[32]

The debate was also carried out in social media, including Mun'im Sirry's own Facebook feed[33] and many others; according to the site where it was originally published, the article was shared more than 700 times. It was also shared on Twitter, most prominently by the liberal scholar Ulil Abshar Abdalla (b. 1967) who, in March 2017, had 664,000 followers. Ulil had previously used the medium to oppose the arguments of anti-LGBT activists, for example by questioning the historicity of the Sodom narrative and asking why God refrains from sending down punishment on contemporary states that tolerate LGBT communities. Like Mun'im Sirry, he had attracted much criticism for his liberal views.[34]

There are a number of direct responses to Mun'im Sirry on various blogs and opinion sites that constitute popular media of intellectual expression in Indonesia. Most of the responses are critical. The conservative scholar Adian Husaini (b. 1965) polemically denounces Mun'im Sirry's opinion as a Jewish, liberal and Satanic exegesis in an opinion piece that was widely shared on Islamist websites.[35] By the same token, although with more references to respectable Islamic scholars, a graduate of al-Azhar describes

Mun'im Sirry's article as a conscious distortion of the meaning of the Qur'ān of the kind that Satan (Iblīs) uses to tempt humans.[36] The idea that Mun'im Sirry is 'playing with the Qur'ān' in the sense of twisting its meaning is uttered by other critics as well.[37] The common notion in all these cases is that Mun'im Sirry's *tafsīr* represents a brand of 'liberal' rethinking of the text that has no legitimacy and will only ever be accepted by members of LGBT communities themselves.

Other responses point to the above-mentioned story of Lot's daughters in Q. 11:78–79 to substantiate the claim that the story of Lot is, in fact, about male–male sexual relations rather than rape or extra-marital sex. One critic embeds this into an attack on Mun'im Sirry's mono-prophetic paradigm, claiming that each prophet had a specific mission and fought against particular evils which, in Lot's case, was homosexuality. He also opposes the idea that anything not expressly forbidden by the Qur'ān is by definition permissible and questions the assumption that public interest (*maṣlaḥa*) would be served by allowing same-sex marriages.[38] Another critic points to the consensus of earlier scholars that homosexuality is sinful and should be punished. He also questions Mun'im's ascription of vehement denunciations of homosexuality to Saudi doctrine, pointing out that much of the vocabulary in the Saudi textbook mentioned by Mun'im is actually Qur'ānic.[39]

Many responses to Mun'im Sirry's interpretation, including some respectful and carefully reasoned pieces, centre on the concept of creation. They frequently adduce as evidence the following two Qur'ānic verses:

> And of everything we created two kinds (or: pairs) so that you might be reminded. (Q. 51:49)

> O people, fear your Lord, who created you from a single soul and who created from it its mate and who spread many men and women from the two of them…(Q. 4:1)

In addition, the story of creation of Adam and his wife – who is unnamed in the Qur'ān – is frequently brought up. Based on this evidence, one critic argues that the exact meaning of the story of Lot is irrelevant. Even if one agrees with Mun'im Sirry that it should not be read as an explicit ban on same-sex relations, the Qur'ān clearly talks about creation and the nature of marriage as a union between a man and a woman with the aim of procreation.[40]

A contribution by Fadhli Lukman that focusses on semantics discusses the Qur'ānic term *azwāj* used in the story of Lot, Q. 26:166. Here, Lot reproaches the men of his people with 'leaving alone their spouses (*azwāj*)' that God has created for them. Fadhli Lukman argues that the term *azwāj*, here, does not refer to 'wives' (*istri*) in the legalistic sense of a spouse of the opposite sex which could easily be replaced by a spouse of the same sex if same-sex marriage was permitted. Rather, it refers to the other half of the pairs as which God created humans: that is, a man to a woman and a woman to a man so they may have offspring.[41]

In contrast to some of the polemical criticism, these last objections need to be taken seriously because they illustrate a fundamental difficulty with thematic approaches to Qurʾānic exegesis: it is hard to draw the line and decide which verses are important and which verses are not. Is it sufficient to analyse all versions of the Lot narrative, or do the verses on creation have to be taken into account? And what do these verses, in turn, say about the gendered vocabulary used in the Lot narrative? The internet controversy on Mun'im Sirry's opinion piece was ultimately too superficial and too polemical to allow for a satisfactory solution to these difficulties. Opinion sites, Facebook and Twitter offer spaces for an exchange of arguments, but rarely encourage a deep and sustained discussion of comprehensive approaches to the Qurʾān.

The Indonesian debate on the story of Lot is deeply embedded in a very real struggle over the social place of LGBT persons and communities in Indonesian society. None of the exegetical opinions uttered in the course of the debate can be entirely understood without taking into account the underlying moral and socio-political attitudes towards this issue and their authors' positions in local power fields. The internet, and more specifically, online media such as opinion sites and blogs that are highly popular in the Indonesian intellectual field, enables even a US-based academic to be part of the local power field and contribute to the debate, and it enables others to interact with him. While this debate took place at a specific moment in time, unlike oral discussions or television debates, it is preserved for all to see in later times and thus open to re-appropriation, should social concerns and social conditions change – as Mun'im Sirry predicted in the introduction to his article, pointing to the possibility that there might come a time at which Indonesian society debates the permissibility of same-sex marriages.

CAUSES FOR CONFLICT

As the example of Mun'im Sirry has shown, the causes of conflicts over the meaning of the Qurʾān go beyond differences in hermeneutical outlook or doctrine. They are also tied in with conflicting visions of state and society and struggles over the authority to define those. There are structural reasons both for the emergence of conflicts and for the power that specific actors in these conflicts possess to vilify or suppress others, or occasionally even threaten their existence. In conflicts of this type, controversies over the correct interpretation ot the Qur'ān are carried from the intellectual arena into real life. The fate of the Egyptian professor Naṣr Ḥāmid Abū Zayd whose marriage was dissolved by a court because he was held to be an apostate due to his theory that the Qur'ān, while being of divine origin, was expressed in human language, is a case in point.[42] Not every intellectual who proposes daring new approaches to the Qur'ān runs the same risk, but some do experience considerable adverse effects of taking such a stand.

Most of the authors who experienced sustained hostile and threatening reactions to their hermeneutical theories and interpretations have in common that they are not part of the academic religious establishment in their countries. They either teach in other subjects, such as Arabic literature as was the case with Abū Zayd, or abroad, as was the case with Fazlur Rahman. Among the notable exceptions to this rule are Iran, where the field of Shi'i *'ulamā'* is very diverse, Turkey and Indonesia. Even in those cases, though, it is likely that exegetes coming from the status group of professional *'ulamā'* or university theologians do not run as high a risk of facing vehement opposition as others do – unless they openly attack the religious establishment, which Abū Zayd did and which was one of the reasons for which he experienced such severe backlash.

Struggles over status and religious authority are thus at the heart of the matter. Another factor is the public Islamisation that occurred since the 1970s in most Muslim societies at varying speed and to varying degrees. In countries such as Egypt, Islamists evolved from a persecuted group to a force that exerted massive moral pressure, causing many other actors, including governments, to pre-emptively distance themselves from anything that might be perceived as blasphemous. Through this mechanism, singular incidents or expressions of opinion can spiral into a situation of moral panic where the tone of the public debate becomes increasingly shrill until it creates the impression that the very foundation of society is at stake.

The fundamental claim undergirding the attacks on Abū Zayd, Fazlur Rahman and others is the existence of a true meaning, or range of meanings, of the Qur'ānic text that is not bound to any specific temporal and personal horizon of comprehension. The prerogative of uncovering this meaning lies with the *'ulamā'*, which explains much of their hostile reactions. This is all the more the case in societies in which, due to the establishment of modern statehood and educational institutions, the *'ulamā'* lost many of their former occupations in the judiciary and in teaching, which caused them to guard all the more jealously the one area in which they may still claim authority: the religious discourse. This includes the right to censorship of religious publications and public utterances. Besides the status interests of *'ulamā'*, the political discourse of many authoritarian regimes emphasised national unity at the expense of diversity and conflicting interests, which were seen as a threat to regimes. The same regimes tried to bolster their legitimacy by co-opting the *ʿulamāʾ* and by setting themselves up as protectors of Islam, which repeatedly caused political interests to intervene in religious controversies.[43]

The most common themes of conflict over the correct interpretation of the Qurʾān are those that touch upon fundamental issue of egalitarianism, acceptance of pluralism and liberalism. This is true of topics such as gender, sexual identity, religious freedom, criminal law and the vision of an Islamic state. Some Muslims read the Qurʾān as a scripture that calls for liberation, diversity and equality. This not only upsets those who see themselves as guardians of an established interpretation of the Qurʾān or aim to purify Islam from what they perceive of as later additions, distortions and innovations. It is also contrary to the interests of nation states that are illiberal, unequal and see pluralism as a threat to a strong unified rule. Under such conditions, it is difficult to publish exegetical ideas that run counter to the hegemonic understanding of the Qurʾān's meaning. But there are always spaces for dissent, and new media greatly facilitate its expression – the fresh and innovative voices coming from states such as Iran and Saudi Arabia clearly demonstrate this.

As long as regimes continue to build their legitimacy upon appeals to religion, however, Qurʾānic exegesis will continue to be carried out in a politically charged climate. The climate is no less problematic in Western countries where many Muslim exegetes reside today. Here, the problem is not so much with a religious establishment and with governments opposing particular approaches to the Qurʾān, but with a hostile public discourse that encourages black-and-white descriptions of either a brutally violent or a peaceful Islam. Nuanced positions, historical analyses and open-minded debate run a risk of being exploited or attacked from either camp. Interpreting the Qurʾān has become a politicised activity to many Muslim intellectuals. Attempts to refute hierarchical and authoritarian readings of the Qurʾān always have a social dimension which is why they so often attract hostile reactions, as the following example shows.

Doubt versus certainty: Aḥmad Khayrī al-ʿUmarī (b. 1970, Iraq) on Q. 21:51–56 and his critics

In 2003, Aḥmad Khayrī al-ʿUmarī, a native of Baghdad and a dentist by training, published his first book: *The Qurʾānic Compass: A Different Kind of Sea Passage in Search of the Lost Map*.[44] While not being a religious scholar and not even having received training in the humanities, the author comes from an illustrious family claiming descent from the second caliph ʿUmar b. al-Khaṭṭāb. His father was the well-known Iraqi historian Khayrī al-ʿUmarī (1925–2003).[45] The book was apparently successful since it saw its eleventh edition by 2016. This time, it was printed by a publisher in Cairo as a high-quality hardcover print. Depending on the edition, it has between 450 and 600 pages and is thus far more than an essay or a pamphlet. Rather, it is a work that wants nothing less than to redefine the Muslim understanding of the Qurʾān, thereby paving the way for a reform of Muslim societies.

The book explains its title thus: it wants to encourage Muslims to finally treat the Qurʾān as it should be treated, not as a talisman, but as a 'compass that leads us (*tahdīnā*) to the way – to escape from our present condition'.[46] This statement evokes the theme of guidance (*hidāya*), a central concept of modernist approaches to the Qurʾān.

Aḥmad Khayrī al-ʿUmarī's approach to the Qurʾān (as exemplified in Excerpt 7.2) evoked acerbic criticism. One need only take a superficial look at that criticism to realise how much the author's emphasis on questions and doubt irked his critics. After all, the very nature of faith is at stake: is it a belief based on unquestioning certitude, or is it the product of questions, doubt and reflection? Do doubts and questions shake the foundations of

Excerpt 7.2

Q. 21:51–65

وَلَقَدْ آتَيْنَا إِبْرَاهِيمَ رُشْدَهُ مِن قَبْلُ وَكُنَّا بِهِ عَالِمِينَ ﴿٥١﴾ إِذْ قَالَ لِأَبِيهِ وَقَوْمِهِ مَا هَٰذِهِ التَّمَاثِيلُ
الَّتِي أَنتُمْ لَهَا عَاكِفُونَ ﴿٥٢﴾ قَالُوا وَجَدْنَا آبَاءَنَا لَهَا عَابِدِينَ ﴿٥٣﴾ قَالَ لَقَدْ كُنتُمْ أَنتُمْ وَآبَاؤُكُمْ فِي
ضَلَالٍ مُّبِينٍ ﴿٥٤﴾ قَالُوا أَجِئْتَنَا بِالْحَقِّ أَمْ أَنتَ مِنَ اللَّاعِبِينَ ﴿٥٥﴾ قَالَ بَل رَّبُّكُمْ رَبُّ السَّمَاوَاتِ
وَالْأَرْضِ الَّذِي فَطَرَهُنَّ وَأَنَا عَلَىٰ ذَٰلِكُم مِّنَ الشَّاهِدِينَ ﴿٥٦﴾ وَتَاللَّهِ لَأَكِيدَنَّ أَصْنَامَكُم بَعْدَ أَن
تُوَلُّوا مُدْبِرِينَ ﴿٥٧﴾ فَجَعَلَهُمْ جُذَاذًا إِلَّا كَبِيرًا لَّهُمْ لَعَلَّهُمْ إِلَيْهِ يَرْجِعُونَ ﴿٥٨﴾ قَالُوا مَن فَعَلَ هَٰذَا
بِآلِهَتِنَا إِنَّهُ لَمِنَ الظَّالِمِينَ ﴿٥٩﴾ قَالُوا سَمِعْنَا فَتًى يَذْكُرُهُمْ يُقَالُ لَهُ إِبْرَاهِيمُ ﴿٦٠﴾ قَالُوا فَأْتُوا
بِهِ عَلَىٰ أَعْيُنِ النَّاسِ لَعَلَّهُمْ يَشْهَدُونَ ﴿٦١﴾ قَالُوا أَأَنتَ فَعَلْتَ هَٰذَا بِآلِهَتِنَا يَا إِبْرَاهِيمُ ﴿٦٢﴾ قَالَ
بَلْ فَعَلَهُ كَبِيرُهُمْ هَٰذَا فَاسْأَلُوهُمْ إِن كَانُوا يَنطِقُونَ ﴿٦٣﴾ فَرَجَعُوا إِلَىٰ أَنفُسِهِمْ فَقَالُوا إِنَّكُمْ أَنتُمُ
الظَّالِمُونَ ﴿٦٤﴾ ثُمَّ نُكِسُوا عَلَىٰ رُءُوسِهِمْ لَقَدْ عَلِمْتَ مَا هَٰؤُلَاءِ يَنطِقُونَ ﴿٦٥﴾

Asking questions: A destructive element for a constructive purpose
[…] When Abraham confronts his people with their superstitions, contradictions and their reality and destroys their idols except for the great one, he uses the technique of asking questions as a strategy of exacerbating what was already a precarious position:

(51) In the past we gave Abraham his rectitude – for We knew him – (52) when he said to his father and his people, 'What are these images to

which you are cleaving?' (53) They said, 'We found our fathers serving them.' (54) He said, 'Then certainly you and your fathers have been in manifest error.' (55) They said, 'Do you bring us the truth, or are you one of those that jest?' (56) He said, 'Nay, but your Lord who originated them is the Lord of the heavens and the Earth, and I am one of those that bear witness unto this. (57) And, by God, I shall outwit your idols after you have turned your backs.' (58) So he broke them into pieces, all but a great one they had, so that they might return to it. (59) They said, 'Who has done this with our gods? Surely he is one of the evildoers.' (60) They said, 'We heard a young man making mention of them, and he was called Abraham.' (61) They said, 'Bring him before the people's eyes, that they shall bear witness.' (62) They said, 'So, are you the man who did this unto our gods, Abraham?' (63) He said, 'No; it was this great one of them that did it. Ask them, if they are able to speak!' (64) So they consulted among themselves, and they said, 'Surely it is you who are the evildoers'. (65) Then they were confounded and said, 'You know that they cannot speak.'

Thus, Abraham here uses the question as a means to destroy the true idols, the mental idols that nest within minds – more so than the pickaxe he uses to destroy the statues. When Abraham spares the great one 'so that they might return to it' according to his plan, the 'return' is *to themselves*. And when Abraham demands of them to ask the idols, they ask themselves in reality. This was exactly the plan Abraham has devised: that the question should be on their tongues, in their minds and in their thoughts. Although the Abrahamic plan was successful in raising doubts among the members of his people, the foundations of a society do not collapse that easily, just by presenting them with a question. The road is longer and harder than that. When it eventually erupts to topple this people's illusions, the essentials of their belief and the foundations of their society, this is the divine guidance that God has provided him with in advance.

Descartes begins his method of scientific inquiry by taking doubt as his starting point and main pillar, designed to change all starting points of inquiry after it, constituting a rational methodology based on the pure scientific scrutiny of things. This method of his is among the most important rational achievements in human thought, which is not surprising in someone whose skill at mathematical-philosophical logical thought ranked as high as Descartes'.

The journey of belief, however, starts with questioning oneself and continues focussing on this while it goes on, considering questions its source of energy, its mode of renewal and the medium through which its agenda for mankind and history is realised, which might seem quite astonishing.

But that astonishment usually comes from a traditional perspective that treats religions as a comprehensive whole, as if all of them revolve around a blind transcendental faith, the aim being for the soul to rest peacefully in that faith which is free of questions and doubts. A belief that has nothing to do with reason: the same belief that emerged from the perceptible miracles upon which the prophets of other religions relied, overwhelming the sensory perceptions and dazzling the emotions.

However, faith in Islam which originally relied on rational interaction with the Qur'ānic discourse applies different criteria: the reliance on questions, the focus on asking questions and the fact that Muslims are more entitled to asking them should no longer be an issue that causes astonishment; but all this is from the outset in agreement with the fabric of this different religion and its distinct nature. That nature removes it from the realm of the traditional perspective on religion with its focus on peace of mind through prayer, worship and asceticism and moves it closer to being a complete way of life [*manhaj*], rather than a way to prayer, exhortation and abstinence.

And whenever religion is a way of life and an outlook on it and the way in which its adherents think, then it starts by asking questions. This is the foundation for a way of thinking out of the depth of faith that is made up of the minds and thoughts of its individual adherents, flowing together to become a faith that does not wither. The act of asking questions keeps it alive and from dying because positive doubt revives it so that it remains renewed and strong in the face of constant changes and transformations.

Unfortunately, this Abrahamic act of asking questions that was the starting point of Islam, and this positive doubt that we are even more entitled to than Abraham – and that enabled him to reach the utmost peace of mind – remained confined to Qur'ānic verses, **while the chance to ground them in Islamic thought was not taken and they were neither rooted firmly nor consolidated in the Muslim mind.** The winds of history were adverse to the ships of faith and brought forth historical intellectual conditions and circumstances on Earth that were far removed from the approach of asking questions by which the true (*ḥanīf*) religion of Islam originated.

These conditions brought forth a way of thought that glorifies inherited certainties and despises questions, considering them an illicit innovation (*bid'a*) that leads to hellfire…And the worst of it is that this way of thinking conceals itself with Qur'ānic verses and *ḥadīth*s, takes them as a cover and exploits them.

[…] These conditions and circumstances did not only influence Islamic thought, but also the character and intellect of Muslims as well as the Muslim individual who has throughout the centuries inherited this heavy burden of history.[47]

belief or can belief only be sound if it has gone through the stages of questions, doubt and reflection?

Time and again, proponents of innovative approaches to the Qurʾān are accused of sowing doubts, undermining certainties and thereby causing discord and sedition. For example, the Syrian scholar Ibrāhīm ʿAbdallāh Salqīnī, scion of a prominent family of Syrian *ʿulamāʾ*, sums up the 'main thoughts' of Aḥmad Khayrī al-ʿUmarī's *Qurʾānic Compass*, from which the above text is an excerpt, as follows:

1. A strong focus on mysteries and the understanding of mysteries, which is the foundation of *bāṭinī* thought.
2. The era of lawgiving [i.e. the first generation of Islam] was the last Golden Age; he [al-ʿUmarī] only suggests this here, but states it plainly in his book *The Fall of Baghdad*. Thus, when Muʿāwiya assumed the caliphate [in 661], this was when the decay in religious and Islamic history began. This is the foundation of the thought of the Rāfiḍa.[48]
3. The veneration of the intellect and giving priority to it over the text, which is the foundation of the thought of the Muʿtazila.[49]
4. Subjecting everything to debate, to the possibility of being freely accepted or rejected; shaking up established principles by [sowing] doubt; declaring doubt the only way to certitude. This is the foundation of the thought of the atheists.
5. Connecting everything exclusively with the material world out of a desire to deny the power of God or even His existence, which is the foundation of materialist thought.
6. The denial of God's control of cause and effect, which is the foundation of the thought of the Qadariyya.[50]
7. Praising secularism and secularists.[51]

This vitriolic criticism, of course, does not do al-ʿUmarī's book justice, nor is it – by its own admission – even based on a thorough reading of the complete book. It is complemented by an *ad hominem* attack on the author's qualification to write about the Qurʾān, him being a dentist and this being his first book – a fairly typical move by *ʿulamāʾ* against persons they perceive as intruders onto their discursive territory. While not particularly intellectually rigorous, Salqīnī's attacks on the *Qurʾānic Compass* are fairly stereotypical. They also demonstrate the extent to which opponents of innovative approaches to the Qurʾān rely on established notions of heresy while setting themselves up as defenders of Sunni orthodoxy against aberrations and threats.

It is maybe not particularly surprising that commonplace conspiracy theories and delegitimisation strategies are employed in such polemics. Besides political conspiracy theories involving Western imperialism or zionism, certain religious themes are recurrent. Exegetes pursuing historical-critical or literary approaches to the Qur'ān are frequently accused of heresy or outright atheism (*ilḥād*), of copying the ideas of Western orientalists or Christian theologians, of promoting the rationalist and non-traditionalist theology of the Mu'tazila and of being part of the Bāṭiniyya. 'Bāṭiniyya' is a derogatory term used for movements who employ an esoteric, allegorical approach to the Qur'ān. It gained particular importance when various strands of the Isma'ili Shi'a, which was frequently equated with the 'Bāṭiniyya', exerted political influence in the Middle East between the tenth and thirteenth centuries CE; and as Salqīnī's text shows, the Bāṭiniyya narrative is still alive. Some of the tendencies Salqīnī accuses al-'Umarī of might appear mutually exclusive, but in Salqīnī's thought they are all part of the same type of heterodoxy. He does not take al-'Umarī's book seriously as an attempt to interpret the Qur'ān, but treats it as a tool of subversion.

It is not subversion, of course, at which al-'Umarī really aims. Using maritime metaphors, he embarks on a personal journey into the Qur'ān's approach and message, searching for the meaning behind the surface narrative – such as the theme of questioning and doubt addressed in this text. That idea seems repulsive to adherents of a more conventional exegesis not only because they do not share his belief in the constructive nature of doubt, but also because his interpretation is far from a literal reading of the story of Abraham as a description of a historical event. While al-'Umarī claims nowhere that the Abrahamic story has not really happened as described in the Qur'ān, his focus is neither on its narrative content nor on its surface theme of Abraham's fight against his people's idols, but on the strategy of inducing his opponents to ask questions. This is what leads Salqīnī to accuse him of being a Bāṭini, that is, searching for some inner meaning of the text while neglecting or even rejecting its obvious 'outer' meaning. Conversely, al-'Umarī levels harsh criticism against traditionalists as well as Salafi paradigms, the latter being alluded to by mentioning those who invoke certitude and reject doubts as *bid'a* ('illicit innovation') which is a central concept for contemporary Salafis.

Al-'Umarī's methodology of analysing the message behind the story is one employed by many modernists; his emphasis on Islam being a complete way of life bears some semblance to Islamist rhetoric. The focus on doubt, however, is more unusual and is closer to a postmodern perspective in which truth and certainty are elusive and it is only from the perspective of the individual that an understanding of the text can be gained. Al-'Umarī places great emphasis on reason and sees spiritual experience as a distraction, an easy road to an uncritical and therefore fragile faith. However, al-ʿUmarī is not so postmodern as to give up the idea of a 'true message' of the Qurʾān, one that he wants to help uncover. In his opinion, doubts, questioning and critical thought are meant to lead believers to that message, not to help deconstruct it. This is a dilemma resulting from many modernist interpretive approaches that encourage critical reasoning, but at the same time expect that reasoning to yield a pre-determined result.

The cultural critique that al-ʿUmarī's Qurʾānic interpretation contains likewise stands in a long tradition of modernist discourses. It describes the Muslim world as being caught up in a process of decadence and decay that is typically perceived of as having started early in Muslim history, possibly – as Salqīnī accuses al-ʿUmarī of claiming – as early as the end of the age of the 'Rightly-Guided Caliphs' (661), or maybe only when traditionalist theology started gaining the upper hand over rationalism in the ninth century or, at the very latest, after the Mongol conquest of Baghdad (1258). All these historical narratives are simplistic, but then, they are not intended to be works of historical scholarship. Rather, their function is to support a contemporary concern: the call for a reawakening, which makes only sense if the premise is that those at whom the call is directed have been asleep.

In reality, the reasons for the prevalence of authoritarian religious discourses are probably more recent. Especially in the post-independence nation states of the Arab world, dictatorial governments have promoted a discourse of unquestionable 'national unity', suppressing critical debate. Often, they co-opted religious scholars to support this repressive discourse on the basis of an equally unquestionable, moralising understanding of Islam.[52] Muslim modernists, however, frequently explain the nature of the resulting discourse with reference to a 'traditional Muslim mindset' that they imagine to be much older than contemporary regimes, transmitted through centuries of religious scholarship and at odds with the 'true message' of the Qurʾān – a message that al-ʿUmarī aims to reconstruct in order to support his call for critical debate. Innovation, according to this reading of the story of Abraham, should be embraced, rather than condemned as *bidʿa*.

POSTMODERN UNCERTAINTIES AND SUBJECTIVE APPROACHES

Many proponents of contemporary Qurʾānic interpretations raise a claim to uncovering the true meaning of the Qurʾān. This is true for Salafis as much as for modernists. They share the idea that there is a definite meaning, a divine intention, inherent in the text, the sole difference being that for a Salafi that meaning has been evident all along while a modernist would assume that premodern exegetes, blinded by the circumstances of the societies they lived in, have been unable to see it.

This is different to what I call the 'postmodern perspective' on the Qur'ān. It is curiously absent from most surveys of contemporary Qur'ānic exegesis or at least not treated as a category of its own. Maybe that is because its aims are often barely distinguishable from those of modernists, and the boundaries between these two categories are blurred. Yet, in hermeneutical terms, the difference between modernist and postmodern approaches could hardly be bigger.

For example, in a recent book on feminist interpretations of the Qur'ān, Aysha A. Hidayatullah writes:

> ...we have been so tied to our attachments to feminist justice that we have been unable to see the historicity and particularity of our positions and have thus produced anachronistic readings of the Qur'an....
>
> Though feminist tafsir has often claimed with certainty that statements on male–female hierarchy in the Qur'an do not reflect the values of the text, I argue that the only thing we can be fully certain of is that *we* prioritize the Qur'an's statements on male–female mutuality; we cannot be certain that the text prioritizes them....We will need to pursue a vision of the Qur'an as a divine text that allows us to imagine justice outside the text's limited pronouncements.[53]

This casts the difference between a modernist and postmodern perspective into sharp relief. Modernists believe that the Qur'ān has been misinterpreted for centuries and, in reality, upholds values such as egalitarianism and liberalism – values that their own interpretation of the Qur'ān is helping to uncover and that are inherent to the true meaning of the text. Postmodernists, on the other hand, might be in search for the same values; but to them, identifying them in the Qur'ān is a conscious act performed by specific readers and in no way the only legitimate understanding of the text. A postmodern approach radically questions the possibility of ever attaining certitude over what the text *really* means. It does not stop at questioning the universal truth of previous interpretations, but also questions the universal nature of its own interpretation. That is not to say that a postmodern approach necessarily doubts the existence of a truth or meaning inherent to the text; it is, however, sceptical of any human's ability to ever identify that truth in any conclusive manner.

Postmodern approaches differ from modernist ones not so much in their ideas on historicity, semantics or the text's literary strategy. Rather, they differ in their focus on the role of the reader to any understanding of the text. To a postmodernist, it is impossible to identify a meaning without a reader who generates it from the text, and thus any interpretation is by necessity subjective. Truth, then, is not a monolithic entity, forever unchanging, which can be mined from the text; rather, the quest for truth is a process that will never be concluded.

This perspective on Qur'ānic interpretation is clearly in line with twentieth-century European hermeneutical ideas, especially those of Hans-Georg Gadamer (1900–2002), and has been much criticised for this perceived Western infiltration by its Muslim opponents.[54] Nevertheless, it has gained significant popularity among Muslim academics in a number of countries, especially those that offer the space to discuss such potentially heretical ideas. There are vibrant – and partly polemical – debates around hermeneutics in Indonesia, and the concept is not foreign to Turkish university theologians either. For example, the Turkish professor Mehmet Paçacı from the Ankara Faculty of Theology aimed for a synthesis between Fazlur Rahman's 'double movement theory' and Gadamer's hermeneutics. As mentioned before, Fazlur Rahman's theory proposes to first situate the Qur'ān in its historical environment, then understand which purpose the ethical and legal norms of the Qur'ān served in that environment and finally come up with rules that serve to implement that purpose in present-day societies. Paçacı notices a gap in this theory where the act of understanding historical and present societies is concerned. According to him, and in line with Gadamer's hermeneutics, such an act of understanding is impossible without taking the exegete's preconditions and precommitments into account, resulting in a subjective and individualised application of the double movement theory.[55]

Hermeneutics and historical-critical readings of the Qur'ān based on the concept are particularly *en vogue* among Iranian Islamic scholars such as Muḥammad Mujtahid Shabistarī (b. 1936). Iranian scholars living in exile have forwarded increasingly daring theories in recent years. For example, Abdolkarim Soroush[56] (b. 1945) proposed to consider the Qur'ān an expression of Muḥammad's entirely human experience, phrased in his own words and based on visions of the Divine that occurred exclusively in dreams, which is an idea that is hotly debated among Iranian scholars, contested by many, but received with interest by others.[57]

A postmodern reading of the Qur'ān paves the way for interpreting the text in the light of external standards, for example universal human rights. Once it is assumed that the readers' dispositions invariably inform their understanding of the text, an extra-Qur'ānic standard of human rights is just as legitimate a source of interpretation as any other, or even a better one since a postmodern exegete is at least conscious of his or her predispositions and honest about them. On the other hand, the more radically subjective the approach, the more urgent the question that Hidayatullah raises: 'In what way is the text still divine?'[58] In what way does God's message to humans manifest itself in the text, and do humans have the capacity to identify it? Is there a realm of fixed, unchangeable meaning in the text, and how can human readers distinguish it from the fluid and the changeable with any amount of certitude? Hidayatullah and others were sharply attacked by the exegete Asma Barlas for taking the view that feminist readings, far from uncovering the Qur'ān's true egalitarian nature, reflect contemporary concerns over a text that might at least just as legitimately read as a patriarchal text. She considers Hidayatullah's position anti-Qur'ānic and essentially levels the same accusation against any hermeneutical approach that, first, assumes that the Qur'ān was revealed in the language of a patriarchal society and, second, doubts that it is possible for any human to uncover its 'true meaning' untainted by the reader's precommitments.[59] The rejection of human capacity to achieve certitude over the Qur'ān's message is thus easily misunderstood as a rejection of the Qur'ān's divinity although this is not the postmodernists' intention as a number of respondents to Asma Barlas pointed out.[60]

One way to deal with the dilemma between the refutation of certain meanings and the belief in a divine message, and one that seems to become more and more popular, is to consciously enter a personal dialogue with the Qur'ān. In this mode of dialogue, the existence of a divine creator and an eternal core to the Qur'ān is not denied; but at the same time, the assumption is that God would and could not expect humans to deny their upbringing, social situation, predispositions, experiences and, most importantly, their conscience when making the Qur'ān's message relevant to their own lives. This personal approach to the Qur'ān is not necessarily based on a sophisticated concept of hermeneutics, but it is based on a decidedly individualistic reading of the Qur'ān that takes into account, and reveals to the reader, the exegete's biography, commitments and relationship to the Qur'ān:[61] 'The Book of God is one, but each of us has his or her own Qur'ān'.[62]

Some exegetes carry these personal musings further: they openly admit when at certain points, the Qur'ān disrupts their relationship with God and clashes with their conscience to a degree that makes it appear insufficient to them to merely contextualise or creatively reinterpret a verse. In some cases, the result is radical rejection of individual verses for the sake of upholding the relationship with the Qur'ān as a whole.[63] The American Muslim scholar Khaled Abou El Fadl (b. 1963) famously argued that, when the Qur'ānic text clashes with a believer's conscience, the reader should make a 'conscientious pause' and reflect about the cause of the friction between text and conscience, which should be the starting point for a thorough investigation. He acknowledges that there are various venues towards a knowledge of God and of what is right, besides the Qur'ān, and that every believer should take his conscience seriously and act in accordance with it.[64]

It is obvious that understanding the Qur'ān as a clear book of guidance, as proponents of all other trends do, does not work with a postmodern approach since the text's meaning is neither clear nor immutable. Rather than guidance, it might be considered inspiration or a broad frame of reference that leaves room for many individual beliefs and practices. That approach, in turn, often enables postmodernists to have a rather more open-minded and respectful attitude towards premodern exegetical traditions than many modernists do since to them, these traditions are not distortions of the Qur'ān's original message, but genuine attempts at making sense of the text that are shaped by their historical context just as much as contemporary efforts are: the exegete's own interpretation is just as time-bound, shaped by fallible human understanding and of limited validity as that of any premodern scholar.

The following text is an example of postmodern Qur'ānic interpretation. I have consciously selected a blog entry, rather than an academic piece of writing, since blog entries and editorials are a fairly common and typically overlooked site of subjective engagements with the Qur'ān. After all, these are types of media that are by definition subjective, and in contrast to many academic writers, the authors using them make no effort to hide the personal nature of their approach.

Subjectivity and Qur'ānic interpretation in a Muslim intellectual's blog: Hakan Turan (b. 1979, Germany) on Q. 5:51

Hakan Turan was born in Ludwigsburg, a town to the north of Stuttgart that boasts both historical sites and a thriving industry. The latter attracted migrant workers from many Mediterranean countries, among them Turan's parents who came from Turkey. Turks, the majority of whom had a rural or working-class background, were the largest group of Muslim immigrants to Germany in the twentieth century. Turan studied physics, mathematics and philosophy and acquired a degree in theoretical physics. He then obtained a teaching diploma for secondary schools and has been working as a teacher since. As such, he participated in the development of a curriculum for Islamic religious education in the schools of his federal state of Baden-Württemberg.

Hakan Turan, in his blog, mentions his interest in Islamic theology, law and Qur'ānic exegesis, and more specifically, in harmonising his religion with the conditions of contemporary German society. He has expressed his interests through lectures, teaching assignments, publications in various media and, of course, his blog.

Andalusian.de, subtitled 'Of heaven, Earth and that which is between them' – covers a variety of topics, from events in Turkey to science. Topics

Excerpt 7.3

Q. 5:51

يَا أَيُّهَا الَّذِينَ آمَنُوا لَا تَتَّخِذُوا الْيَهُودَ وَالنَّصَارَىٰ أَوْلِيَاءَ بَعْضُهُمْ أَوْلِيَاءُ بَعْضٍ وَمَن يَتَوَلَّهُم مِّنكُمْ
فَإِنَّهُ مِنْهُمْ إِنَّ اللَّهَ لَا يَهْدِي الْقَوْمَ الظَّالِمِينَ ﴿٥١﴾

(51) O you who believe, do not take the Jews and the Christians as *awliyā'* (friends/protectors/allies/helpers); they are awliyā' of each other. Whoever of you makes them his awliyā' becomes one of them. God does not guide the evildoers.

May Muslims take Jews and Christians as friends?

When I was at primary school, my circle of friends contained all kinds of nationalities: Germans, Italians, Spanish, Portuguese – all of them classmates. In the mornings, we were running around the school yard together, and in the afternoons, we were sitting at our C64 computers playing *Giana Sisters* or roaming the streets of town. There were nearly no Turks. My best friend was Italian. He stood in for me with his fists when two German classmates clobbered me nearly on a daily basis on my way to school – I had attracted their anger by the imprudent claim that Turks have much more courage than Germans. One of them invited me to his wedding twenty years later. Sometimes I was invited to dinner with the Italian. Often, we strolled across the fields before sunset and talked about our parents' home towns or the jobs of our dreams. He wanted to become an architect at the time and me, a doctor.

My parents appreciated my good relationship with my classmates and I would never have thought that it could meet with anyone's disproval – until one day I met an elderly Turk who identified with political Islam which was on the rise in Turkey at the time, and he told me something that curdled my blood:

You may not be friends with these people – for the Qur'ān says: Do not take the Jews and Christians as friends. They are friends of each other.

I replied that this could not be true. Until then, I had only ever heard things about Islam that I liked, and my religion was very important to me. But my friends were important to me, too. And each attempt to internally distance myself from them broke my heart. I settled the issue by concluding, in a somewhat resigned manner, that my friends might be Christian, but that I got along with them much better than with the few Turkish children I knew at the time. God was going to understand, I was certain of that. I was equally certain that something about the Qur'ānic verse I had been presented with was not quite the way my zealous acquaintance had conveyed to me. Unfortunately, I was at the time far from able to explore the issue more thoroughly.

Years went by, but this verse, which was Q. 5:51, could be heard again and again from various quarters. Either it was from politicised pious Muslims who dreamed of an Islamic state in Turkey, who handed out their pamphlets among the Turkish population in Germany and asserted their influence in some mosques as well. Or it was from German Islamophobes who used it to rebut Muslim advocates of dialogue or in order to demonstrate that Islam is the enemy of the Western world and that a believing Muslim could, for religious reasons, never be the friend of an ordinary German. Thus, they considered superfluous each attempt to treat Muslims as citizens and humans on a par with them. For in their view, Muslims despise 'unbelievers' and therefore refuse to be a part of German society. The above-mentioned Qur'ānic verse was proof enough to them. There was no need to ask actual Muslims for their opinion.

Since then, nothing has changed about the verse and about the two positions mentioned above. What has changed, however, is my own knowledge of this verse and the Qur'ān. Through that knowledge, I had the chance to develop my own position. Taking this verse as an example, it is possible to gain insights into a host of general issues concerning the Qur'ān and Islam. Those, in turn, helped me a lot with regard to an understanding of Islam that suits the German context. I'll try to present the most important steps and arguments here, some of which are not logically dependent on each other. Let's start with the most direct approach.

1. Philology, or: does the verse really say 'to take as friends'?

My mind was put at ease when I found publications in German that problematised the wording of the verse openly. Thus, I was not the only one who had stumbled upon this verse and had been unable to harmonise it at first glance with my habits. For example, some German as well as Turkish authors pointed out that the singular *walī* of the term *awliyā'*, translated as 'friends', may mean other things as well such as 'helper', 'protector', 'leader' or even 'religious leader'. Others also considered meanings such as 'representative' or 'religious representative'. Accordingly, the verse roughly says that one is forbidden from taking Jews and Christians as spiritual leaders. I could live with that. [...] If someone had taught me earlier in my life how vast the room for interpretation is where such controversial Qur'ānic terms are concerned, I would probably have realised on my own that the Qur'ānic term *awliyā'* may have quite different meanings, most notably including some that are a lot less problematic to me. The even later realisation that Arabic offers more likely terms for the meaning of 'friend' such as *ṣadīq* and *ṣāḥib* (cf. Q. 53:2) bolstered my confidence in this interpretation.

It was thus through philological expertise that seemingly irrefutable fundamentalist arguments could be defused.

2. Consistency, or: why should we be allowed to marry someone we are forbidden from taking as friends?

I came upon the next discovery when I read a translation of the entire *sūra* for the first time. Here, you need to understand that an immediate reading of the Qur'ān is not the most common way of inquiry about Islam among Muslims. Actually, the immediate engagement with Qur'ān translations in general continues not to be particularly popular among Muslims, which explains many Muslims' striking ignorance with respect to the Qur'ān despite the fact that it is holy to them. Anyway, in the course of my reading of the Qur'an, I came across another verse, in the same *sūra* as the one mentioned above, that from my perspective made an interpretation along the lines of 'do not take Jews and Christians as friends' impossible.

For in Q. 5:5, marriage with Jewish and Christian women is explicitly permitted – without any requirement for them to change their religion. The classical Islamic law of the jurists has confirmed this rule. So, if a Muslim may marry a Christian woman and thus not only makes a Christian woman his life partner, but also turns her Christian family into relatives of his, without any necessity for a change of religion, then it is impossible, for purely logical reasons, to forbid friendship with humans of Christian faith. Logic! It's that simple.

When I met the Islamist zealot, who was basically a nice guy, again one day, I proudly confronted him with this argument which I had brooded over in restless nights and judged to be ingenious. His reaction was priceless: 'No, this is only an option if the woman converts to Islam!' So, I produced a Qur'ān translation and shoved *sūra* five under his nose (just as my friends, the critics of Islam, like to do with me). The next response was hilarious as well: 'No, I don't trust this translation'. But I had already sufficiently established from other sources that this was not a question of translation.

It was a simple question of logic, or more precisely: of logical reconcilability, that is, the consistency of Qur'ānic interpretation as a whole – coupled with a solid knowledge of seemingly contradictory sources that in reality explain each other and help to find plausible interpretations of ambiguous passages.

3. Coherence, or: what do we find if we look for greater contexts?

There were also Muslim authors who [...] pointed out that this verse might talk of Christians and Jews, but of particular Christians and Jews, rather than all of them. Specifically, it refers to those who deride the faith of Muslims. The argument of these authors was simple. One need only read a bit further in the Qur'ān to find 'Take not as your friends such as mock your faith and make a jest of it, be they from those who were given the Book before you (i.e., Jews and Christians – HT), or from the deniers' (5:57). This is a similar wording as that of 5:51, but with a decisive explanatory addition: the injunction is not to take as friends *those who ridicule Islamic faith* from among the Christians and Jews. If it was obligatory to avoid all Jews and Christians anyway, the additional descriptor in the verse would be superfluous. [...]

This means taking into account the entire textual context of a verse as it is already required in the classical theory of Qur'ānic exegesis in order to adequately understand the Qur'ān. If we read Q. 5:51 and 5:57 together they basically say: 'Do not take Jews and Christians as friends...those Jews and Christians who mock your faith and make a jest of it'.

It was thus the demand of logical interdependency, or coherence, that made it possible to read one verse as an explanation or qualification of another verse, particularly if both verses belong to the same section and can thus be understood as being associated with each other – a hermeneutical technique that is altogether known and systematised in classical Qur'ānic exegesis.

4. Reduction, or: does anyone find the actual fundamental principle?

The Qur'ān repeatedly claims to be complete and perfect in some sense. Considering the erratic and seemingly disjointed structure of many *sūra*s, this might appear to be absurd. If we understand this claim in the sense of a type of logical, rather than legalistic, completeness, however, it turns out to be extremely fruitful. Our working hypothesis would then be, just as in the previous section:

The Qur'ān, despite all its diversity, does not merely consist of individual statements that occasionally complement or explain each other; rather, it is possible to arrange them logically in a way that results in a cohesive and coherent system of meaning.

It is up to the exegete himself to recognise or produce that coherence in order to come to the really relevant meanings of the Qur'ān.

A system of clauses made coherent only becomes truly beautiful, however, when it is possible to identify fundamental principles that reduce the huge diversity to simple maxims. That means: if I find in a set of clauses one that contains or implies all others in some sense, then I can continue my actual work based on this specific clause, for the other clauses do not deliver fundamentally new information anyway. Rather, they constitute applications and examples of the more general principle.

In order to simplify matters, I will call these special generalised clauses fundamental principles. In a structure as complex as Islam, it might not be possible to reduce the entire system of thought to a single fundamental clause (or rather, we are not competent to do so), but we can certainly identify a limited number of special clauses of the kind described

Might it thus be possible to find a passage in the Qur'ān that explains the fundamental principle behind the verse 'Do not take the Christians and Jews as *awliyā'*'? Or is the verse itself already a fundamental principle and thus essential for Islam as many critics of Islam claim? The good news is this: there is a passage that makes the answer to this question abundantly clear to the detriment of the critics of Islam:

'Perhaps God may establish friendship/love (Ar., *mawadda* – HT) between you and those of them with whom you are at enmity. God is mighty and God is forgiving and compassionate.

God does not forbid you to act virtuously and with justice towards those who have not fought you over your faith and have not driven you from your houses. God loves those who act justly.

God only forbids you to make friends of those who have fought you over your faith or have driven you from your houses or helped in your expulsion. Those who make friends of them, those are the evildoers' (Q. 60:7–9).

Those passages originate (fortunately!) from the Medinan period in which the Prophet was actively leading wars, probably from the seventh or eighth year after the Muslims' exodus to Medina (the Prophet died in the eleventh year after the *hijra*). We are thus not dealing with a passage from the Meccan period in which Muslims were generally forbidden from fighting. Many critics of Islam ardently believe that the peaceful Meccan verses were abrogated by the generally martial Medinan verses, having lost their practical relevance. And they react aggressively to dissent (which is not true for the more respectable critics of Islam).

But we are not only dealing here with a relatively late Medinan passage, but it also emerged in the context of war with the idolaters from Mecca. According to a tradition, the mother of one of the Prophet's wives who was an idolater from Mecca wanted to visit her daughter in Medina despite the state of war between the cities. This verse gave her permission to do so and explained that the enemy who needs to be fought is not simply any non-Muslim, but it is those non-Muslims who fight Muslims and expel them from their homes or support that expulsion, that is, the military aggressors.

These verses not only elucidate when and why war against people of different faiths may be legitimate, but they also clarify when, exactly, friendship with people of different faiths is forbidden: when the person of different faith fights me because of my faith, expels me from my home or helps those who expel me to do so.

Now, any reasonable person and every pluralist society should be able to live quite comfortably with that qualification. […]

The passage from *sūra* 60 can be considered the more fundamental one because it drew the red lines under more extreme conditions and in a more precise manner.

Incidentally, we have demonstrated more here than we had originally intended, for verse 60:9 clearly states that even friendship with peaceful and benevolent idolaters is not forbidden. […] This is an important aspect since we are dealing, in our society, not only with Christians and Jews, but also with atheists, agnostics and adherents of other religions. Of course, these are nearly never 'idolaters'. Still, the Qur'ānic reference to the idolaters is important because these are not considered to belong to the People of the Book and at the time were the main enemies of Islam. If even those may be taken as friends as long as they are peaceful and respectful, then such friendships are surely not forbidden either where ethically fair-minded atheists and agnostics are concerned. […] One look at everyday experience demonstrates that my scenario is quite realistic and usually does not pose any problems unless one insists on creating a society based on the ideas of the classical jurists.

This, then, is my result:

Genuine friendship with non-Muslims is forbidden only under the condition that those humiliate, fight, persecute or expel me (or those close to me) because of my faith unjustly and in a degrading manner.

[…] I need to slightly put this into perspective by pointing out that it is always possible to make a text coherent in the sense of some meaning or other through the use of interpretive techniques – however, there are few possibilities of making a text coherent *in a simple and natural way*, without permanent additional assumptions, exceptions and unprovable claims of abrogation. […] The only question is: which interpretation is the most plausible and most easily reconciled with the rest of the text?

And, yes: I suspect that we have found here a very plausible interpretation and one that may be universalised.

It follows: those who do not interpret the verses discussed above as I do, but as a general prohibition against friendship with Jews and Christians will also find arguments for their point of view. However, they will come across much greater contradictions and tensions within the text than the approach presented here. The permission to marry Jewish and Christian women without any need for conversion in and by itself makes a reading of the Qur'ān that is averse to friendship [with non-Muslims] unlikely.

Thus, it is the identification of fruitful fundamental principles in the Qur'ān which imply or explain other verses that helps to remove ambiguity and 'defuse' problematic passages by reference to the Qur'ān. This makes it possible to reduce the content of individual statements to more general principles. Of course, this requires a good knowledge of the entire text and of the room for interpretation it allows.

5. Finally: the pragmatist confession

Now we have discussed Qur'ānic interpretations at length. […] The argument I have presented here culminated in the attempt, to identify those verses of the Qur'ān that may be considered fundamental principles because they implicitly contain the remainder of Qur'ānic statements. And it resulted in the conclusion that those fundamental principles differentiate and finally solve many apparent problems in a rationally comprehensible manner.

But:

I want to be honest. The deeper reason for which I become friends with non-Muslims in actual practice probably does not lie in any of the arguments I have presented, not even the entirety of these arguments.

Rather, it lies in the fact that I have grown up with these people. That I have sung and played with them in kindergarten when I was a small child. That I was welcome to their homes as a child and that even their parents had time for me. That I discovered the world of libraries, of computers and science through them. That we've been together through thick and thin, in adolescence and afterwards. That they were there for me when I needed them, just as my family and many Muslims were there for me when I needed them. That they acquainted me with philosophy, with music and with theoretical physics. That we laughed and sang together, philosophised and argued. That I have learned from them to look at my faith both from an inside and an outside perspective. That I realised that everyone considers the things he is familiar with to be the most self-evident and plausible. It was thus clear to me that non-Muslims are not per se evil deniers of an obvious truth, but that most of them have grown up with experiences completely different from mine which makes it entirely plausible for their lives to take a different path from mine.

Finally, it lies in the fact that according to what I have experienced at all stages of my life, non-Muslims might sometimes be the better Muslims.

What, now, is the logical human response to good things one experiences from one's fellow humans?

Should the reward of goodness be anything other than goodness? (Q. 55:60)

These are my biographical reasons for my friendships with non-Muslims. Those were what triggered my effort to work through the theory of Islam with regard to this matter.

But isn't it always like that in life?

I advise everyone to be honest about this and not to leave the false impression that we do everything we do only because Islam wants us to do it in precisely this manner. With many – not all – things, it is rather ourselves who want to do something and then try to provide theoretical justification in hindsight.

This does not mean that anyone can or should twist everything to get the result they want. Whoever does this will ultimately only cheat themselves. Such behaviour, that is, the conscious omission, twisting or denial of something obvious, will always be incompatible with sincere faith.

Rather, the inner desire for something in one's life may be a reason to deal with the theory behind it in more detail. Afterwards, we should be honest enough to admit to ourselves where there is compatibility and where there can be no compatibility.

How you want to live in the end is yet another question.

I thank God for having given me the opportunity to devote my attention to this fundamental issue and to come to a positive result. My endeavour might just as well have resulted in failure – in which case I would most likely have continued my positive relationship with the Germans around me, but with mixed feelings, knowing that my religion actually forbids these friendships.

But my reflections on the Qur'ān have brought me to a point where I think that my attitude towards friendship with non-Muslims is correct from an Islamic point of view. […] I admit willingly and openly that the wish was father to the thought. However, this is not a problem for me since I ended up finding good arguments. The *validity* of those arguments does thus not depend on their *genesis*. Which is, in turn, another of my working hypotheses.

Therefore, the pragmatist insight is as follows: there are pre-religious dispositions in life that largely shape our later perspective on religion. Depending on the nature of these predispositions, the logical approach to religion that comes later may confirm them to a greater or lesser extent.

In any case, we should have the courage to trust our inner feelings, and when we later study our religion, we should persevere until the end and should not allow parrots or dinosaurs to discourage us. […]

This kind of theorising might be interesting to Muslims and non-Muslims with theoretical interests. For all others, that is, the vast majority, interpersonal relations out there in real life while observing the ordinary rules of respectful coexistence are completely sufficient. They make a much greater difference than any kind of Qur'ānic exegesis, however substantiated it may be.

Therefore: Love each other and occasionally say so.

And don't think too much about ideology and *Weltanschauung* when what actually matters is merely for people to like each other and spend time with each other. Our time in this world is too short to make life difficult for ourselves and others.

On this note, *wassalām*...

Glory be to You. The only knowledge we have is what You have taught us; verily, You are the knowing, the wise...(Q. 2:32)[65]

related to Islam and interreligious dialogue play a particularly important role. This includes the description of personal spiritual experiences, conference reports, theological reflections and new interpretations of the Qur'ān, often with a modernist impetus, but respectful towards the Islamic intellectual heritage. The author's familiarity with, and affinity to, logic are apparent in many of his blog posts which are often extensive and thorough. Turan primarily uses the blog as a medium of expressing his thoughts, not so much as a site of debate. It is possible to leave a comment, but this does not happen frequently. One of his blog posts is devoted to an extensive and substantial discussion of Q. 5:51 (see Excerpt 7.3).

A blog is by definition a public diary; it presents the blog owner's personal musings, often in an informal, colloquial, sometimes humorous style. It is precisely on that consciously subjective note that the author begins and ends his reflections on Q. 5:51, a verse that constitutes one of the most central points of contention with respect to the role of Islam in pluralist societies. Q. 5:51 frequently receives attention for many reasons, one of them being the Salafi focus on *al-walā' wa'l-barā'*, the exclusive loyalty to their in-group and simultaneous severance of all ties with outsiders. Their reading of Q. 5:51 seems to confirm this principle.

The verse has also been the subject of great political controversy in Indonesia in 2016 and 2017, centring on the candidacy of a Christian for the post of governor of Jakarta. Opponents relied on Qur'ān translations that translated the term *awliyā'* in Q. 5:51 as 'leaders' (*pemimpin*), a legacy from the colonial period. Many Islamists reproached the Indonesian Ministry of Religion for having replaced that translation with 'friends' (*teman*) in a later edition, not because the prohibition against having non-Muslim friends infuriated them, but because they were convinced that the verse has a political meaning.[66]

Hakan Turan's attitude to the verse is different from that of Indonesian Muslims because his circumstances and his point of departure are different. He tackles Q. 5:51 not for political reasons, but because it creates practical and emotional problems for Muslims growing up in predominantly non-Muslim societies. Moreover, the author is aware that the verse is problematic not only to himself, but also from an outside perspective. He thus repeatedly refers in his argument to critics of Islam. In Germany, as in any other Western context, these critics of Islam have become one of the main groups who negotiate the relevance and even the meaning of the Qurʾān today, and therefore they also have become part of the audience of many exegetical texts.

The blog post does not limit itself to addressing critics of Islam or non-Muslims in general; it talks to Muslims, too, probably primarily so. The original blog post is even longer than the translation presented here and offers more detailed ideas on terminology and context. It also emphasises that this is no fatwa, no claim to religious authority, but a personal approach that might be relevant to others struggling with the same problems. The stylistic level is on the colloquial side as is appropriate for a public diary. At the same time, it strives for objectivity even when describing the subjective. The author's affinity to formal logic is obvious in the structure and the way he phrases his arguments. The matter-of-fact, real-life approach to language is also apparent in the way he writes about groups such as Turks, Muslims and Germans without any attempt to linguistically represent complex multiple identities as is rarely done in everyday communication, however much it might be thought to be desirable in cultural studies.

The repertoire of exegetical techniques is wide and mainly based on the author's own ideas. While he occasionally mentions methods of premodern Qurʾānic interpretation, he does not quote any named exegete's opinion on the verse and on the various exegetical problems it contains. Nor is it his aim to perform a full exegesis of Q. 5:51. Turan is not so much interested in explaining the verse, he is interested in its practical application, and therefore he focusses on the theme of friendship with non-Muslims.

His first approach to that theme is semantic. It concerns the meaning of the term *awliyāʾ* which is among the main exegetical problems raised by the verse. The problem is exacerbated by the use of translations because those frequently reduce or eliminate the ambiguity inherent in the Qurʾānic term *walī*.[67]

While the semantics of that term have been discussed by practically all premodern exegetes, the contextualising approaches employed by Turan take a distinctly modernist turn. This is particularly true for the connection he establishes between the themes of friendship and marriage. It probably would have occurred to few premodern exegetes to see the two institutions as interrelated since their concept of marriage involved a clear hierarchy. The modernist hermeneutical impetus is even clearer when Turan pursues the idea that the Qurʾān has 'fundamental principles', which seem to be a synonym of what other authors call *maqāṣid*. The methodology he develops in order to identify the fundamental principle governing relationships with non-Muslims is framed in logical terms. It takes into account chronology and historical context, but not in the sense of the classical abrogation theory.

Rather, the reason for which Q. 60:7–9 constitutes a higher principle than other verses, according to Turan, is the fact that this *sūra* emerged during a state of war. If even then personal relationships and fair behaviour between Muslims and non-Muslims were not categorically forbidden, Turan reasons, then the rule can be universally applied to both states of conflict and peace.

Maybe the most striking feature of Turan's hermeneutical outlook, however, is his distinctly postmodern attitude that is not merely subjective, but also aware of its own subjectivity. Turan puts his cards on the table. He knows his predispositions. He knows that his solution to the exegetical problem at hand is the solution he *wanted* to find, and he knows that it might be perfectly possible to read the Qur'ān and come to entirely different conclusions. The Qur'ān, thus, ceases to be the only arbiter of what is true and false, right and wrong; it can neither negate the exigencies of everyday life nor the reader's conscience. This is not to mean that Turan does not believe in any truth or meaning inherent to the text; he does, just as he believes in the existence of non-negotiable methods of critical inquiry that enable a reader of the Qur'ān to come closer to the truth. At the same time, he is aware of the subjectivity and imperfection of any human attempt to approach that truth.[68]

While a Qur'ānic commentary typically offers no space for such expressions of subjectivity, a blog post is the perfect media for this type of postmodern exegesis. It might be a combination of this media framework and his radically subjective and pragmatist approach that allows Turan to go further in his interpretation than most. Interpretations that allow for friendship with Christians and Jews are commonly – though not consistently – found among modernists, and some – especially in South and Southeast Asia – also consider it possible to accommodate friendships with adherents of other religions such as Hinduism and Buddhism. Atheism and agnosticism, though, are a different matter altogether. Few exegetes dare go as far as to involve atheists and agnostics in a plea for friendly relations with non-Muslims. However, as Turan's text makes clear, context matters. In Germany, 36% of the population were estimated to not adhere to any religion in 2015 while the proportion of Christians is steadily decreasing.[69] Agnostics and atheists constitute a large part of German society, and shunning them might come at a high social and personal cost. It is therefore unsurprising – although by far not commonplace – that a Muslim based in Germany would consider including this segment of the non-Muslim population into his thought process.

Recent transformations in media and media use make it likely that we will see an upswing in this type of personal approach to the Qur'ān. Individuals today – provided they have internet access – have an ever-increasing number of venues at their disposal that allow them to expose their lives, thoughts and experiences to others. The creation and publication of content on the internet has become a popular activity, and the subjectivity of that content is a given. It is not conceived as a drawback, but as a self-evident precondition of active media use. This provides a framework quite different from that of a printed work of *tafsīr* or a televangelist's sermon – a framework quite ideally suited to accommodate a postmodern reflection on the Qurʾān.

NOTES

1. Muslim feminists often point to the existence of premodern female scholars and religious authorities, but these seem to have been active predominantly in *ḥadīth* scholarship and Sufism, not in Qurʾānic exegesis, at least not where written works are concerned.
2. Written between the 1950s and 1970s; see Khurrām Shāhī, *Dānishnāmih*, vol. 1, 754.
3. The Qurʾān – if understood in a straightforward manner – gives men permission to have intercourse with the female slaves he owns (Q. 23:5–7). In actual fact, the verses, if taken literally, give women permission to have intercourse with male slaves they own as well. Exegetes have taken pains to explain why the verse only refers to men; cf. Pink, *Sunnitischer Tafsīr*, 148–153.
4. Cf. Bauer, *Gender Hierarchy in the Qur'ān*, 240–241.
5. For the English-language feminist exegetical discourse as well as the problem with the term 'feminism', see Hidayatullah, *Feminist Edges of the Qur'an*; see also Navarro, 'Approaching Feminism from the Margin'.
6. Abū Bakr, *Al-Mar'a wa-al-jindir*.
7. Lamrabet, *Femmes et hommes dans le Coran*; Lamrabet, *Le Coran et les femmes*.
8. Doorn-Harder, *Women Shaping Islam*; Mudzakir, 'Indonesian Muslim Women'.
9. The focus, here, is on problems related to the interpretation of the Qurʾān, of course, to the exclusion of other concerns of women's rights activists such as female genital mutilation which is justified by *ḥadīth*s.
10. For a discussion of exegetical approaches to that verse, see page 284, 'Epilogue: The Qurʾān, textual interpretation and authority, or: may husbands beat their wives?'
11. For a discussion of masculinity in Islam, see De Sondy, *The Crisis of Islamic Masculinities*.
12. This is a translation that lends itself to queer-friendly interpretations of the Qurʾān because it neither suggests that all humans are either male or female nor does it suggest that only male–female relationships are allowed. See Kugle, *Homosexuality in Islam*, 1.
13. Hidayatullah, *Feminist Edges of the Qur'an*, 110–123.
14. One of the foundational texts for such an approach is Esack, *Qur'an, Liberation & Pluralism*. For a larger overview, see Rahemtulla, *Qur'an of the Oppressed*.
15. El-Rouayheb, *Before Homosexuality in the Arab-Islamic World, 1500–1800*.
16. Bauer, *Die Kultur der Ambiguität*, 268–311.
17. Geissinger, 'Islam and Discourses of Same-Sex Desire'.
18. See Kugle, *Homosexuality in Islam*; Siraj, 'Islam, Homosexuality and Gay Muslims'; Shannahan, 'Some Queer Questions' with a focus on Lesbian Muslims; Hendricks, 'Islamic Texts: A Source for Acceptance.'.

19. See Mun'im Sirry's profile at <http://lsi.co.id/lsi/2012/09/17/profile-denny-ja>.
20. Sirry, 'Islam, LGBT, dan Perkawinan Sejenis'.
21. Email communication with Mun'im Sirry, 18 March 2017.
22. Sirry, *Fiqih lintas agama*; translated into English as Sirry, *Interfaith Theology*.
23. Sirry, *Scriptural Polemics*.
24. See Mun'im Sirry's faculty profiles at <http://theology.nd.edu/people/faculty/munim-sirry> and <http://kroc.nd.edu/facultystaff/faculty/munim-sirry>.
25. See Paramaditha, 'The LGBT Debate'; The Straits Times, 'Debate in Indonesia'; Lamb, 'Why LGBT Hatred Suddenly Spiked'; Feder and Hindryati, 'Indonesia is Fighting'.
26. See Lamb, 'Indonesian Police Arrest More than 140 Men'.
27. See, especially, the 2010 book by Kugle, *Homosexuality in Islam*.
28. Sirry, 'Ulama-Ulama Homoseksual'.
29. For (largely sympathetic) reports on that talk, see Florene, 'Benarkah Islam mengajarkan penolakan pada LGBTQ?'; Konde Institute, 'Melihat keberagaman seksualitas dan identitas gender secara humanis'.
30. Sirry, 'Mun'im Sirry Menafsir Kisah Nabi Luth Secara Berbeda'. Text originally in Indonesian. The translation has been approved by Mun'im Sirry and contains a few suggestions for improvement he made that correlate with the Indonesian original.
31. The pro-LGBT counterargument to this – which Mun'im Sirry does not explicitly put forward in this specific discussion – is that Lot's offer was made out of a desire to protect his guests, not because they were male, but because of the fundamental standards of hospitality that would have made an assault on one's guests an outrageous crime. See Geissinger, 'Islam and Discourses of Same-Sex Desire', 83; Kugle, *Homosexuality in Islam*, 54.
32. For this quotation and to gain a general impression of the debate see the reader comments at Sirry, 'Mun'im Sirry Menafsir Kisah Nabi Luth Secara Berbeda'.
33. Without further comment, he shared the link to his *Inspirasi.co* article at <https://www.facebook.com/masirry/posts/10153873201354373>. For a sample of criticism on social media, see Saputra, 'Ustadz Armansyah'.
34. See Ulil Abshar Abdallah's tweets of 8 February 2016 (<https://twitter.com/ulil/status/696701433278631937> and <https://twitter.com/ulil/status/696699385598464000>). For an example of the criticism he received, see Munir, 'Ulil, LGBT, dan Al-Quran'.
35. Husaini, 'Tafsir Yahudi [1]' and 'Tafsir Yahudi [2]'. The author also shared this piece on Facebook and it was published on the website of the Islamist pressure group *Front Pembela Islam* (content was lost after a change of URL).
36. Salim, 'Mengkaji "reinterpretasi" Quran'.
37. Alim, 'Menafsiri LGBT'.
38. Muhaimin, 'Islam, LGBT dan Perkawinan Sejenis'. The piece had also been shared on the website of the Islamist pressure group *Front Pembela Islam* (content was lost after a change of URL).
39. Dzulhadi, 'Gagal membela LGBT'.
40. Alifurrahman, LGBT perlu direhabilitasi.
41. Lukman, 'Islam dan pernikahan sejenis', and the subsequent clarification: Lukman, 'Tentang penciptaan, bukan pernikahan'.
42. Bälz, 'Submitting Faith to Judicial Scrutiny'.
43. Wielandt, 'Wurzeln der Schwierigkeit'.

44. Published by Dār al-Fikr, Damascus.
45. See his personal website: <http://akomari.com/السيره-الذاتيه>.
46. Al-ʿUmarī, *Al-Būṣala al-Qurʾāniyya*, back cover.
47. Ibid., 56–58. Text originally in Arabic.
48. A derogatory term for the Imami Shiʿa.
49. A rationalist school of theology that came to be associated with doctrines such as the createdness of the Qurʾān and the free will of humans and was rejected by the mainstream of Sunni Islam, especially by its more scripturalist adherents.
50. A derogatory term often used to denote a theological school that asserts that humans have free will. In fact, it has been applied to a wide variety of theological trends, but the implication was always to accuse them of denying God's omnipotence.
51. Salqīnī, *Qirāʾa fī kitāb Aḥmad Khayrī al-ʿUmarī.*
52. Wielandt, 'Wurzeln der Schwierigkeit'.
53. Hidayatullah, *Feminist Edges of the Qurʾan*, 172–173.
54. See, for example, Hidayatullah.com, 'Hermeneutika'.
55. Körner, *Revisionist Koran Hermeneutics in Contemporary Turkish University Theology*, 76–79.
56. Soroush, *Reason, Freedom, and Democracy in Islam.*
57. See Sadrzadeh, 'The Shia Shakedown'.
58. Hidayatullah, *Feminist Edges of the Qurʾan*, 194.
59. Asma Barlas, 'Secular and Feminist Critiques of the Qurʾan'.
60. Barlas' statement as well as the responses by Kecia Ali, Karen Bauer, Amina Wadud, Aysha Hidayatullah and Fatima Seedat were published in a symposium titled Feminism and Islam: Exploring the Boundaries of Critique in the *Journal of Feminist Studies in Religion* 32, no. 2 (2016), 121–142.
61. See, for example, Sardar, *Reading the Qurʾan*, 3–11.
62. Al-Bāz, *Al-Qurʾān fī Miṣr*, 277.
63. The most famous issue that this principle is applied to is the question of whether Q. 4:34 allows a husband to beat his wife. See Chaudhry, 'The Problems of Conscience and Hermeneutics'. For Muslim positions in that debate, see page 284, 'Epilogue: The Qurʾān, textual interpretation and authority, or: may husbands beat their wives?'
64. Abou El Fadl, *Speaking in God's Name*, 213.
65. Turan, 'Dürfen sich Muslime Juden und Christen zu Freunden nehmen?'. Text originally in German.
66. See, for example, Emont, 'Does the Quran Forbid Electing Christians?'
67. For a discussion of Q. 5:51 and the take of Qurʾānic commentaries on its interpretation, see Pink, 'Tradition and Ideology'.
68. Communication with the author, 26 April 2017.
69. Forschungsgruppe Weltanschauungen in Deutschland. 'Religionszugehörigkeiten in Deutschland 2015'.

EPILOGUE: THE QURʾĀN, TEXTUAL INTERPRETATION AND AUTHORITY, OR: MAY HUSBANDS BEAT THEIR WIVES?

In 2010, a Turk called Enbiya Yıldırım turned to the international, Arabic-speaking users of a Salafi message board with the following question in Arabic:

> These days, some professors at Turkish universities interpret the verse 'and beat them' [Q. 4:34] as meaning 'to avoid them, be annoyed with them, sever your relationship with them' and similar. They say that the word 'to beat' (*al-ḍarb*) is not used here in the sense of actual beating and they refer to dictionaries to support this. Moreover, these people justify their position by pointing out that beating is not appropriate in our age which is why they change the meaning of the verse. I want to ask two things: what do you think of this? And does the Arabic language give room to this kind of interpretation, meaning that when you read the verse, does this meaning come to your mind?[1]

The thread starter refers to what might be the most embattled Qurʾānic verse in the recent past: Q. 4:34, a verse that seems to give permission to a husband to beat his wife.

Q. 4:34

الرِّجَالُ قَوَّامُونَ عَلَى النِّسَاءِ بِمَا فَضَّلَ اللَّهُ بَعْضَهُمْ عَلَىٰ بَعْضٍ وَبِمَا أَنفَقُوا مِنْ أَمْوَالِهِمْ فَالصَّالِحَاتُ
قَانِتَاتٌ حَافِظَاتٌ لِّلْغَيْبِ بِمَا حَفِظَ اللَّهُ وَاللَّاتِي تَخَافُونَ نُشُوزَهُنَّ فَعِظُوهُنَّ وَاهْجُرُوهُنَّ فِي الْمَضَاجِعِ
وَاضْرِبُوهُنَّ فَإِنْ أَطَعْنَكُمْ فَلَا تَبْغُوا عَلَيْهِنَّ سَبِيلًا إِنَّ اللَّهَ كَانَ عَلِيًّا كَبِيرًا ﴿٣٤﴾

(34) Men are in charge of (or: responsible for?) women because of what God has granted some of them in preference to others and because of the possessions which they spend. The righteous women are obedient, guarding [for?] the invisible, because God has guarded [them?]. Admonish those women whose rebelliousness (?) you fear, shun them in the beds and hit them [*wa-ḍribūhunna*]. If they obey you, do not seek a way against them. God is Exalted and Great.

The translation above could be replaced by any number of rather different ones that claim to better represent the meaning because the verse is long, complex and contains several exegetical problems. But the thorniest issue it addresses is whether there might be any justification, at the beginning of the twenty-first century, for a husband to beat his wife. Regardless of what construct of marriage and gender hierarchy one holds to be preferable or even God-given, it is hard to see the act of beating his wife as a man's natural right today in the same unconcerned way that an exegete in the nineteenth or early-twentieth century might have done. For exactly that reason, the debate to which the above-mentioned thread starter refers has emerged: a debate on whether the Arabic word for 'beating', 'striking' or 'hitting', *ḍaraba*, might have an entirely different meaning here. That opinion has increasingly been promoted since the 1990s in the context of a debate on marital violence in particular and gender equality in general.[2]

The thread starter refers rather derisively to Turkish professors of theology who doubt that the Qur'ān permits husbands to beat their wives. He neglects to mention that he himself is a professor of *ḥadīth* at a theological faculty known for its modernist leanings, that of Ankara, and therefore probably involved in a controversy with his colleagues against whom he seeks ammunition. In a further statement in the thread, he claims that Turkey suffers from great problems due to its openness towards the West. One of the symptoms, according to him, is the existence of a Turkish translation of Muhammad Asad's (1900–1992) modernist English Qur'ān translation despite the fact that Asad doubts the historicity of the miracles described in the Qur'ān. Predictably, since the message board is almost exclusively frequented by Salafis, he receives much support for his stance. Respondents cite any number of Qur'ānic commentaries, from al-Ṭabarī and Ibn Kathīr to twentieth-century Saudi publications, in support of a conservative reading of the verse and bemoan the prevalence of secularist ideas. One reply particularly protests the fact that 'secularists' want to introduce legislation against marital violence in Algeria. Referring to that last piece of information, one respondent jokes that if that law is passed, and before it is enacted, one could simply hurry to beat one's wife so severely that it is sufficient for the next twenty years. Others complain about the ignorance of non-native speakers of Arabic; one person adduces evidence from a Qur'ānic verse about Job (Q. 38:44) from which, he says, it is clear that *ḍaraba* means 'to beat'. One contributor sums up the general opinion as follows:

> They want to keep up with the times and to prevent the image of Islam from being blemished, or so they claim. As if the Qur'ān gave the order to beat women as a first resort! They are at odds with the *tafsīr* of the early authorities. […] The problem is that there are all kinds of people who, when they are confronted with some accusation against Islam, start bending it [Islam] and trying to come up with baseless justifications. […For example:] 'The Qur'ān gives the order to beat women'. – Yes, it

> does, but [the important thing to ask is] are there constraints and conditions to that and should they be beaten as a first resort?[3]

Thus, the respondent points to the consensus of earlier authorities and suggests that the concerns of modernists about domestic abuse should not be answered by doubting that a husband has the right to beat his wife, but by detailing the restraints and conditions that govern the application of this rule. As other respondents explain at great detail, based on the opinions of exegetical authorities, the beating should not be severe (*ghayr mubarriḥ*), possibly only with a small implement such as a *siwāk* used for cleaning one's teeth; it should not be in the face, not be disfiguring and not break any bones – the latter provision rather calling into question whether a symbolic strike with a *siwāk* is really what the verse talks about. The quotation above emphasises that beating is not a first resort, but the last. Actually, and much in contrast to the Salafi claim to strict literalism, this cannot unequivocally be derived from the wording from the verse which says: 'Admonish those women […], shun them in the beds and hit them'. Are these three options a husband may freely choose from, should he even apply all of them, or are they consecutive, meaning that he should only hit his wife when the preceding two options have not worked? Most exegetes lean towards the last reading, probably in an attempt to restrict the applicability of wife-beating somewhat, a tendency to which the nineteenth-century exegete al-Shawkānī responds: 'The literal meaning of the Qur'ānic syntax is that the husband may do all these things when he fears *nushūz*'.[4] As the discussion on the message board shows, however, even Salafis, who often set great store by al-Shawkānī's literal readings, prefer not to go quite as far and rather present beating as a last resort. Obviously, even many of those Muslims who think that a literal application of the Qur'ān is all that is required feel a certain pressure to legitimise the verse as the following text, which is widely shared on Indonesian Salafi websites, shows:

> The enemies of Islam do not cease to throw a bad light on Islam because this religion permits the beating of wives whereas they consider that to be degrading for women. We, on the other hand, tell them: 'The Islamic sharia certainly permits the beating of wives. But we need to ask *when* beating is allowed and *who* may be beaten'.
>
> Of course, corporal punishment is administered when nothing else has worked. Good advice and shunning her in bed could not cure the wife from her immoral behaviour. When that is the case, what is better: indulging the wife in her deviation, again and again in her damaging and reprehensible behaviour that will ultimately destabilise the family and rip it apart completely? Or to take her hand in order to lead her to goodness? […] Which is better, to hit the wife lightly in order to return her to

> the straight path, or to indulge her until ultimately a divorce decision is taken through which the whole family will be split?[5]

Hitting one's wife is thus portrayed as the only means to prevent a behaviour that will lead to the destruction of one's family. This line of argument is by no means a prerogative of Salafis. The Gülenist[6] Qur'ān translator Ali Ünal, whose work has a distinct tendency towards Islamist apologetics, explains in an extensive note on Q. 4:34:

> As a general rule, God has given men greater physical strength than women and endowed them with a greater capacity for management, as the fact that even in the modern world, administrators are usually men proves. God has also charged men with the financial responsibility for the family. Again, this is not true to the same degree of all men and women; there will, of course, be some women who are better managers than some men. This is why He has made men the head of the family. [...] Men are generally responsible for the well-being and prosperity of the family members and for the management of the family. So, while the verse directs men as to how they should treat rebellious women who are of bad conduct, it guides them to a gradual means of education. [...] It should be noted that these measures are aimed at education and saving the marriage from collapse in case of a wife's rebelliousness. [...] [T]his punishment is only applicable to a truly rebellious person who is of evil conduct, a person who displays obstinacy, not only not doing her duty in the home but also one who does not care about good moral conduct; in short, such a woman is not only wronging her family, she is also wronging herself. [...] Furthermore, the Messenger condemned any unjustifiable beating'.[7]

Many authors offer even more scientific-sounding explanations for the different roles of husbands and wives within marriage and family life. For example, the Indonesian scholar Muhammad Quraish Shihab (b. 1944) who is by no means a radical opponent of women's rights explains at length how men differ from women physically and psychologically, including the common argument that women are more prone to mood swings and have less control of their emotions than men. For several pages, he tries to support this argument by appealing to the authority of Western scientists. The only of those I could identify is Anton Nemilov who published a book called *The Biological Tragedy of Women* in 1930. The other persons cited are one 'Professor Reek', supposedly an American psychologist, and one 'Cleo Dalon', another female psychologist, both of whom are said to be the authors of lengthy quotations outlining the innate differences between men and women. For example, according to these quotations, what women most long to hear from their husband is 'I love you', while what men most long to hear from their wife is 'I am proud of you'. It is impossible to find any of these persons other than on any number of apologetic Muslim websites that all copy from each other. The real source seems to be the Arabic translation of a book by an Iranian Shiʿi scholar, Murtaḍā Muṭahharī (1919–1979), called *Niẓām ḥuqūq al-mar'a* (The System of Women's Rights), who cites these persons from a Persian women's magazine in Arabic transliteration (*Rīk* or *Rayk* and *Klīf* or *Klayf Dālsūn*, but since the person is identified as female, Quraish Shihab's 'Cleo' might be correct) as witnesses for his argument that men and women have innate differences and therefore need different rights and duties.[8]

This type of scientific 'evidence' is both obscure and arbitrary, but it is also very common;[9] thus, there seems to be a need for it. In contrast to some of the Salafis who advise Enbiya Yıldırım on their message board, for the majority of Muslims dealing with Q. 4:34 today, the authority of the text is not enough. The authority of science is needed in order to bolster the authority of a more or less literal reading of the text. And that more or less literal reading with an emphasis on the light or possibly symbolic nature of the stroke and the example of the Prophet, who is said to never have beaten his wives, is what unites most Muslim scholars and intellectuals interpreting the verse.

Of course, the problems that the modernist Turkish university professors whom the thread starter mentions so disparagingly have with the verse will not be addressed by any of the justifications mentioned so far. Why should modernists feel bound by the opinions of premodern exegetical authorities when these exegetes were restrained by the prejudices of a patriarchal society? Would the beating of wives suddenly become acceptable just because the stick is rather small and is only used after having tried other means of punishment? Has God created humans in such an unequal way that it is legitimate for one type of human to hold the authority to punish the other type of human, however lightly or symbolically? These are questions raised by many modernists today, and they are hardly satisfied with the above-mentioned responses.

'Even once is too much. For if the Qur'an allows the believing men to hit the believing women, it is sanctioning domestic violence.'[10] The British writer Ziauddin Sardar (b. 1951) here, by evoking the rather recent concept of 'domestic violence', points to a problem inherent to the verse and its traditional interpretation: once the Qur'ān is seen to allow husbands to administer physical punishment to their wives, who will ensure that husbands deal with that right as responsibly as contemporary apologists usually assume they would? More fundamentally, should we consider women to be subordinate to man in any way? Sardar's response is twofold. For one thing, Sardar argues for the possibility that *ḍaraba* might not even mean 'to beat' at all. Secondly, he applies a prominent modernist approach, Fazlur Rahman's double movement theory. According to this approach, in the Qur'ān's original environment the verse constituted a step towards limiting the physical power of husbands over their wives, rather than giving them license to beat them as they liked. Seventh-century Arabia could not have accommodated a more radical change. However, the 'moral goal is to move towards a society totally free from both polygamy and misogyny and their expression through domestic violence.'[11] In contemporary societies, it is important to implement the moral goal of the verse, rather than applying it literally.[12]

The debate about these questions reveals deep-seated uncertainties, in at least parts of both camps, over the authority of the Qur'ānic text. When some modernists such as Sardar, with reference to Arabic dictionaries, strive to assign the verb *ḍaraba* a different meaning than 'to beat' or at least to question whether 'to beat' is the only possible meaning, they try to justify the authority of the text at a time at which an increasing number of non-Muslims and Muslims have difficulties with a straightforward permission or even command to a husband to physically discipline his wife. The Iranian-American clinical psychologist Laleh Bakhtiar wrote an entire English Qur'ān translation with the main intent to offer an alternative reading of Q. 4:34. Specifically, she translated *ḍaraba* as 'to go away from them', which is also a central sales argument for her book.[13]

Many modernists situate this semantic solution to their problem in a Qur'ānic interpretation that points at the fundamentally egalitarian nature of men and women in the creation narrative. They also emphasise the central doctrine of *tawḥīd*, the oneness of God which, in their opinion, makes it impossible for any created being to raise an ontological claim to authority over others.[14] The problem with finding the solution to the seemingly patriarchal message of Q. 4:34 on the semantic level, however, is that it seems rather construed which is exactly what the thread starter, in the above example, was getting at. It is akin to quoting the English expression 'realisation hit him' from a dictionary in order to show that 'to hit' does not necessarily mean 'to strike' or 'to beat'. In the phrase 'the man hit his wife', however, no native speaker of English would assume that this refers to some kind of insight, rather than a physical blow.

Even if it is assumed that *ḍaraba* might mean something different from hitting one's wife, or is at least open to such a meaning, the question would still be why God chose to use a wording that could so easily be misunderstood and continues to be understood as condoning marital violence by a large portion of Muslim scholars: the 'rereadings of verse 4:34 generally neglect to account for the existence of the word *ḍaraba* in the text of the verse at all'.[15] That word does not only lend itself to being understood as hitting, striking or beating one's wife, but as evidence shows, it was and still is extremely frequently understood that way. And this problem persists even if one argues, as an anonymous exegete does, that God has used the presumably ambiguous word *ḍaraba* in order to test men and distinguish between the morally good and the violent.[16] After all, the contributors to the message board mentioned above clearly assume, based on the verse, that the Qur'ān does not legitimise legislation against marital violence, in Algeria or elsewhere.

This is an important consideration because modernist interpretations face the same kind of impasse in other cases as well. The Qur'ān might well be understood to aim at the abolition of slavery or polygamy, but it does mention these practices in a way that makes them seem permissible. Historically, this contributed to their continuing legitimation and this is often still the case today. Legislation in order to abolish polygamy, for example, is frequently considered by Islamists as well as *'ulamā'* to be at odds with the sharia. And even if one cites the example of the Prophet in order to categorise certain practices, such as the beating of wives, as morally reprehensible, that does not change anything about the laws that grant husbands permission to do so.

Two solutions to this dilemma, in particular, come with the promise of internal consistency, but also with their own inherent problems. One of them is the Salafi approach: to radically affirm the authority of the text above all other considerations. As long as one does not allow other factors such as contemporary human rights ideals to interfere with that approach, it makes perfect sense; but we have seen that even Salafis are not always willing to fully commit to this method.

The other solution is the exact opposite and one that is currently a highly visible, but also rather marginal position. Just as Salafis radically affirm the absolute authority of the text, a small number of postmodern exegetes radically deny the absolute authority of the text. Rather, they situate it within a broader vision of God, religion and the quest for truth. While not necessarily questioning the existince of a 'true meaning' to the text, they question human capacity to identify that meaning with any certainty.

The first step towards such an attitude is to make room, in the modernist project of reading the Qur'ān as unambiguous guidance, for doubt – doubt raised by the exegete's conscience or by an instinctive reaction to the text. Khaled Abou El Fadl openly admits that his inquiries into the meaning of Q. 4:34 are motivated by his repulsion at the idea of a husband beating his wife. His quest for beauty and his repulsion by ugliness constitute standards by which he measures his understanding of the text, and his concept of God transcends the specifics of individual Qur'ānic statements:

> We search for God in the permutations of the rejuvenating text, in the enticement of beauty, in the revulsions of ugliness, in the restitutions of conscience, and in the wonders of creation. I ask my God for a guideline,

> and I always find it in beauty, for my guide is beautiful and sublime. How can The Beautiful demand of us anything but the beautiful?...I see much beauty in reason. We do not worship an irrational god; all creation testifies to the beauty of His reason....Do you know of a woman who finds beauty or dignity in a beating?...Before I ascribe to God something that torments the heart, before I admit to men the power of execution, I must weigh the possibilities in my head. If there is the glimmer of beauty to be pursued then my mind will search the subtleties of what has been said. If I have a shadow of doubt I will run to the refuge of the beautiful....By God, my sister, this is a test. For the wife beaters will be content but all others will want to scrutinize the text....I promised no conclusions, for the flow of thought can only know tentative resolutions. But if I managed to create a shadow of doubt about the permissibility of wife beatings then the pious will stay away from situations of doubt.... If I find in my heart revulsion and consternations, I take it to my Lord.[17]

Taking one decisive further step from here, the African-American Muslim intellectual and activist Amina Wadud (b. 1952) explicitly distinguishes between the divine creator and the Qur'ān which is an expression of God's intention in the imperfect, human language of seventh-century Arabia.

> Allah's knowledge could not be adequately or accurately expressed in the existing Arabic epistemology. [...] Human language limits Allah's Self-disclosure. If revelation through text must be in human language, in order for humans to even begin to understand it, then revelation cannot be divine or Ultimate. [...] the mind of the Prophet acts as a filter through which the divine disclosure takes place. Just as "Islam" reminds us that the Prophet was an ordinary, albeit exceptional, human being, he was also an ordinary, albeit exceptional, male. He was also a member of seventh-century Arabia...[18]

After a decades-long struggle to maintain the authority of the Qur'ān by reinterpreting it in a way that is compatible with gender equality, Wadud concludes, first, that new theoretical approaches to interpreting the Qur'ān will by themselves not change much about gender inequality, just as slavery was not abolished by specific Muslim scriptural interpretations.[19] Nevertheless, the Qur'ānic revelation is open to new meanings that transcend the limits of the language used to express it. These are 'directly proportionate to the facility of perception' of the recipient.[20] Still, Wadud identifies two aspects of the Qur'ān where the attribution of new meanings remains unsatisfactory to her.

> Besides the imbalanced expression of human sexuality in terms most specific to masculine, heterosexual dominance, the second place of dissatisfaction when grappling with textual inadequacies is verse 34, *surat al-nisa'*. [...] There is no getting around this one, even though I have

> tried through different methods for two decades. I simply do not and cannot condone permission for a man to 'scourge' or apply *any kind* of strike to a woman. [...] This leads me to clarify how I have finally come to say 'no' outright to the literal implementation of this passage. [...It is] unjust in the ways that human beings have come to experience and understand justice, and hence unacceptable to universal notions of human dignity.[21]

Wadud describes her own history with reading Q. 4:34 as a movement from a 'yes, but' to saying 'no' to the verse. What is more, she applies a standard of justice that is above and beyond the text, asserting that the 'text is not the only representative of the divine'.[22] Just as it was possible to abolish slavery despite the fact that the Qur'ān depicts it as permissible, gender equality can be established despite a Qur'ānic patriarchal discourse, she maintains.

This is possible, in a sense, because Wadud fundamentally questions the authority of the text in two ways. First, she argues that 'no one text can ever completely disclose the full nature of Allah and therefore can be the complete and exclusive articulation of it', thereby establishing a need for other sources, such as the reader's conscience, idea of justice and notion of human dignity. Second, she calls for Muslims to acknowledge the fact that they have always manipulated the text in accordance with the standards of their age and will continue to do so, in order to 'finally arrive at a place where we *acknowledge that we intervene* with the text'.[23] This approach assigns agency to humans in their dealing with the sacred text. At the same time, it raises the pressing question to what extent the text is still an articulation of the divine.

Where modernists have moved the Qur'ān into the centre of Muslim religious discourse in order to modernise their societies, postmodernists are questioning the Qur'ān's centrality for precisely the same reason. This involves acknowledging the existence of other sources of knowledge and standards of justice besides and even above the text. It also, very often, involves explicit criticism of the idea that the text in its present form is the exact word of God and contains God's complete and perfect message to mankind.

This is currently a fairly marginal position although it seems to become ever more visible, particularly in Iran through the ideas of Abdolkarim Soroush and others who think along similar lines. The dilemma it tries to solve is not exactly new, however. At a time at which the 'hot topic' of Qur'ānic exegesis was not the concept of gender roles, but, for example, the attributes of God, quite similar issues were at stake. What does it mean when the Qur'ān says about a fully transcendental God that he has a face, hands and a throne? Is it obligatory to believe in these things or do they have to be taken as metaphorical attributes because a different standard, that of reason, tells us to?[24] Here, too, the Qur'ān was situated in a larger framework informed by theological dogma and logic that might induce exegetes to refuse to read the text literally.[25] Ultimately, exegetes search for coherence not only within the text but also between the text and a larger frame of reference; a broader notion of truth. The particularity of the postmodern position is that it openly admits to doing so. Thus, Farid Esack wrote: '… if a choice has to be made between violence towards the text and textual legitimization of violence towards real people, then I would be comfortable to plead guilty to charges of violence against the text'.[26]

This statement points to the important fact that the concrete social ramifications of gender hierarchies are very different from those of a literal understanding of God's face. Marital violence is a real problem that, while not being caused by the Qur'ānic text, exists in legal and social spaces that are informed by notions of Islamic law, sanctioned by the Qur'ān. Consequently, and in contrast to the rather scholarly discourse on God's attributes, the discourse on marital violence is led, to a significant extent, by women activists. The field of Qur'ānic exegesis has been opened to new voices and this fact has a direct bearing on the range of Qur'ānic interpretations negotiated today.

Are there still limits to the interpretation of the Qur'ān? The answer to that question depends on an exegete's conception of the authority of the text and on the larger framework in which they embed the text. On the one hand, if the text in its transmitted form is considered divine, perfect and self-contained, there are limits to its reinterpretation, defined by its 'outer' (*ẓāhir*) meanings. On the other hand, meanings that are not apparent from the text can also be upheld, just as they have always been, because the text's authority is frequently subjugated to other factors such as *ḥadīth*, logic, theological doctrine or esoteric knowledge. The limits of interpretation are thus constantly contested and shaped by this interaction between the text itself and a larger framework of truth. However, their very existence, legitimacy and appropriateness is taken for granted by the large majority of Muslim readers of the Qur'ān today because they believe that this is the only way to ensure that the text retains both its authority and its centrality to Muslims.

There is another parallel between the debate over Q. 4:34 and the earlier debates on God's attributes. The struggle over the correct understanding of the text and its authority was embedded in power fields then and it is embedded in power fields today. What may be said and written about the Qur'ān and what reactions this entails depends on who says it where and to whom.

However, changes in media and audiences as well as the immense differences between various local and national exegetical contexts open up spaces for an ever-growing plurality of opinions. External pressures contribute to this, the most recent of those probably being the resurgence of the Jihadi-

Salafi trend in the form of the 'Islamic State' in Iraq and Syria (ISIS) – an event that compelled many Muslims to take a stand in some way or other.

My aim in this book was to describe the genealogy of contemporary Muslim engagement with the Qur'ān. This approach does not lend itself well to predictions of the future, nor would that be a plausible endeavour. Some of the roads that Muslims have taken in past decades and centuries to explore the meaning of the Qur'ān might be dead ends, but most of them continue, whether they run straight ahead, take unexpected turns, fork or intersect. Who would be able to say what future the budding trend towards postmodern scepticism has vis-à-vis the Salafi paradigm that is currently so successful? Or whether they will both flourish and engage in bitter conflicts? Will traditional scholars hold their ground or will they become insignificant? The text might be divine, but its interpretation is very much subject to human agency.

NOTES

1. Yildīrim et al., 'Fa''iẓūhunna wa'hjurūhunna fī'l-maḍāji' wa'ḍribūhunna', post no.1.
2. The debate on the verse is extensive, far exceeding the discussion of the meaning of *ḍaraba* that I outline here, and a substantial amount of scholarly literature has been produced on its interpretation. See, among others, Chaudhry, *Domestic Violence and the Islamic Tradition*; Marín, 'Disciplining Wives'; Bauer, '"Traditional" Exegeses of Q 4:34'; Scott, 'A Contextual Approach to Women's Rights in the Qur'ān'; Bauer, *Gender Hierarchy in the Qur'ān*; Klausing, 'Two 20th-Century Exegetes between Traditional Scholarship and Modern Thought'; Mahmoud, 'To Beat or Not to Beat'.
3. Yildīrim et al., 'Fa''iẓūhunna wa'hjurūhunna fī'l-maḍāji' wa'ḍribūḥunna', post no.4.
4. Al-Shawkānī, *Fatḥ al-qadīr*, vol. 1, 738.
5. This segment is found in at least two different texts on Q. 4:34, attributed to different authors. See Yahya, 'Menjawab'; Al-Atsariyyah, 'Pukulan'. Texts originally in Indonesian.
6. The movement following the Turkish religious thinker Fethullah Gülen who had a Sufi background, but was also influenced by some modernist and Islamist ideas. Instead of founding a political party, he called for a reform of Islam through education. His network embraces globalization and modern technology, but at the same time promotes a conservative morality. The Turkish government held it responsible for the failed coup of 2016 and has since branded it a terrorist organization.
7. Ünal, *The Qur'ān*, 193.
8. Shihab, *Tafsir al-Mishbāh: Pesan, kesan dan keserasian Al-Qur'an*, vo. 2, 425–427; Muṭahharī, *Niẓām ḥuqūq al-mar'a fī'l-Islām*, 198–200, 206–207.
9. See also the many examples in Bauer, *Gender Hierarchy in the Qur'ān*, 219–240.
10. Sardar, *Reading the Qur'an*, 301.
11. Ibid., 302.
12. Hidayatullah, *Feminist Edges of the Qur'an*, 65–86.

13. See the website of the project at <http://www.sublimequran.org>. For the translation of *ḍaraba*, see Bakhtiar, *The Sublime Quran*, 76.
14. Hidayatullah, *Feminist Edges of the Qur'an*, 87–122.
15. Ibid., 106.
16. Wakas M. [username], 'Wife Beating in Islam?'
17. Abou El Fadl, 'Excerpt'.
18. Wadud, *Inside the Gender Jihad*, 214.
19. Ibid., 183–184.
20. Ibid., 214.
21. Ibid., 199–200.
22. Ibid., 201.
23. Ibid., 204.
24. For a brief introduction to the debate that was central to the entire tradition of *kalām*, see Gilliot, 'Attributes of God'.
25. Norman Calder called this the 'measuring of the quranic text against…ideological structures'. See Calder, 'Tafsīr from Ṭabarī to Ibn Kathīr'.
26. See Chaudhry, *Domestic Violence and the Islamic Tradition*, 185–186, n. 162.

BIBLIOGRAPHY

Abdel Haleem, M. A. S. *The Qur'an: A New Translation*. Oxford: Oxford University Press, 2008.

ʿAbduh, Muḥammad. *Tafsīr al-Fātiḥa*. Cairo: al-Manār and Maṭbaʿat Bāb al-Khalq, 1901.

Abou El Fadl, Khaled. 'Excerpt by Khaled Abou El Fadl: "On The Beating of Wives".' *Scholar of the House*. Accessed 29 January 2018. <http://www.scholarofthehouse.org/exbykhabelfa.html>.

— *Speaking in God's Name: Islamic Law, Authority and Women*. Oxford: Oneworld, 2001.

al-Abṭaḥī, Muḥammad al-Bāqir al-Muwaḥḥid. *Al-Madkhal ilā al-tafsīr al-mawḍūʿī lil-Qurʾān al-karīm*. Najaf: Maṭbaʿat al-Ādāb, 1969.

Abū ʿAzīz, Saʿd Yūsuf Maḥmūd. *Tafsīr al-Qurʾān al-karīm lil-aṭfāl wa'l-usra al-muslima*. Cairo: Dār al-Tawfīqiyya lil-Turāth, 2010.

Abū Bakr, Umayma. *Al-Marʾa wa'l-jindir: ilghāʾ al-tamyīz al-thaqāfī wa'l-ijtimāʿī bayn al-jinsayn*. Damascus: Dār al-Fikr, 2002.

Abu Waleed. 'Refuting the Ahmadiyya Claim that Quran 16:20-21 Proves that Isa ﷷ Died.' *Exposing Ahmadiyya Community*, 25 March 2015. Accessed 18 May 2017. <http://exahmadi.blogspot.de/2015/03/refuting-ahmadiyya-claim-that-quran.html>.

Adams, Charles J. 'Abū l-Aʿlā Mawdūdī's *Tafhīm al-Qurʾān*.' In *Approaches to the History of the Interpretation of the Qurʾān*, ed. Andrew Rippin. Oxford: Clarendon, 1988, 307–323

Admin [username]. 'Edip Yuksel.' *19.org*, 7 April 2016. Accessed 6 September 2018. <http://19.org/posts/edip-yuksel>.

Al Arabiya News. 'Britain Bans Controversial Saudi Cleric al-Arifi.' *Al Arabiya English*, 25 June 2014. Accessed 26 April 2017. <http://english.alarabiya.net/en/News/world/2014/06/25/Controversial-cleric-al-Arifi-banned-from-UK-.html>.

Al-Atsariyyah, Ummu Ishaq. 'Pukulan Dalam Rangka Mendidik.' *Asy Syariah Online*, 23 April 2012. <http://asysyariah.com/pukulan-dalam-rangka-mendidik>. Also available at *Salafys.com*, February 2017. <http://www.salafys.com/2017/02/pukulan-dalam-rangka-mendidik.html>. Both accessed 23 May 2017.

Albawaba News. 'Saudi Officials Arrest Sunni Cleric.' *Al Bawaba*, 19 October 2014. Accessed 10 May 2017. <http://www.albawaba.com/news/saudi-officials-arrest-sunni-cleric-613805>.

Ali, A. Yusuf. *Qur'ān: An English Interpretation of the Holy Qur'ān, with Full Arabic Text*. Lahore: Kashmiri Bazar, 1975.

Ali, Maulvi Muhammad. *The Holy Qur-án: Containing the Arabic Text with English Translation and Commentary*. Woking: The 'Islamic Review' Office, 1917.

Alifurrahman. 'LGBT perlu direhabilitasi.' *SEWORD*. Accessed 17 March 2017. <https://seword.com/sosbud/lgbt-perlu-direhabilitasi-2rj4>.

Alim, Syahirul. 'Menafsiri LGBT.' *Coretan dan Pemikiran*, 24 February 2016. <http://fushilati.blogspot.com/2016/02/manafsiri-lgbt.html>. Also available at *Kompa-*

siana, 4 March 2016. <https://www.kompasiana.com/syahirulalimuzer/56d8f9aac8afbdab306878a6/menafsiri-lgbt>. Both accessed 17 March 2017.

Al Islam. 'Jesus.' *Al Islam: The Official Website of the Ahmadiyya Muslim Community*, n.d. Accessed 18 May 2017. <https://www.alislam.org/library/jesus>.

Al-Muwahhid, Sayfuddin. *Tafsir ad-Da'iya: Der Tafsir des Verkünders*. Istanbul: Hak Yayınları, 2014.

Al-Rasheed, Madawi. *A History of Saudi Arabia*. New York: Cambridge University Press, 2nd ed., 2010.

Alshech, Eli. 'The Doctrinal Crisis within the Salafi-Jihadi Ranks and the Emergence of Neo-Takfirism: A Historical and Doctrinal Analysis.' *Islamic Law and Society* 21 (2014): 419–452.

Ambros, Arne A. 'Beobachtungen zu Aufbau und Funktionen der gereimten klassisch-arabischen Buchtitel.' *Wiener Zeitschrift für die Kunde des Morgenlandes* 80 (1990): 13–57.

al-ʿAnqāʾ [username]. 'Īrān takhtariq al-Azhar al-sharīf wa-taṭbaʿ tafsīr al-Qurʾān al-karīm bi'l-shiʿr.' *Muntadayāt Aghnām* (internet forum), 11 March 2012. Accessed 22 May 2017. <http://www.aghnam.com.sa/vb/showthread.php?t=167192>.

Answering Islamic Skeptics. 'Evolution in Islam.' *Answering Islamic Skeptics*, n.d. Accessed 6 February 2017. <http://www.answeringislamicskeptics.com/evolution-in-islam-overview.html>.

Arberry, Arthur J. *The Koran Interpreted*. 2 vols. London: Allen & Unwin, 1955.

al-ʿArīfī, Muḥammad. 'Maʿānī sūrat al-Fātiḥa.' *YouTube*, 12 March 2015. Accessed 26 April 2017. <https://www.youtube.com/watch?v=zePahio0nMI>.

Arnaldez, Roger. 'Al-Insān al-Kāmil.' In *Encyclopaedia of Islam, Second Edition*. Leiden: Brill, 1978, vol. 4, 1237.

Asad, Muhammad. *The Message of the Qurʾān*. Bristol: The Book Foundation, 2003.

Asad, Talal. *The Idea of an Anthropology of Islam*. CCAS Occasional Paper Series. Washington: Georgetown University, 1986.

Asharq al-Awsat. 'Al-Azhar Hails First Female Interpretation of the Quran.' *Asharq al-Awsat*, 25 January 2009. Accessed 6 September 2018. <https://eng-archive.aawsat.com/theaawsat/features/al-azhar-hails-first-female-interpretation-of-the-quran>.

Asma Barlas. 'Secular and Feminist Critiques of the Qurʾan: Anti-Hermeneutics as Liberation?' *Journal of Feminist Studies in Religion* 32, no. 2 (2016): 111–121.

al-ʿAssāfī, Zabin ʿAzīz. *Al-Ibrīz fī'l-tafsīr al-mawḍūʿī li-Kitāb Allāh al-ʿazīz*. Sanaa: Markaz al-Mutafawwiq, 2012.

Ateş, Süleyman. *Kuran'da nesh meselesi*. Istanbul: Yeni Ufuklar, 1996.

Azra, Azyumardi, Dina Afrianty and Robert W. Hefner. 'Pesantren and Madrasa: Muslim Schools and National Ideals in Indonesia.' In *Schooling Islam: The Culture and Politics of Modern Muslim Education*, ed. Robert W. Hefner and Muhammad Qasim Zaman. Princeton: Princeton University Press, 2007, 172–198.

Bakhtiar, Laleh. *The Sublime Quran*. Chicago: Kazi, 15th ed., 2012.

Baljon, J. M. S. *Religion and Thought of Shāh Walī Allāh Dihlawī, 1703–1762*. Leiden: Brill, 1986.

— *Modern Muslim Koran Interpretation (1880–1960)*. Leiden: Brill, 1968.

Bälz, Kilian. 'Submitting Faith to Judicial Scrutiny through the Family Trial: The "Abû Zayd Case".' *Welt des Islams* 37, no. 2 (1997): 135–155.

al-Bannā, Ḥasan. *Five Tracts of Ḥasan al-Bannāʾ*, trans. Charles Wendell. Berkeley: University of California Press, 1978.

Bano, Masooda. *Contesting Ideologies and Struggle for Authority: State-Madrasa Engagement in Pakistan*. Religions and Development Research Programme. Birmingham: International Development Department, University of Birmingham, 2007.

Bar-Asher, Meir M. *Scripture and Exegesis in Early Imāmī Shiism*. Leiden: Brill, 1999.

al-Barbarī, Ḥusayn. 'Īrān takhtariq al-Azhar al-sharīf wa-taṭba' tafsīr al-Qur'ān al-karīm bi'l-shi'r.' *Dunyā al-waṭan*, 18 May 2012. Accessed 6 September 2018. <https://www.alwatanvoice.com/arabic/news/2012/05/18/279613.html>.

Bauer, Karen. *Gender Hierarchy in the Qur'ān: Medieval Interpretations, Modern Responses*. New York: Cambridge University Press, 2015.

— 'Justifying the Genre: A Study of Introductions to Classical Works of *Tafsīr*.' In *Aims, Methods and Contexts of Qur'anic Exegesis (2nd/8th–9th/15th c.)*, ed. Karen Bauer, 39–65. Oxford: Oxford University Press, 2013.

— '"Traditional" Exegeses of Q 4:34.' *Comparative Islamic Studies* 2, no. 2 (2006).

Bauer, Thomas. *Die Kultur der Ambiguität: Eine andere Geschichte des Islams*. Berlin: Verlag der Weltreligionen, 2011.

Bayyinah.com. 'History.' *Bayyinah.com*, n.d. Accessed 26 April 2017. <http://bayyinah.com/history.html>.

al-Bayyūmī, Muḥammad Rajab. 'Hādhā l-manhaj li'l-tarbiyya al-dīniyya yuthīr tasā'ulāt khaṭīra.' *Al-Akhbār*, 11 June 1999, 41.

al-Bāz, Muḥammad. *Al-Qur'ān fī Miṣr*. Cairo: Rawāfid lil-Nashr wa'l-Tawzī', 2016.

Bazargan, Abdolali. *In the Presence of the Sublime Qur'an: A Commentary on Part 30, Chapters 78–114*, ed. Hamid Mavani, trans. Mohammad Fani and Amir Douraghy. Laguna Hill: Payam, 2016.

— 'Kilās-i Qur'ān.' *Bazargan.org*, n.d. Accessed 6 September 2018. <http://www.bazargan.com/abdolali/main0.html>.

— 'Maqālāt wa-āthār-e qalamī: Sharḥī bar sūra-hā-ye Qur'ān.' *Bazargan.org*, n.d. Accessed 28 March 2017. <http://www.bazargan.com/abdolali/main3.html>.

— Sūra-yi 'Aṣr. *Bazargan.org*, n.d. MP3 file. Accessed 29 March 2017. <http://www.bazargan.com/abdolali/MP3/103-001-003.mp3>.

— 'Tafsīr-i sūra-yi 'Aṣr'. *Bazargan.org*, n.d. Accessed 29 March 2017. <http://www.bazargan.com/abdolali/Assr.htm>.

— 'Zindigīnāmih.' *Bazargan.org*, n.d. Accessed 29 March 2017. <http://bazargan.com/abdolali/main4.html>.

Belal, Abdul Wahid Osman. 'Ahmadiyya Refuted.' *Usislam.org*. Accessed 18 May 2017. <http://www.usislam.org/cults/ahmadiyya_refuted.htm>.

Bell, Richard and William Montgomery Watt. *Introduction to the Qur'ān*. Edinburgh: Edinburgh University Press, 1990.

Berkey, Jonathan Porter. *The Formation of Islam: Religion and Society in the Near East, 600–1800*. New York: Cambridge University Press, 2003.

Bigliardi, Stefano. 'The "Scientific Miracle of the Qur'ān": Map and Assessment.' In *Islamic Studies Today: Essays in Honor of Andrew Rippin*, ed. Majid Daneshgar and Walid A. Saleh. Leiden: Brill, 2016, 339–353.

al-Biqā'ī, Burhān al-Dīn. *Maṣā'id al-naẓar lil-ishrāf 'alā maqāṣid al-suwar*. Riyad: Maktabat al-Ma'ārif, 1987.

Biyografya. 'Talip Özdeş.' *Biyografya: Encyclopedia of Turkey's Famous People*, n.d. Accessed 17 January 2017. <http://www.biyografya.com/biyografi/2604>.

Boberg, Dirk. *Ägypten, Nağd und der Ḥiğāz: Eine Untersuchung zum religiös-politischen Verhältnis zwischen Ägypten und den Wahhabiten, 1923–1936, anhand von in Kairo veröffentlichten pro- und antiwahhabitischen Streitschriften und Presseberichten*. Bern: Peter Lang, 1991.

Brigaglia, Andrea. '*Tafsīr* and the Intellectual History of Islam in West Africa: The Nigerian Case.' In *Tafsīr and Islamic Intellectual History: Exploring the Boundaries of a Genre*, ed. Andreas Görke and Johanna Pink. Oxford: Oxford University Press, 2014, 379–415.

Brown, Daniel W. *Rethinking Tradition in Modern Islamic Thought*. Cambridge: Cambridge University Press, 1999.

van de Bruinhorst, Gerard C. '"I Didn't Want to Write This": The Social Embeddedness of Translating Moonsighting Verses of the Qur'an into Swahili.' *Journal of Qur'anic Studies* 17, no. 3 (2015): 38–74.

Buehler, Arthur F. *Recognizing Sufism: Contemplation in the Islamic Tradition*. London: I. B. Tauris, 2016.

al-Buḥayrī, Aḥmad. 'Majmaʿ al-buḥūth al-islāmiyya yuwāfiq ʿalā awwal tafsīr li'l-Qurʾān al-karīm tataqaddam bihī imrȧa.' *Al-Miṣrī al-Yawm*, 23 December 2008. Accessed 6 September 2018. <https://today.almasryalyoum.com/article2.aspx?ArticleID=191639>.

Burge, S. R. 'Jalāl al-Dīn al-Suyūṭī, the *Muʿawwidhatān* and the Modes of Exegesis.' In *Aims, Methods and Contexts of Qur'anic Exegesis (2nd/8th–9th/15th C.)*, ed. Karen Bauer. Oxford: Oxford University Press, 2013, 277–307.

Calder, Norman. '*Tafsīr* from Ṭabarī to Ibn Kathīr: Problems in the Description of a Genre, Illustrated with Reference to the Story of Abraham.' In *Approaches to the Qur'ān*, ed. Abdul-Kader Shareef and G. R. Hawting. London: Taylor & Francis, 1993, 101–140.

Campanini, Massimo. *The Qur'an: Modern Muslim Interpretations*. London: Routledge, 2011.

Carré, Olivier. *Mysticism and Politics: A Critical Reading of* Fi Zilal al-Qur'an *by Sayyid Qutb (1906–1966)*. Leiden and Boston: Brill, 2003.

Chaudhry, Ayesha S. (ed.). *Domestic Violence and the Islamic Tradition: Ethics, Law, and the Muslim Discourse on Gender*. Oxford Islamic Legal Studies. Oxford: Oxford University Press, 2013.

— 'The Problems of Conscience and Hermeneutics: A Few Contemporary Approaches.' *Comparative Islamic Studies* 2, no. 2 (2006): 157–170.

Comité Jeunesse de la mosquée Assakina de Farciennes. 'Qui est Sofiane Kabir?' *Sagesse Musulmane*, 6 December 2011. Accessed 26 April 2017. <https://sagesse-musulmane.wordpress.com/2011/12/06/qui-est-sofiane-kebir>.

Communauté Islamique Ahmadiyya. 'La mort de Jésus-Christ (a.s) selon le Saint Coran'. *Communauté Islamique Ahmadiyya*, 5 November 2015. Accessed 18 May 2017. <https://www.islam-ahmadiyya.org/croyance-doctrine-ahmadiyya/130-la-mort-de-jesus-christ-selon-le-saint-coran.html?showall=&start=7>.

Coppens, Pieter. Seeing God in this World and the Otherworld: Crossing Boundaries in Sufi Commentaries on the Qurʾān. PhD thesis, Universiteit Utrecht, 2015.

— *Seeing God in Sufi Qur'an Commentaries: Crossings between this World and the Otherworld*. Edinburgh: Edinburgh University Press, 2018.

Daily News Egypt. 'Quranists Still behind Bars despite Court Decision.' *Daily News Egypt*, 8 August 2007. Accessed 11 January 2018. <https://dailynewsegypt.com/2007/08/08/quranists-still-behind-bars-despite-court-decision>.

Dallal, Ahmad. 'The Origins and Objectives of Islamic Revivalist Thought, 1750–1850.' *Journal of the American Oriental Society* 113, no. 3 (1993): 341–359.

Daneshgar, Majid. 'An Approach to Science in the Qur'ān: Re-Examination of Ṭanṭāwī Ǧawharī's Exegesis.' *Oriente Moderno* 95, no. 1–2 (2015): 32–66.

Dar-us-Salam Publications. 'Safi-ur-Rahman al-Mubarakpuri.' *Dar-us-Salam Publications*, n.d. Accessed 20 October 2016. <https://dar-us-salam.com/authors/safiur-rahaman.htm>.

Darwaza, Muḥammad ʿIzza. *Al-Tafsīr al-ḥadīth: Tartīb al-suwar ḥasab al-nuzūl*. Beirut: Dār al-Gharb al-Islāmī, 2nd ed., 2000.

De Sondy, Amanullah. *The Crisis of Islamic Masculinities*. New York: Bloomsbury Academic, 2014.

Departemen Agama RI (ed.). *Al-Qur'an dan tafsirnya*. Jakarta: Departemen Agama RI, 4th ed., 2009.

Derveze, Izzet. *Et-tefsirü'l hadîs*. Bursa: Ekin, 2nd ed., 1997.

al-Dhahabī, Muḥammad. *Al-Tafsīr wa'l-mufassirūn*. Cairo: Dār al-Kutub al-Ḥadītha, 1961.

van Doorn-Harder, Pieternella. 'Teaching and Preaching the Qur'ān.' In *Encyclopaedia of the Qur'ān*, ed. Jane Dammen McAuliffe. Leiden: Brill, 2006, vol. 5, 205–231.

— *Women Shaping Islam: Indonesian Women Reading the Qur'an*. Urbana: University of Illinois Press, 2006.

Dressler, Markus. *Writing Religion: The Making of Turkish Alevi İslam*. Reflection and Theory in the Study of Religion. New York: Oxford University Press, 2013.

Droge, Arthur J. *The Qur'ān: A New Annotated Translation*. Bristol, CT: Equinox, 2013.

al-Dubayshī, Muḥammad. *Al-Taqwā fī'l-Qur'ān al-karīm: Dirāsa fī'l-tafsīr al-mawḍūʿī*. Cairo: Dār al-Muḥaddithīn lil-Baḥth al-ʿIlmī wa'l-Tarjama wa'l-Nashr, 2008.

Dzulhadi, Qosim Nursheha. 'Gagal membela LGBT (catatan untuk Mun'im Sirry.' *Tempo.co*, 10 March 2016. Accessed 17 March 2017. <https://indonesiana.tempo.co/read/66041/2016/03/10/adianh/gagal-membela-lgbt-catatan-untuk-mun-im-sirry>.

El-Muvahhid, Seyfuddin. *Davetçinin tefsiri*. Istanbul: Hak Yayınları, n.d.

El-Rouayheb, Khaled. *Before Homosexuality in the Arab-Islamic World, 1500–1800*. Chicago: University of Chicago Press, 2005.

Elshakry, Marwa. *Reading Darwin in Arabic, 1860–1950*. Chicago: The University of Chicago Press, 2016.

Emont, Jon. 'Does the Quran Forbid Electing Christians?' *The Atlantic*, 18 April 2017. Accessed 7 September 2018. <https://www.theatlantic.com/international/archive/2017/04/indonesia-ahok-muslim/523002>.

Ende, Werner. 'Ehe auf Zeit (*mutʿa*) in der innerislamischen Diskussion der Gegenwart.' *Die Welt des Islams* 20, no. 1 (1980): 1–43.

Ennaifer, H'mida. *Les commentaires coraniques contemporains: Analyse de leur méthodologie*. Rome: Pontificio Istituto di Studi Arabi e d'Islamistica, 1998.

Ersan, Mehmet Özgür. 'Elif -Lam -Mim.' *Mehmet Özgür Ersan*, 25 November 2014. Accessed 8 November 2016. <http://mehmetozgurersan.com/?p=367>.

Esack, Farid. *Qur'an, Liberation & Pluralism: An Islamic Perspective of Interreligious Solidarity against Oppression*. Oxford: Oneworld, 2002.

Fachrudin, Azis Anwar. 'The Face of Islam Nusantara.' *Jakarta Post*, 24 July 2015. Accessed 12 March 2017. <http://www.thejakartapost.com/news/2015/07/24/the-face-islam-nusantara.html>.

Feder, J. Lester, and Rin Hindryati. 'Indonesia is Fighting about LGBT Rights Like it Never Has Before.' *BuzzFeed.News*, 18 February 2016. Accessed 17 March 2017. <https://www.buzzfeed.com/lesterfeder/indonesia-is-fighting-about-lgbt-rights-like-it-never-has-be>.

Federspiel, Howard M. *Popular Indonesian Literature of the Qur'an*. Ithaca: Cornell University Press, 1994.

Fischer, Wolfdietrich. *Grammatik des klassischen Arabisch*. Wiesbaden: Harrassowitz, 2nd ed., 1987.

FreeQuranEducation. 'The Life of Nouman Ali Khan – VIP Show.' *YouTube*, 16 March 2014. Accessed 26 April 2017. <https://www.youtube.com/watch?v=Vqc6eEJDNZc>.

Florene, Ursula. 'Benarkah Islam mengajarkan penolakan pada LGBTQ?' *Rappler Indonesia*, 22 June 2016. Accessed 7 September 2018. <https://www.rappler.com/indonesia/137204-pandangan-islam-mengenai-lgbt>.

Forschungsgruppe Weltanschauungen in Deutschland. 'Religionszugehörigkeiten in Deutschland 2015.' *Fowid.de*, 20 December 2016. Accessed 9 March 2017. <https://fowid.de/meldung/religionszugehoerigkeiten-deutschland-2015>.

Friedmann, Yohanan. 'Aḥmadiyya.' In *Encyclopaedia of Islam, THREE*. Leiden: Brill, 2007. Accessed 5 September 2018. <http://dx.doi.org/10.1163/1573-3912_ei3_COM_0007>.

— *Prophecy Continuous: Aspects of Ahmadī Religious Thought and its Medieval Background*. New Delhi and New York: Oxford University Press, New ed., 2003.

Fudge, Bruce. 'Qurʾānic Exegesis in Medieval Islam and Modern Orientalism.' *Welt des Islams* 46, no. 2 (2006): 115–147.

— *Qurʾānic Hermeneutics: Al-Ṭabrisī and the Craft of Commentary*. London: Routledge, 2011.

Garland, David. 'What is a "History of the Present"? On Foucault's Genealogies and their Critical Preconditions.' *Punishment & Society* 16, no. 4 (2014): 365–384.

Gätje, Helmut. *Koran und Koranexegese*. Zurich: Artemis, 1971.

Geissinger, Aisha. 'Islam and Discourses of Same-Sex Desire.' In *Queer Religion*, ed. Donald L. Boisvert and Jay Emerson Johnson. Santa Barbara, CA: Praeger, 2012, vol. 1, 70–83.

al-Ghazālī, Muḥammad. *Naḥwa tafsīr mawḍūʿī li-suwar al-Qurʾān al-karīm*. Cairo: Dār al-Shurūq, 12th ed., 2011.

Gilliot, Claude. 'Attributes of God.' In *Encyclopaedia of Islam, THREE*. Leiden: Brill, 2007. Accessed 5 September 2018. <http://dx.doi.org/10.1163/1573-3912_ei3_COM_0163>.

— 'ʿAbdallāh b. ʿAbbās.' In *Encyclopaedia of Islam, THREE*. Leiden: Brill, 2012. Accessed 5 September 2018. <http://dx.doi.org/10.1163/1573-3912_ei3_COM_23549>.

Goldziher, Ignác. *Die Richtungen der islamischen Koranauslegung*. Leiden: Brill, 1920.

Görke, Andreas. 'Die Spaltung des Mondes in der modernen Koranexegese und im Internet.' *Welt des Islams* 50 (2010): 60–116.

— 'Redefining the Borders of *tafsīr*: Oral Exegesis, Lay Exegesis and Regional Particularities.' In *Tafsīr and Islamic Intellectual History: Exploring the Boundaries of a Genre*, ed. Andreas Görke and Johanna Pink, 363–380. Oxford: Oxford University Press, 2014.

Griffel, Frank. 'What Do We Mean By "Salafī"? Connecting Muḥammad ʿAbduh with Egypt's Nūr Party in Islam's Contemporary Intellectual History.' *Welt des Islams* 55 (2015): 186–220.

Ḥabannaka al-Maydānī, ʿAbd al-Raḥmān Ḥasan. *Maʿārij al-tafakkur wa-daqāʾiq al-tadabbur: Tafsīr tadabburī lil-Qurʾān al-karīm bi-ḥasab tartīb al-nuzūl wafqa manhaj kitāb 'Qawāʿid al-tadabbur al-amthal li-kitāb allāh ʿazza wa-jalla.'* Damascus: Dār al-Qalam, 2000.

Haidar, Hamza. 'After the Prophet.' *The International Reporter*, 31 January 2016. Accessed 10 May 2017. <https://theinternationalreporter.org/2016/01/31/after-the-prophet>. Site deleted; archived content available at <https://web.archive.org/web/20180611115342/https://theinternationalreporter.org/2016/01/31/after-the-prophet>, accessed 6 September 2018.

Halm, Heinz. *Shi'ism*. New York: Columbia University Press, 2nd ed., 2004.

Ḥamza, Karīmān. *Al-Lu'lu' wa'l-marjān fī tafsīr al-Qur'ān*. Cairo: Maktabat al-Shurūq al-Duwaliyya, 2nd ed., 2011.

— *Riḥlatī min al-sufūr ilā al-ḥijāb: Fī ṭarīq al-nūr*. Cairo: Dār al-I'tiṣām, 1981.

Haykel, Bernard. 'On the Nature of Salafi Thought and Action.' In *Global Salafism: Islam's New Religious Movement*, ed. Roel Meijer. London: Hurst, 2009, 33–57.

— *Revival and Reform in Islam: The Legacy of Muhammad al-Shawkanī*. Cambridge: Cambridge University Press, 2003.

Hegghammer, Thomas. 'Jihadi-Salafis or Revolutionaries? On Religion and Politics in the Study of Militant Islamism.' In *Global Salafism: Islam's New Religious Movement*, ed. Roel Meijer. London: Hurst, 2009, 244–266.

Hendricks, Muhsin. 'Islamic Texts: A Source for Acceptance of Queer Individuals into Mainstream Muslim Society.' *Equal Rights Review* 5 (2010): 31–51.

Hidayatullah, Aysha A. *Feminist Edges of the Qur'an*. Oxford: Oxford University Press, 2014.

Hidayatullah.com. 'Hermeneutika dan Infiltrasi Kristen.' *Hidayatullah.com*, 3 April 2004. Accessed 20 February 2017. <http://www.hidayatullah.com/kolom/catatan-akhir-pekan/read/2004/04/03/2486/hermeneutika-dan-infiltrasi-kristen.html>.

Ḥijābī 'Affāfī [username] et al., 'Mā al-farq bayn qawlihī ta'ālā "tajrī min taḥtihā al-anhār" wa-qawlihī "tajrī taḥtahā al-anhār".' *Multaqā Ahl al-Ḥadīth* (internet forum), thread started 20 October 2011. Accessed 20 April 2017. <http://www.ahlalhdeeth.com/vb/showthread.php?s=0e89c6a3781df28a35facd8b04781eea&t=263816>.

Hirschkind, Charles. *The Ethical Soundscape: Cassette Sermons and Islamic Counterpublics*. Cultures of History. New York: Columbia University Press, 2006.

Hourani, Albert. *Arabic Thought in the Liberal Age, 1798–1939*. Cambridge: Cambridge University Press, 1983.

Hubeali.com (ed.). *Tafseer Abu Hamza Sumali*, n.d. Accessed 22 March 2017. <http://www.hubeali.com/tafseer>.

Husaini, Adian. 'Tafsir Yahudi, Tafsir Liberal, Tafsir Iblis [1].' *Hidayatullah.com*, 6 March 2016. Accessed 17 March 2017. <https://www.hidayatullah.com/kolom/catatan-akhir-pekan/read/2016/03/06/90634/tafsir-yahudi-tafsir-liberal-tafsir-iblis-1.html>.

— 'Tafsir Yahudi, Tafsir Liberal, Tafsir Iblis [2].' *Hidayatullah.com*, 6 March 2016. Accessed 17 March 2017. <https://www.hidayatullah.com/kolom/catatan-akhir-pekan/read/2016/03/06/90642/tafsir-yahudi-tafsir-liberal-tafsir-iblis-2.html>.

Husayn, Nebil A. 'Pro-Alid Sunnis.' *Nebil A. Husayn, Ph.D.*, n.d. Accessed 10 May 2017. <http://scholar.princeton.edu/nhussen/links/pro-alid-sunnis-المنزهون%C2%A0من%C2%A0اهل%C2%A0الحديث>.

Ibn Kathīr, Abū al-Fidā' Ismā'īl b. 'Umar. *Tafsīr al-Qur'ān al-'aẓīm*. Riyad: Dār Ṭība, 1999, vol. 7.

Ibn Kathīr, 'Imād al-Dīn Ismā'īl b. 'Umar. *Al-Miṣbāḥ al-munīr fī tahdhīb Ibn Kathīr*, ed. Ṣafī al-Raḥmān al-Mubārakpūrī. Cairo: al-Maktaba al-Islāmiyya, 2008.

Idara Dawat-o Irshad. 'Qadiani Changes to the Translation of the Holy Quran.' *Idara Dawat-*

o-Irshad, n.d. Accessed May 18. 2017. <http://irshad.org/exposed/translation.php>.

Ijaz, Tahir. 'Death of Hazrat Jesus (as).' *Al Islam: The Official Website of the Ahmadiyya Muslim Community*. Accessed 18 May 2017. <https://www.alislam.org/library/articles/death-of-hazrat-jesus>.

Ikhwan, Munirul. An Indonesian Initiative to Make the Qur'an down-to-Earth: Muhammad Quraish Shihab and His School of Exegesis. PhD thesis, Freie Universität Berlin, 2015. Accessed 5 September 2018. <https://refubium.fu-berlin.de/handle/fub188/8572>.

— 'Fī taḥaddī al-dawla: "Al-Tarjama al-tafsīriyya" fī muwājahat al-khiṭāb al-dīnī al-rasmī lil-dawla al-Indūnīsiyya.' *Journal of Qur'anic Studies* 15, no. 3 (2015): 121–157.

Islam Q & A. 'More Women in Hell than Men?' *Islam Question and Answer*, 11 June 2002. Accessed 4 March 2017. <https://islamqa.info/en/21457>.

Izutsu, Toshihiko. *God and Man in the Koran: Semantics of the Koranic Weltanschauung*. Tokyo: Keio Institute of Cultural and Linguistic Studies, 1964.

al-Jābirī, Muḥammad ʿĀbid. *Fahm al-Qurʾān al-ḥakīm: Al-Tafsīr al-wāḍiḥ ḥasab tartīb al-nuzūl*. Beirut: Markaz Dirāsāt al-Waḥda al-ʿArabiyya, 2008.

— *Madkhal ilā al-Qurʾān al-karīm: Fī'l-taʿrīf bi-l-Qurʾān*. Beirut: Markaz Dirāsāt al-Waḥda al-ʿArabiyya, 2nd ed., 2007.

Jādd, ʿAmr. 'Tafsīr Karīmān Ḥamza li'l-Qurʾān laysa awwal tafsīr tuqaddimuhū imraʾa.' *Al-Yawm al-sābiʿ*, 23 December 2008. Accessed 22 February 2017. <http://www.youm7.com/story/2008/12/23/تفسير-كريمان-حمزة-للقرآن-ليس-أول-تفسير-تقدمه-امرأة/58169>.

Jalbani, Ghulam Husain. *Life of Shah Wali Allah*. New Delhi, India: Kitab Bhavan, 2006.

Jamāl al-Dīn, Murtaḍā. *Al-Uṣūl al-manhajiyya lil-tafsīr al-mawḍūʿī fī'l-Qurʾān al-karīm*. Karbala: al-Amāna al-ʿāmma lil-ʿataba al-Ḥusayniyya al-muqaddasa, 2016.

Jansen, J. J. G. *The Interpretation of the Koran in Modern Egypt*. Leiden: Brill, 2nd ed., 1980.

Jomier, Jacques. 'La revue "Al-ʿOrwa al-Wothqa" (13 mars – 16 octobre 1884) et l'autorité du coran.' *Mélanges de l'Institut Dominicain d'Études Orientales du Caire* 17 (1986): 9–36.

Jones, Alan. *The Qur'ān: Translated into English*. Cambridge: Gibb Memorial Trust, 2007.

Jung, Dietrich. *Orientalists, Islamists and the Global Public Sphere: A Genealogy of the Modern Essentialist Image of Islam*. Comparative Islamic Studies. Sheffield, UK and Oakville, CT: Equinox Pub, 2011.

Kabir, Sofiane. 'Explication de la sourate al Fâtiha.' *YouTube*, 8 September 2012. Accessed 26 April 2017. <https://www.youtube.com/watch?v=n5bhqeDlcr0>.

Karaman, Hayreddin, Mustafa Çağrıcı, İbrahim Kâfi Dönmez and Sadrettin Gümüş. *Kur'an yolu: Türkçe meâl ve tefsir*. Ankara: Diyanet İşleri Başkanlığı, 5th ed., 2014.

Keeler, Annabel and Sajjad Rizvi. 'Introduction.' In *The Spirit and the Letter: Approaches to the Esoteric Interpretation of the Qur'an*, ed. Annabel Keeler and Sajjad Rizvi, 1–47. Oxford: Oxford University Press, 2016.

Kementerian Agama Republika Indonesia, ed. *Al-Qur'an dan terjemahnya*. Jakarta: Kementerian Agama Republika Indonesia, 2013.

Kepel, Gilles. *Muslim Extremism in Egypt: The Prophet and Pharaoh*. Berkeley: University of California Press, 2003.

Kermani, Navid. 'From Revelation to Interpretation: Nasr Hamid Abu Zayd and the Literary Study of the Qur'an.' In *Modern Muslim Intellectuals and the Qur'an*, ed. Suha Taji-Farouki. Oxford: Oxford University Press, 2004, 169–192.

— 'From Revelation to Interpretation: Nasr Hamid Abu Zayd and the Literary Study of the Qur'an.' In *Modern Muslim Intellectuals and the Qur'an*. Oxford: Oxford University Press, 2006, 169–192.

Khālid, ʿAmr. *Khawāṭir Qur'āniyya: Naẓarāt fī ahdāf suwar al-Qur'ān*. Cairo: al-Dār al-ʿArabiyya lil-ʿulūm, 2004.

Khan, Ahmad. 'Islamic Tradition in an Age of Print: Editing, Printing, and Publishing the Classical Heritage.' In *Reclaiming Islamic Tradition: Modern Interpretations of the Classical Heritage*, ed. Elisabeth Kendall and Ahmad Khan. Edinburgh: Edinburgh University Press, 2016, 52–99.

Khan, Naveeda. 'Nineteen: A Story.' *Anthropological Theory* 10, no. 1–2 (2010): 112–122.

Khan, Nouman Ali. '*FULL* Divine Speech ~ Nouman Ali Khan ~ Surah Fatiha Tafsir ~ New Malaysia 2014!!' *YouTube*, 22 June 2014. Accessed 26 April 2017. <https://www.youtube.com/watch?v=KCTYgprsCAo>. Shortened version of the same lecture: 'Divine Speech - Tafsir of Surah Al Fatiha - Nouman Ali Khan - Malaysia 2014 (New).' *YouTube*, 22 June 2014. Accessed 26 April 2017. <https://www.youtube.com/watch?v=rj404-I7XPg>.

— 'Deeper Look at Al Fatihah Part 5.' *YouTube*, 12 October 2018. Accessed 6 November 2018. < https://www.youtube.com/watch?v=0RVN9byZB1o&t=804s>.

— 'GET TO KNOW: Ep. 1 - Surah Al-Fatihah - Nouman Ali Khan - Quran Weekly.' *YouTube*, 6 June 2016. Accessed 27 April 2017. <https://www.youtube.com/watch?v=_8I6BZQED7E>.

— 'Rediscovering the Fatihah Full.' *YouTube*, 1 October 2015. Accessed 26 April 2017. <https://www.youtube.com/watch?v=gja_tG3Rp88>.

Khorchide, Mouhanad. *Islam ist Barmherzigkeit: Grundzüge einer modernen Religion*. Freiburg im Breisgau: Herder, 2012.

Khurrām Shāhī, Bahā' al-Dīn. *Dānishnāmih-yi Qur'ān va Qur'ān pazhūhī*. Tehran: Dūstān-Nāhīd, 1377.

Klar, Marianna. 'Ibn Kathīr's (d: 774/1373) Treatment of the David and Uriah Narrative. The Issue of Isrā'īliyyāt and the Syrian School of Exegesis.' In *Warrior, Poet, Prophet and King: The Character of David in Judaism, Christianity and Islam*, ed. Marzena Zawanowska. Leiden: Brill, forthcoming in 2019.

Klausing, Kathrin. 'Two 20th-Century Exegetes between Traditional Scholarship and Modern Thought: Gender Concepts in the *tafsīr* of Muḥammad Ḥusayn Ṭabāṭabā'ī and al-Ṭāhir Ibn ʿĀshūr.' In *Tafsīr and Islamic Intellectual History: Exploring the Boundaries of a Genre*, ed. Andreas Görke and Johanna Pink. Oxford: Oxford University Press, 2014, 419–440.

Körner, Felix. *Revisionist Koran Hermeneutics in Contemporary Turkish University Theology*. Würzburg: Ergon, 2005.

Konde Institute. 'Melihat keberagaman seksualitas dan identitas gender secara humanis.' *Konde*.co, June 2016. Accessed 7 September 2018. <http://www.konde.co/2016/06/melihat-keberagaman-seksualitas-dan.html>.

Kugle, Scott Siraj al-Haqq. *Homosexuality in Islam: Critical Reflection on Gay, Lesbian and Transgender Muslims*. Oxford: Oneworld, 2010.

Kurzman, Charles (ed.). *Modernist Islam, 1840–1940: A Sourcebook*. Oxford: Oxford University Press, 2002.

Lacroix, Stéphane. 'Between Islamists and Liberals: Saudi Arabia's new "Islamo-

Liberal" reformists.' *Middle East Journal* 58, no. 3 (2004): 345–365.

Lacunza-Balda, Justo, and David Westerlund. 'Translations of the Quran into Swahili, and Contemporary Islamic Revival in East Africa.' In *African Islam and Islam in Africa: Encounters between Sufis and Islamists*, ed. Eva Evers Rosander, 95–126. London, 1997.

Lamb, Kate. 'Indonesian Police Arrest More than 140 Men at Alleged Gay Sauna Party.' *The Guardian*, 22 May 2017. Accessed 29 May 2017. <https://www.theguardian.com/world/2017/may/22/indonesian-police-arrest-more-than-140-men-at-alleged-gay-sauna-party>.

— 'Why LGBT Hatred Suddenly Spiked in Indonesia.' *The Guardian*, 22 February 2017. Accessed 17 March 2017. <https://www.theguardian.com/global-development-professionals-network/2017/feb/22/why-lgbt-hatred-suddenly-spiked-in-indonesia>.

Lamrabet, Asma. *Le Coran et les femmes: Une lecture de libération*. Lyon: Editions Tawhid, 2008.

— *Femmes et hommes dans le Coran: Quelle égalité?* Ozoir-la-Ferrière: Albouraq, 2012.

Lauzière, Henri. 'The Construction of Salafiyya: Reconsidering Salafism from the Perspective of Conceptual History.' *International Journal of Middle East Studies* 42, no. 3 (2010): 369–389.

— *The Making of Salafism: Islamic Reform in the Twentieth Century*. Religion, Culture, and Public Life. New York: Columbia University Press, 2016.

— 'What We Mean Versus What They Meant by "Salafi": A Reply to Frank Griffel.' *Welt des Islams* 56 (2016): 89–96.

Lukman, Fadhli. 'Islam dan pernikahan sejenis: Catatan untuk Mun'im Sirry.' *Catatan Fadhli*, 25 February 2016. Accessed 18 March 2017. <https://fadhlilawang.com/2016/02/25/islam-dan-pernikahan-sejenis-catatan-untuk-munim-sirry>.

— 'Tentang penciptaan, bukan pernikahan.' *Catatan Fadhli*, 26 February 2016. Accessed 18 March 2017. <https://fadhlilawang.com/2016/02/26/tentang-penciptaan-bukan-pernikahan>.

Luṭfī, Wāʾil. 'Tamwīl ajnabī li-manāhij al-fitna al-ṭāʾifiyya.' *Rūz al-Yūsuf*, 13 March 1999, 13–15.

Mac23190 [username]. 'Refutation of the Ahmadiyya/Qadiyaniyya Claims that 'Isa (as) is Dead.' *Ghuraba Publications*, 5 February 2014. Accessed 18 May 2017. <https://ghurabapublications.wordpress.com/2014/02/05/refutation-of-ahmadiyyaqadiyaniyya-claims-that-isa-as-is-dead>. Site deleted; archived content available at <https://web.archive.org/web/20150703193505/https://ghurabapublications.wordpress.com/2014/02/05/refutation-of-ahmadiyyaqadiyaniyya-claims-that-isa-as-is-dead>. Accessed 6 September 2018.

Mahmoud, Mohamed. 'To Beat or Not to Beat: On the Exegetical Dilemmas over Qurʾān 4:34.' *Journal of the American Oriental Society* 126 (2006): 537–550.

al-Mālikī, Ḥasan b. Farḥān. 'Tafsīr ṣādim li-sūrat al-Fātiḥa khilāfan li-mā qālahū al-mufassirūn – al-shaykh Ḥasan b. Farḥān al-Mālikī.' *YouTube*, 15 July 2013. Accessed 24 April 2017. <https://www.youtube.com/watch?v=6cRavmWeaAo>.

Malti-Douglas, Fedwa. *Medicines of the Soul: Female Bodies and Sacred Geographies in a Transnational Islam*. Berkeley: University of California Press, 2001.

Mansour, Ahmed [Aḥmad Ṣubḥī Manṣūr]. 'Polytheists and Disbelievers in the Quranic Sharia Legislations of Marriage in Islam', trans. Ahmed Fathy. *Ahl al-Qurʾān*, 23 August 2017. Accessed 29 November 2017. <http://www.ahl-alquran.com/English/show_article.php?main_id=17112>.

— 'the quranists as persecuted muslim scholars', posted by Stefan. *truth booth online*, 19 November 2007. Accessed 11 January 2018. <https://pressthat.wordpress.com/2007/11/19/the-quranists-as-persecuted-muslim-scholars>.

Manṣūr, Aḥmad Ṣubḥī. 'Al-Kāfirūn fī tashrīʿ al-zawāj al-islāmī.' *Ahl al-Qur'ān*, 23 August 2017. Accessed 29 November 2017. <http://www.ahl-alquran.com/arabic/show_article.php?main_id=17107>.

— 'Al-Masjid al-aqṣā al-ḥaqīqī fī arḍ Miṣr.' *Ahl al-Qur'ān*, 6 January 2018. Accessed 11 January 2018. <http://www.ahl-alquran.com/arabic/show_article.php?main_id=17798>.

— 'Hādhā "al-Aqṣā" fī al-Quds huwa masjid ḍarār.' *Ahl al-Qur'ān*, 9 January 2018. Accessed 11 January 2018. <http://www.ahl-alquran.com/arabic/show_article.php?main_id=17806>.

— 'Kitāb: Lā nāsikh wa-lā mansūkh fī'l Qur'ān al-karīm.' *Ahl al-Qur'ān*, n.d. Accessed 11 January 2018. <http://www.ahl-alquran.com/arabic/book_main.php?page_id=5>.

al-Marāghī, Aḥmad Muṣṭafā. *Tafsīr al-Marāghī*. Cairo: Muṣṭafā al-Bābī al-Ḥalabī wa Awlāduh, 1946.

Marín, Manuela. 'Disciplining Wives: A Historical Reading of Qur'ān 4:34.' *Studia Islamica* 97 (2003): 5–40.

Martin, Richard C. 'Inimitability.' In *Encyclopaedia of the Qur'ān*, ed. Jane Dammen McAuliffe. Leiden: Brill, 2002, vol. 2, 526–536.

Maududi, Syed Abul Aala. *Tafheemul Quran*, ed. Hafiz Khan. Ebook. San José, 2011. <http://www.quranalmajid.com/quran_tafheem.php>.

Mawsūʿat al-Nābulūsī. 'Al-Sīra al-dhātiyya li-faḍīlat al-duktūr Muḥammad al-Rātib al-Nābulusī.' *Mawsūʿat al-Nābulūsī li'l-ʿulūm al-Islāmiyya*, n.d. Accessed 26 April 2017. <http://nabulsi.com/blue/ar/biography.php>.

McAuliffe, Jane Dammen. 'The Genre Boundaries of Qur'ānic Commentary.' In *With Reverence for the Word: Medieval Scriptural Exegesis in Judaism, Christianity, and Islam*, ed. Jane Dammen McAuliffe, Barry D. Walfish and Joseph W. Goering. Oxford: Oxford University Press, 2003, 445–461.

McLarney, Ellen Anne. *Soft Force: Women in Egypt's Islamic Awakening*. Princeton: Princeton University Press, 2015.

Menk, Ismail. 'About.' *Mufti Menk*, n.d. Accessed 6 September 2018. <https://www.muftimenk.com/about-mufti-menk>.

— 'Mufti Menk – Tafseer of Surah Al Fatiha.' *YouTube*, 26 February 2011. Accessed 26 April 2017. <https://www.youtube.com/watch?v=qNA203TKo_o>.

— 'Tafseer of Surah Al Fatiha – Mufti Ismail Menk.' *YouTube*, 31 March 2013. Accessed 26 April 2017. <https://www.youtube.com/watch?v=oi00HycOQ1w>.

Messick, Brinkley Morris. *The Calligraphic State: Textual Domination and History in a Muslim Society*. Berkeley: University of California Press, 2000.

Minority Rights Group International. 'Egypt: Quranists of Egypt.' *Minority Rights Group International*, October 2017. Accessed 11 January 2018. <http://minorityrights.org/minorities/quranists-of-egypt>.

Mir, Mustansir. 'Some Features of Mawdudi's *Tafhim al-Qur'an*.' *American Journal of Islamic Social Sciences* 2 (1985): 233–244.

— 'The *Sūra* as a Unity: A Twentieth-Century Development in Qur'ān Exegesis.' In *Approaches to the Qur'ān*, ed. Abdul-Kader Shareef and G. R. Hawting. London: Routledge, 1993, 211–224.

Miracles of Quran. 'Ants: Wingless ants are all females.' *Miracles of Quran*, n.d. Accessed 27 January 2017. <http://www.speed-light.info/miracles_of_quran/ants.htm>.

— 'Evolution.' *Miracles of Quran*, n.d. Accessed 6 February 2017. <http://www.speed-light.info/miracles_of_quran/evolution.htm>.

Mirza, Younus. 'Ibn Kathīr, ʿImād Al-Dīn.' In *Encyclopaedia of Islam, THREE*. Leiden: Brill, 2012. Accessed 5 September 2018. <http://dx.doi.org/10.1163/1573-3912_ei3_COM_30853>.

Mirza, Younus Y. 'Ibn Taymiyya as Exegete: Moses' Father-in-Law and the Messengers in *Sūrat Yā Sīn*.' *Journal of Qur'anic Studies* 19, no. 1 (2017): 39–71.

Mohammed, Hafiz Sher. 'The Death of Jesus according to Islamic Sources', trans. Zahid Aziz. *The Lahore Ahmadiyya Movement*, n.d. Accessed 18 May 2017. <http://www.muslim.org/islam/deathofj.htm>.

Montasser, Khaled. 'The Mistaken Crusade against Quranists and Baha'i.' *Egypt Independent*, 7 July 2015. Accessed 11 January 2018. <https://www.egyptindependent.com/mistaken-crusade-against-quranists-and-baha-i>.

al-Mubarakpuri, Shaykh Safiu-Rahman (trans.). *Tafsir Ibn Kathir (Abridged)*. 10 vols. Riyad: Dar-us-Salam, 2nd ed., 2003.

Mudzakir, Ro'fah. 'The Indonesian Muslim Women's Movement and the Issue of Polygamy: The Aisyiyah Interpretation of Qur'an 4:3 and 4:129.' In *Approaches to the Qur'an in Contemporary Indonesia*, ed. Abdullah Saeed, 175–192. Oxford: Oxford University Press, 2005.

Mühlbeyer, Katharina. 'Aid al-Qarni – Der saudische Guttenberg.' *Alsharq*, 24 February 2012. Accessed 26 May 2017. <http://www.alsharq.de/2012/arabischehalbinsel/saudi-arabien/aid-al-qarni-der-saudische-guttenberg>.

Muhaimin, A. Wafi. 'Islam, LGBT dan Perkawinan Sejenis.' *Hidayatullah.com*, 27 February 2016. Accessed 7 September 2018. <https://www.hidayatullah.com/artikel/tsaqafah/read/2016/02/27/90233/islam-lgbt-dan-perkawinan-sejenis.html>.

Munir, Rinaldi. 'Ulil, LGBT, dan Al-Quran.' *Catatanku*, 15 February 2016. Accessed 17 March 2017. <https://rinaldimunir.wordpress.com/2016/02/15/ulil-lgbt-dan-al-quran>.

Musa, Ali Masykur. *Membumikan Islam Nusantara: Respons Islam terhadap isu-isu aktual*. Jakarta: Serambi Ilmu Semesta, 2014.

Muslimah Media Watch. 'Kariman Hamzah: Giving us a Woman's Interpretation of the Qurʾān.' *Patheos*, 31 December 2008. Accessed 22 February 2017. <http://www.patheos.com/blogs/mmw/2008/12/karim-hamzah-giving-us-a-womans-interpretation-of-the-quran>.

Mustaqim, H. Abdul. *Tafsir Juz 'Amma for Kids*. Yogyakarta: Madania Kids, 2012, vol. 2.

Muṭahharī, Murtaḍā. *Niẓām ḥuqūq al-marʾa fī'l-Islām*. Iran: Dār al-Kitāb al-Islāmī, 2005.

al-Nābulusī, Muḥammad Rātib. 'Tafsīr sūrat al-Fātiḥa 001.' *YouTube*, 9 February 2014. Accessed 26 April 2017. <https://www.youtube.com/watch?v=xX-Fw-Rnp_4&list=PLf23n9TTOK4c-nNoHSRioIOkDz1rm3dzV>.

— 'Tafsīr sūrat al-Fātiḥa 002.' *YouTube*, 9 February 2014. Accessed 26 April 2017. <https://www.youtube.com/watch?v=XKylDE_w3pY>.

— 'Tafsīr sūrat al-Fātiḥa kāmila.' *YouTube*, 27 May 2015. <https://www.youtube.com/watch?v=XmtgzGoX_ro&t=78s>; and 24 April 2013. <https://www.youtube.com/watch?v=i5adJ4pQu_A>. Both accessed 26 April 2017.

Naguib, Shuruq. 'Bint Al-Shāṭiʾ's Approach to *Tafsīr*: An Egyptian Exegete's Journey from Hermeneutics to Humanity.' *Journal of Qur'anic Studies* 17, no. 1 (2015): 45–84.

Nasr, Seyyed Hossein (ed.). *The Study Quran: A New Translation and Commentary*. New York: HarperOne, 2015.

Navarro, Laura. 'Approaching Feminism from the Margins: The Case of Islamic Feminisms.' *Alternatif Politika* (February 2016): 82–94.

Neubauer, Anna. Celle qui n'existe pas: Soufisme et autorité féminine à Istanbul. PhD thesis, Université de Neuchâtel, 2009. Accessed 5 September 2018. <https://doc.rero.ch/record/12708/files/th_NeubauerA.pdf>.

Neuwirth, Angelika. 'Form and Structure of the Qur'ān.' In *Encyclopaedia of the Qur'ān*, ed. Jane Dammen McAuliffe. Leiden: Brill, 2002, vol. 2, 245–266.

Nigeria Research Network. *Islamic Actors and Interfaith Relations in Northern Nigeria*. Policy Paper No. 1, March 2013. Accessed 4 March 2017. <https://www.qeh.ox.ac.uk/sites/www.odid.ox.ac.uk/files/nrn-pp01.pdf>.

Nispen tot Sevenaer, Christian van. *Activité humaine et Agir de dieu: le concept de 'Sunan de Dieu' dans le commentaire coranique du Manār*. Beirut: Dar El-Machreq, 1996.

Noyan Dedebaba, Bedri. *Kur'ân-ı Kerim (Manzum Meâl)*. Ankara: Feryal, 2nd ed., 2007.

NU Online. 'Apa yang dimaksud dengan Islam Nusantara?' *NU Online*, 22 April 2015. Accessed 12 March 2017. <http://www.nu.or.id/post/read/59035/apa-yang-dimaksud-dengan-islam-nusantara>.

Nur Ichwan, Moch. 'Differing Responses to an Ahmadi Translation and Exegesis: *The Holy Qur'ân* in Egypt and Indonesia.' *Archipel* 62 (2001): 143–161.

O'Connor, Kathleen Malone. 'Popular and Talismanic Uses of the Qur'ān.' In *Encyclopaedia of the Qur'ān*, ed. Jane Dammen McAuliffe. Leiden: Brill, 2004, vol. 4, 163–182.

Office of Ayatollah Sayid Mortadha Al-Qazwini. 'Biography.' *Office of Ayatollah Sayid Mortadha Al-Qazwini*, n.d. Accessed 20 August 2018. <http://alqazwini.org/biography.htm>.

The Oxford Dictionary of Islam. 'Ahl al-Quran.' *Oxford Islamic Studies Online*. Accessed 4 March 2017. <http://www.oxfordislamicstudies.com/article/opr/t125/e75>.

Özdeş, Talip. *Kur'an ve nesh problemi*. Ankara: Fecr, 2005.

Paçacı, Mehmet. 'Sola scriptura?' In *Alter Text – neuer Kontext: Koranhermeneutik in der Türkei heute*, ed. Felix Körner. Freiburg: Herder, 2006, 130–163.

Pandya, Sophia. 'Religious Change among Yemeni Women: The New Popularity of 'Amr Khaled.' *Journal of Middle East Women's Studies* 5, no. 1 (2009): 50–79.

Paramaditha, Intan. 'The LGBT Debate and the Fear of "Gerakan".' *The Jakarta Post*, 27 February 2016. Accessed 17 March 2017. <http://www.thejakartapost.com/news/2016/02/27/the-lgbt-debate-and-fear-gerakan.html>.

Pink, Johanna. 'Ein Monopol aufs Paradies? Innermuslimische Kontroversen über die Frage der Exklusivität des Zugangs zum jenseitigen Heil.' In *Zeitgenössische islamische Positionen zu Koexistenz und Gewalt*, ed. Tilman Seidensticker. Wiesbaden: Harrassowitz, 2011, 59–81.

— 'Form Follows Function: Notes on the Arrangement of Texts in Printed Qur'an Translations.' *Journal of Qur'anic Studies* 19, no. 1 (2017): 138–150.

— '"Literal Meaning" or "Correct *'aqīda*"? The Reflection of Theological Controversy in Indonesian Qur'an Translations.' *Journal of Qur'anic Studies* 17, no. 3 (2015): 100–120.

— *Neue Religionsgemeinschaften in Ägypten: Minderheiten im Spannungsfeld von Glaubensfreiheit, öffentlicher Ordnung und Islam*. Würzburg: Ergon, 2003.

—'Riḍā, Rashīd.' In *Encyclopaedia of the Qur'ān Supplement*. Leiden: Brill, 2017. Accessed 5 September 2018. <http://referenceworks.brillonline.com/entries/encyclopaedia-of-the-quran/rida-rashid-EQCOM_050503>.

— 'Striving for a New Exegesis of the Qur'ān.' In *The Oxford Handbook of Islamic Theology*, ed. Sabine Schmidtke. Oxford: Oxford University Press, 2016, 765–792.

— *Sunnitischer Tafsīr in der modernen islamischen Welt: Akademische Traditionen, Popularisierung und nationalstaatliche Interessen*. Leiden: Brill, 2011.

— 'The Fig, the Olive, and the Cycles of Prophethood: Q 95:1–3 and the Image of History in Early 20th-Century Qur'anic Exegesis.' In *Islamic Studies Today: Articles in Honor of Andrew Rippin*, ed. Walid Saleh and Majid Daneshgar. Leiden: Brill, 2016, 317–338.

— 'The Global Islamic Tradition and the Nation State in the Contemporary Muslim Exegesis of the Qur'an.' In *New Trends in Qur'anic Studies*, ed. Mun 'im Sirry. International Qur'anic Studies Association Series, forthcoming.

— 'Tradition and Ideology in Contemporary Sunnite Qur'anic Exegesis: Qur'anic Commentaries from the Arab World, Turkey and Indonesia and their Interpretation of Q 5:51.' *Welt des Islams* 50, no. 1 (2010): 3–59.

— 'Tradition, Authority and Innovation in Contemporary Sunni Tafsir: Towards a Typology of Qur'anic Commentaries from the Arab World, Indonesia and Turkey.' *Journal of Qur'anic Studies* 12 (2010): 56–82.

— 'Where Does Modernity Begin? Muhammad al-Shawkānī and the Tradition of *Tafsīr*.' In *Tafsīr and Islamic Intellectual History: Exploring the Boundaries of a Genre*, ed. Johanna Pink and Andreas Görke. Oxford: Oxford University Press, 2014, 325–362.

— ''Abduh, Muḥammad.' In *Encyclopaedia of the Qur'ān Supplement*. Leiden: Brill, 2015. Accessed 5 September 2018. <http://referenceworks.brillonline.com/entries/encyclopaedia-of-the-quran/abduh-muhammad-EQCOM_050483>.

Poonawala, Ismail K. 'Taʾwīl.' In *Encyclopaedia of Islam, Second Edition*. Leiden: Brill, 2000, vol. 10, 390–392.

— 'Translatability of the Qur'an: Theological and Literary Considerations.' In *Translation of Scripture: Proceedings of a Conference at the Annenberg Research Institute May 15–16, 1989*. A Jewish Quarterly Review Supplement. Philadelphia, 1990, 161–192.

porus [username]. 'Syedna Is a Star Created by Imam Hussain.' *Dawoodi Bohra Forum* (internet forum), 3 April 2011, post no. 74. Accessed 8 November 2016. <http://www.dawoodi-bohras.com/forum/viewtopic.php?t=5911&start=60>.

Preckel, Claudia. 'Islamische Reform im Indien des 19. Jahrhunderts: Aufstieg und Fall von Muḥammad Ṣiddīq Ḥasan Ḫan, Nawwāb von Bhopal.' In *Die islamische Welt als Netzwerk: Möglichkeiten und Grenzen des Netzwerkansatzes im islamischen Kontext*. Würzburg: Ergon, 2000, 239–256.

Qadhi, Yasir. 'Tafsir Surat al-Fatihah 18: The path of those who are astray ~ Dr. Yasir Qadhi | 24th July 2014.' *YouTube*, 28 July 2014. Accessed 26 April 2017. <https://www.youtube.com/watch?v=Xtoylv5U8Xk>.

— 'Shaykh Dr Yasir Qadhi: Official YouTube Channel.' *YouTube*, n.d. Accessed 26 April 2017. <https://www.youtube.com/user/YasirQadhi/about>.

al-Qarnī, ʿĀʾiḍ b. ʿAbdallāh. *Al-Tafsīr al-muyassar*. Riyad, 2nd ed., 2007.

Qarʿāwī, Sulaimān b. Ṣāliḥ. *Dirāsāt min al-tafsīr al-mawḍūʿī*. Riyad: Dār al-Tadmuriyya, 2003.

al-Qāsimī, Ẓāfir. *Jamāl al-Dīn al-Qāsimī wa-ʿaṣruhū*. Damascus: Maktabat Aṭlas, 1965.

al-Qazwīnī, Murtaḍā. 'Tafsīr al-Qur'ān al-karīm: Sūrat al-Fātiḥa al-ḥalqa (3) al-āya 6 – Āyat Allāh al-Sayyid Murtaḍā al-Qazwīnī.' *YouTube*, 24 December 2014. Accessed 26 April 2017. <https://www.youtube.com/watch?v=m-awmUsmGt4>.

QTafsir.com. *Quran Tafsir Ibn Kathir*. Accessed 18 October 2016. <http://www.qtafsir.com>.

Quṭb, Sayyid. *Al-'Adāla al-ijtimā'iyya fī'l-Islām*. Cairo: 'Īsā al-Bābī al-Ḥalabī, 5th ed., 1958.

— *Sayyid Qutb and Islamic Activism: A Translation and Critical Analysis of Social Justice in Islam*, trans. William E. Shepard. Leiden: E. J. Brill, 1996.

Rahemtulla, Shadaab. *Qur'an of the Oppressed: Liberation Theology and Gender Justice in Islam*. New York: Oxford University Press, 2017.

Rahman, Fazlur. *Islam and Modernity: Transformation of an Intellectual Tradition*. Chicago: University of Chicago Press, 1982.

— *Major Themes of the Qur'ān*. Minneapolis: Bibliotheca Islamica, 1980.

— 'Some Key Ethical Concepts of the Qur'ān.' *Journal of Religious Ethics* 11 (1983): 170–185.

Rahman, Yusuf. 'The Controversy around H. B. Jassin: A Study of His *Al-Quranu'l-Karim Bacaan Mulia* and *Al-Qur'an Al-Karim Berjawah Puisia*.' In *Approaches to the Qur'an in Contemporary Indonesia*, ed. Abdullah Saeed, 85–105. Oxford: Oxford University Press, 2005.

Raven, Wim. 'Sīra and the Qur'ān.' In *Encyclopaedia of the Qur'ān Supplement*. Leiden: Brill, 2016. Accessed 5 September 2018. <http://referenceworks.brillonline.com/entries/encyclopaedia-of-the-quran/sira-and-the-quran-supplement-2016-EQCOM_050498>.

Riexinger, Martin. 'Islamic Opposition to the Darwinian Theory of Evolution.' In *Handbook of Religion and the Authority of Science*, ed. Olav Hammer and James R. Lewis. Leiden: Brill, 2011, 483–510.

— 'Propagating Islamic Creationism on the Internet.' *Masaryk University Journal of Law and Technology* 2, no. 2 (2008): 99–112.

— 'Responses of South Asian Muslims to the Theory of Evolution.' *Die Welt des Islams* 49, no. 2 (2009): 212–247.

Rippin, Andrew. 'Abrogation.' In *Encyclopaedia of Islam, THREE*. Leiden: Brill, 2013. Accessed 5 September 2018. <http://dx.doi.org/10.1163/1573-3912_ei3_COM_0104>.

— 'Occasions of Revelation.' In *Encyclopaedia of the Qur'ān*, ed. Jane Dammen McAuliffe. Leiden: Brill, 2003, vol. 3, 569–573.

— 'The Contemporary Translation of Classical Works of *Tafsīr*.' In *Tafsīr and Islamic Intellectual History: Exploring the Boundaries of a Genre*. Oxford: Oxford University Press, 2014, 467–489.

Robinson, Francis. 'Perso-Islamic Culture in India from the Seventeenth to the Early Twentieth Century.' In *Turko-Persia in Historical Perspective*, ed. Robert L. Canfield. Cambridge: Cambridge University Press, 1991, 104–131.

Robson, James. 'Ḥadīth.' In *Encyclopaedia of Islam, Second Edition*. Leiden: Brill, 1971, vol. 3, 23–29.

Rock, Aaron. 'Amr Khaled: From *Da'wa* to Political and Religious Leadership.' *British Journal of Middle Eastern Studies* 37, no. 1 (2010): 15–37.

Saad, Elias N. *Social History of Timbuktu: The Role of Muslim Scholars and Notables, 1400–1900*. Cambridge Studies in Islamic Civilization. Cambridge: Cambridge University Press, 2010.

Sadrzadeh, Ali. 'The Shia Shakedown.' *Qantara.de*, 16 November 2016. Accessed 30 March 2017. <https://en.qantara.de/content/iranian-scholars-in-exile-the-shia-shakedown?nopaging=1>.

Sagir, Fatma. *Diversität und Anerkennung: Eine kritische Studie der Texte des zeitgenössischen islamischen Denkers Asghar Ali Engineer (Indien 1939–2013)*. Berlin: Wissenschaftlicher Verlag, 2015.

Sairio, Anni, and Minna Palander-Collin. 'The Reconstruction of Prestige Patterns in Language History.' In *The Handbook of Historical Sociolinguistics*, ed. Juan Manuel Hernández-Campoy and Juan Camilo Conde-Silvestre. Chichester, UK: Wiley, 2012, 626–638.

Saleh, Fauzan. *Modern Trends in Islamic Theological Discourse in 20th Century Indonesia: A Critical Survey*. Leiden: Brill, 2001.

Saleh, Walid A. 'A Fifteenth-Century Muslim Hebraist: Al-Biqāʿī and his Defense of Using the Bible to Interpret the Qurʾān.' *Speculum* 83, no. 3 (2008): 629–654.

— 'Ibn Taymiyya and the Rise of Radical Hermeneutics: An Analysis of *An Introduction to the Foundations of Qurʾānic Exegesis*.' In *Ibn Taymiyya and His Times*, ed. Yossef Rapoport and Shahab Ahmed. Oxford: Oxford University Press, 2010, 123–162.

— 'Preliminary Remarks on the Historiography of *Tafsīr* in Arabic: A History of the Book Approach.' *Journal of Qurʾanic Studies* 12 (2010): 6–40.

— *The Formation of the Classical* Tafsīr *Tradition: The Qurʾān Commentary of al-Thaʿlabī (d. 427/1035)*. Leiden: Brill, 2004.

— 'The Gloss as Intellectual History: The *Ḥāshiyah*s on *al-Kashshāf*.' *Oriens* 41 (2013): 217–259.

Salim, Fahmi. 'Mengkaji "reinterpretasi" Quran soal homoseksual.' *Hidayatullah.com*, 29 February 2016. Accessed 17 March 2017. <https://www.hidayatullah.com/artikel/tsaqafah/read/2016/02/29/90308/mengkaji-reinterpretasi-quran-soal-homoseksual.html>.

Salqīnī, Ibrāhīm ʿAbdallāh. *Qirāʾa fī kitāb Aḥmad Khayrī al-ʿUmarī: Al-Būṣala al-Qurʾāniyya*. 29 February 2016. Accessed 17 January 2017. <https://isalkini.com/2016/02/29/قراءة-في-كتاب-أحمد-خيري-العمري-البوصلة>.

Sands, Kristin Zahra. 'Making it Plain: Sufi Commentaries in English in the Twentieth Century.' In *The Spirit and the Letter: Approaches to the Esoteric Interpretation of the Qur'an*, ed. Annabel Keeler and Sajjad Rizvi. Oxford: Oxford University Press, 2016, 155–176.

Saputra, Dimas. 'Ustadz Armansyah menantang debat terbuka Mun'im Sirry, jawaban untuk Inspirasi.co.' *Dimas Saputra*, February 2016. Accessed 17 March 2017. <http://dimaskung.blogspot.com/2016/02/ustadz-armansyah-menantang-debat.html>.

Sardar, Ziauddin. *Explorations in Islamic Science*. London and New York: Mansell, 1989.

— *Reading the Qur'an: The Contemporary Relevance of the Sacred Text of Islam*. Oxford: Oxford University Press, 2011.

Sargut, Cemalnur. *Âyetü'l-kürsî*, n.p.: n.p., 2013.

— *Kur'an ile var olmak*. Ed. Ferda Yıldırım, 2014.

Sauer, Rebecca. '*Tafsīr* between Law and Exegesis: The Case of Q. 49:9.' In *Tafsīr and Islamic Intellectual History: Exploring the Boundaries of a Genre*, ed. Andreas Görke and Johanna Pink. Oxford: Oxford University Press, 2014.

Scott, Rachel M. 'A Contextual Approach to Women's Rights in the Qur'ān: Readings of 4:34.' *The Muslim World* 99, no. 1 (January 2009): 60–85.

Sedgwick, Mark J. *Muhammad Abduh*. Makers of the Muslim World. Oxford: Oneworld, 2010.

Sevea, Iqbal Singh. 'The Ahmadiyya Print Jihad in South and Southeast Asia.' In *Islamic Connections: Muslim Societies in South and Southeast Asia*, ed. R. Michael Feener and Terenjit Sevea, 134–148. ISEAS Series on Islam. Singapore: Institute of Southeast Asian Studies, 2009.

Seyyid Hakkı. 'Elif-Lam-Mim sıfatları.' *Seyyid Hakkı*, n.d. Accessed 8 November 2016. <http://uludivan.de.tl/Elif_Lam_Mim-s%26%23305%3Bfatlar%26%23305%3B.htm>.

Shafīq, Sulaymān. 'Al-tasāmū…al-farīḍa al-ghā'iba fī Miṣr al-ān.' *Al-Ahālī*, 26 May 1999, 1.

Shaltūt, Maḥmūd. *Tafsīr al-Qur'ān al-karīm: Al-ajzā' al-'ashara al-ūlā*. Cairo: Dār al-Shurūq, 12th ed., 2004.

Shannahan, D. S. 'Some Queer Questions from a Muslim Faith Perspective.' *Sexualities* 13, no. 6 (2010): 671–684.

al-Sha'rāwī, Muḥammad Mutawallī. 'Tafsīr sūrat al-Fātiḥa li'l-shaykh al-Sha'rāwī al-ḥalqa al-ūlā.' *YouTube*, 9 July 2011. Accessed 26 April 2017. <https://www.youtube.com/watch?v=ZQIpwI1APHY&list=PL47BCDC254119AFB9>.

al-Sharq al-Awsaṭ. 'Karīmān Ḥamza: Tafsīrī laysa nisā'iyya…bal yukhāṭib al-rijāl wa'l-nisā' wa'l-kibār wa'l-ṣighār fī shakl "ḥawādīth" ḥāniyya.' *Al-Sharq al-Awsaṭ*, 24 February 2009. Accessed 6 September 2018. <http://archive.aawsat.com/details.asp?section=17&article=508379&issueno=11046#.W5E4gC3aGis>.

Shavit, Uriya. 'The Evolution of Darwin to a "Unique Christian Species" in Modernist-Apologetic Arab-Islamic Thought.' *Islam and Christian–Muslim Relations* 26, no. 1 (2 January 2015): 17–32.

al-Shawkānī, Muḥammad. *Fatḥ al-qadīr al-jāmi' bayn fannay al-riwāya wa'l-dirāya min 'ilm al-tafsīr*, ed. 'Abd al-Raḥmān 'Amīra. Cairo: Dār al-Wafā', 1994.

Shihab, Muhammad Quraish. *Tafsir al-Mishbāh: Pesan, kesan dan keserasian Al-Qur'an*. 15 vols. Jakarta: Lentera Hati, 2000.

— *Tafsir al-Qur'an al-Karim: Tafsir atas surat-surat pendek berdasarkan turunnya wahya*. Bandung: Pustaka Hidayah, 1997.

— *Wawasan al-Quran: Tafsir tematik atas pelbagai persoalan umat*. Bandung: Mizan, 2013.

al-Shihrī, 'Abd al-Raḥmān. 'Ṣadara ḥadīthan Al-Durr al-nathīr fī ikhtiṣār Ibn Kathīr li'l-duktūr Muḥammad Mūsā Āl Naṣr.' *Multaqā Ahl al-tafsīr* (internet forum), 26 December 2006. Accessed 10 March 2017. <https://vb.tafsir.net/tafsir7065/#.WMJs7LH_VGM>.

al-Sibā'ī, Iqbāl. 'Qaṣā'id shi'r li-tafsīr al-Qur'ān.' *Masress*, 3 October 2009. Accessed 19 May 2017. <http://www.masress.com/rosaweekly/21552>.

Siraj, Asifa. 'Islam, Homosexuality and Gay Muslims: Bridging the Gap between Faith and Sexuality.' In *Queering Religion, Religious Queers*, ed. Yvette Taylor and Ria Snowdon. New York: Routledge, Taylor & Francis Group, 2014, 194–210.

Sirry, Mun'im A. (ed.). *Fiqih lintas agama: Membangun masyarakat inklusif-pluralis*. Jakarta: Yayasan Wakaf Paramadina/Asia Foundation, 2004.

— (ed.). *Interfaith Theology: Responses of Progressive Indonesian Muslims*. Jakarta, Indonesia: International Center for Islam and Pluralism, 2006.

— 'Islam, LGBT, dan Perkawinan Sejenis.' *Tempo.co*, 2 March 2016. Accessed 17 March 2017. <https://indonesiana.tempo.co/read/64822/2016/03/02/masirry/islam-lgbt-dan-perkawinan-sejenis>.

— 'Mun'im Sirry Menafsir Kisah Nabi Luth Secara Berbeda.' *Inspirasi.co*, 20 February 2016. Accessed 16 March 2017. <https://www.inspirasi.co/post/detail/5806/munim-sirry-menafsir-kisah-nabi-luth-secara-berbeda>.

— *Scriptural Polemics: The Qur'an and Other Religions*. Oxford: Oxford University Press, 2014.

— 'Ulama-Ulama Homoseksual.' *GeoTimes*, 16 September 2016. Accessed 17 March 2017. <http://geotimes.co.id/ulama-ulama-homoseksual/#gs.Z44F4hs>.

Smith, Jane I. *An Historical and Semantic Study of the term 'Islām' as Seen in a Sequence of Qur'ān Commentaries*. Missoula: Scholars Press, 1975.

Soileau, Mark. 'Conforming Haji Bektash: A Saint and his Followers between Orthopraxy and Heteropraxy.' *Welt des Islams* 54 (2014): 423–459.

Solihu, Abdul Kabir Hussain. 'The Earliest Yoruba Translation of the Qur'an: Missionary Engagement with Islam in Yorubaland.' *Journal of Qur'anic Studies* 15, no. 3 (2015), 10–37.

Soroush, Abdolkarim. *Reason, Freedom, and Democracy in Islam: Essential Writings of Abdolkarim Soroush*, ed. Mahmoud Sadri and Ahmad Sadri. Oxford: Oxford University Press, 2002.

Stewart, Devin. 'Rhymed Prose.' In *Encyclopaedia of the Qur'ān*, ed. Jane Dammen McAuliffe. Leiden: Brill, 2006, vol. 4, 476–484.

The Straits Times. 'Debate in Indonesia on LGBT Issue.' *The Straits Times*, 24 February 2016. Accessed 17 March 2017. <http://www.straitstimes.com/asia/se-asia/debate-in-indonesia-on-lgbt-issue>.

Sulaymān, Muṣṭafā. 'Mashrūʿukum al-taʿlīmī yushʿil al-nār fī Miṣr.' *Al-Usbūʿ*, 31 May 1999, 12.

Sulṭān, Maḥmūd. 'Manāhij tahmīsh al-dīn wa-qatl al-intimāʾ wa'ghtiyāl al-waḥda al-waṭaniyya.' *Al-Shaʿb*, 23 March 1999, 4.

Ṭāhā, Maḥmūd Muḥammad. *Al-Risāla al-thāniya min al-Islām*. Khartoum: al-Munaẓẓama al-Sūdāniyya li-Ḥuqūq al-Insān, 1992.

— *The Second Message of Islam*. Syracuse: Syracuse University Press, 1987.

Taji-Farouki, Suha. 'An Islamist Tafsir in English: The Ascendant Qur'an by Muhammad al-'Asi (b. 1951).' In *The Qur'an and its Readers Worldwide: Contemporary Commentaries and Translations*, ed. Suha Taji-Farouki. New York: Oxford University Press, 2015, 377–427.

— (ed.). *Modern Muslim Intellectuals and the Qur'an*. Oxford: Oxford University Press, 2004.

— (ed.). *The Qur'an and its Readers Worldwide: Contemporary Commentaries and Translations*. New York: Oxford University Press, 2015.

Taştan, Osman. 'Hüseyin Atay's Approach to Understanding the Qur'an.' In *Modern Muslim Intellectuals and the Qur'an*, ed. Suha Taji-Farouki. Oxford: Oxford University Press, 2006, 241–262.

Tazul Islam. 'Maqāṣid al-Qurʾān: A Search for a Scholarly Definition.' *Al-Bayan* 9, no. 1 (2011): 189–207.

Tazul Islam and Amina Khatun. 'Objective-Based Exegesis of the Qurʾān: A Conceptual Framework.' *Quranica* 7, no. 1 (2015): 37–54.

The Telegraph. 'Egyptian Quranist Detained, Released.' *The Telegraph*, 15 February 2011. <http://www.telegraph.co.uk/news/wikileaks-files/egypt-wikileaks-cables/8326926/EGYPTIAN-QURANIST-DETAINED-RELEASED.html>.

Thaver, Tehseen. The Ambivalences of Modernity in Contemporary Turkish Sufism: CemalNur Sargut's Living Qur'an Community. Unpublished paper.

Theoretical [username]. 'Is This for Real?' *Scienceforums.net* (internet forum), thread started 4 January 2015. Accessed 4 April 2017. <http://www.scienceforums.net/topic/87209-is-this-for-real>.

Tilifizyūn al-Kūt. 'Barnāmaj sīrat al-nabī al-akram – j. 2 – al-ḥalqa 3.' *YouTube*, 13 July 2013. Accessed 24 April 2017. <https://www.youtube.com/watch?v=COjRrcpqYaE>.

Tim Rumah Qurani. *Komik-Qu: Komik al-Quran*! Jakarta: PT Mizan Publika, 2008.

Topan, Farouk. 'Polemics and Language in Swahili Translations of the Qur'an: Mubarak Ahmad (d. 2001), Abdullah Saleh al-Farsy (d. 1982) and Ali Muhsin al-Barwani (d. 2006).' In *The Qur'an and its Readers Worldwide: Contemporary Commentaries and Translations*, ed. Suha Taji-Farouki. New York: Oxford University Press, 2015, 473–498.

Tottoli, Roberto. 'Interrelations and Boundaries between *Tafsīr* and Hadith Literature: The Exegesis of Mālik b. Anas' *Muwaṭṭà* and Classical Qur'anic Commentaries.' In *Tafsīr and Islamic Intellectual History: Exploring the Boundaries of a Genre*, ed. Andreas Görke and Johanna Pink. Oxford: Oxford University Press, 2014.

— 'Origin and Use of the Term *Isrā'īliyyāt* in Muslim Literature.' *Arabica* 46, no. 2 (1999): 193–210.

Turan, Hakan. 'Dürfen sich Muslime Juden und Christen zu Freunden nehmen?' *Andalusian.de*. Accessed 8 March 2017. <http://blog.andalusian.de/duerfen-sich-muslime-juden-und-christen-zu-freunden-nehmen>.

al-ʿUmarī, Aḥmad Khayrī. *Al-Būṣala al-Qur'āniyya: Ibḥār mukhtalif baḥthan ʿan kharīṭa lil-nuhūḍ*. Cairo: Dār al-Maʿrifa, 11th ed., 2016.

Ünal, Ali. *The Qur'ān: With Annotated Interpretation in Modern English*. Clifton, NJ: Tughra Books, 2013.

Vaktidolu, Adil Ali Atalay. *Kuran'ı Kerim: Manzum meali ve tefsir özeti*. Istanbul: Can Yayınları, 2nd ed., 2010.

Valentine, Simon Ross. *Islam and the Ahmadiyya Jama'at: History, Belief, Practice*. London: Hurst, 2008.

Wadud, Amina. *Inside the Gender Jihad: Women's Reform in Islam*. Oxford: Oneworld, 2006.

Wagemakers, Joas. 'Framing the "Threat to Islam": Al-Walà wa al-Barà in Salafi Discourse.' *Arab Studies Quarterly* 30, no. 4 (2008): 1–22.

— 'Revisiting Wiktorowicz: Categorising and Defining the Branches of Salafism.' In *Salafism After the Arab Awakening*, ed. Francesco Cavatorta and Fabio Merone, 7–24. Oxford: Oxford University Press, 2017.

— 'Salafi Source Readings between Al-Qaeda and IS.' *Oasis* 12, no. 23 (2016): 55–62.

— '"The *Kāfir* Religion of the West": *Takfīr* of Democracy and Democrats by Radical Islamists.' In *Accusations of Unbelief in Islam: A Diachronic Perspective on* Takfīr, ed. Camilla Adang, Hassan Ansari, Maribel Fierro and Sabine Schmidtke. Leiden: Brill, 2016, 327–353.

— 'The Transformation of a Radical Concept: *Al-Wala' wa-l-Bara'* in the Ideology of Abu Muhammad al-Maqdisi.' In *Global Salafism: Islam's New Religious Movement*, ed. Roel Meijer. London: Hurst, 2009, 81–106.

Wakas M. [username]. 'Wife Beating in Islam? The Quran Strikes Back.' *Meine-Islam-Reform*, 1 April 2010. Accessed 18 February 2018. <http://meine-islam-reform.de/index.php/artikel/eglischeartikel/529-wifebeating.html>.

Wesselhoeft, Kirsten. 'A Hermeneutics of Intimacy: A Discussion of Recent Work on

Gender and Sexuality in the Islamic Tradition.' *Journal of Religious Ethics* 45, no. 1 (2017): 165–192.

Wielandt, Rotraud. 'Exegesis of the Qur'an: Early Modern and Contemporary.' In *Encyclopaedia of the Qur'ān*, ed. Jane Dammen McAuliffe. Leiden: Brill, 2002, vol. 2, 124–142.

— 'Wurzeln der Schwierigkeit innerislamischen Geprächs über neue hermeneutische Zugänge zum Korantext.' In *The Qur'an as Text*, ed. Stefan Wild. Leiden: Brill, 1996, 259–282.

Wikipedia contributors. 'Ḥasan Farḥān al-Mālikī.' In *Wikipedia Arabic*, 8 May 2017. Accessed 10 May 2017. <https://ar.wikipedia.org/wiki/حسن_فرحان_المالكي>.

Wiktorowicz, Quintan. 'Anatomy of the Salafi Movement.' *Studies in Conflict & Terrorism* 29, no. 3 (2006): 207–239.

Wild, Stefan. 'Muslim Translators and Translations of the Qur'an into English.' *Journal of Qur'anic Studies* 15, no. 3 (2015), 158–182.

Wilson, M. Brett. 'Ritual and Rhyme: Alevi-Bektashi Interpretations and Translations of the Qur'an in Turkey (1953–2007).' *Journal of Qur'anic Studies* 17, no. 3 (2015): 75–99.

— *Translating the Qur'an in an Age of Nationalism: Print Culture and Modern Islam in Turkey*. Oxford: Oxford University Press, 2014.

Wise, Lindsay. 'Amr Khaled: Broadcasting the Nahda.' *Arab Media & Society*. 1 November 2004. Accessed 5 September 2018. <https://www.arabmediasociety.com/amr-khaled-broadcasting-the-nahda>.

Wright, Sue. 'Language Policy, the Nation and Nationalism.' In *Cambridge Handbook of Language Policy*, ed. Bernard Spolsky. Cambridge: Cambridge University Press, 2012, 59–78.

Yahya, Emye. 'Menjawab Fitnah QS 4:34 Memicu KDRT.' *Dzul Kifayatain_Tis'ah*, 15 March 2013. <http://slayersalibis9.blogspot.de/2013/03/menjawab-fitnah-qs-434-memicu-kdrt.html>; also available at *Menjawab Fitnah Misionaris*, 5 July 2012. <http://menjawabfitnahmisionaris.blogspot.com/2012/07/menjawab-fitnah-qs-434-memicu-kdrt_04.html>. Both accessed 23 May 2017.

Yanbuʿī, Muḥammad. *Mafhūm al-āya fī 'l-Qur'ān al-karīm wa 'l-ḥadīth al-sharīf: Dirāsa muṣṭalaḥiyya wa-tafsīr mawḍūʿī*. Cairo: Dār al-Salām, 2014.

Yuksel, Edip. 'Another Quranist is Arrested in Egypt.' *Discover True Islam*, 29 October 2008. Accessed 11 January 2018. <https://free-minds.org/forum/index.php?topic=9597318.0>.

Yildīrim, Anbiyā et al. 'Fa'ʿiẓūhunna wa'hjurūhunna fī'l-maḍājiʿ wa'ḍribūhunna.' *Multaqā Ahl al-Ḥadīth* (internet forum), thread started 2 February 2010. Accessed 22 May 2017. <http://www.ahlalhdeeth.com/vb/showthread.php?t=202132>

Zadeh, Travis. *The Vernacular Qur'an: Translation and the Rise of Persian Exegesis*. Oxford: Oxford University Press, 2012.

al-Zamakhshsarī, Abū 'l-Qāsim Jār Allāh Maḥmūd b. ʿUmar. *Al-Kashshāf ʿan ḥaqāʾiq al-tanzīl wa-ʿuyūn al-aqāwīl fī wujūh al-taʾwīl*. Cairo: Muṣṭafā al-Bābī al-Ḥalabī, 1966.

Zaman, Muhammad Qasim. *The Ulama in Contemporary Islam: Custodians of Change*. Princeton: Princeton University Press, 2002.

Zawadi, Bassam. 'The Ahmadis are not Muslims: A Response to Nabeel Qureshi's Video "Nabeel Qureshi, Ahmadiyyat and Islam: Are Ahmadis Muslim?"' *Call to Monotheism*, n.d. Accessed 18 May 2017. <http://www.call-to-monotheism.com/the_ahmadis_are_not_muslims>.

INDEX

ʿAbd al-ʿAzīz b. Suʿūd, 62, 182
Abdalla, Ulil Abshar, 255
ʿAbduh, Muḥammad, 11, 18–20, 25, 32, 45, 50–51, 61–63, 75, 95, 126, 192
Abdul Mustaqim, 95–100
Abou El Fadl, Khaled, 268, 290–291
Abraham, 150, 260–262, 264–265
abrogation, 141–149, 166, 172, 231, 279
Abū Bakr, Umayma, 245
Abū Zayd, Naṣr Ḥāmid, 133, 209, 258
Adam and Eve, 42, 45–46, 48, 256
al-Afghānī, Jamāl al-Dīn, 18–19, 61–62
Afghanistan, 70, 113
ahl al-bayt, 49, 94, 121, 204–206, 228
ahl al-kitāb, *see* People of the Book
ahl-i ḥadīth movement, 82
ahl-i Qurʾān, 157
Aḥmad, Mīrzā Ghulām, 27, 230–231, 233–234, 236
Ahmadiyya Movement, 27, 114, 219, 230–239
  Lahore Ahmadiyya Movement, 27, 230, 235–236
ʿĀʾisha bt. Abī Bakr, 174
Aisyiyah, 245
āl al-bayt, *see* ahl al-bayt
al-Albānī, Nāṣir al-Dīn, 64
alcohol, 141, 193
Alevism, 28, 202–207, 218
Algeria, 285
ʿAlī b. Abī Ṭālib, 91, 94, 203–206, 221–222
  Nahj al-Balāgha, 86
ʿAlī Zayn al-ʿĀbidīn, 205
Ali, Kecia, 245
ʿAlī, Muḥammad, 27, 230
ʿAlī, Yūsuf, 237
allegorical interpretations, 37, 205–206, 218, 222, 227
Āl Naṣr, Muḥāmmad b. Mūsā, 60
Altafsir.com, 83
Amīn, Sayyida Nuṣrat Baygum, 244
al-amr biʾl-maʿrūf waʾl-nahy ʿan al-munkar, 91–92
angels, 199
Ankara Faculty of Theology, 143, 212, 267, 285
An-Na'im, Abdullahi Ahmed, 143, 208–209
Anthropomorphism, 292
apostasy, 69, 143, 158, 230, 239, 258
apps, 84, 89
ʿaqīda, 16
al-ʿArīfī, Muḥammad, 103, 106–110, 112, 120
Asad, Muhammad, 6, 126, 142, 148, 285
asbāb al-nuzūl, *see* occasions of revelation
Ashʿarism, 40, 49, 61, 220
Atalay, Ali Adil ('Vaktidolu'), 202–207
Atatürk, Mustafa Kemal, 207
Ateş, Süleyman, 149–150
atheism, 263-264, 280
audio sermons, 108–109
authoritarianism (governance), 258–259, 265
āya (semantics of the term), 147–148
Ayverdi, Sâmiha, 225–226, 228
al-Azhar, 40, 65, 126, 140–141, 152–154, 158, 173, 210, 212–213, 220–221, 255
  Islamic Research Council (*Majmaʿ al-buḥūth al-islāmiyya*), 1–3, 173
al-Baghawī, Ḥusayn b. Masʿūd, 69
Baghdad, Mongol conquest of, 263, 265
al-Bahī, Muḥammad, 154
Bahrain, 221
Bakhtiar, Laleh, 289
al-Bannā, Ḥasan, 25
Barlas, Asma, 245, 268
bāṭin (inner meaning of the Qurʾān), 223–224, 226

Bāṭiniyya (polemics), 263–264
al-Bayḍawī, ʿAbdallah b. ʿUmar Abū al-Khayr Nāṣir al-Dīn, 15, 52, 66, 213
Bayram-ı Velî, 228
al-Bāz, Muḥammad, 2–3
Bazargan, Abdolali, 85–94
Bazargan, Mehdi, 85, 149
Beirut, 50, 197
Bektashi Sufi order, *see* Sufism
Belal, Abdul Wahid Osman, 233–235
Bible, 19, 26–27, 45–46, 56, 91, 144, 180–181, 192, 194, 198–199, 217, 234
bidʿa, 20, 63, 112, 264–265
Bint al-Shāṭīʾ, ʿĀʾisha ʿAbd al-Raḥmān, 153, 186, 244
al-Biqāʿī, Burhān al-Dīn, 41, 71, 128
birth control, 245
Blachère, Régis, 149
blogs, 269–281
Bucaille, Maurice, 194–195, 209
Buddhism, 45, 164, 224, 234, 280
al-Bukhārī, Muḥammad b. Ismāʿīl, 57
cabbalism, 224
Cairo, 50, 62, 82
  printed edition of the Qurʾān, 28, 140–141, *see also* al-Azhar
caliphate, 230
Caliphs, 'Rightly-Guided', 228, 265
censorship, 213, 258
Central Asia, 212, 224
Chakralavi, Abdullah, 157
children, *see* education; pedagogy
Christianity, 46, 50, 55, 100, 111–112, 114, 120–121, 132, 150, 164, 179–181, 198–199, 227, 231–233, 236, 247–248, 264, 270–280
  Copts, 159, 181
  missionaries, 18, 26–27, 172, 179, 192, 236
  Protestantism, 25–28, 181
  Roman Catholic church, 181
  Trinity, 226
Christians, *see* Christianity
chronology of the Qurʾān, 136, 140–141, 143, 148, 204, 279
colonialism, 62, 179, 192, 208–209, 230, 233, 278
comic strips, 21–24, 94
communism, 183
companions (of the Prophet), 49, 63, 156, 228
concubinage, *see* slavery
conspiracy theories, 255, 263–264
corruption, 99–100
cosmology, 192, 196
creationism, *see* 'Darwinism'
Damascus, 45, 50, 61
dars (teaching session), 109, 114
Darwaza, Muḥammad ʿIzzat, 129, 135, 140, 168n.36, 186
'Darwinism', 196–197
David, 53–60
  and Bathsheba, 56
daʿwa, 27, 29–32, 89–90, 108, 197, 209, 231, 237, 239
Dawoodi Bohra, *see* Ismāʿīli Shiʿa
democracy, 15, 143, *see also* shūrā
Denny JA (Denny Januar Ali), 247
al-Dhahabī, Muḥammad, 50
al-Dihlāwī, Walī Allāh, 17–19
Diyanet İşleri Başkanlığı, *see* Turkey: Directorate of Religious Affairs
divorce laws, 244–245, 247
domestic violence, 244–245, 284–293
dreams, 59–60
economy, 129, 218
education, 18, 125, 159, 173, 211–212, 258, 269, *see also* dars
  tertiary, 211–212
Egypt, 1–3, 5, 21, 23, 25–26, 29–32, 45, 65, 69, 153–154, 157–159, 172–182, 187–191, 217, 220, 245, 249, 258, *see also* al-Azhar; Cairo
  Ancient Egypt, 195, 199
  'marriage crisis', 180
Elmalılı Hamdi Yazır, 149, 213, 229
El-Muvahhid, Seyfuddin, 66–71
Elsaie, Adel, 233
embryology, 194, 196–197, 199
Engineer, Asghar Ali, 223
Esack, Farid, 208, 293
Europe, 18–19, 29, 85, 107, 149, 179, 192, 211
evolution, theory of, *see* 'Darwinism'
Facebook, 255, 257
faḍāʾil traditions, 59
Fahd b. ʿAbd al-ʿAzīz, 82
Fanous, Raef, 197

al-Farāḥī, Ḥamīd al-Dīn, 186
al-Farmāwī, ʿAbd al-Ḥayy, 154
Fāṭima bt. Muhammad, 205, 221
fatwa, 16, 279
feminism, *see* gender; women's rights activism
film, 2
fiqh, 15–16, 39, 164–165, 212, 222
Fodio, Usman Dan, 32 n.2
Foucault, Michel, 8–10
France, 106, 233
Futuḥ Miṣr, *see* Ibn ʿAbd al-Ḥakam
Gabriel, 206
Gadamer, Hans-Georg, 267
gender, 40, 125–126, 129, 134, 142, 158, 165, 191–192, 222–223, 226, 230, 244–247, 266, 284–293
  of exegetes, 33 n.9, 103, 173–174, 225–229, 244–245, 259, 268
Germany, 269–280
ghayba, 221
al-Ghazālī, Muḥammad, 154
al-Ghazālī, Zaynab, 173
Goldziher, Ignác, 219
government (systems of), 70, 92, 125, 129, 259
Great Britain, 230
Greek antiquity, 180
Gülen movement, 287
Gulf War, second (1991), 72
Ḥabannaka al-Maydānī, ʿAbd al-Raḥmān Ḥasan, 167 n.33
Hadhramaut, 40
Hagar, 47
ḥadīth(s), 16–17, 19, 37, 47, 49, 57, 61–65, 69, 74–76, 89, 92, 111–113, 120, 132, 142, 151, 155–158, 173–174, 182, 184, 204, 212, 220, 226, 234, 236–237, 293
ḥākimiyya, 69–70
Ḥamza, Karīmān, 172–181
Ḥasan al-ʿAskarī, 221
al-Ḥasan b. ʿAlī
ḥāshiya, 51
Ḥawwā, Saʿīd, 185–187
headscarf, 172, 229
hermeneutics, 127–128, 267–268
hidāya, 19–20, 25, 125, 174, 184, 260, 269
Hidayatullah, Aysha A. 5, 266–268
ḥijāb, *see* headscarf
hijra, 74
Hinduism, 280
historical context (of the Qurʾān), 11, 121, 125, 129–134, 151–152, 279
'homosexuality', *see* marriage: same-sex; sexual identity
Husaini, Asdia, 255
al-Ḥusayn b. ʿAlī, 92, 205, 221
Ḥusayn, Ṭāhā, 152
Ibādism, 219
Iblīs, *see* Satan
Ibn ʿAbbās, 140, 217
Ibn ʿAbd al-Ḥakam, Abū al-Qāsim ʿAbd al-Raḥmān b. ʿAbdallāh, 217
Ibn ʿArabī, Muḥyī al-Dīn, 223, 225, 228
Ibn ʿĀshūr, al-Ṭāhir, 129
Ibn Bāz, ʿAbd al-ʿAzīz, 113
Ibn Ḥazm of Cordoba, 253
Ibn Kathīr, Ismāʿīl b. ʿUmar ʿImād al-Dīn, 5–6, 9, 24, 35, 46, 49–61, 65–66, 69–70, 82, 95, 209, 213, 255, 285
Ibn Saud, *see* ʿAbd al-ʿAzīz b. Suʿūd
Ibn Taymiyya, Taqī al-Dīn Aḥmad, 17, 20, 35, 45–46, 49–51, 61–63, 75, 82, 113, 155–156
Ibrāhīm, Saʿd al-Dīn, 159
Ijaz, Tahir, 232–233
iʿjāz al-Qurʾān, 81, 187, 194, 231
  'numerical miracle', 195
  'scientific miracle', 173, 191, 194–199, 209, 231
ijmāʿ 36, 48, 72, 219
ijtihād, 64
India, 17–18, 50, 52, 61, 82, 182, 221, 223, 230, 233
Indonesia, 3, 5, 21–24, 27–28, 40–48, 72, 95–100, 102, 135, 154, 207–208, 210–212, 245, 247–258, 267, 278, 286–287
  Council of Indonesian *ʿulamāʾ* (*MUI*), 248–249
  Ministry of Religion, 95, 212–218, 278
  Pancasila, 213
inheritance law, 141, 245
al-insān al-kāmil, 223, 228

internet, 5–6, 81, 83–85, 100–121, 159, 209, 213, 247, 249, 280, *see also* blogs; social media
Iran, 3, 85–86, 89, 92, 127, 208, 219, 221–223, 258–259, 267, 288–289, 292
  Islamic Revolution, 85, 211
Iraq, 221, 259–265
ISIS, 134, 159, 166, 294
ishārī interpretations, *see* allegorical interpretations
islām (semantics of the term), 150
Islam nusantara, 240 n.27
ʿiṣma (of the prophets), 56
Ismāʿīli Shiʿa, 223, 264
Israel (state), 112
Israel, lost tribes of, 234
isrāʾīliyyāt, 20, 50–51, 55–56, 60, 156
Istanbul, 82
Izutsu, Toshihiko, 133
al-Jābirī, Muḥammad ʿĀbid, 136–141
jāhiliyya, 182
al-Jalālān, *see* Tafsīr al-Jalālayn
Jamāʿat-e Islāmī, 182
Java, 95, 248
al-Jazāʾirī, Abū Bakr, 78 n.59
Jesus, 45–46
  death of, 231–239
Jews, *see* Judaism
Jibrīl, *see* Gabriel
jihad, 73, 91, 113, 125, 230, 239, *see also* war
jihadism, 65, 69–70, 113, 159, 221
  Jihadi-Salafi movement, 185, 233, 237–239, 293–294
al-Jīlānī, ʿAbd al-Qādir, 228
al-Jīlī, ʿAbd al-Karīm, 228
Job, 285
Jordan (state), 72, 83, 241
Joseph, 215–218
Judaism, 20, 50, 55, 111–112, 114, 120–121, 150, 180, 231–232, 255, 270–280
juzʾ ʿamma, 88
Kabir, Sofiane, 103, 106, 108–112, 120
kalām, *see* theology
Karbala, 221, 228
Kashmir, 234, 239
Khalaf Allāh, Muḥammad Aḥmad, 152–153
Khālid, ʿAmr, 29–32, 187–191
Khalifa, Rashad, 157–158, 195, 210, 230
Khan, Nouman Ali, 6, 84, 104–105, 108–110, 112, 209
Khān, Sayyid Aḥmad, 142, 181
Khān, Ṣiddīq Ḥasan, 82
al-Kharaqānī, Abū al-Ḥasan, 228
Khārijism, 219
Khomeini, Ayatollah, 85
al-Khūlī, Amīn, 151–153, 195
King Fahd Complex for the Printing of the Holy Qurʾān, 27, 57, 120
Kuwait, 113–114
Lamrabet, Asma, 245
Lebanon, 197–199, 221
letters, disjointed, at beginning of *sūra*s, 206, 227
LGBTQ, *see* sexual identity
literary exegesis, 151–154, 249
Lot, 247–257
Lukman, Fadhli, 256–257
Luther, Martin, 181
madhāhib, *see* schools of law
Madjid, Nurcholish, 248
madrasa, 15, 36, 51, 73, 212
maghāzī literature, 132
Maḥmūd, ʿAbd al-Ḥalīm, 172
Malay world, the, 82
al-Mālikī, Ḥasan b. Farḥān, 103, 111, 113–121
al-Manār, 45, 82–83
manhaj, 11, 63, 184
Manṣūr, Aḥmad Ṣubḥī, 157–166
maqāṣid al-Qurʾān, 125, 128–131, 165, 191, 279
al-Marāghī, Aḥmad Muṣṭafā, 45, 48, 126
marriage, 130, 190–191, 222, 245, 247, 256, 279, 284–293
  interreligious, 159–166, 248
  same-sex, 247–257
  temporary (*zawāj al-mutʿa*), 222, *see also* polygamy, same-sex marriage, domestic violence
martyr, *see* shahīd
masculinity, 245, 291, *see also* gender
al-Māturīdī, Abū Manṣūr, 144
Mavani, Hamid, 90
al-Mawdūdī, Abū al-Aʿlā, 69–70, 182–185, 209
Menk, Ismail, 103, 105, 108–111

Messianism, 27, 195, 230, 236
migration, 89–90, 209
Miracles of Quran (website), 197–199
moral panic, 248, 258
Morocco, 136–141, 245
Moses, 45–46, 69–70, 184, 193
mosques, 203, 206
Muʿāwiya b. Abī Sufyān, 94
al-Mubarakpuri, Safiur-Rahman, 52–60
Mughal Empire, 17
Muḥammad, 45–46, 69, 100, 121, 131–134, 150, 158, 164–165, 194–195, 205–206, 228, 233, 288, 290, *see also* ḥadīths
Muhammadiyah (Indonesia), 27
munāsaba, 186, 217
music, 2
Muslim b. al-Ḥajjāj, 57
Muslim Brotherhood, 2, 25, 38, 69, 72, 100, 182, 185
Muṭahharī, Murtaḍā, 288
Muʿtazila, 71, 218, 263–264
muwāṭana, 165
mysticism, *see* Sufism
al-Nābulusī, Muḥammad Rātib, 107–110, 112
Naik, Zakir, 209
naskh, *see* abrogation
Nasserism, 182
nation state, 7, 202, 207, 210–218, 222, 258-259
nationalism, 3, 18, 135, 152, 203, 206–207
naẓm (of the Qurʾān), 89, 183, 185–191
Nemilov, Anton, 287
New Order regime, *see* Suharto
niẓām, 11
Noah, 31, 42
Nöldeke, Theodor, 140–141
Noyan, Bedri, 202, 206–207
Numayrī, Jaʿfar Muḥammad, 143
'numerical miracle', *see* iʿjāz al-Qurʾān
occasions of revelation, 16, 95, 131–132, 136, 183
Old Order Regime, *see* Sukarno
order of revelation, *tafsīr* in the, 134–141, 187, 204
Orientalism, 28, 132, 149, 156, 172, 179, 192, 264
Ottoman Empire, 179, 203, 207–208, 210, 220, 228
Özdeş, Talip, 143–150
Paçacı, Mehmet, 267
Pacifism, 159
Pahlavī, Muḥammad Riḍā, 85
Pakistan, 183, 211, 230
  International Islamic University, Islamabad, 248
Paloh, Surya, 102
Pancasila, 213
Paramadina Foundation, Jakarta, 248
Paris, 19
pedagogy, 20–21, 95–100, 215, 218
People of the Book, 165
philosophy (*falsafa*), 15, 20, 50, 61, 224
Pickthall, Muhammad, 237
pluralism, religious, 102, 248, 259, 278
poetry, 1–3, 202–207
polygamy, 130, 174–181, 193, 245, 289–290
polytheism, *see* shirk
pork, prohibition on, 193, 195
prayer, 15, 58, 70, 103, 139, 193, 195, 203, 226, 229
preaching, 17, 20, 31–32, 39, 85, 100–121
proselytising, *see* daʿwa
punishments, Qurʾānic, 156, 158, 185, 230, 239, 259
Qadariyya, 263
Qadhi, Yasir, 103–104, 108–112
Qādyān, 230
al-Qāʿida, 134, 159
al-Qarnī, ʿĀʾiḍ b. ʿAbdallāh, 5, 72–76
al-Qāsimī, Jamāl al-Dīn, 45–46, 48, 75, 82
Qatar
  Al Jazeera, 101
al-Qazwīnī, Āyatollāh al-Sayyid Murtaḍā, 103, 107–111, 120
queerness, *see* sexual identity
Quraish Shihab, Muhammad, 40–48, 73, 95, 102, 154, 287
Qurʾānism, 157–166, 210, 230
Quṭb, Sayyid, 32, 38, 48, 66, 69–70, 75, 142, 173, 182–186, 191, 195, 209, 213, 246
Rābiʿa al-ʿAdawiyya, 228
racism, 246

Rahman, Fazlur, 121, 129–130, 150, 154, 157, 208–209, 258, 267, 288–289
Ramadan series, 2, 40, 101, 104–105, 109–110, 113–114
rape, 255-256
al-Rāzī, Fakhr al-Dīn, 49, 51–52
recitation (of the Qur'ān), 15, 19, 21, 94, 110
retaliation, 142
rhyme, *see* poetry
Riḍā, Muḥammad Rashīd, 50–51, 62, 75, 82 84, 129, 183 184, 186
ridda, *see* apostasy
al-Rifā'ī, Aḥmad, 228
Rifā'i, Ken'an, 225, 228
Rifā'iyya Sufi order, *see* Sufism
Roman antiquity, 180
Royal Aal al-Bayt Institute for Islamic Thought, 83
Rückert, Friedrich, 204
al-Rūmī, Jalāl al-Dīn, 225, 228
ṣabr, 92
al-Ṣābūnī, Muḥammad 'Alī, 95, 150
Saeed, Abdullah, 208
ṣaḥāba, *see* companions (of the Prophet)
Saheeh International (Qur'ān translation), 82
saj', 204
Ṣaḥwa, 72
ṣalāt, *see* prayer
Salqīnī, Ibrāhīm 'Abdallāh, 263
Sam'ānī, Aḥmad, 228
al-Sanūsī, Muḥammad, 32
Sardar, Ziauddin, 196, 288
Sargut, Cemâlnur, 225–229
Sargut, Meşküre, 225
Satan, 68, 100, 255–256
'Satanic verses', 133
Saudi Arabia, 3, 27, 51–57, 61–62, 65–66, 72–76, 82, 101, 103, 113–114, 120, 127, 143, 159, 166, 199, 210, 212, 219–221, 252–253, 259, 285, *see also* King Fahd Complex for the Printing of the Holy Qur'ān
schools of law, 16, 18–20, 40, 61, 220
  Ḥanafi school, 220
  Shāfi'i school, 41, 58–59
science, 92, 172, 181, 191–199, 224, 287–288
'miracle', scientific, of the Qur'ān, *see* i'jāz al-Qur'ān
script, 208
semantics, modernist use of, 121, 133, 143, 147–151, 154, 165
sexual identity, 125, 230, 259, 246–257, 259, 291, *see also* marriage: same-sex
sexuality, 291
Shābistarī, Muḥammad Mujtahid, 267
shahīd, 111, 120
Shaltūt, Maḥmūd, 153, 173
al-Sha'rāwī, Muḥammad Mutawallī, 29, 32, 101, 103, 106, 108–110, 112
Sharī'atī, 'Alī, 122 n.17
al-Shāṭibī, Abū Isḥāq, 126
al-Shawkānī, Muḥammad, 32 n.2, 36, 65, 75, 82, 286
Sher Mohammad, Hafiz, 235–236
Shi'a, 3, 37, 49, 63, 85–86, 88–94, 107, 113, 121, 127, 132, 149, 153, 155, 203–204, 205–206, 218, 220–223, 228, 288
  Rāfiḍa (anti-Shi'i polemics), 263, *see also* Ismā'īli Shi'a, Zaydi Shi'a
al-Shinqīṭī, Muḥammad al-Amīn, 66, 155
shirk, 62–63, 66–70, 121, 165, 226
shūrā, 185, *see also* democracy
Ṣidqī, Muḥammad Tawfīq, 45
sīra literature, 132, 136, 138–139
Sirry, Mun'im, 247–257
slavery, 25, 31, 125, 129, 131, 134, 142, 179, 193, 290–292
  concubinage, 178–179, 245
social justice, 85, 100, 184, 191
social media, 107, 119, 247, 255, *see also* YouTube; Twitter; Facebook
Solomon, 198
Soroush, Abdolkarim, 86, 267, 292
Soviet Union, 212, 224
successors (of the Prophet's companions), 49, 156
Sudan, 142–143
Sufism, 17–18, 20, 28, 37, 48, 63, 74, 158, 218, 220, 223–229
  Bektashi order, 202–203, 207
  'Muḥammadan path' (*al-ṭarīqa al-Muḥammadiyya*), 229
  Rifā'i order, 225–229

Suharto, 40, 100, 102, 214
Sukarno, 214
Sunna, *see* ḥadīth(s)
Sunni Islam, 36, 94, 113, 121, 132, 140, 156, 158, 203, 206, 218–223, 228, 230, 263
al-Suyūṭī, Jalāl al-Dīn, 59, 65, 217, *see also* Tafsīr al-Jalālayn
symbolism, 206
Syria, 158, 185, 263
  Greater Syria (pre-WWI), 62
al-Ṭabarī, Abū Ja'far b. Jarīr, 41, 48, 50, 95, 178, 285
Ṭabāṭabā'ī, Muḥammad Ḥusayn, 48, 154, 186
tābi'ūn, 49
al-Ṭabrisī, Abū 'Alī Faḍl b. al-Ḥasan, 222
Tafsīr al-Jalālayn, 15, 73
tafsīr al-Qur'ān bi'l-Qur'ān, 120, 154–155
tafsīr bi'l-ma'thūr, 50
tafsīr bi'l-ra'y, 50
tafsīr mawḍū'ī, *see* thematic tafsīr
ṭāghūt, 66, 69–70, 184
Ṭāhā, Maḥmūd Muḥammad, 142
Ṭāhā, Muḥammad Sayf al-Dīn, 1–3
takfīr, 65, 70–71, 237
Ṭanṭāwī Jawharī, 94, 192
taqlīd, 125, 129
Ṭarābīshī, Georges, 158
tawḥīd, 63, 226, 246, 289
ta'wīl, *see* allegorical interpretations
taysīr, 126
television, 5, 29, 32, 38–40, 72, 81, 84, 94, 100–102, 106–107, 113–114, 172, 225, 257
  televangelism, 29, 281
terrorism, 165–166
al-Tha'labī, Aḥmad b. Muḥammad, 51
Thanawī, Ashraf 'Alī, 186
thematic *tafsīr*, 40, 153–154, 249–257
theology, 15–16, 19–20, 25, 37, 50, 61, 126, 220, 222, 265, 292–293
translation (of the Qur'ān), 25–28, 57–58, 90, 120, 149, 204, 212, 214, 230–231, 237
Trinity, *see* Christianity
Ṭu'ma b. Ubayriq, 69–70
Turan, Hakan, 269–280
Turkey, 3, 66, 127, 135, 143–150, 157, 196, 202–207, 212–213, 225–229, 258, 267, 269–271, 279, 284–285, 288
  Directorate of Religious Affairs, 214
al-Ṭūsī, Abū Ja'far Muḥāmmad b. al-Ḥasan, 222
Twitter, 247, 255, 257
al-'Umarī, Aḥmad Khayrī, 5, 259–265
Ünal, Ali, 287
United States, the, 72, 85–94, 134, 157–159, 165, 196, 237, 245, 248–249, 254, 268, 289
al-'Urwa al-wuthqā, 18–20, 82
'Vaktidolu', *see* Atalay, Ali Adil
verses, numbering of (in the Qur'ān), 204, 242 n.94, 243 n.99
Wadud, Amina, 208, 245, 291–292
waḥdat al-wujūd, 223
Wahhābism, 51, 62–63, 70, 72, 113
al-walā' wa'l-barā' 64, 70, 278
walī, semantics of, 270–280
war, 19, 64, 91, 125, 129, 141–142, 158, 280, *see also* jihad
wasaṭiyya, 40, 83, 220
West Africa, 28
Wiktorowicz, Quintan, 65
women, *see* gender; marriage; women's rights activism
women's rights activism, 127, 244–245, 266, 293, *see also* gender
Yahya, Harun (a.k.a. Adnan Oktar), 197
Yemen, 40
Yıldırım, Enbiya, 284–285, 288
Yıldırım, Ferda, 226–227
YouTube, 5–6, 38, 72, 84, 102–121
Yüksel, Edip, 157
Yunus, Mahmud, 123 n.35
al-Zamakhsharī, Abū 'l-Qāsim Jār Allāh Maḥmūd b. 'Umar, 15, 41, 71, 88–89, 144–145, 148
Zayd b. Ḥāritha, 133
Zaydi Shi'a, 218–219, 241 n.39
Zaynab bt. Jahsh, 133
Zionism, 264

INDEX OF QUR'ĀNIC CITATIONS

sūra	*verse*	*page*
1		15, 102–110, 139, 226
1	6–7	111–121
2	21	204–207
2	143	40
2	255	229
2	256	19
3	19	150
3	55	231–239
3	67	150
3	85	150
4		189–191
4	1	256
4	3	130, 172–181
4	34	245, 284–293
4	48	68
4	69	111, 120
4	116	66–71
5	51	169–280
6	108	199
6	151	121
8	12	134
8	65	91
9	93	1
9	112	72–76
11	78–79	256
12	54–55	214–218
14	24–26	222
16	101	143–150
21	5	204
21	51–65	260–265
21	105	183
23	1–11	29–32
23	5–7	25, 281 n.3
26	160–173	250
27	18	197–199
27	54–58	250
29	28–30	251
31	17	86, 92
31	22	19
36		226
36	69	3
38	21–25	52–60
38	44	285
42	14–15	199
47	4	134
49	12	21–24
49	13	246
51	49	256
52	30	204
54	1	193
54	33–37	251
66	5	73
69	41	3, 204
95	1–3	40–48
103	3	85–94
104		95-100, 123 n.35
109		136–141
112		225–229

www.ingramcontent.com/pod-product-compliance
Lightning Source LLC
Chambersburg PA
CBHW052057230426
43662CB00036B/1147